ENTERING THE CIRCLE

ENTERING THE CIRCLE

HERMENEUTIC INVESTIGATION IN PSYCHOLOGY

edited by
Martin J. Packer and
Richard B. Addison

State University of New York Press

Published by
State University of New York Press, Albany

Printed in the United States of America

For information, address State University of New York
Press, State University Plaza, Albany, N.Y., 12246

Library of Congress Cataloging in Publication Data

Entering the circle: hermeneutic investigation in psychology/edited
    by Martin J. Packer and Richard B. Addison.
        p.   cm.
    Bibliography: p.
    ISBN 0-7914-0014-X.   ISBN 0-7914-0015-8 (pbk.)
    1. Hermeneutics.   2. Psychology—Research—Methodology.
    I. Packer, Martin J.   II. Addison, Richard B., 1949-
    BF76.6.H47E58 1989
    150. 19--dc 19   88-24908
                                                                 CIP

10 9 8 7 6 5 4 3 2

Contents

Overview

Martin J. Packer and Richard B. Addison

Hermes was messenger to the Greek gods. (He went by the name Mercury, too.) Himself the god of travel, commerce, invention, eloquence, cunning, and thievery, he acquired very early in his life a reputation for being a precocious trickster. (On the day he was born he stole Apollo's cattle, invented the lyre, and made fire.) His duties as messenger included conducting the souls of the dead to Hades, warning Aeneas to go to Italy, where he founded the Roman race, and commanding the nymph Calypso to send Odysseus away on a raft, despite her love for him. With good reason his name is celebrated in the term 'hermeneutics,' which refers to the business of interpreting.

Hermes brought messages of advice, warning, and instruction to humans from the gods. Since we don't have a godly messenger available to us, we have to interpret things for ourselves. This century has been a time for special recognition of the importance of messages, of translation and interpretation. It has also been marked by an appreciation that these all have a tricky side to them. We've come to appreciate that misunderstanding is as common as understanding, and that not only those we disagree with show prejudice. We've come to see that the past, and cultures foreign to us, can be reappropriated, comprehended and studied only in a partial manner.

Yet we've also come to realize that interpretation of messages is central to our existence. This is not a consequence of the disappearance of Hermes (or not literally so); rather it has been a matter of increased awareness that we are cultural and social beings, rather than natural creations or biological entities. And it comes from changes in life style that have left many of us dealing with human messages far more often than natural phenomena. An awareness of the importance of interpretation has stirred in popular culture. William Safire, pundit to the people, wrote in the *New York Times* Sunday magazine in early 1988 that Hermes brought him a message: "He's back in the news." Safire says of hermeneutics, "Watch that word; when it gets tied firmly to a concept in many people's minds, it will be taken as a sign of our times."

1

Interpretation of messages takes much of our time. We worry about the message that television conveys, and frown over the latest press release from the White House. We advise each other to 'give clear signals' in our relationships. Some among us argue about such arcane topics as the difficulty of divining the intentions of the framers of the American Constitution. We even talk of the messages in cellular DNA that are read when cells are built. Some of this talk confuses texts and codes, languages and logics, but this only confirms that Hermes is a tricky fellow.

This is no small change. It represents, in the eyes of some, the failure of the Enlightenment project, of modernism, of the idea that progress is to be achieved through the scientific accumulation of knowledge with which to design and build a utopian world. The shapers of the Enlightenment emphasized the autonomy of the individual, in both ethical and epistemological matters, distinct from church and state. They were confident that reason—exemplified by Galileo's physics—would free us from our passions, our history, our traditions. The end results of this project have been positivist objectivism and ethical relativism. The project has self-destructed, its limits and mistakes exposed in part by its undeniable successes. But where do we go next? A powerful sense of who we are and what we should be doing, one that went unchallenged for two centuries, is now crumbling.

Heidegger's hermeneutic investigation of human being in *Being and Time*, published in 1927, has become one source for our modern (or postmodern) understanding of the centrality of interpretation. For Heidegger, our everyday action always embodies an interpretation of who we are, albeit one generally concealed and misunderstood. Each of us grows up in and into a traditional way of interpreting ourselves, which lays out possibilities for our being. Grasping these possibilities, we take a stand on our existence. Heidegger's analysis loosens up and dissolves the hardened paint of the traditional picture of individuality, subjectivity and objectivity, knowledge, reason and emotion, thought and action, identity, and inquiry. Sixty years later, the flux he initiated continues to swell.

The behemoth that is psychology is stirring under the impact of all of this. Research psychologists become aware that some tricky and problematic assumptions underlie the research methods that have been customary to many of them. Clinicians recognize they sometimes take for granted the interpreting that is central to their practice. A professional journal like the *American Psychologist* becomes the arena where a variety of novel approaches are paraded: hermeneutic, phenomenological, constructionist, humanistic, dualistic, Aristotelian (e.g., Aanstoos 1985; Faulconer & Williams 1985; Gergen 1985; Jennings 1986; Packer 1985a; Silverstein 1988) along with fierce and heady debates on the philosophy of science (e.g., Champion 1985; Dar 1987; Farrell 1986; Gholson & Barker 1986; Kimble 1984; Krasner &

Houts 1984; Manicas & Secord 1983; Messer 1985; Serlin & Lapsley 1985; Unger 1985).

This book springs from the ferment of all this activity. The concern behind it is to present a selection of accounts of exemplary interpretive research projects in developmental, clinical, social and educational psychology. A wealth of literature exists that examines the philosophical and metatheoretical bases of the interpretive approach (and much of it is referred to in the chapters of this book). The reader who absorbs this literature will be in a position to critique the metatheoretical assumptions that lie, unexamined, behind much research and theory in the human sciences. Yet such a reader will find little in this literature to guide her or him in actually conducting an interpretive inquiry. There is comparatively little published writing that addresses the practical and methodological aspects of research conducted from the hermeneutic stance. In addition, and compounding the problem, relatively few psychological journals publish or encourage the submission of reports of interpretive research, so that few exemplars of such research are available for study. There are indications, though, that this too is changing: in the past few years mainstream journals have indicated a tentative willingness to publish interpretative research.

The chapters of this book are arranged in a manner that reflects three phases that can be distinguished in interpretive inquiry. The first phase is that of entering the hermeneutic circle in the right way: discovering an appropriate workable perspective from which interpretation can proceed. The second is the conduct of inquiry within that perspective. The third phase is one of critical reflection upon and evaluation of the interpretive account that is the outcome of inquiry. Chapters in the first section describe how a new approach to the understanding and interpretation of a phenomenon is sought, or how an existing perspective is found unsatisfactory. Those in Section Two describe inquiry where an established perspective is the basis for interpretive articulation of a phenomenon. Chapters in Section Three critique the perspective of their own or another's inquiry. Some of the investigations embody elements of more than one phase; in such cases we have placed the chapter in the section that represents the authors' major emphasis.

In the Introduction we draw a comparison between interpretive inquiry and the two dominant perspectives in psychology that, together, embody the traditional world-view: empiricism and rationalism. Individual research programs and theoretical schools unreflectively adopt one of these two perspectives to provide their root metaphors, common-sense notions about the world, basic conceptions of explanation and description, and standards of judgment and evaluation (Brown 1986). We contrast the traditional world-view with the hermeneutic perspective in four respects: the kind of domain that inquiry is considered to be directed toward; the origin or source of knowledge; the form of explanation that is seen as the goal of inquiry; and the manner of inquiry that is considered most appropriate. One of our aims is to draw a distinction between the traditional view of method as interpretation-free procedure or technique and, on the other hand, an interpretive view of method as establishing a point of view from which inquiry can proceed, and evaluating the account produced. We think this distinction is germane to an understanding and appreciation of the interpretive research described in the other chapters of this volume.

Section One. The first section includes chapters that describe the *initiation* of an interpretive research program, and discuss how a new interpretive perspective is adopted. One of the major thrusts in research described in these chapters is reaching an appropriate starting point for interpretation.

1. As a clinician and researcher, Richard Addison (chapter one) is concerned with the problem of the professional socialization of family physicians. His approach is one of participant observation and interviewing, immersing himself in the everyday world of family practice resident-physicians. Spending considerable time with the residents as they saw patients, attended conferences and lectures, ate, and slept in the hospital, Addison kept detailed notes of what he saw and how he felt as he became involved in the residents' efforts at "surviving." These observations became the basis for an account of two "modes of being" that dominated the residents' lives: "covering-over" and "over-reflecting." Addison developed a narrative account of how these modes developed and came to be problematic. He also developed an account of a more integrated way of being. At the residents' request he led a group to help them cope with the stress of residency and integrate the maladaptive modes of being (see Addison, in press). In doing so, he acknowledged his stance as a critical researcher within the hermeneutic circle.

After laying out his grounded interpretive approach, Addison discusses some of the key hermeneutic elements of his method. These include the circular relationship between understanding and interpretation, the importance of background context in interpreting actions, the contribution of a researcher's preunderstanding to the writing of a narrative account, and the role a narrative account can play in opening up possibilities for researcher, research participants, and the structure of residency training.

2. Robert Selman is a researcher and clinician working in the area of children's social development (cf., Selman 1980). In chapter two Selman and his colleagues Lynn Hickey Schultz, Brina Caplan and Katherine Shantz look at the social interactions that take place in the context of the "Pair Therapy" of two troubled adolescents. These interactions are "fixed" as a text by video recording and narrative accounts by observers and the therapist. The researchers begin analysis of the clinical sessions by outlining a set of four hierarchically organized developmental levels that, as descriptions of compe-

tence, reflect the structuralist perspective they are moving from. But they discovered these levels unable to account for the rich interpersonal context they believed to be the source of change, and for the detailed course of interaction during the therapy sessions.

The researchers were led to articulate a set of "interaction indices" that organize their analysis by pointing out key aspects of the interactions between therapist and adolescents. They were moved to change their method of inquiry by a recognition that forms of understanding already embodied in their clinical practice were eluding their study. The accounts they developed articulate their practical understanding of the troubled adolescents and their concerns. Theory and practice are in a circular and dialogical relationship here; practice is guided in part by theoretical conceptions of development and change, but those conceptions are modified as a result of reflexive and interpretive examination of practice. And Selman perhaps comes closest to being a modern Hermes, as he transforms messages from each boy into a form more suited for the other.

3. In chapter three, Martin Packer discusses occasions of betrayed agreement among college students in an analog task setting. The textual records here are video recordings of the students' exchanges. Packer describes a self-consciously circular analysis, beginning with the choice of a conceptual approach to action that provided entry to the circle of interpretation.

For Packer, three aspects of interaction became conspicuous: the interpersonal distance people maintained, relative moral status, and the "mythology" of what was talked about. He interprets the conflicts over betrayal (cf. Packer 1985b) in terms of three sequential phases that followed the "burning" (as the young people called the broken agreement): an initial reaction to it, followed by accusation and response, and ending with articulation or standoff. Unspoken "concerns" over responsibility and trust shaped action in the first phases, while explicit "issues" were talked about in the final phase.

Working notes made during the research are used to explicate the circular movements of interpretation. Drawing on Heidegger's (1927/1962) hermeneutic approach, Packer discusses the relationship between interpretation and understanding, and the manner in which a researcher's preliminary understanding of a text or text-analog provide an essential, but corrigible, access to it and a starting place for interpretation. He addresses the need to prepare for an interpretive analysis, and suggests ways to foster the articulation of understanding, including writing "simple descriptions," focusing on the problematical, tolerating and sustaining ambiguity in order to avoid premature interpretive closure, and seeking both confirmation and refutation.

4. John Mergendoller also deals, in chapter four, with a lived moral issue, that of draft resistance. He addresses the considerations and problems he met in using interview texts as the basis for, first, narrative portraits of the consci-

entious objectors he talked with and, then, a comparative analysis of the communalities among these individual histories of resistance to the war in Vietnam. Mergendoller argues convincingly that writing a narrative portrait is not a matter of summarizing the events chronicled in the interview transcript so much as it is a reflection on and renewal of the dialogue between researcher and interviewee. As a reconstruction it is, then, already an interpretation.

The comparative analyses became for Mergendoller a reflective process of repeated rereading of the portraits and interviews, during which the question guiding the research (draft resistance as moral action) became re-examined and reformulated. Moral deliberation and moral enactment were two aspects that came to the fore, both linked to the reaffirmation of moral identity in the face of a situation challenging that identity. Resisters related their actions to two aspects of identity in their narratives: selfhood and tradition. Mergendoller concluded that the acts of resistance generally provided an affirmation, and sometimes an extension, of moral identity.

Section Two. The second section is made up of chapters that describe research conducted from an interpretive perspective that has already been identified. These studies aim to move beyond the discovery stage of research, utilizing an established perspective to investigate and articulate social action.

5. In chapter five, Lyn Brown, Mark Tappan, Carol Gilligan, Barbara Miller and Dianne Argyris report on their work interpreting narratives from open-ended interviews concerning moral conflict and choice. They regard these narratives not as the products of an underlying competence—the cognitive-developmental position adopted by Kohlberg—but as texts where different "voices," that speak from distinct orientations or perspectives, can be discerned. Their method of reading is one that aims, (after an initial perusal of the text in which the dramatic form of the story becomes established,) to identify the two moral voices of care and of justice, and the manner in which the interviewee places self in the narrative (cf. Gilligan 1982). In this way they begin to see how an individual constructs a moral conflict. The two moral voices reflect and find their source in the premise that we experience our relationships with one another in terms of attachment and equality; that we all have concerns over intimacy and power. It is noteworthy that in Brown et al.'s analysis one portion of the text may be evidence for both a justice reading and a care reading; there is no one-to-one matching between text and interpretation, as would be the case if one were "stage-scoring" the narrative.

Brown et al. proceed to place their narratives within a categorical typology based on the presence and relative dominance of the two moral voices, and on the alignment of self with those voices. Such a categorization permits them to ascertain degree of agreement among interpreters, and to assess group differences.

6. Robert Elliott's inquiry (chapter six) focuses on significant change events that occur during therapy: incidents that clients themselves identify as helpful and important occasions. The texts that Elliott and his coworkers work from are transcriptions of audio-recorded conversation between client and therapist during the therapeutic hour. His "Comprehensive Process Analysis," as the approach is named, aims at a consensual expansion of the factors contributing to change events, and the impact of these events. Portions of client-therapist discourse are expanded as series of propositions, and their event "pathways" charted. Elliott characterizes the approach as exploratory, discovery-oriented and theory-generating rather than hypothesis-testing.

The perspective that Elliott previously worked within, and which he came to find inadequate, was an empiricist one. Ratings of isolated therapist and client behaviors proved devoid of clinically or theoretically significant findings, despite Elliott's awareness as a clinician of those aspects of the therapeutic intervention apparently responsible for change. The empiricist approach imposed distorting assumptions upon the phenomena of study; assumptions such as the independence of events from their setting, the desirability of objective measurement, and the need to find mechanistic causal links. Recognition of the inadequacy of these assumptions provoked Elliott into developing the alternative approach he describes here. Nonetheless, Elliott remains closer than the other contributors (perhaps excepting Spence) to the possibility of an objective account of the interaction between therapist and client, an account of what they are "really" saying, free from "contamination" by observers.

7. Theodore Sarbin has developed a form of interpretation that seeks out "tropes"—figures of speech—and other rhetorical devices. The texts he examines are accounts of the everyday experience of emotions, typically anger. Sarbin regards the human events that we call emotions or passions as being best considered "narrative emplotments," organized as narratives, with plot, actors, and setting. Sarbin has expanded on the general application of the narratory principle elsewhere (Sarbin 1986). Here (chapter seven) he narrows his focus to illustrate the way in which roles, plot, and the rhetorical actions that make up an emotion can be identified: the acts such as insult and retribution that constitute an "attack" of anger. The rhetorical aspect of emotions is to be located, Sarbin argues, in the cultural prescriptions at work behind all dramatistic acts. These prescriptions themselves take a largely narrative form, as myths, parables, songs and stories. Each is "a symbolized account of actions of human beings that has a temporal dimension to it" (Sarbin 1986, 3), and each one develops or solves a moral problem in a manner that alters the valuation of the protagonists' social and moral identity.

Section Three. The chapters in the third section critique the unidentified, unacknowledged, and unexamined perspective of the research studies of

others. They do so from an explicitly acknowledged and spelled out hermeneutic or interpretive perspective. These chapters explicitly refer to the way
interpretation involves reflection upon ways of understanding and thinking
that have become taken for granted and customary, but which turn out to
be illusory.

8. The chapters by Donald Spence and Robert Steele provide an interesting contrast in several respects. Donald Spence has compared narrative
truth and historical truth (cf. Spence 1982). His textual target here (chapter
eight) is the published account of a psychoanalytic case study, which he sub-
mits to a critical examination of its forms of argumentation. Spence focuses
on a contrast between "rhetorical" and "evidential" arguments. The former
aims to persuade by appeal to authority, is secretive, protective of theory, and
shows repeated shifts from assumption to putative fact. Evidential argument,
in contrast, is egalitarian, objective and participatory, with its procedures and
data in the public domain. The case-study tradition in psychoanalysis, he
argues, shows disturbing parallels, in its reliance on such elements as metaphor and the substitution of word for thing, with the occult tradition of
alchemy. Since case studies are employed frequently in interpretive research,
Spence's remarks have application beyond their immediate psychoanalytic
focus. And of course Spence's chapter is itself an analysis of a single text, with
the consequence that his interpretation becomes intriguingly reflexive.

9. Robert Steele (chapter nine) also aims to uncover the rhetoric he sees
at work in a text. But while Spence wants to expunge rhetoric, Steele delights
in it. His view is that "rhetoric . . . [is] a living, if denied, part of a text." Steele's
previous work has included an analysis of Freud's and Jung's psychologies as
"two model hermeneutic systems which . . . provide complementary schemata
which can both be used to restore human lives" (Steele 1982, viii). Like Spence,
Steele here examines a published journal article. His deconstructionist
approach is "to make visible that which by training and custom has been
rendered invisible," starting with the "average expectable reading" of a text
and reading what is "between the lines." The text must be viewed from odd
angles and different perspectives in order to seek out its tropes and hidden
meanings, and articulate them. Reality, declares Steele, is contradictory and
ambiguous, and we must read with a radical eye in order to make sense of it.

10. In chapter ten Kenneth Gergen explores the constraints—or rather
the absence of constraint—on the common-sensical interpretation of reports
of opinion and behavior. Gergen has developed a constructionist position (cf.
Gergen 1982, 1985) that, while not identical to hermeneutics, shares with it a
common ground. Many personality researchers have adopted the armamentarium of psychometrics with vigor in an effort to infer consistent personality
characteristics ("traits") on the basis of surveyed opinions. The assumption
that motivations and dispositions comprise a stable, underlying structure to

personality, one that can as a consequence be objectively measured, has been critiqued by those of an interpretive persuasion (e.g., Shweder & D'Andrade 1980). Gergen found when he asked people to "read counter" (see Steele, chapter 9, this volume) to their regular readings of typical personality-test statements that this was an easy task for them. The statements were items from a commonly used personality assessment measure, the Rotter measure of perceived locus of control. An opinion like "Who gets to be boss depends on who was lucky enough to be in the right place first" turned out to be interpreted just as easily as an expression of oversensitivity as one of boldness, as the reader supplied a plausible context to replace the one stripped away by the psychometrician. And in constructing these diverse interpretations, Gergen's readers show us that the apparent orderliness of items in a personality measure is a deceptive result of non-critical and non-contextual reading.

11. The chapter by Dieter Misgeld and David Jardine (chapter eleven) further illustrates the way in which interpretation can involve scrutiny of a taken-for-granted approach whose justification proves on examination to be illusory. Their work is a "reflective investigation of the interpretive grounds of phenomena relevant to psychological-educational research." The text whose analysis exemplifies this approach is a document concerning the educational mission of elementary schooling. Misgeld and Jardine uncover within it an unquestioned technical understanding of childhood and adulthood, and of development and maturity. They point out that research in educational psychology has frequently adopted Piaget's structuralist genetic epistemology and defined adult "competencies" as end-points toward which development proceeds and which education must foster. The technical objectivism of psychometrics has then been brought to bear, resulting in an effort to define competencies in objective, value-free terms so that educational processes and their outcome can be assessed and evaluated.

Misgeld and Jardine point out that the hermeneutic orientation is often assimilated into this technical approach by being considered simply one more technique to be picked from a selection. But they argue that, unlike the technical procedures of rationalist and empiricist inquiry, hermeneutics involves "reflectively explicating the assumptions, prejudices, or understandings in which we already live." From the hermeneutic stance understanding cannot be separated from self-understanding, and interpretive inquiry is critical of technical approaches on the ground that they distort our understanding of ourselves. And hermeneutic inquiry is pedagogical rather than theoretical, moving us to action as it leads us to gain a deeper understanding of ourselves and others.

12. In chapter twelve the editors consider the question of the evaluation of interpretive accounts. We argue that several reasonable approaches to evaluation already have been suggested, but they have sometimes been suggested

for the wrong reasons, and sometimes rejected for similar incorrect reasons. Evaluation cannot be reduced to validation by means of interpretation-free procedures. On too many occasions efforts are made to evaluate interpretive accounts in terms of the correspondence theory of truth. We propose instead that Heidegger's account of truth as "uncovering" provides a new sense of what we do when we evaluate an interpretation.

Taken together, these chapters direct our attention to many aspects of interpretive inquiry. Interpretation works with a text, but this can be a written text, an interview narrative, narrative observations, or action that has been "fixed" in the way Ricoeur (1979) describes. Gergen shows us that such a text is qualitatively distinct from the isolated statements, stripped from context, that can be found in so many psychological tests and coding forms. We learn that an interpreter must read the text in both a usual manner and a special manner, a radical manner, deliberately shifting perspectives. Brown et al. talk of the different "voices" that a text can reveal; Steele of the "extraordinary text" that must be read; Selman et al. of "indices" that direct attention to the various aspects of interaction. Several authors talk of the complexity disclosed in a text when it is read in this way, and they emphasize the need to recognize and be tolerant of ambiguity, to be aware of the possibility of multiple perspectives.

The outcome of interpretation, of course, varies widely from chapter to chapter, and depends on the aim with which inquiry was undertaken. But it is possible to say in general that reading leads to an articulation, a more explicit laying out of forms of understanding that have their source in the two "poles" involved in the reading process: interpreter and text. In part the reading discloses what the interpreter brings to the text, and so Spence can talk of the autobiographical element in his explication de texte, and Selman et al. can draw out and make more explicit their experience as clinicians, their practical "know how," in understanding what transpires in Pair Therapy. And in part the interpretation uncovers themes, arguments and concerns that were hidden in the text, and so Steele talks of the "textual unconscious"; Sarbin of the textual character of emotion as being disguised by reifications; Misgeld and Jardine of tacit manipulative tendencies. These are not elements that lie "behind" the text, as an abstract structure that could replace it, but facets "within" the text that become obvious only as it is scrutinized from various perspectives.

Looking over the chapters we can see that interpretive reading can be guided by forms of analysis that have been developed for studying written texts: analyses of the rhetorics of justification, influence and persuasion, of plot, character and figures of speech (Sarbin; Steele; Spence). Or reading can be guided by a sense of the character of concerns that "move" us in our conduct together: concerns over care and justice (Brown et al.), intimacy, autonomy and status (Caplan et al.; Packer), identity (Mergendoller). These two forms of analysis reflect different emphases in the metaphorical connection between action and text: the first regards text as the primary term, and considers human action understandable only in narrative terms. The second places priority on action, and argues that texts can have dramatic organization only because life itself has a dramatic character.

We remarked above that academic psychology has been dominated by two perspectives that stem from a single world-view. *Empiricist* approaches such as behaviorism, social learning theory, and experimentalism are complemented by *rationalist* approaches such as structuralism, cognitive-developmentalism, and cognitive science, with its computer-models and flow-diagrams. Empiricism and rationalism are twin perspectives because, despite obvious surface differences, they share many of the same assumptions about reality, knowledge, science, and the kind of explanation science provides. Hermeneutics counters this traditional world-view, calling into question many of these basic assumptions. In so doing it opens up fresh possibilities for psychology (some say a can of worms!) that we have only just begun to explore. The following are some of these possibilities:

The possibility that our accustomed and accepted means for reporting our research is not always appropriate. The accepted format for publishing research reports rests upon and expresses questionable assumptions about the way we do research, and may need rethinking. Students are groomed to write in "APA format," where a manuscript is divided into parts they are told reflect the stages in the research process. But division into "introduction, method, results and discussion" imposes a linearity that research does not possess, even in its most hard-nosed experimental manifestations.

The possibility that we should reconsider the traditional way we treat the people we study. We describe them as our "subjects" (meaning, presumably, that the researcher should be treated like royalty!). In the name of scientific necessity we have come to accept that these subjects must be spied on from behind screens and one-way mirrors, manipulated, and deceived. But all these devices stem from a mistaken view of science.

The possibility that the research training we give our undergraduate and doctoral students is inappropriate. Rigor and professionalism have been equated with quantification and statistical analysis. We tell students that we are training them to be neutral, objective, and value-free. We tell them they will be investigating a reality whose existence is independent of them, a reality about which there are objective "facts," and which is value-neutral. From the hermeneutic perspective, these are all false claims.

Even students who will become practicing clinicians are required to demonstrate familiarity with experimental design and analysis, when most of them will never use these skills again. Wouldn't it make more sense to help them hone and develop their interpretive abilities? Particularly with the growing acceptance of the Psy.D. degree as an equal to the Ph.D., there is an opportunity now to reconsider the research component of doctoral-level professional training.

The possibility that we can renew the communication between practitioners and researchers. At a time when the American Psychological Association appears to be undergoing a painful meiosis into scientist and practitioner camps, the notion that they might be able to talk together in a shared language about interpretation, as a phenomenon common to both psychotherapy and the world of research, is an intriguing one.

The possibility that we should rethink the relationship between theory and practice in psychological research. The practical implementation of research results, whether it is in clinical, educational, or commercial settings, is looked down on by some researchers. Science, they feel, is detached observation, description and explanation, and so implementing the results of this work in practical settings is mere application that follows after the real work. In contrast, from the hermeneutic perspective the researcher is intrinsically involved in whatever inquiry is directed toward, and should not take steps to shake off that involvement. Detachment is not an essential prerequisite to objective, undistorted description and explanation. On the contrary, it is a distorting move that removes or covers up the practical involvements—cultural, social and personal—that enable us to understand other people in the first place. This suggests that psychological research, to the extent that it becomes interpretive, is intimately tied to practical issues.

All that is still required from us at this point is to invite the reader to feast on what lies ahead, and to do so in the spirit of excitement and exploration that has motivated the contributors to this volume.

Introduction

MARTIN J. PACKER AND RICHARD B. ADDISON

Twin perspectives have come to rule research and theory in contemporary psychology: the twins of empiricism and rationalism. They are stances taken and attitudes adopted on the concern of how best to be psychologists (even on the question of how best to *be*). They have been dominant in our discipline, and in our intellectual culture, for so long that they go unnoticed and unquestioned. They provide the taken-for-granted background assumptions that run throughout modern psychology, from empiricist approaches such as social learning theory and positivist experimentalism to rationalist approaches such as structuralism and much of cognitive science. The empiricist perspective endorses talk of stimulus and response, of dependent and independent variable, of significance test. Rationalism shapes discussion of information-processing, memory retrieval, scheme and structure, sensory input. Along with ways of talking they regulate techniques of inquiry. Experimental manipulation of variables and the prediction and testing of observable associations are empiricist programs. Computer simulation and formal modeling are rationalist lines of attack. The story of this dual hegemony is as manifold and complex as the branches of institutionalized psychology, and so we shall content ourselves here with giving a brief overview of these perspectives and some of the claims they make about the world and the proper place of psychology in it. We shall consider arguments that these claims are mistaken, even though they have come to be seen as undeniable. And we shall draw a comparison between these twin perspectives and hermeneutics.

A project to evaluate the competing claims of traditional and interpretive approaches to inquiry in psychology would, if done properly, need to make manifest the assumptions fundamental to both rationalism and empiricism, show where and how these assumptions are flawed, and then demonstrate what interpretive inquiry uncovers to deal with the difficulties. (And difficulties of this kind are not always dealt with by being resolved, as we shall see.) A simple review of the various efforts (by Heidegger, MacIntyre, Taylor, Dreyfus, Bernstein and several others) to accomplish this project is in itself too large a task for this introduction. What we shall provide instead is more a thumbnail sketch of what lines of argument have been drawn out by these writers.

Even attempting this simpler task, we soon stumble over the difficulties of conducting an argument about perspectives as broad as those of empiricism, rationalism and hermeneutics. Terms and lines of argument that make sense in one perspective can seem meaningless when viewed from a second. Guiding values for one ("objectivity," say) are understood as misleading myths or chimeras from within another. Forms of argumentation become incommensurate: formal proof stands against narrative history. And we are working at a level where, ex hypothesi, there is no higher level to move to in order to arbitrate the conflict. It would be easy, and very tempting, to relax and say that it is all relative: that the choice between an empiricist, a rationalist, or a hermeneutic perspective is arbitrary; they are equally valid alternatives. This route has often been taken, but it is one we want to avoid here. It can lead to a nihilistic skepticism that can only undercut the concrete inquiries we conduct. We believe that interpretive inquiry is not just another alternative alongside more familiar methodologies.

We shall follow a path that seems the only route possible: arguing that hermeneutics provides a *better* perspective on the world than the traditional twins. Sometimes the argument is straightforward, and the traditional perspectives fall into self-contradiction, failing in terms of their own standards of logic and truth. At other times one can only see the flaws in empiricism or rationalism by shifting to the interpretive perspective. On such an occasion, the argument turns into something close to a brawl: once empiricism and rationalism are shown to be flawed, then cracked open on their flaw-lines, hermeneutics becomes the only game left in town. As Sherlock Holmes declared, "Once the impossible has been eliminated, whatever remains, no matter how improbable, must be true."

Comparing World-Views

Although the origins of empiricism and rationalism (and indeed hermeneutics) can be traced as far back as ancient Greece, we shall begin our account with what has been called the beginnings of modernity, in the seventeenth century. It was then that Descartes (1641/1968) made his first programmatic moves in what was to become a dominant mode of philosophical analysis, one which has found expression in psychology too, via Kant, Piaget, Chomsky, Kohlberg, Miller, and many others. And it was then, too, that Locke (1690/1975) articulated a related account of the person, of the world, and of the character and limitations of knowledge and scientific inquiry; an account whose descendants are also multiple in contemporary psychology. Descartes, of course, was a progenitor of modern rationalism; Locke, a founding father of modern empiricism (as well as democratic constitutionalism). Descartes' and Locke's accounts seem opposites in key respects: Descartes emphasized the dubitable status of sensory knowledge and the need for mind to examine itself in an active and systematic manner; Locke in contrast wrote of the primary qualities of objects in the world—"solidity, extension, figure, motion or rest, and number"—and of ideas in the mind being copies or "resemblances" of these qualities. In one account mind is essentially active, doubting and questioning, in the other mind is largely passive, mirroring an external reality. But the two accounts are complements rather than genuine opposites. Two sides of a single coin, struck from the same metal, they share unexamined assumptions about reality and knowledge. This communality reflects Descartes' and Locke's common admiration of the new developments in the sciences of their time, especially Galileo's geometry and optics, and also their common abandonment of elements of Christian dogma. Common to both accounts is a dualistic view of mind and world as two distinct realms, a belief that they had identified the source of genuine knowledge, and a view that physical science provided a clear and satisfactory model for all analytical inquiry. What both these early statements of empiricism and rationalism celebrated (and to a large extent invented) was the *individual,* as a kind of inquirer after and a carrier of knowledge distinct from both church and state. What was, understandably, brushed aside was the interdependence of individual and larger institutions. Two results of this emphasis on individual knowing were, first, a habit of mind we now call naturalism—a belief in the fixed objective character of both mind and world—and, second, the earliest account of what Taylor (1985, p. 9) calls the "disengaged modern identity." Locke in particular adopted a naive realism, a belief that our ideas of the world (at least as far as primary qualities are concerned) correspond to qualities that "do really exist in the bodies themselves." Here lie the roots of the "correspondence theory" of truth, which have twisted themselves hidden through the ground of contemporary research practice, and trip us still.

Four Areas of Comparison

Rationalist, empiricist and interpretive inquiry can be usefully compared in four areas: In terms of (a) the kind of domain that inquiry is considered to be directed toward; (b) the origin or source of knowledge; (c) the form of explanation that is seen as the goal of inquiry; and (d) the manner of inquiry that is deemed most appropriate. In each of these four—object, origin, explanation, and method—interpretive inquiry makes a radical break with empiricism and rationalism (cf. Palmer 1969; Bleicher 1980).

	Empiricism	Rationalism	Hermeneutics
Domain of inquiry	Independent entities with absolute properties	Formal structures underlying appearances	Action in context; Texts and text analogues
Ground of knowledge	Foundation provided by interpretation-free facts; brute-data	Foundation provided by axioms and principles	Starting place provided by practical understanding; articulated and corrected
Character of explanation	Statements of regularities among data. Causal laws	Formal, syntactic reconstruction of competence	Narrative accounts; a reading of the text
Method: relationship to researched	Objective, value-neutral stance	Detachment; abstraction from context	Familiarity with practices; participation in shared culture
Method: justification of explanation	Assess correspondence with reality	Assess correspondence with intuitions of competent person	Consider whether interpretation uncovers an answer to its motivating concern

Figure 1

Comparing Empiricist, Rationalist, and Hermeneutic Perspectives

Objects, Abstractions, or Everyday Activity?

Every kind of systematic inquiry requires that assumptions be made about the characteristics of the domain studied. Empiricism, rationalism, and hermeneutics each construe the domain of inquiry differently, so that investigators work within quite different preconceptions of the sorts of entity toward which their inquiry is properly directed. This is not to say that the three simply have *different* domains of inquiry, but rather that they interpret a common reality in incompatible ways.

In empiricist inquiry it is taken for granted that the world is made up of basic objects or elements that can be described in a manner that involves no interpretation. These building blocks have properties that are independent of human concerns and practices. The task of scientific inquiry in psychology, from this stance, is to take these elements as its object and describe their properties and interactions. But on closer examination there is a hidden context to this preconception, that of 17th-century mechanical science. Empiricist inquiry in the human sciences today inhabits essentially the same world that Locke borrowed from Galileo (as distinct from, for instance, the world of modern quantum physics): a world where physical objects have absolute, context-independent properties such as size, mass, position, and velocity that can be measured unambiguously with simple procedures and instruments, and a world where such measurements allow precise prediction of subsequent behavior (analogous to Galileo's prediction of a body's movement down an inclined plane). By analogy, people can be described in terms of objective properties such as personality traits, intelligence quotients, or attachment strengths, that are assessed in categorical or quantitative terms with psychometric tests and measures. Modern psychometrics assumes the mental and behavioral worlds are each made up of independent entities that can be collated and measured. The objects of empiricist inquiry are literally objects—entities whose behavior and characteristics are analogous to those of the physical entities whose mechanical interaction was studied by Galileo. Far from this being the only, natural, objective way of seeing the world, it is a product of particular social and intellectual circumstances. There are, perhaps, excuses for the belief of the time that the **true** way of understanding reality had finally been achieved by the new "scientific method." There is no longer any excuse, though, for this naive realism of 17th-century empiricism to continue unabated in contemporary psychological research. It is time to acknowledge that so-called objective reality is a product of human invention.

While empiricist inquiry undertakes to discover lawful generalizations about events in an objective universe, rationalist approaches have, in general, taken on the task of reconstructing a portion of human knowledge or experience. Rationalists are concerned with a realm of formal abstraction to which they give greater credence than everyday appearances. Descartes and Kant, both rationalist philosophers, took on the task of reconstructing human knowledge in its entirety, and determining the conditions for and limits to genuine knowledge; structuralist researchers—one contemporary form of rationalism—have dealt with more restricted subdomains in the same way: de Saussure (1915/ 1959) and Chomsky (1957, 1965) examine language; Piaget (1977) studies the domain of operational intelligence; Kohlberg (1971) looks at the realm of moral judgment. In each case the aim has been to provide an orderly reconstruction that would introduce clarity and indubitability into a realm that is seen as filled with ambiguity and error. Speech, for Chomsky, and action, for Piaget, are occasions of mere "performance," and are distorted by errors, memory constraints and other cognitive limitations. Performance is also shaped in a way structuralists find uninteresting (or, at most, secondary) by the demands of specific situations, and by concrete concerns and interests. The structuralist aim is that of all rationalist approaches: to reconstruct a "competence" or "deep structure" that underlies this performance. Abstract systems of language (de Saussure's "la langue"; Chomsky's "transformational grammar") are held to underlie the speech one uses in everyday conversation; intellectual operations (Piaget's "schemes") are posited to underlie a child's actions with objects and people.

A rational reconstruction of competence provides a transcendental structure whose subject is also a transcendental one: the "ideal speaker-hearer" for Chomsky; the "epistemic subject" for Piaget; one who would operate in "the ideal speech situation" for Habermas. Performance, on the other hand, is viewed as unhappily tied to a subject who is an individual in particular historical, cultural, social and personal conditions. The internal relations of the abstract system of competence are considered far more interesting than the connections between action and setting, which are merely "external."

Furthermore, the underlying structures are assumed to be formal ones, composed of syntactic rules and elements (Williams 1978): rules whose application can proceed automatically, in a definite and established manner that requires no interpretation or judgment. (The computer program is the contemporary exemplar par excellence of a syntactic rule.) So while rationalist inquiry doesn't deal with the simple isolated elements of empiricism, the structures it reconstructs have only formal internal relations, and are stripped of all relationship to context and setting. Piaget recounts a central structuralist postulate "that structures are self-sufficient and that, to grasp them, we do not have to make reference to all sorts of extraneous elements" (Piaget 1970, 4).

The object or domain of rationalist inquiry is, as rationalists describe it, not an immediately apparent one; it lies behind appearances. But rationalists are faced in the first place, just like the rest of us, with occasions of situated speech and action, and their inquiry must do something with these in order that the underlying structures become apparent. As Piaget puts it, "Structures are not observable as such, being located at levels which can be reached only by abstracting forms of forms or systems of the nth degree; that is, the detection of structure calls for a special effort of reflective abstraction" (Piaget 1970, 136). This abstraction is one that removes an utterance or action from its immediate context, from the particular circumstances of a human situation, and from individual interests and concerns.

So, unlike the mechanical world of empiricism, with its inclined planes and swinging pendulums, rationalist inquiry recognizes a non-mechanical interdependence among psychological entities, but one where the connections are purely formal syntactic ones, and the context of human concerns and projects is considered something that can, indeed must, be stripped away. Is anything wrong with this position?

The central criticism of rationalism has been that when human action (including speech) is abstracted from its context it is, unfortunately, not cleaned up but distorted. The assumption that skilled human performance is just sloppy competence, as structuralists would have it, is a distorting one. Distorting in what way? The cost of abstraction is that the object is "mummified, as everything becomes when it is torn out of its context" (Musil 1930/ 1979).[1] The counter claim from the hermeneutic stance is that action and context are not separable without consequences that undercut the aims of rationalist inquiry. Performance and context cannot be teased apart; what abstraction really does is introduce a "privation," an absence of practice. Rationalism sees a dirty baby splashing in scummy bathwater and pulls her out to spruce up and put her on display in pristine condition. The hermeneutic argument is not that the baby gets washed out with the bathwater but that she turns out to be a water-baby who dies on dry land, and so must be studied in her original setting.

One way this argument has been made is to say that the "indexicality" of action—the way in which aspects of context are pointed out and used to bear meaning when we act and talk—is destroyed by rationalist abstraction (Garfinkel 1967; cf. Packer, this volume). Practical activity is intrinsically linked to its context and has a complex temporal organization: the very things that an analysis of competence is designed to eschew. A hermeneutic stance focuses our attention on these contextual and temporal aspects of action; the structures of action are unspiritual and worldly rather than transcendental and eternal.

What might be the consequences of abandoning both empiricism's naive realism and rationalism's inclination to abstraction? What follows once we regard reality as a historical and cultural construction, and recognize action's mundane indexicality? Once empiricism's historical origin in 17th-century mechanics is uncovered, the search by psychologists for mental and behavioral entities analogous to the physical objects studied by Galileo comes to seem an inappropriate strategy of inquiry. (This is true whether the inquiry is psychological, sociological, anthropological or historical, of course). In the empiricist stance the constituents of human life are objects. In the hermeneutic stance they are events and entities that have status and significance by virtue of involvement in our practices. We deal daily with books, cars, VCRs, computers, lovers, pets, plants, classes, universities, relatives, cafes, bureaucracies, regulations, permits. Empiricist inquiry sanctions the effort to study and describe these as though their character and properties are independent of the parts they play in human lives, and their relevance to human concerns and projects. Interpretive inquiry embraces the view that these phenomena cannot be understood independent from human interests and activities, and considers claims to have done this mistaken.

Interpretive inquiry focuses on human activity situated in context and the offspring of such activity: institutions, histories, accounts, records, texts, stories, lives. It makes no sense to imagine any of these existing in the absence of beings like ourselves, who wish to study them and, conversely, it would make no sense to think that we could exist, as psychologists and inquirers, apart from or independent of a whole range of practices, institutions, and accounts. People both constitute and are constituted by their social world;

we contribute to sustaining it as what it is (or changing it); it made us what we have become. We are not, and cannot become, the neutral and dispassionate observers that both empiricism and rationalism would have us be.

A Foundation to Knowledge, or a Starting Place for Inquiry?

The three perspectives differ in their assumptions about the origin or source of the knowledge that inquiry (hopefully) leads to. Throughout the 300-year span of the empiricist stance a recurrent theme has been the claim to have identified the basic components of knowledge: elements that are simple, irreducible and ultimate; terms "for which the correspondence between name and experience is immediately understood" (von Mises 1956, 80). For Locke these basic building blocks of knowledge were "simple ideas, the materials of all our knowledge" (p. 75). In more recent times the logical positivists proposed similar candidates. Ernst Mach, the physicist whose epistemological views were admired by the Vienna Circle founders of logical positivism, considered all experience to consist of elemental sensations: "colors, sounds, warmths, pressures, spaces, times, etc." and their compounds (cited in von Mises, op cit). For the logical positivists, logic is used to connect and manipulate statements about these basic givens, and logic itself is empty of content, being merely the tautological restatement of truths in new forms that may be more convenient and economical (cf. Hahn 1930/1980). Simple ideas or experiences provide the foundation upon which all knowledge is built; logic is just the mortar that holds the bricks together.

Although logical positivism has been declared dead many times, its underlying empiricist assumptions haunt us still. Psychology and the other human sciences resound with nervous and hollow appeals to the self-evidence of objective information. Taylor's definition of these brute facts can hardly be bettered: they are claimed to be:

> data whose validity cannot be questioned by offering another interpretation or reading, data whose credibility cannot be founded or undermined by further reasoning. If such a difference of interpretation can arise over given data, then it must be possible to structure the argument so as to distinguish the basic, brute data from the inferences made on the basis of them. (1979, p. 30)

Data of this kind are commonly taken to be the basis of psychological theories in many contemporary research reports. And what is wrong with this? The major difficulty stems from the claim that any data are self-evident: observed and recorded without interpretation. If the phenomena we study are not isolated independent objects with fixed properties, then we can't observe them in a primordial, objective experience that makes reference neither to their setting nor our concerns.

Even in the natural sciences, which the logical positivists considered the epitome of value-free description, seemingly objective and interpretation-free observations turn out to be dependent on contexts of several kinds. It has become recognized that what counts as an observation depends on current theory; observations are "theory-loaded" (Hanson 1958, and cf. Dreyfus 1980). Successive theories are incommensurable in the sense of requiring radical translation between superficially equivalent terms. With the shift in physics from the Newtonian to the Einsteinian paradigm, basic terms like "mass" and "inertia" changed their meaning, and were applied in different ways to natural phenomena (Kuhn 1970b, 267; cf. Hacking 1983, 167ff).

Positivist efforts to catalog simple observables and prescribe the objective manner by means of which they can be identified have run into many problems. But statements with a positivist tone still linger in introductory psychology texts, and serve to obscure the role that an understanding of culture and humanity inevitably plays in the very identification and description of actions and events; they deny that the observer "presupposes an interpretation of the behavior as having a certain point, as situated within a cultural and institutional framework, as obeying or infringing relevant norms, rules, or expectations, and so on" (McCarthy 1978, 148).

Empiricism, then, claims to have identified a foundation for scientific inquiry in the form of unquestionable observables that are directly given to the senses. Rationalist inquiry seeks a foundation too, but one whose validity is provided by the consistent procedures of formal logic. Rationalism seeks to establish a scaffolding of indubitable principles, preferably formal ones, from which structures that reconstruct human phenomena can be logically generated. Descartes described his aim "to build anew from the foundation, if I wanted to establish any firm and permanent structure in the sciences" (1641/1969, p.144), "... to discover [at least] one thing only which is certain and indubitable" (p. 149), and he aimed to do this through the systematic application of reason, examining each of his beliefs to ascertain the degree of its certainty. In this way he believed he could arrive at an Archimedian point on which to base his reconstruction of all genuine knowledge: the famous "cogito." Descartes's "Cogito ergo sum" was the base upon which he was able to build a proof of the existence of God and of order in the natural world.

Chomsky's structuralist linguistics (here described by Piaget) has an analogous beginning:

> Instead of looking for an inductive step-by-step procedure to help us collect the properties of particular languages and ultimately language in general, Chomsky inquires: What grammatical postulates are necessary and sufficient to describe the universal principles of language structure and to furnish a general method for selecting a grammar for any given particular language? (Piaget 1970, 84).

Here again a foundation is sought in the form of basic principles from which the rules that make up any particular grammatical competence can be derived. In Piaget's own work on the cognitive-developmental analysis of intelligence, basic structures are described that underlie a child's overt actions, and these themselves are products of "functional invariants" or biologically-based tendencies: assimilation and accommodation. Piaget was interested in describing underlying structures of intelligence, stages of development that ignore setting and activity, and so he was only indirectly interested in the thought and action that a child engages in when confronting a puzzling task.

But the foundation sought in rationalist inquiry, the basic principles or axioms from which a formal reconstruction can be logically derived, has proved as unreachable, or at least as misleading, as the empiricist foundation. Members of the Vienna Circle (e.g., Hahn 1933/1980) were happy to point out that formal logic is unable to bear the weight that rationalists wish to place upon it: logic cannot provide a foundation for knowledge about either the world or the mind. Newton's cosmology and Euclid's geometry, once thought to be fruits of a universal logic and, at the same time, true statements about empirical reality have turned out to be neither. They turn out to be conventions: two among the many possible ways of describing physical phenomena. Relativity theory displaced Newton's universe, and the discovery in the late 19th century of alternatives to the "natural" geometry of Euclid showed that it was a mistake (the "shipwreck of formalism"; Rosen, 1987, 153) to think that logical propositions somehow match reality; rather, their explanatory power is a product of the contingent choice of their axioms. That is to say, Newton's and Euclid's systems both worked because they were ingenious systems for representing natural phenomena in a manner relevant to our need to control and manipulate nature, not because they mirrored an objective reality. Furthermore, Godel's theorem (Nagel and Newman 1958) showed that a system of formal logic may be incomplete and inconsistent; hardly properties that are desirable for a truth-preserving instrument of thought.

So both these attempts to establish a foundation on which inquiry could build final truths have run into major difficulties. It seems time to say that foundationalist efforts have failed, and also time to recognize that scientific inquiry does not require an indubitable foundation. Rationalist axiomatic reconstructions and empiricist brute-data building blocks are both Rube Goldberg devices designed to enable people to escape from what they fear is a vicious circle: the circle of interpretation, the *hermeneutic circle*. The gadgets don't work; the foundations have crumbled; and the hermeneutic circle turns out to be an inevitable part of our efforts to understand human phenomena.

Discarding the apparatus that is supposed to make psychology truly scientific, and the efforts to avoid the fearsome circularities of interpretation, is proving to be no casual matter. The problems that foundationalist moves have run into have given rise to what Bernstein (1983, p. 18) calls "Cartesian Anxiety": "not just radical epistemological skepticism but the dread of madness and chaos where nothing is fixed, where we can neither touch bottom nor support ourselves on the surface." Researchers working within the empiricist stance fear that if their search for a method that achieves objectivity fails then relativism must be an inevitable result, and inquiry will reflect only subjective opinions. And when those who have embarked on the never-ending rationalist quest for total explicitness become confronted by the recognition that there is unavoidable ambiguity in human affairs and understanding, their fear is a similar one, that this ambiguity will be a total one, leading inexorably to the same relativism.

Hermeneutics is repeatedly challenged to explain its apparently relativist position. The difficulty in meeting this challenge stems from the challengers' expectation that the solution to the puzzle must take the form of procedures or criteria, whereas the guarantees against relativism (and against totalitarian objectivism, for that matter) lie in our practices (MacIntyre 1984, 1988; Kuhn 1977, 320ff; Bernstein 1983, 223ff).

Both everyday understanding and scientific knowledge have their starting place in practical activity: in our direct, everyday practical involvement with tools, artifacts, and people in the world. Geertz (who describes his own anthropological work as hermeneutic) points out that "science owes more to the steam engine than the steam engine owes to science" (1983, p. 22). A similar practical starting point is the place where we, as psychologists, inevitably begin our research, but it is located in human interactions, not mastery of the environment. One might say that psychology owes more to the cocktail party than the cocktail party owes to psychology (we think of Cherry 1953). Both our everyday actions and our research are embedded in the social practices of our home, our workplace, our society. This practical activity is distinct from any psychological theorizing we do, and it would continue if we stopped forming theories. Practical understanding is not an origin for knowledge in the sense of a foundation; it is, instead, a **starting place** for interpretation. Interpretive inquiry begins not from an absolute origin of unquestionable data or totally consistent logic, but at a place delineated by our everyday participatory understanding of people and events. We begin there in full awareness that this understanding is corrigible, and that it is partial in the twin senses of being incomplete and perspectival. Understanding is always moving forward. Practical activity projects itself forward into the world from its starting place, and shows us the entities we are at home among. This means that neither common sense nor scientific knowledge can be traced back to an origin, a foundation.

Explanation and Understanding

We have considered views of the domain of inquiry in each of the three perspectives and conceptions of the origin or starting place of the knowledge sought in each approach to inquiry. Our third topic is intimately related to both of these: the form or character that an explanatory account is taken to have.

The programmatic statements of logical positivism still influence many psychologists' notions of what makes an adequate explanation. For many, an explanation has been provided when observation-statements are linked to form theoretical-statements. An explanation is a hypothesized lawful relationship of co-occurrence that has been tested through empirical observation; a combination of a general law and description of specific conditions. Conceived in this way, as a statement of regularities, explanation has the same formal character as prediction. If certain conditions exist, laws such as Newton's allow one to deduce (i.e., predict) a future outcome. Conversely, a particular outcome is explained if, given a general law, one can show that the requisite initiating conditions transpired. The billiard ball entered the pocket because the cue ball hit it with specified velocity and angular momentum; the child moved toward her mother because appearance of a stranger induced anxiety that was reduced by closer proximity.

From this stance, a scientific theory is often viewed as merely restating factual observations in a simple, handy and economical form: it aims to be "a complete and clear inventory of the facts of a domain" (Mach 1896/1986, 415). Explanation is provided by laws, and laws express regularities in the observable data. "The general laws of physics ... are not essentially different from descriptions" (op. cit., p. 396). Newton's laws of motion are paragons of explanation. Consider for instance the First Law of Motion: $v = u + at$. This general statement permits calculation of a body's velocity (v) at any future time (t), given knowledge of the initial conditions: the acceleration acting upon it (a) and its initial velocity (u).

We have described how a rationalist explanatory account takes the form of a reconstruction: a precise formal delineation of structures underlying performance. Here, explanation is provided by a set of rules, an algorithm, whose relationship to the domain of inquiry is that of a formal logic to the set of well-formed statements deducible from its axioms. For example, Chomsky's (1957) transformational grammar generates all and only the grammatically well-formed sentences of American English. Cognitive scientists set great store by computer models of psychological processes such as depth-perception, semantic memory, or text comprehension, because the formal algorithms and data structures involved in such a model provide, from this stance, a full explanatory account of the process. The widespread interest in machine intelligence reflects this deeper quest for a successful reconstruction in logical terms of some area of human understanding, a success that would finally vindicate the rationalist project. Minimal progress has been made in this effort at reconstruction, however (cf. Dreyfus 1979; Dreyfus & Dreyfus 1986).

One telling criticism of both causal laws and formal reconstructions is that such explanations are what they claim to be (interpretation-free and fully explicit descriptions of reality) only when the elements they operate on are uninterpreted ones. The measurements of objective properties and the syntactic units that make up a system of competence are indeed claimed to be uninterpreted. But we have already outlined the case for the hermeneutic view that human understanding is not made up of elements of this kind, and that it traffics instead in "thick concepts" that meld fact and value (Williams 1985). To the extent that an explanatory account of human action has its starting place in human understanding, it will not be formal. Instead, interpretive inquiry yields narrative accounts and "thick descriptions" (Geertz 1983). MacIntyre argues that:

> In successfully identifying and understanding what someone else is doing we always move towards placing a particular episode in the context of a set of narrative histories, histories both of the individuals concerned and of the settings in which they act and suffer. ... It is because we all live out narratives in our lives and because we understand our own lives in terms of the narratives that we live out that the form of narrative is appropriate for understanding the actions of others. (MacIntyre 1984, 211).

Even if agreement were reached that the elements in causal laws are context-bound and that interpretation plays a part in their identification, the search for regularities and predictive laws remains a far from satisfactory mode of psychological explanation. First, prediction is impossible in many cases where we may nonetheless achieve understanding. For instance, society changes through conceptual, practical, and technological revolutions whose form cannot be predicted (the introduction of computers into business, government and research provides a powerful contemporary example), and one consequence is that we cannot predict the terms in which the future will be understood (historical changes in notions of trading, for instance, illustrate this). Furthermore, social life has a game-like quality to it that can be identified only in retrospect, if at all, and so evades prediction ("the problem about real life is that moving one's knight to QB3 may always be replied to with a lob across the net," MacIntyre 1984, 98). Third, the outcomes of individuals' decisions effect social life at the cultural, institutional and personal levels, but cannot be predicted. (Which social scientist anticipated Gorbachev's introduction of Glasnost?) Pure contingency has had profound consequences that we may comprehend without anticipating. (The length of Cleopatra's nose played a role in the declaration of war.) Human life resembles the weather in being an open system that never reaches equilibrium; like the weather we can recognize what transpires (storms, sunny days) even when unable to say what comes next.

Predictive laws are inadequate explanations for a second reason. The few generalizations in social science that hold up are qualified by *certeris paribus* conditions; they hold true "other things being equal," meaning their scope of application is extremely ill-defined. They are secondary phenomena, the results of social practices and institutions whose functioning is symbolic and representational, not causal. They are the consequence of factors such as the necessity for scheduling and coordinating our actions (brushing teeth after eating breakfast). They reflect the way that knowledge of statistical regularities shapes our action. (We know we catch more colds in winter, and predictably stock up on Vitamin C.) They work only because our understanding of the causal regularities of nature constrains social life. (Storm clouds bode rain, so we tend to seek shelter when thunderclouds form.) (Cf. MacIntyre 1984, 93ff; Taylor 1979, 69ff).

Both empiricist and rationalist inquiry seek a kind of explanation that only makes reference to interpretation-free elements and formal rules. In the natural sciences such an approach works because scientists can forget the conceptual and practical framework they are working within: the accepted paradigm. In a human science like psychology the same approach leads to distortions and trivial "findings," because it suppresses the framework of concerns and interests of the people being studied. It also assumes, falsely, that researchers have reached consensus on the best perspective from which to conduct their inquiries.

What is "Scientific Method" in Psychology?

We have examined arguments that say that both empiricist and rationalist forms of inquiry concern themselves with domains of inquiry that exclude and deny context and setting, that both seek an unattainable foundation of certainty upon which to construct scientific knowledge, and that both seek explanations in the form of elements and rules that avoid both interpretation and human interests and concerns. And we have reviewed arguments that both rationalism and empiricism inevitably require interpretation of the phenomena they aim to explain, at the same time as they deny doing so.

We can now consider the conception of method that is involved in each form of inquiry. If interpretive inquiry makes a radical break with the fictions of a pre-existing, independent object to scientific investigation and of an epistemological foundation upon which objective theories can be based, the break in the view of what is appropriate method is a radical one, too. It is easy to set up a straw man when discussing conceptions of scientific method. In a sense there are as many methods in psychology as there are research programs. But the fact remains that over the centuries various programmatic statements have been made about proper scientific method, and psychology has been more than susceptible to their appeal.

In both empiricist and rationalist inquiry, method is what is considered necessary to obtain foundational knowledge and systematically generate an appropriate kind of explanation. In empiricist inquiry, procedures are necessary to collect reliable data under selected or manipulated conditions, and then to identify regularities among these data that meet stringent and objective criteria (generally levels of statistical significance). In rationalist inquiry, formal principles must be defined that will serve as the basis for an axiomatization of the domain of knowledge under investigation. In both stances method is considered a matter of procedure or technique, involving analytical operations that require no involvement of human judgment and valuation. This is no surprise; since the grounding (in a foundation of either brute data or formal axioms) and the explanation (by description of regularities, or formal derivations) are by intention interpretation-free, it follows that the method linking them must also be interpretation-free. If either the empiricist or the rationalist program is to succeed, reflection, judgment and evaluation must be replaced by technique. And, equally, if both an interpretation-free foundation and a value-neutral explanation turn out to be fictional notions in the human sciences, then method will not prove to be reducible to procedure. Within both rationalist and empiricist approaches to inquiry there are two aspects of method we shall discuss: establishing a *point of view* from which to proceed, and *evaluating* the explanation produced.

Empiricism

The Objective Point of View. The empiricist researcher aims to achieve what might be called an absolute perspective; a God's eye view, from which the world could be described in objective terms. Such a perspective would be distinct from that of any particular observer. The researcher must try to become detached from any personal involvement and adopt what Nagel (1986) calls "the view from nowhere." But cultivating the appropriate "scientific attitude" is hardly a matter of mere procedure. Being value-neutral, free from prejudice, objective and unbiased (to the small extent that these are possible at all) involves adopting a special posture of distance from or denial of one's personal interests and concerns. And being unconcerned or disinterested is as little achieved through procedures and techniques as is being concerned. Paradoxical though it sounds, detachment is itself a kind of perspective, a way of viewing the world, that cannot be reduced to technique. Computers, though they implement procedures, are not detached: they are blind. They don't see from nowhere: they see nothing.

The Correspondence Problem. In empiricism, evaluating an explanation is, in large part, a matter of employing techniques or procedures that aim to assess correspondence with a reality independent of the researcher. This of course is where positivism placed its weight: improving the hygiene of science by specifying operations, checks and rules that would ensure that theories and statements were grounded through chains of logic to the bedrock of fundamental data. Bacon and Hume appealed to inductive logic to guarantee the truth of a theory; since Popper the claim has been that the logic of falsification guarantees rejection of false theories. In either case truth is viewed as a matter of fit between theory and reality. But the whole enterprise of employing procedures that will validate a hypothesis or theory is based on a conundrum: the impossible "correspondence theory" of truth that began with Locke and was continued by Mach and the Vienna Circle positivists. Scientific procedures are, on this account, those that establish and maintain a correspondence between theory and world: that provide accurate descriptions of an independent reality. But how could such a correspondence ever be assessed? Who can be in a position to decide whether our ideas, our theories, or even our observations correspond with an independent reality? Locke himself saw the paradox:

> It is evident that the mind knows things not immediately, but only by the intervention of the ideas it has of them. Our knowledge therefore is real only so far as there is conformity between our ideas and the reality of things. But what shall be here the criterion? How shall the mind, when it perceives nothing but its own ideas, know that they agree with things themselves? (Locke 1690/1975).

Locke tried to finesse his way out of this problem with an unconvincing appeal to a correspondence "ordained and adapted to" "by the wisdom and will of our Maker" (op. cit.). Again we find that method cannot be a matter of procedure. Validating an explanatory account by establishing degree of correspondence with reality cannot be done by procedure, because no procedure could possibly accomplish the desired comparison.

The logic of falsification (Popper 1959) seems at first glance to avoid the correspondence problem, but it does not. This logic runs, in brief, as follows. From the theory to be assessed, a hypothesis is derived. This hypothesis makes explicit prediction about the character or co-occurrence of states of affairs, given specified conditions (that may be brought about through manipulation, if needed). The hypothesis is counted as falsified if the prediction is observed to be false. A theory stands or falls, is "corroborated" or uncorroborated, on the basis of its power to make unfalsified predictions. Through rebuttal of predictions that are not realized, theories are refuted and rejected. We hang onto a theory whose predictions are not false, always bearing in mind that it may just have been lucky; a theory is never verified, it just escapes falsification. We never make positive claims that a theory is valid; only negative claims that it has survived the tests that its competitors failed.

Thus far, we seem to need no reference to notions and claims of correspondence. But note that the hypotheses, the conjectures or predictions, must be tested through observation of the states of affairs they describe. It is still assumed, then, that there are factual states of affairs that can be objectively, neutrally, described. Indeed, Popper believes that the correspondence theory has been "rehabilitated" (1979, p. 314) because, he claims, we can develop metalanguages that both refer to the statements in a theory and describe facts about the world, and so put them side by side for comparison. Popper fails to see this merely shifts the problem's location: how does a metalanguage get the access to reality, to "a certain fact" (op. cit., 315) that would be needed to know that its "description" is correct? Kuhn (1970, p. 283) sees the need that falsification retains to somehow relate sentences and actual observations and experiments, and argues that Popper "is entirely silent about how it can do so." Kuhn concludes that "rather than a logic, Sir Karl has provided an ideology; rather than methodological rules, he has supplied procedural maxims" (op. cit., 283). Even in the guise of falsificationism, empiricist method is actually a matter of maxims, not rules.

Rationalism

The Detached Point of View. The rationalist researcher aims for a viewpoint that is similar to that sought after in empiricism: an attitude of detachment from the concerns and interests of everyday life that supposedly leads, through abstraction, to clarity. Descartes' own account of his meditations provides a clear example of this aim. Descartes deliberately cultivated a special attitude of detachment; to prepare himself he made a concerted effort to abstract himself from all practical involvements and their attendant cares, predicaments and significances, in order to engage in exercises of reflection and cogitation. He aimed for a physical setting and a state of mind where he could be devoted solely to his inquiry, with no other interests or distractions, generally by retreating to a comfy chair by the fire. "Sitting by the fire, wearing a dressing gown" (1641/1968, p. 96) he describes his technique: "I shall now close my eyes, stop up my ears, turn away all my senses, even efface from my thought all images of corporeal things" (op. cit., 113), aiming to get to a point where "my mind is free from all cares" (op. cit., 95).

This aspect of Descartes' method is an unwitting attempt to establish the kind of engagement that Heidegger calls the "present-at-hand" (Heidegger 1927/1962; cf. Packer 1985). This is a mode of detachment from practical activity, and Heidegger argues that it is derivative and privative: experience in this mode is distorted, a shadow of the kind of understanding provided by concerned involvement. Again it is evident that what is going on here is not the application of an interpretation-free procedure; it is the adoption of a certain kind of "detached involvement" with the world, a short-lived laying aside of one concerns and interests. Rationalist method also turns out not to be what it claims to be.

Intuitions of Correctness. Recall that a rationalist account of a psychological phenomenon aims at a reconstruction of the formal structures that underlie appearances. For instance, slips of the tongue might be explained with a computer simulation of cognitive processes of retrieval from memory, limited-capacity processing, and output production. Now the phenomena themselves don't provide any guidance for assessing the reconstruction. Rather, this is a matter of showing that a reconstruction is consistent and complete. In practice this means, first, demonstrating that the system follows its own rules and, second, that the output carries a sense of appropriateness; that it accords with "the intuitive knowledge of competent subjects" (Habermas 1979, 9). For instance, in our tongue-slip example, the program should not only be able to use its rules to generate slips we've observed, it should also make new slips of its own. And these should seem appropriately "slippy" to us. Similarly, the syntactic rules of a Transformational Grammar can be examined to see that they will generate sentences, and novel sentences must be examined to decide whether they seem "grammatical." The first of these is a straightforward matter, but the second leads to problems. Appeals of this type, to an intuitive sense that a particular rational reconstruction satisfies the relevant criterion—be it one of logical indubitability, linguistic equivalence, moral adequacy, or slippyness—can be found from Descartes to Chomsky. Descartes resolved to "accept nothing in my judgments beyond what presented itself so clearly and distinctly to my mind, that I should have no occasion to doubt it" (Descartes, cited in Williams 1978, 32). Saussure made the same assumption that indubitable intuitions can be found. He "seems to assume that the native speaker is normally able to make a correct identification of features of linguistic structure, by some simple process of introspection and reflection" (Harris 1987, 11). Harris points out that this appeal to intuition is *central* to Saussure's structuralist project, not just an afterthought: "The theoretical significance of this assumption it would be difficult to exaggerate. Only its unquestioned acceptance will justify Saussure's lack of concern with providing any systematic 'discovery procedure' for the identification of linguistic signs." In just the same way, for Chomsky the reconstruction of linguistic competence must "meet the empirical conditions of conforming, in a mass of crucial and clear cases, to the linguistic intuition of the native speaker" (Chomsky 1965, 21).

Despite their long history, intuitions of this kind provide, at best, dubious validation of a formal explanatory reconstruction. First, intuition and logic can go in contrary directions. For this reason, in mathematics there has long been an effort to replace intuitions of validity with formal proof (Hahn 1933/1980). Second, intuitions may carry a sense of clarity and certainty that turns out to be illusory. We have seen that empiricist inquiry involves a hidden, and indefensible, assumption that an observer has direct, unproblematic access to the real world. Rationalist inquiry involves an equally suspect assumption that we can have accurate intuitive knowledge about the operation of some portion of our cognitive apparatus. (Psychologists especially should doubt this!) Habermas apparently finds acceptable the consequence that "linguistic intuitions can be 'false' only if they come from incompetent speakers" (1979, p. 212). Such a view ignores the likelihood that even people we would not consider incompetent (researchers included) may have a partial, incomplete or distorted understanding of themselves and what they are doing. It also overlooks the fact that the judgments being requested (grammatical well-formedness, semantic equivalence, moral adequacy) require supposition of a putative setting or usage. Intuitions draw upon and reproduce a background understanding of typical situations and usual aims, an understanding which is however not part of the reconstructed competence. And, viewed in this light, intuitive judgments turn out to involve interpretation: they appeal to and grow out of areas of know-how, skill, style, and expertise that elude formalization. So, to return to our main theme, the appeal to intuitions as a basis for evaluating a reconstruction can hardly be said to involve the simple application of procedures or operations.

In light of the dubious status of their claims to successfully define scientific method in terms of interpretation-free procedures or techniques, it is perhaps not too strong to say that rationalism and empiricism are fundamentally ideological stances. Reports of research framed within each of these perspectives (accounts both ancient and modern) deal not so much with what *is* done in systematic inquiry as with what it is wished *could* be done. Unwarrantable claims are made, and both empiricism and rationalism cover up the role and particular character of human interests and concerns. For if method cannot be reduced to procedure and technique, it follows that, here as before, what empiricist and rationalist researchers do is not what they claim to be doing. If the two aspects of traditional objectivist inquiry that we have discussed—establishing a point of view and evaluating an explanation—are not procedures, what is going on? Both empiricism and rationalism turn out to contain a hidden interpretive component. Psychological inquiry involves the researcher forming a relationship with research participants, and assessing and evaluating, communicating and acting on what has been learned. The relationship will involve an attitude or posture on the researcher's part; the evaluation will appeal to shared values and norms.

Does Interpretive Inquiry Have a Method?

The tacit assumption in traditional psychological inquiry that scientific method must involve only technique or procedure explains a curious anxiety about method that runs through the interpretive research literature. In large part, the attraction of an interpretive approach lies in the relief it offers from the procedural strictures of experimentalist psychology, which many of us feel loosens our grip on the baby in an effort to ensure that the bathwater is handled properly. Experimental design and statistical analysis, for example, are often taught as though they are keys that will unlock any psychological puzzle-box, rather than as adjuncts to an understanding of people and their actions.

Perhaps in reaction to these strictures, some who have adopted an interpretive stance have argued that hermeneutics has *no* method. In this volume Misgeld and Jardine come closest to this position. They cite Gadamer's claim that "the problem of hermeneutics goes beyond the limits that the concept of method sets to modern science. The understanding and the interpretation of texts is not merely a concern of science, but is obviously part of the total human experience of the world. The hermeneutic phenomenon is basically not a problem of method at all. It is not concerned with a method of understanding, by means of which texts are subjected to scientific investigation like all other objects of experience" (Gadamer 1960/1986, xi). But what Gadamer calls "Method" (with capital M) and sets up in opposition to "truth" is not the actual methods of science but the sloganistic statements of positivism; explicitly the canons of induction laid out by Hume and Mill, and by extension the procedures of hypothesis and deduction asserted by Popper. As Bernstein points out:

> Gadamer tends to rely on an image of science which the postempiricist philosophy and history of science have called into question.... Method [in natural science] is more like hermeneutical understanding than Gadamer frequently acknowledges, and when it comes to validating competing understandings and interpretations we are confronted with the type of critical problems that are so fundamental for understanding scientific inquiry (Bernstein 1983, 168).

In other words Gadamer's distinction between Method and understanding is somewhat overdrawn, and perpetuates a mythology about the way the natural sciences operate (and cf. Warnke 1987; Weinsheimer 1985). The same mythology, of course, finds expression in the empiricist (especially, but the rationalist also) conception of proper research method in psychology. A fundamental change in our role as researchers and inquirers—such as a hermeneutic stance requires—surely involves a correlative change in our sense of the appropriate way to conduct our inquiries. Our understanding of method must change. But to throw method away entirely, as Gadamer does, is to accept the very mythology that needs to be debunked.

Scientific method is *not* interpretation-free procedure and technique. We have suggested that even in the traditional stances it involves two aspects: establishing a point of view, and evaluating the account that results. If this is so, then interpretive inquiry has a method that can be called scientific, because the chapters in this volume are amply involved with both these aspects. Of course the point of view is not one of objectivity or detachment, and evaluation does not take the form of validation. Furthermore, in the myth of procedure, these two aspects of method are described as two poles, the start and end of inquiry. First, we are told, develop the objective, detached attitude that will be necessary to observe and reflect. Then build a theory (or at least a hypothesis). Finally, end by evaluating what you have by applying rigorous validity tests. From the interpretive stance, the researcher's point of view and the evaluation of explanatory accounts are not seen as being separated in this way, but as in a constant dialogue. Rather than opposite ends of a straight line, they are on the circumference of a circle: the hermeneutic circle. Establishing a point of view, a perspective, is the forward arc, and evaluation forms the reverse arc. Getting a perspective, adopting a point of view, is a forward movement because of a phenomenon which Heidegger identified and analyzed, and which he called "projection."

The Essential Circularity of Understanding

One of Heidegger's foremost contributions to our views of both philosophy and science has been to show that there is a *circularity* to understanding. When we try to study some new phenomenon we are always thrown forward into it. Unless it is totally alien we will have some preliminary understanding of what kind of phenomenon it is, and of what possible things might happen to it. This means that we both understand it and at the same time misunderstand it; we inevitably shape the phenomenon to fit a "fore-structure" that has been shaped by expectations and preconceptions, and by our lifestyle, culture and tradition. Understanding always takes place within this horizon or framework that is "projected" by human being ("Dasein"):

[U]nderstanding has in itself the existential structure which we call *"projec-tion"* [Entwurf] .... Projecting has nothing to do with comporting oneself towards a plan that has been thought out, and in accordance with which Dasein arranges its Being. On the contrary, any Dasein has, as Dasein, already projected itself; and as long as it is, it is projecting. As long as it is, Dasein always has understood itself and always will understand itself in terms of possibilities (Heidegger 1927/1962, 185).

It is important to emphasize that the hermeneutic circle is ontological rather than simply epistemological or methodological. Projection is, first of all, a structure of our way of being in the world, our living, our actions and interactions, before it characterizes our knowledge and our sciences. "Under-standing is projective because the Being of Dasein is projective" (Caputo 1987, 61). Projection is an existential structure; our existence is such (unlike that of the objects around us) that we are thrown into future ways of acting that are made possible by our cultural and personal history. We live toward a future whose possibilities are both created and limited by the present and the past.

Because this circularity is essential, intrinsic and unavoidable, the empiricist and rationalist attempts to break away from interpretation and reach an epistemological foundation were inevitably futile. As Caputo (1987, p. 61) puts it, "to understand means to project a certain horizonal framework within which the being is to be understood. Entities can appear only insofar as a certain horizon of Being has already been laid out for them in advance .... [This means] there are no pure, uninterpreted facts of the matter but only beings already set forth in a certain frame, projected in their proper Being."

The circularity of understanding, then, is that we understand in terms of what we already know. But the circularity is not, Heidegger argues, a "vicious" one where we simply confirm our prejudices, it is an "essential" one without which there would be no understanding at all. And the circle is complete; there is accommodation as well as assimilation. If we are persevering and open, our attention will be drawn to the projective character of our under-standing and—in the backward arc, the movement of return—we gain an increased appreciation of what the fore-structure involves, and where it might best be changed.

In interpretive inquiry, projection has finally become acknowledged as an inevitable and essential part of our understanding, both everyday and scientific. Consequently, the choice of a point of view or perspective often becomes a careful and deliberative one. And it is often seen to involve establishing a relationship with those who participate with us, and working out a mode of engagement with them. Far from being detached and neutral, we need to adopt a perspective that is engaged and concerned. In our science as much as in our everyday living we shouldn't try to throw away either our culture or our past. Knowledge can't be built (or even rebuilt) from scratch, nor can it be guaranteed satisfactory for all people and all times.

We talked earlier of an anxiety about method in interpretive research, an anxiety, we argued, that drove Gadamer to deny that interpretive inquiry *has* a method. The same anxiety can be seen in the fact that one issue seems to arise again and again in discussions of interpretation: that of ensuring "validity in interpretation" (to borrow a phrase from the title of an early and influential book on this topic, Hirsch 1967). Not surprisingly this issue is raised by empiricist and rationalist critics of interpretive inquiry, but it also recurs among practitioners. There is a central concern behind this issue of validity: that interpretations should not turn out to reflect the prejudices and biases of the interpreter. And this concern in turn stems from a recognition, although often not fully explicit and articulated, of the circularity of understanding.

The concern is not an unreasonable one: every day we are confronted with one-sided accounts of events, political and personal, that claim to be "interpretations" but are partisan and slanted. But the answer to it will not be the identification of "validation procedures" for interpretation. Rather, the answer lies in an examination of the flip side of the circle, the reverse movement of evaluation. This aspect deserves detailed consideration in its own right, but we shall postpone this to an Endpiece.

Some Final Thoughts

We've said that when we conduct hermeneutic inquiry we must look for a starting place, one that will vary from inquiry to inquiry, and not an absolute foundation. Something more follows from this. Objectivist psychology, rationalist or empiricist, has sought a foundation in order to build something that will rest upon it: a fixed construction, an edifice. Generally the plans for this construction have sketched it as a unification of all the sciences; an accumulation and systemization of all knowledge. Hermeneutic inquiry is not oriented toward such a grand design. Any final construction that would be a resting point for scientific inquiry represents an illusion that must be resisted. If all knowledge were to be at last collected in some gigantic encyclopaedia this would mark not the triumph of science so much as the loss of our human ability to encounter new concerns and uncover fresh puzzles. So although hermeneutic inquiry proceeds from a starting place, a self-consciously interpretive approach to scientific investigation does not seek to come to an end at some final resting place, but works instead to keep discussion open and alive, to keep inquiry under way. Seen in that light, the chapters that follow make exciting, provocative reading.

Our purpose here has been to provide an inoculation against the twin maladies of rationalism and empiricism; ills that we feel are stunting our discipline. Once the reader has been protected from them we hope the chapters that follow will, in their accounts of interpretive investigations, induce a fever of a more energizing character. We are aware we have not provided a neat, succinct account of how interpretive inquiry escapes the pitfalls and solves the problems we have argued traditional inquiry has fallen into. In part this is the role of the other chapters in this volume. But in part we must admit we find ourselves in agreement with Clifford Geertz when he says:

> I do not believe that what 'hermeneutics' needs is to be reified into a para-science, as epistemology was, and there are enough general principles in the world already .... The stuttering quality of not only my own efforts along these lines but of interpretive social science generally is a result not (as is often enough suggested by those who like their statements flat) of a desire to disguise evasion as some new form of depth or to turn one's back on the claims of reason. It is a result of not knowing, in so uncertain an undertaking, quite where to begin, or, having anyhow begun, which way to move. (Geertz 1983, 5).

PART ONE

Finding a Perspective
From Which to Interpret

CHAPTER 1

Grounded Interpretive Research:
An Investigation of Physician Socialization[1]

RICHARD B. ADDISON

Psychologists and other social scientists have tried to court respectability by carrying out research that aims to be "scientific." Such research based on empiricist or rationalist assumptions has shown itself to be inadequate for capturing the meaning of social activity for individuals and social structures. It has also proved itself inadequate for illuminating the conditions and context within which that social action takes place. Increased awareness of these inadequacies has given rise to renewed interest in and development of interpretive research approaches.

In this chapter, I will describe and discuss an interpretive investigation I conducted. I will begin by laying out the problem with which I began my inquiry. I will then describe my grounded interpretive method of investigation: the preliminary steps I took, how I developed an interpretive account (along with a brief summary of the account I developed), and how I refined the account. And finally I will discuss four central aspects of interpretive research that are embodied in my approach: the relationship between immersion, understanding, and interpretation, the fore-structure of interpretation, the background context, and how interpretive accounts can open up possibilities.

The Problem of Becoming a Physician

I have always been interested in what is commonly referred to as the socialization of primary-care physicians.[2] Not only is this topic of interest to me, it is also problematic for the individuals involved. Becoming a physician has become increasingly focused on the technology of medicine. Medical costs and malpractice claims have increased tremendously. Patients expect physicians to be medically knowledgeable, technically proficient, and ruthlessly compulsive. Primary-care physicians in particular are also expected to be patient, kind, caring, wise, and infallible. When they inevitably prove themselves fallible, the public becomes dissatisfied and disillusioned. At the same time, the incidence of stress, burnout, poor patient care, isolation, marital problems, substance abuse, depression, and suicide among physicians has increased.

The medical internship, that year following graduation from medical school when the individual begins to practice as a physician, has long been recognized to be the most stressful period in the process of becoming a physician (Bloom 1963; Light 1980; Miller 1970; Mumford 1970). This is the time when individuals begin practicing as physicians, the period when they begin forming habits and patterns of behaving and interacting that often extend beyond the internship and residency into their personal and professional lives (Bloom 1963).

I wanted to better understand what becoming a physician was like for the individuals involved as well as the implications of the process for the structures of medical training and health care; how their practices became problematic for themselves, their patients, patients' families, and others; whether positive alternatives were possible for individuals and for the structure of medical training; and what resident-physicians actually did as they started practicing medicine. These are the types of concerns that are best addressed by a grounded interpretive investigation.

My Approach to the Problem

In part, the choice of a method of investigation depends on the problem to be investigated. The method chosen must fit the problem and goal of the investigation. In part, the choice of a method and the perception, definition, and framing of the problem also depend on the researcher's preunderstanding of the world. (See my discussion of Heidegger's notion of fore-structure below.)

Survey research on physicians' attitudes and beliefs about the relationship between their training and their stress would provide me with little more than a shallow comprehension of the process of becoming a physician. Self-report measures or questionnaires are inadequate for capturing an understanding of the everyday social practices and context of participants in ongoing social situations. These methods are insufficient for understanding the depth and complexity of social interactive processes that occur during residency training.

I was intrigued by and attracted to grounded theory,[3] a systematic inductive procedure for gathering and analyzing "data" for the purpose of generating a theory or account. Although grounded theory addresses some of the inadequacies of positivist research methods, as I conducted my investigation, I learned how it falls short of being a consistently interpretive or hermeneutic method of research. Examining certain tenets and practices of grounded theory may help elucidate both its interpretive strengths and limitations.

1. Both grounded theory and interpretive research are constantly comparative; that is, they adopt the stance of always questioning gaps, omissions, inconsistencies, misunderstandings, and not-yet understandings. This practice is a central feature and strength of both grounded theory and hermeneutic research.

2. Grounded theorists stress that theory should be processual rather than static or fixed. If Glaser and Strauss mean that processual theory should be like a narrative account, this would be a major improvement over traditional positivist research.

3. Grounded theorists recognize the importance of context and social structure. Glaser (1978) talks about context and conditions that contribute to social situations, and their effect on social structure. However, he also talks about contingencies, causes, consequences, and covariance, terms usually associated with a more mechanized view of social interaction than a fully interpretive approach holds.

4. Grounded theorists do not believe it necessary to observe individuals' practices. For generating grounded theory, interviewing alone is acceptable. Interpretive researchers recognize and take a stand on the priority of individuals' practices over their beliefs and attitudes.

5. Grounded theorists recommend that the researcher "jointly collects, codes, and analyzes his data" (Glaser & Strauss 1967, 45). This statement implies the recognition that data collection, coding, and analysis cannot be separated. This is a strength in that it is an improvement over traditional positivist research that divorces these actions from each other. But grounded theorists also speak as if field notes can be neatly separated into categories of data: observational notes, methodological notes, personal notes, theoretical notes, and theoretical memos. I found this separation of fact and theory to be artificial in practice.

Use of the term "data" often carries the implication of concrete, independent, objective fact (see also Taylor 1979). I prefer merely to talk about my notes and materials, hoping to express a more fluid sense of what I was working with, without sacrificing my connection to the notes: that is, without forgetting that I was the one who was taking notes, asking questions in the interview, and selecting what aspects of documents and literature were significant for my purposes.

6. Grounded theory is an inductive process: theory must grow out of the data and be grounded in that data; theory must not become just the construction of the researcher. In contrast, in interpretive research, theory building is a co-constitutive process: the researcher begins with preunderstandings that affect how he or she perceives the world and selects "data." Theory must be

built not just from the bottom up, but hermeneutically co-constituted in a dialogical manner that involves much self-reflection by the researcher.

Grounded theory seems to hold the naive realist assumption of inductively discovering some "basic social process" that "emerges" to accurately describe, at a theoretical level, something that corresponds with "reality." Interpretive research emphasizes that the researcher must *not* act as if he or she is a value-free researcher who can objectively see things as they "really" are, or that the "data" collected is, in some way, independent of the person who collects it. This is one of the thorniest shortcomings of grounded theory: that the effects of the researcher's preunderstandings are not taken into account in reporting "theory" that "emerges."

Although grounded theorists admit the perspective of the researcher changes while doing research, they seem to limit the change in the researcher to learning about the world of the participants rather than examining his or her own preunderstandings. This is an important hermeneutic principle: that as the researcher learns about the social interaction he or she is researching, he or she also learns about him or herself. In interpretive research, the researcher's understanding of the situation transforms researcher, participants, and setting in a widening of horizons (Gadamer 1976.)

Even though I recognized these limitations of grounded theory, I still appreciated its strengths, especially its emphasis on systematically developed, processual, contextual accounts of social behavior. This strength made it possible for me to utilize many aspects of grounded theory. With my hermeneutic background, I proceeded to modify its shortcomings, calling the result a grounded interpretive method.

What follows is a broad brush-stroke description of how I generated a grounded interpretive account of the first year of residency training: that crucial period when individuals began practicing as physicians.

Preliminary Steps

In order to gain a sense for the best way to spend my time, I began by looking at many different training situations and talking to different people who were involved in the training of physicians. My initial forays consisted of visiting various residency programs, talking with practicing physicians, medical educators, and social scientists who had done previous research on physician socialization and stress, and attending and participating at colloquia on doctor-patient communications.[4] I visited training sites of different medical specialities (family practice, pediatric, internal medicine and emergency medicine residencies) in different areas (rural, semi-rural, and urban) with different affiliations (university-based, university-affiliated, and community-based).

After about nine months of preliminary observations, I decided I would gain a much richer and deeper understanding of becoming a physician by concentrating my efforts on one residency program. I chose a university affiliated family practice residency program with nine incoming residents, located at a community hospital in a semi-rural area.

I felt it important to narrow my focus to these nine residents in one program in order to gain a better understanding of the subtlety and complexity of their existence. I decided to follow these nine individuals intensively through the stressful and formative first year of their postgraduate training.

I presented myself as a psychologist and researcher who was studying the process of becoming a physician. There is some question as to the best way to present oneself when undertaking a field study: if the researcher tells the people being observed that they are being observed or tells them exactly what he or she is interested in, will their behaviors be influenced or "biased?" On one level, in any participant-observation study, the answer would be yes, awareness of observation and awareness of subject matter can influence behavior. In this study, in the short run, the residents may have been influenced by my presence and by knowing the focus of my study. However, even if they did change their behavior due to my presence in selected incidents, over the length of time I spent with them, they were unable to repeatedly assume such a calculated stance. This is why it is important, when trying to understand a culture, to immerse oneself in that culture for a significant period of time. It is also ethically important to present oneself and one's intentions as clearly and openly as possible to build trust with the individuals being observed. On another level, observation always influences performance, and to think otherwise is naive.

I followed the residents, observing them in almost every aspect of their lives. I openly recorded observations about what I saw, what I felt, how I was doing research, what I understood and did not understand, and what I thought was important. I interviewed them, their spouses, and others associated with their education and training, asking questions about what I observed. I read the seemingly endless memos, schedules, and documentation that were churned out by the hospital, the residency, and the residents themselves. Although I also reviewed the literature on physician stress and physician socialization, the bulk of my notes consisted of observations, interviews, understandings, interpretations, and self-understandings.

Developing an Interpretive Account

The purpose of recording and analyzing field notes is to make sense of the participants' world by organizing one's understandings and preunderstandings of the participants' understanding of their world into a cohesive, narrative account. This happens not in discrete, linear steps, but rather in uneven, circular, and often unpredictable fits and starts.

In my investigation, I generated a narrative account that was grounded in the everyday practices of the individuals involved. I do not assume that the account corresponds with, represents, or reconstructs "reality." Rather, I generated an interpretive account that looks at a crucial period in the process of becoming a physician, provides an interpretation of how distress developed and was maintained, describes the conditions, context, and problematic atmosphere of the process, discusses the costs and significance of the process for residents and the structure of medicine, and suggests directions for improving physician training. My account is one that can grow and be modified as time, social conditions, and individuals change.

In order to make sense out of the world I was immersed in and organize my understanding of that world, I began reflecting on and analyzing my notes and interviews as soon as they were transcribed. This analysis initially involved noticing any common or recurring practices or behaviors I thought might be a significant part of their process of becoming a physician. Eventually I began to see patterns, flows, and directions in their behaviors. While still continuing my observations and interviews, I wrote further notes about patterns, put these notes on index cards, and sorted them into provisional categories. For example, I developed a category of the stressful immediate issues residents were confronted by as they began the residency. This category included work and information overload, time pressures, sleep deprivation, problem patients, dying patients, their own uncertainty and inexperience, responsibility, authority, autonomy and control issues. At the same time, I tried to understand the relationship or flow between the categories I was finding.

After about three to four months, I began to see what grounded theory calls a "core concept." I saw it repeated in field notes, interviews, and interactions. It seemed to be the central question that organized the practices of the first year residents: How to "survive" the residency.

Residents never explicitly addressed either the process of becoming a physician or the notion of socialization. Instead, they talked about trying to "survive" the residency. A term such as "surviving" is both analytic and descriptive; it reflects the everyday experience of the residents while unifying and making sense of their experience. As I began to interpret their existence and practices as focused on surviving, the horizon of my understanding widened and deepened. I saw their everyday practices as part of the larger narrative whole of "surviving" the residency.[5] The story of how the residents survived the residency is a fascinating one.[6] In brief summary, when the residency began, the new residents found themselves in a situation that one resident called "totalizing." They were confronted by the immediately stressful issues mentioned above, their year was completely scheduled for them, and they felt controlled and dominated by requirements and responsibilities.

At the same time residents began forming social relationships with patients, nurses, receptionists, attending physicians, private physicians, residency faculty, and other residents. Many also had relationships outside of the residency, with friends, spouses, and family members. These relationships were sometimes experienced as a source of comfort, help, and growth. Sometimes they were experienced as another source of stress for residents. The residents adopted various strategies for dealing with these relationships and immediate issues. These strategies included "learning the ropes" (see also Geer, et al, 1968), asking for help, helping others, covering for each other, "dumping," "punting," and isolating themselves.

I began to see that these immediate issues, social interactions, and coping strategies lay in front of certain conflicts and contradictions in the fabric of residency training . Residents experienced conflict and contradiction in several areas.

One of these areas was what I call their spheres of existence: work, education, and life outside of residency. When they began the residency, the residents acted as if the three spheres should be equally balanced. The original purpose of work was to take good care of patients; the purpose of education was to learn family medicine; and the purpose of life outside was to maintain some quality of life. Over the first six to nine months, the purpose of work deteriorated into getting done; education degenerated into learning from clinical experience; and life outside became whatever was left over. Work expanded to become far more important than education; and life outside was reduced to next to nothing.

A second area of conflict and contradiction for the residents was focused on their models of medicine. Teachers of three competing part models—the biotechnical model, the "reality" model, and the psychosocial model—competed for teaching time and influence over the residents' educational experience.

In the hospital, the biotechnical model of specialists and subspecialists held sway. Family physicians were rarely found in the hospital where residents initially spent most of their time. Instead, residents learned how specialists saw and treated patients. Residents also learned the types of knowledge and facts specialists looked for: specialized biomedical knowledge that ignored more humanistic aspects of patient care.

In the clinics, the "reality" model prevailed. This model was championed by older family physicians who were trained as general practitioners. It assumed that in order to survive financially, family physicians in practice had to see a large number of patients quickly and efficiently. Therefore residents were required to see a certain number of patients per clinic. Moreover, every few months, this number was increased to push residents to become even more efficient. Residents did not merely become more efficient; they also developed the habit of dispatching patients as quickly as possible to try to get through with their work (see also Mizrahi 1986.) This approach left them extremely frustrated with "problem patients" who were not amenable to quick interventions and who slowed the residents down in their clinics.[7]

The psychosocial model, put forth by psychologists who consulted on a part-time basis, had the most to offer residents about treating these problem patients. Although most family physicians who had been in practice for a few years recognized their greatest shortcoming was in the area of psychosocial aspects of medicine, during the residency there was little time allotted for psychosocial training. Residents soon forgot how helpful it could be to attend to the doctor-patient relationship, patients' families, and their social situation. Also, residents had little time or patience to learn the more intangible, harder-to-grasp knowledge and skills of the psychosocial model while they struggled to learn biomedical means of keeping patients alive.

In large part the competitive tension among the three models reflected the general tenuous relationship between specialists and family physicians. Specialists and family physicians had a relationship that was both competitive and dependent in the community and in the residency. Residents learned by assisting with procedures on the specialists' hospital patients. They also needed consultation from these specialists. But if residents became too accomplished, they might take business away from specialists. Because specialists in the community needed referrals, they tried to maintain working relationships with the family physicians-to-be.

Over time, residents found themselves losing touch with their images, goals, and ideals. What they did as residents was not what they imagined they would be doing when they decided to become family physicians. Their practices were in conflict with their ideals.

As these contradictions became more painful, residents alternately fell into two extremely disparate and rigid modes of being in order to "survive": *Covering-Over* and *Over-Reflecting*. In the Covering-Over mode, they performed their everyday tasks and learned to master the necessary skills and procedures of doctoring, but were unable to reflect on themselves and their practices. At times they became so Covered-Over that they appeared callous, saw patients as objects, ignored the importance of the doctor-patient relationship, and lost touch with their images and ideals. One resident described her version of the typical Covered-Over resident:

> It's like the person who's real aggressive, gets in there and does everything, wants to be really invasive and is always exaggerating. . . . They make it seem like they are in life-and-death situations. . . . He really loves codes because he can get in there and do these great procedures on the people.

One third-year resident told me that in the Covering-Over Mode:

> You don't have the energy to communicate . . . and so, you tend to just not deal with it. You just stop. And so, that cuts off from other people the things that are extremely important that are going on within you.

In the other mode, the Over-Reflecting mode, residents became so overwhelmed and discouraged when they did reflect on the habits they were developing that they began to doubt themselves, their abilities, their decisions, and their career choice. In this mode, they sometimes felt like quitting medicine. They told me that "If the shit hits the fan, that person many times will be a little ambivalent, wait a little too long." In April another resident told me that:

> Depression and crying all the time is still an almost everyday occurrence. . . . When you get into that category of detaching yourself and feeling like there's no hope, . . . quitting is a real alternative, and it's kind of like a freeing mechanism.

The conditions under which residents moved between Covering-Over and Over-Reflecting and the manner in which they moved between the two modes were complex. The way residents experienced and dealt with conflicts and contradictions often determined what extreme mode they found themselves dwelling in. When they found contradictions too painful, they tended to dwell in the Over-Reflecting mode. When they were able to ignore contradictions, they tended to dwell in the Covering-Over mode.

The movement between these extreme modes was jarring and dysfunctional. When residents became stuck in the repetitive, painful, inflexible and uncontrollable movement between Covering-Over and Over-Reflecting, they were at risk of becoming burned out, depressed, isolated, and even suicidal, as well as having marital discord, substance-abuse problems, and delivering substandard patient care or quitting medicine. Integrating these two extreme modes was not easy. For some residents, integration did not occur during residency. A few residents achieved some degree of integration during their third year of residency; only one resident in the group I followed began to integrate Covering-Over and Over-Reflecting in the first year.

When it happened, this integration consisted of two aspects: *positive involvement in everyday practices* and *productive personal reflection.* Together, positive involvement in everyday practices and productive personal reflection constituted co-aspects of a single integrating mode of being.

Positive involvement in everyday practices is the ability to learn skills, perform procedures, and master everyday tasks. It entails getting involved flexibly in work. It does not entail the rigid blocking out of emotion and personal reflection characteristic of Covering-Over. Suppressing emotional responses and personal reflection is done temporarily and flexibly.

Productive personal reflection is the ability to see oneself in the process of becoming a physician. This includes reflection on everyday practices as well as on images of the kind of physician a resident wants to become. Self-reflection is also necessary to develop an understanding of the subtleties, complexities, and possibilities of the doctor-patient relationship. When done flexibly and in the context of residents' everyday activities, this self-reflection constitutes productive personal reflection. Productive personal reflection embodies the understanding that feelings, emotions, desires, goals, images, and relationships are all an important part of becoming and being a physician. Productive personal reflection does not entail the extreme doubt, uncertainty, disaffection, and inability to become involved that are characteristic of the extreme mode of Over-Reflecting.

The residents who achieved this integrating mode were able to move flexibly between positive involvement in their everyday practices and productive personal reflection without being lost in Over-Reflection or Covered-Over in their everyday practices. They were able to recognize their shortcomings as well as their abilities. Doubt was experienced along with anxiety and feelings of failure, but not to the extent that residents became paralyzed and unable to act when the situation called upon them to do so.

Contradictions in their training were seen and recognized as worth struggling to sort out. Residents attended both to getting their work done and to caring for patients. They were interested in learning those procedures performed by family physicians. They worked at recognizing their own needs and at setting realistic limits to their time at work so that their life outside medicine could regain some substance.

Residents in the integrating mode looked toward role models who maintained a good balance among their spheres of existence and who actively embodied the principles of family medicine. Although residents were often dissatisfied with the compromises they saw themselves making, they struggled to reassess their own images, goals, and ideals in light of their practices. Part of this struggle was expressed in negotiating to change the structural requirements of the residency.

The integrating mode proved to be a positive solution for the problem of becoming habituated in the extreme modes of Covering-Over and Over-Reflecting. The continued personal and professional development of resident-physicians is dependent on learning to move flexibly between positive involvement in everyday practices and productive personal reflection (Addison in press).

Refining the Account

As I felt more confident in the coherence of certain areas of my developing account, I moved to explore still other areas. I looked at practices, relationships, and situations I did not yet understand. The guiding focus for these observations was unearthing contradictions, inconsistencies, and gaps in the account.

For example, I was told by one of the members of the faculty that residents were required to see a great number of patients in their outpatient clinics to prepare them "realistically" for their experience in private practice after residency.At the same time, I also talked to family physicians in practice who chose not to lead such a harried pace. Only through continued questioning of residents, faculty, and administrators did I come to understand that the hospital counted on the income from these clinic visits. Economic factors were significant in dictating educational requirements for the residents. Because of the hurried pace in clinics, residents developed unfortunate patterns of relating to their clinic patients that generalized beyond crowded and rushed clinics. Thus, by pursuing my not-yet understanding residents' rushed and antagonistic patterns of relating to patients in clinic, I was able to reach a more comprehensive understanding of how economic conditions affected the residents' everyday practices.

Another key element in refining my account was presenting the account to residents, medical educators, and social science colleagues. My social science colleagues helped me to reflect critically on gaps in the overall logic and structure of the account. Medical educators helped me to reflect critically on the perspective I had adopted by immersing myself in the residents' world. Residents' comments were by far the most valuable for refining my account. They told me what they thought I had missed, what they thought I had conceptualized incorrectly, or what their associations were to various aspects of the model. I not only found residents' comments essential to flesh out certain portions of my account, but I also found their reactions fascinating. Whenever I presented the account to a resident for the first time, he or she quickly became overwhelmed and anxious; no one was able to endure an overview of the account at one sitting. After I showed one resident a version of the account, he told me:

> I had an incredible amount of anger about everything that was on that sheet. I mean, everything that was bothering me was on there in some way, . . . and all the arrows went exactly the way the arrows in my brain were going . . . but I was unaware of a lot of them at the time. . . . And I looked at them all and . . . within 15 seconds my eyes were just welling up with tears . . . It just made me feel so uncomfortable.

Eventually I began to interpret the strength of his and others' reaction to this new way of seeing as confirmation of the significance and intelligibility of my account.

Interpretive Aspects

Certain aspects of my approach stand out as distinctive of hermeneutic or interpretive research. Understanding and making sense out the residents' everyday practices by immersing myself in their world, reflecting on my own preunderstanding of their existence, and placing my interpretations within a larger background context are central elements of a grounded interpretive approach. That the account opened up possibilities for residents and for the education of primary-care physicians is also characteristic of an interpretive approach. In the following sections of this chapter, I will discuss in more detail how my approach embodies these four interpretive aspects.

Immersion, Understanding, and Interpretation

One of my goals was to understand what the everyday lives of the residents were like. I did this by following them, observing them, and immersing myself in most of their everyday and everynight activities, not only to learn *what* they did , but to understand what it was *like* for them to be residents, to understand what their practices *meant* to them. If I had only interviewed them, I would have learned a great deal about what they *said* they were doing, but perhaps little about their actual practices, which may not have been congruent with what they said. In order to learn about their practices I immersed myself in their local culture for prolonged periods of time and questioned them about what I observed them doing.

Thus when generating an account of social practices, it is crucial that researchers base their accounts not on self-reports or interviews alone, but include their observation, understanding, and interpretation of the everyday practices of the participants.

One illustration of how my involvement in the residents' existence allowed me to understand the significance of their practices centers on my interpretation of being "on call." Being on call entailed coming to the hospital at seven a.m., working through that day and through the night when the other residents went home. The residents then continued to work through the next day. This meant they could be awake and working for thirty-six hours straight. If one of their clinic patients delivered a baby on the night before or the night after their call night, they might be awake for most of two or three nights in a row. At all times during this period they were expected to operate at full capacity. Their duties might include admitting patients to the hospital, presenting these patients to the third-year resident who was supervising their work, checking the status of these patients, seeing their clinic patients, charting, attending conferences and rounds with attending physicians, and assisting in surgery. While assigned to an inpatient rotation, residents were on call every fourth night. This was clearly an important and central activity for them; they talked about it often and with great intensity.

To try to understand what it was like for them, I accompanied them while they were on call, observing, taking notes, and asking questions. Afterwards, I recorded the following field note:

> As I drove away from the hospital yesterday, it was raining, a slight drizzle and the sky was grey. Even though I was tired and groggy and had enough for now, I felt a kind of sadness. I realized that I was tearing myself away from the hospital, from the intensity of the residents' work. There was a part of me that did not want to leave this extremely exciting and intense setting; a part of me that felt an emptiness in the absence of this intensity. Why so intense? First, because at any moment, another human's life could be in their hands; second, because of the intimacy with which people allow them to enter their lives; third, because there was always something to be learned—this constant learning atmosphere, never to be mastered, is a challenge; and fourth, being with another resident or other health professionals in this process allows for the possibility of intensely intimate bonding to occur, often to the disruption of one's life outside of the hospital, if such a thing exists after three years of this process.

Another note I recorded after accompanying them on call read:

> As I leave this time I have a coke and some candy bars. Here I start eating junk food again (just like the residents did). This kind of staying up all night, this kind of schedule can't be good for one's health.

This latter interpretation was corroborated by residents' complaining about gaining weight and being out of shape and of how disturbing these changes were for them. I also wrote:

> All the time I've left after call, I've really had no energy to say goodbye to people like _____ and _____. It just shows how my emotional reactions are 'off' in a sense after being up most of the night, and what this must be like for them. I notice that being on call the second time, that is, last Friday night, didn't seem to tire me out quite so much as the first time. My guess is that I'm getting used to not sleeping, and the residents must also get used to their schedules. There is this effect where one can get used to anything.

I learned that as the residents tried to master the requirements of the residency, their emotional reactions became blunted, and habits of health, exercise, and nutrition fell by the wayside. As my understanding of the residents' practices grew, I also began to formulate issues that were significant for them: how the intensity of their experience in the hospital affected their life outside of medicine; and how their life outside often paled by comparison, especially when they were sleep-deprived from being on call every fourth night. These interpretations allowed me to reimmerse myself and understand their practices at a deeper and richer level. This richer understanding allowed me to build a more comprehensive account of their practices. This circular movement between understanding the residents' practices by immersing myself in their culture and providing an interpretation of those practices is an important hermeneutic movement to grasp.

The Fore-structure of Interpretation

At the same time that I reflected on my understandings, interpretations, and developing account, I was examining what Heidegger (1927/1962) calls the "fore-structure" of interpretation. Heidegger argues that in order to know anything at all, we must have some pre-understanding of what is knowable. This pre-understanding, or fore-structure, remains largely in the background as taken-for-granted. However, when the object of investigation is human activity, it is important to recognize the influence of our fore-structure in order to arrive at a more explicit interpretation or account (Dreyfus 1980, in press.)

The interpretive tradition emphasizes that there is no detached, privileged standpoint from which one objectively records "reality." In my research, I must recognize that I already work within an interpretive framework or paradigm, am predisposed to looking for certain aspects and away from others in the situation, and have a taken-for-granted way of doing research, of being a researcher, and of interacting with the participants involved.

If I try to spell out this framework, I might say that I approach the world and interact with it as if events or social acts are not seen as things-in-themselves; meanings of events are not fixed or given in pre-established categories; meaning or significance emerges and changes over time. At the same time, I believe and operate as if this interpretive activity is not completely free: Meaning is always in a particular context and based upon a background of shared cultural practices; meaning is not a fundamentally unique, privatized property of individuals nor is it independent from the practical situations of social interaction; meaning is negotiated in our ongoing, everyday interactions with others in the world. I cannot help but bring this framework to my research endeavors. Acknowledging this connects me with the account I am building.

In hermeneutically circular fashion, as I learned about the residents' existence, I also learned about the way I was predisposed to perceiving and making sense of their world. For example, one of my taken-for-granted assumptions was that individuals chose to specialize in family medicine over other more lucrative and technical specialties because they wanted to be altruistic healers rather than technicians. I found this was not nearly as central a factor in choice of specialty as I had assumed. Residents chose family medicine because they wanted to be challenged, because they did not want to limit their knowledge and expertise to one area, because they thought they would not be accepted in other specialities, as well as because they saw themselves as altruistic. I also discovered that the healer-technician split was more of an issue for me in my own choice of profession than it was for them: I became a clinical psychologist/practicing psychotherapist who abhors prescriptive techniques and cookbook approaches to psychotherapy. The relationship between what I was looking for in the residents' practices and what I stood for in my own profession was not clear to me until I was in the midst of my research, yet it influenced my understanding and interpretations from the outset, especially in the kinds of questions I asked residents. When I recognized that I had been looking for this healer-technician split, I became free to look in other directions.

Thus examining the fore-structure of my understanding and its effect on my developing account was an integral part of my research approach. Even though it is never possible to divest oneself completely of preunderstandings, it was important for me to become as clear as possible about the way the fore-structure of my understanding influenced my account; otherwise the account would be in danger of becoming my own preunderstandings projected onto the process I was investigating.

The Background Context

At the same time I was immersing myself in the residents' everyday activities and reflecting on the fore-structure of my understanding, I was also attempting to look at the larger background context of the residents' everyday practices. This is another important aspect of the hermeneutic circle and the interpretive process. In developing narrative accounts of social behavior, researchers must attend to the way in which practices are embedded in a larger background context.

Looking at these practices without reference to the context within which they occur leaves researchers at a disadvantage for making sense out of these practices. For example, the residents termed certain problem patients "RTPs," or "Resident Torture Patients." These were patients who had headaches, backaches or other vague complaints that were very difficult to diagnose and treat. Taken at face value, one might have concluded that residents were simply callous and insensitive to objectify patients and minimize their problems in this manner. However, when I came to understand the larger background context—that is, that residents were struggling to "survive" in the "totalizing" atmosphere of residency training—my understanding widened to tell a richer and more complex story: residents had little time in their schedules to pay attention to psychosocial or relationship aspects of the doctor-patient interaction; they needed to master the biotechnical procedures of medicine in order to "survive" professionally. They had to cope with stressors such as work and information overload, time pressures, and sleep deprivation. As a result, they understood difficult patients as just one more source of "abuse." Residents were not given the opportunity to learn how to deal with these problem patients nor were they helped to explore their feelings about such patients. with reference to the larger context of trying to survive residency, their practice of referring to patients as "RTPs" made more sense; both residents and patients were victims of the effects of residency training. In turn, the structure of residency-training programs depended on larger institutions such as medical-training governing bodies and economic factors of the health-care industry (see also Starr 1982).

How residents understood time provided another example of the importance of the background context for making sense out of particular social practices. Residents were always late: They were late for the noon-time conferences; they were late leaving the hospital; they were late to eat meals; they were late to meet their significant others and family; they were late returning to the hospital to take over from other residents on their team who had been covering for them; and they were late to see patients. When residents were running late, were overscheduled, or had to wait for consults from attending physicians, they became rushed, harried, and impatient, and they often provided incomplete and unsatisfactory care. Also, ordinary clock time faded in importance for residents in the face of life-and-death situations which could not be scheduled, planned or anticipated.

I refer to the residents' implicit understanding of time as "Doctor's Time": When a resident said he or she would be back in five minutes, that could mean anywhere from ten minutes to two hours; when a resident told a patient he or she would be back soon, that could mean anywhere from fifteen minutes to three days. Since patients were unaware of the meaning of "Doctor's Time," they became anxious, frustrated, and angry waiting for the doctor. No matter how important the patient's schedule was, it was assumed the doctor's was more important; the patient waited for the doctor, the doctor never waited for the patient. Thus by understanding the background conditions of residents' temporal existence, I was able to give a more complete account of why residents often developed antagonistic relationships with patients.

Opening up Possibilities

By developing an understanding of the first-year residents' everyday activities, reflecting on the preunderstandings with which I perceived their behavior, and considering the larger background context of their existence, I formed a narrative, interpretive account of this period in their process of becoming physicians. This account has the potential to open up new ways of looking at social practices for the researcher and the individuals involved.[8] Bleicher believes that:

> Participant-observation requires constant self-reflection and learning. It's dialogical in that subject and object remain in communicative contact in the course of which a fusion of horizons may occur: the sociologist has to become socialized in the particular form of life of his object while being able to widen the 'horizon' of the latter through offering a differing account of a given situation (1982, 143).

In my case, I immersed myself in the world of the residents, and reflected on what I found and on the fore-structure of my understanding. I was in dialogue with the residents, trying to understand their existence. I identified with the residents as I became socialized in their world. For a time, our horizons became fused.

At the same time, my account is more than just what the residents experienced; it is an interpretation of the residents' experience and practices. It is not how they would describe their experience, but rather, my interpretation of their experience. I offered them a "differing account" that opened up possibilities for them.

The recognition that narrative accounts of social practices can open up possibilities for the subjects raises some questions about the "validity" of accounts: In interpretive research, validity, in the positivist sense of the word, is not at issue. Instead, appeals are made to the account's comprehensiveness, comprehensibility, intelligibility, credibility, meaningfulness, significance, and fruitfulness for opening up new possibilities. The question of how to assess the value of narrative accounts is hotly debated among interpretive researchers. The arguments range in a continuum from something close to objectivism to total relativism (See Bernstein 1976, 1983.) Some qualitative or naturalistic researchers believe that it is very important to find respectable standards to judge naturalistic research. They have looked to concepts such as credibility, transferability, dependability, confirmability, and reflexivity to substitute for the positivist standards of internal validity, generalizability, reliability, objectivity, and investigator bias (See Guba and Lincoln 1981). Others believe that attempting to judge the adequacy of non-positivist research by reference to these qualitative correlates is nothing more than a misguided attempt to apply a thinly disguised template of positivist standards to research carried out in a non-positivist paradigm (See Smith & Heshusius 1986). Interpretive researchers in this volume take a variety of stands on this question.

In positivist research, the researcher assumes he or she is developing an account that corresponds to a "reality" that is "out there." The closer an account comes to describing that reality, the better it is. In interpretive research, truth is seen as an ongoing and unfolding process, where each successive interpretation has the possibility of uncovering or opening up new possibilities. Again Bleicher argues:

> If ... theory is a 'reading,' then it cannot be verified or falsified, but only clarified, i.e., made more comprehensive and comprehensible. Interpretations proffered cannot be judged in reference to reality 'out there,' but only in relation to their fruitfulness, i.e., their potential for opening-up new ways of seeing, thereby initiating new practices (1982, 142).

In this same vein, Habermas stresses that:

> The interpretation of a case is corroborated only by the successful continuation of a self-formative process, that is by the completion of self-reflection (1971, 277).

In such a view, the criterion for assessing the credibility and/or significance of the results of interpretive research is whether the interpretation encourages the completion or continuation of self-reflection. Was this the case in my research?

I believe that the answer is affirmative on both an individual and structural level. In addition to their reactions upon seeing my account, the residents requested that I lead a group for them to talk about stressful aspects of their everyday activities as they struggled to "survive" the residency and become family physicians. In part, I viewed their request as added confirmation of the credibility and meaningfulness of my account.[9] I am still leading these groups now, six years later. The residents also negotiated for other changes in the structure of residency training that allow them the opportunity to reflect on their everyday practices and to make their practices more congruent with their images of what family physicians need to learn. These changes have helped residents integrate the Covering-Over and Over-Reflecting modes. In addition they lobbied for and received the resignation of the residency director. The new residency director supports and encourages self-reflection. He has also provided funds to hire new faculty members who are enthusiastic about teaching residents. The structure of residency training continues to change in this and other residency programs; self-reflection seems to be continuing.

Any theory, model, or narrative account of human activity is always open to modification and refinement. Although my account has achieved a certain degree of cohesiveness and comprehensiveness, as times, conditions, and context change, the account will also change. For example, if I were to repeat the study in the same setting now, with different residents, the immediate issues might be different. Specific conflicts and contradictions experienced by residents would probably be different. If I were to study other residency programs or other specialties, areas of conflict and contradiction would be very likely to change. There are some features of the account that will be germane to other situations and other contexts over time. It is likely that "surviving" by the disjunctive movement between the two extreme modes of Covering-Over and Over-Reflecting is central to becoming a physician in most residency programs, as well as to becoming a professional in many other fields.

In this chapter I have described how a grounded interpretive method of research can be used to provide a narrative account of a crucial phase of becoming a family physician. The account, grounded in the everyday practices of the residents, described how a problematic situation developed and was maintained, and indicated directions for positive change. The account helped to widen the horizons of the participants and the researcher. It continues to open up possibilities for others who read it.

CHAPTER 2

The Development of Close Relationships: Implications from Therapy with Two Early Adolescent Boys

ROBERT L. SELMAN, LYNN HICKEY SCHULTZ, BRINA CAPLAN, AND KATHERINE SCHANTZ[1]

I. The Clinical Context and its Theoretical Underpinnings

Introduction

Arnie, at age thirteen, claims to need no friends. In class, he sits off in a corner by himself. At lunch, he usually eats alone; and as he walks down the corridors, his eyes are cast down, his vision turned inward. His "interpersonal life" is filled not with friends, but with fictional characters from other worlds. Half kidding and half serious, he is preoccupied with a need to be able to "stand alone," protecting himself from the dangers in the science fiction and horror comics and books he carries around with him constantly. He broods over autonomy ("I don't need to rely on nobody"), but this is often belied by his intense and sudden anger when a counselor he is willing to talk to is a few minutes late for a meeting or when a teacher on whom he depends does not give him the attention he demands. Often Arnie appears sad and lonely.

Arnie's classmate Mitchell is also thirteen and friendless, but not for lack of effort. Mitchell would desperately like to have a friend, but he does not know how to go about making or keeping one. Mitchell virtually throws himself onto peers, trying to be included in the interactions of his classmates, but seldom if ever succeeding. Part of the problem is that his style of interacting is more like that of someone half his age. He giggles uncontrollably, does not focus his attention on the social scene, and often misunderstands the social subleties and nuances of his peers' interactions. He tattles one day and expects his victims to be his friends the next. When even slightly rebuffed, he reacts with epithets and curses, then expects forgetfulness if not forgiveness. Desperate for early adolescent intimacy, Mitchell is confused and lonely.[2]

59

Arnie and Mitchell attend a day-treatment school for children with emotional and interpersonal difficulties, and the boys are in *pair therapy* together there. Pair therapy is a program of clinical intervention and developmental research we began almost ten years ago. Its general aim is to help troubled children develop the capacity to establish and maintain close friendships. The treatment requires two pre-or early adolescents to meet regularly (typically once a week for about an hour) with a pair therapist. The therapist plays a crucial role, facilitating and mediating the pair's social interactions and providing them with a third-person perspective. Therefore, the treatment is both social interaction-based and insight-oriented. This dual focus encourages the pair to do things together, and, with the crucial help of the therapist, to reflect on both the degree of success and the level of maturiy of "how we did." Thus, the treatment program provides what Harry Stack Sullivan (1953) described as an opportunity for "consensual validation," a process of social communication that serves to restructure the children's immature interpersonal functioning and world views.

Pair therapy is the vehicle we use to achieve the general goal of our developmental research: to characterize the developmental and dynamic qualities of close friendships. More specifically, our goal is to examine the therapeutic process of pair therapy by delineating details of the ongoing social interaction between the three participants to illuminate development in the construction of the relationship between the two children. Our method unites three complementary perspectives on the therapeutic process on successive levels of analysis—that of the individual, the dyad, and the triadic system (Bronfenbrenner 1979).

The first perspective is that of each child's *development level* of interpersonal maturity. When we began to observe pair therapy sessions, our focus was on expanding the children's repertoire of interpersonal negotiation strategies, and our heuristic tool was social perspective coordination from the structural-development tradition (Selman 1980). Thus, our starting point was cognitivist, with a tendency to focus on the individual.

The second perspective is that of the relation between two dyadic *social-regulation processes*. When developing the initial account of the development of autonomy and our associated research methodology, we had limited our developmental analyses to one aspect of social regulation processes—the specific autonomy process of interpersonal negotiation strategies (Selman & Schultz 1988). In so doing, we struck a balance between the ever present tensions between reductionism and quantitative data on the one hand, and richness and detail on the other, in one circumscribed area of social interaction. As our work progressed we began to include observation and facilitation of processes of intimacy (e.g., the capacity to share experience) as well as those of autonomy (e.g., the capacity to negotiate interpersonal conflict). In this more recent effort to describe the interplay of the development of complementary social regulation processes we have expanded the scope of the phenomenon we study to include intimacy processes, specifically by studying occasions of shared experience (e.g., Selman & Yeates 1987).

With the case of Arnie and Mitchell, we have integrated a third, more hermeneutically-informed "systems" perspective: that of *interaction indices*. This perspective addresses social interaction at a systems level, a triadic system comprised of three dyads (child1-child2, child1-adult, child2-adult). By *"interaction"* we mean all the "things that are going on" in the pair therapy room, things that reveal persons' existing relation to, ongoing relating with, active creation of, and even intentions regarding their animate and inanimate environment. By *"indices"* we mean pointers to key aspects of that context, aspects that provide a variety of cues and clues for observers. With these tools we expanded the method as well as the scope of our study of social interaction. In this chapter we describe these interaction indices, their integration with our first two perspectives and levels of analysis, and how the dynamic interplay of these different perspectives provides a valuable methodology for the study of pair therapy or any social interaction context.

The three perspectives of our research methodology reflect three corresponding goals of our clinical practice. The individual, developmental goal of pair therapy is to establish a context in which each child can move toward an ability to use mutual and collaborative actions when dealing with other individuals in close one-to-one relationships. This capacity for mutual collaboration, in our structural-development model, is based upon the developing ability to coordinate perspectives on the social interaction between the self and a significant other. The level of social-perspective coordination underlying interpersonal collaboration is usually achieved in pre-or early adolescence. It allows the self to reflectively step outside of itself and fully experience the interaction between self and other from what we have called a "third-person point-of-view" (Selman 1980). This capacity is similar to what Anna Freud (1966) in a different context termed the development of the "observing ego".

A second, dyadic goal of pair therapy is to facilitate the dyad's ability to regulate its own social interactions rather than to depend on an external force or source. Our clinical interest is in using what we understand of forms of shared experience and interpersonal negotiation as guides to the broad and long-range goals of pair therapy. On the one hand, we ask what the therapist can do to facilitate the "glue" of pair therapy, the fostering of more advanced levels of shared experience. On the other hand, we are interested in how the therapist can help both members of the pair to "structure" their own autonomy, to act with a greater sense of collaboration in sorting out their own needs and the needs of their pair partner in interpersonal negotiation.

The third specific goal of pair therapy, corresponding to our research perspective on interaction indices, is a systems goal: to facilitate the children's ability to achieve synchrony in their relationships with more than one other person at a time. Each member of the pair develops a close relationship with two other persons in the course of pair therapy, the other child and the therapist. The ability to coordinate these two relationships in social interaction in the same physical and psychological space is usually deficient in troubled children. This ability is an important part of children's socialization needs, however, particularly as they enter the increasingly complex social world of adolescence.

The First Perspective: Developmental Level of Social Interaction

In previous work (e.g., Selman & Schultz 1988) we examined extensively one critical manifestation of the capacity for autonomy: the strategies children use for interpersonal negotiation. *Interpersonal negotiation strategies* are defined as the ways in which individuals in situations of social conflict ("contexts for interpersonal negotiation") deal with the self and a significant other to gain control over inner and interpersonal disequilibrium. Normal children growing up, we have proposed, develop an expanding repertoire of these strategies based upon the ontogeny of levels in the child's developing capacity to coordinate psychosocial perspectives (Selman 1980). The sequence of levels, reflecting Werner's (1948) orthogenetic and comparative notion of development, ranges from the primitive, global, and undifferentiated to the psychologically complex and hierarchically differentiated and integrated.

Interpersonal negotiation strategies classified as level 0 are primarily impulsive, physicalistic strategies (e.g., impulsive fight or flight). These methods of resolving social problems do not clearly distinguish between and acknowledge the perspectives of the self and the significant other.

Level 1 strategies reflect recognition that the significant other's perspective may differ from the self's in the particular context. However, these strategies are action-based and do not coordinate, that is, simultaneously consider, the perspectives of the self and the significant other. Strategies classified as level 1 include one-way commands and assertions, and conversely, simple and unchallenging accommodation (giving in) to the perceived needs and requests of the significant other.

Strategies classified as level 2 are psychologically-based reciprocal exchanges that reflect an understanding of both the self and the significant other as planful, capable of reflection, and having opinions, feelings, and behaviors that influence the other person. These strategies embody the ability to reflect upon the self's needs from a second-person perspective. They include trades, exchanges, verbal persuasion, convincing others, making deals, or suggesting other behaviors designed to protect the subjective interests of the self in negotiation. The self may go second, but not yet yield completely.

Level 3 strategies, akin to Sullivan's notion of collaboration, integrate the interests of self and other as viewed from a third-person perspective. These strategies involve compromise, dialogue, process analysis, and the development of shared goals. They reflect an understanding that concern for the relationship's continuity over time relates to the solution of any immediate problem.

Specific stategies falling into each of these four levels (0 to 3) can be further classified according to which predominant interpersonal style or orientation the child adopts. In strategies in the *self-transforming orientation,* the individual acts predominantly on the self to accommodate to the other; in strategies in the *other-tranforming orientation,* the individual tries to change the other to accommodate to the self. At advanced developmental levels, the interpersonal orientations become less polarized, culminating in a *collaborative orientation,* which strategies are neither self-nor other-transforming but balanced and integrated. The interpersonal orientation aspect of our developmental model plays an important role in the course of the therapeutic process in pair therapy. We have observed that the relative orientations of the two children change in predictable ways as they construct their relationship, ways that interact with developmental level, as we describe below. In addition, the differentiation of levels into orientations reminds us of Werner's (1948) point that surface behaviors that appear "different" may be based on the same underlying level or organization.

The Second Perspective: Intimacy and Autonomy Processes

The pair therapy project began with a focus on helping children with poor peer relationships become more adept at getting along, and so it was their fights, disagreements, and conflicts that caught our eye and called for attention. As we refined our techniques for helping these children improve their negotiations and conflict resolution skills on an individual level, we began to see the complementary difficulties they were having in establishing and maintaining a sense of closeness with peers. Indeed, the intimacy the children experienced with each other in pair therapy seemed to encourage them to try new and unfamiliar (at least more reciprocal, if not collaborative) negotiations strategies. Therefore, more recently, we have used pair therapy to explore an important manifestation of intimacy; here our interest has been in delineating evolving forms or levels of *shared experience* (e.g., Selman & Yeates 1987). These forms of shared experience are more clearly in the interaction of the dyad rather than "in the individual," providing a counterpoint to the forms of interpersonal negotiation.

With this dual perspective on the nature of personality development, we view the capacity for mutual collaboration as the result of the codevelopment of two basic aspects of social regulation. The first is the capacity for *intimacy,* interpreted in our work as the ability to share experiences with another person. The second aspect of social regulation is the capacity for *autonomy,* defined not in the inner sense of establishing a separate and distinct identity, as emphasized by Erikson (1968), but in an interactional sense, as the ability to understand, coordinate, and negotiate one's own needs with the needs of another person, particularly when they potentially conflict. In our view, the terms intimacy and autonomy do not describe static phenomena, nor are they early, late, or final achievements (i.e., particular stages of life). Instead, these terms describe psychological processes that function *throughout* life, from infancy to old age. They are not simply achieved (have/don't have) products or properties within an individual, but potentially ever-developing, ever-consolidating aspects of the self's actions in ongoing relationships with others (Stern 1985; Erikson 1963). Conversely, at all points they are vulnerable to regression and de-differentation.

Optimally, the capacity for mutual collaboration continues to broaden, deepen, and be transformed as a function of the developmental tasks and contextual challenges of social interactions encountered across one's lifetime. The component processes of mutual collaboration—intimacy and autonomy—function from birth onward, but the forms they take change and fluctuate with time and experience. Furthermore, during development, these processes can be arrested and the forms they take can become fixated or regressive or unstable. If the capacities for intimacy and autonomy are developing adequately, both separately and together, the child growing into adolescence can begin to use a collaborative attitude, exercising first reciprocal and cooperative, then mutually collaborative methods of relating to significant others. As Blatt & Shichman (1973) have pointed out, the developmental lines toward higher forms of intimacy and autonomy normally develop in a complex dialectical process (cf., Cooper, Grotevant, & Condon 1983; Gilligan 1982). Accordingly, various forms of psychopathology are best considered as distortions of *both* processes, but are more blatantly manifest in one or the other of these two fundamental developmental lines. But what does "developing adequately" mean, and what do distortions actually look like, in concrete and observable terms?

With this question in mind and this theoretical orientation in hand, we returned to our corpus of data—the videotapes and narratives in our library of past pair therapy sessions—to seek instances of social interactions that might be considered exemplars of different forms of shared experience. Once again, we borrowed the notion of comparative development from Werner and the levels in the coordination of social perspectives from our earlier work to describe the following four tentative levels of shared experience.

At the most primitive level (0), what seems to be shared (more literally "spread" in an unreflective way) is one child's impulsive and motoric activity. The experience often starts with one actor's expressiveness and appears to be transmitted to the other through a *process of contagion.* This kind of activity is often poorly managed, such that often an outside agent (e.g., a parent, teacher, therapist, or peer) is needed to control the expression of the common action should it become overstimulating.

At the next higher level (1) children appear to "share" actions more consciously but in a somewhat paradoxical way. One actor "commands" the other to participate, not necessarily or only through orders or dictates but rather through a kind of expressive enthusiasm. And the other takes pleasure in following. Often this *unilateral* form of shared experience—a term meant to capture its paradoxical nature—is seen in fantasy and role-play situations in which turns are taken at being in control (although one partner usually determines the switching of roles).

In contrast, shared experiences at the next level (2) involve *reciprocal reflection* on the experience of actions. In other words, the accent falls on reflecting *with* another who has had the same or a similar observation or experience. Both children participate equally; however, the "cooperative" experience is shared primarily for the sake of each self's own satisfaction still, without a strong or clear sense of interconnection. A common kind of shared experience at this level is one in which each member of the pair is intent on gaining consensual validation on the meaning of the actions of a third party (e.g., a teacher both participants share or a peer with whom each interacts).

A more *mutually collaborative* form of reflective shared experience consists of communications in which the other person's concerns are felt to be as significant as one's own. At this level (3), each participant clearly regards the other as part of a mutually experienced "we." A collaborative attitude in the context of intimate shared experience, no less than in autonomy-oriented interpersonal negotiation, can be best observed in social interactions *over time,* in the cues and clues that are observed in ongoing interpersonal relationships (cf. Hinde 1979, Sroufe & Fleeson 1986).

Table 1 integrates the first and second perspectives, showing the comparison between developmental levels of shared experience (intimacy) and those of interpersonal negotiation strategies (autonomy).

Our Third Perspective: Interaction Indices

The levels of intimacy and autonomy processes we tentatively identified are admittedly limited heuristics to help us understand the various forms, functions, and fluctuations of social regulation. When we began to observe the course of Arnie's and Mitchell's pair therapy, we wanted to describe the process—the social interactions—through which the pair achieved greater degrees of closeness and collaboration. However, the categories of shared experience and interpersonal negotiation shown in Table 1 failed to account for the complexity that every session presented, and seemed inadequate to fully illuminate the relationship-building process of pair therapy. Therefore, we decided to further expand our method in a hermeneutic direction to more fully explicate the *meaning* of the social interaction and describe the rich interpersonal context of social interchange in which developmental change takes place (Mischler 1979).

Table 1

Intimacy Function (Sharing Experience)	Core Developmental Levels in the Capacity to Coordinate Social Perspectives	Autonomy Function (Negotiating Interpersonal Conflict)
Shared experience through collaborative empathic reflective processes	Mutual Third-Person Level (3)	Negotiation through collaborative strategies oriented toward integrating needs of self and other
Shared experience through joint reflection on similar perceptions or experiences	Reciprocal Reflective Level (2)	Negotiation through cooperative strategies in a persuasive or deferential orientation
Shared experience through expressive enthusiasm without concern for reciprocity	Unilateral One-Way Level (1)	Negotiation through one-way commands/orders or through automatic obedience strategies
Shared experience through unreflective (contagious) imitation	Egocentric Impulsive Level (0)	Negotiation through unreflective physical strategies (impulsive fight or flight)

For the first eight months of Arnie's and Mitchell's therapy, the weekly, approximately hour-long sessions in the pair therapy room were recorded on videotape and simultaneously observed by two members of our research team through a one-way mirror. Each observer focused on one member of the pair, making note of his actions, mood, language, and interests during the session. The observers met with the pair therapist regularly after each session to discuss the interactions and see whether their perspectives matched, whether patterns seen from outside were also visible inside the room. The layout of the pair therapy room is shown in Figure 1. Note that "room" has two meanings in our analyses of social interaction, representing a physical space (the room) and a psychological space (as in "room" to grow, or "room" between us, or not enough "room" in this town for both of us).

With this intensive, "triangulated" (three-person) method of observation we identified "interaction indices" that directed our attention to what seemed to be the most significant aspects of the social interaction in each session. The result was the development of observational constructs ("interaction indices") with which we could attempt to more fully capture these hermeneutic aspects of the social interaction. The six "interaction indices" described below—spacing, pacing, mood, shared history, personal themes, and therapist's acts—point to key aspects of the physical and psychological interaction at a given point in time, and changes in the interaction over time. The interaction indices are not hard and fast categories, but signs or indicators of various aspects of the social environment. They are tools for contextualizing and amplifying a whole spectrum of social regulation, from the most conflict-laden interpersonal negotiation to the most intimate shared experience.

Spacing. All three participants in a pair therapy session place themselves at chosen spots in the room and at chosen distances from and orientations toward one another. We believe the resulting physical geometry has a social meaning, on the assumption that changes indicate altered patterns of remoteness or intimacy. In other words, we regard "physical closeness" as not just a metaphor but a necessary (nonverbal) index of the degree of interpersonal comfort, trust, and collaboration in a given interpersonal situation. We have used this index to map a host of physical movements, including altered posture and dyadic and triadic repositionings.

Pacing. In addition to expressing meaning with speech, individuals act and talk in characteristic temporal patterns, including pace, response tempo, and degree of synchrony with others. By pacing we mean how the pair's speech patterns and the verbal content of speech manifest themselves, and the degree to which each actor is attuned to the communicative ability of the other actor(s). Pacing will vary, of course, depending on circumstances; factors such as social pressure, a dull but inescapable task, or a wish to impress others can alter the speed and harmony of a person's communicative actions. Nonetheless, there is usually a pattern and consistency to the pace or way we talk and act, and how we use feedback from others to modify or regulate the pace.

With the pacing index, we keep track of the distinctive pace set by each participant, as well as "what he said," of similarities and divergences in the boys' verbal orientation and level of comprehension, of discrepancies in communication that may indicate some greater problem, and the odd verbal note that may be a sign of some greater disharmony. In addition to providing a

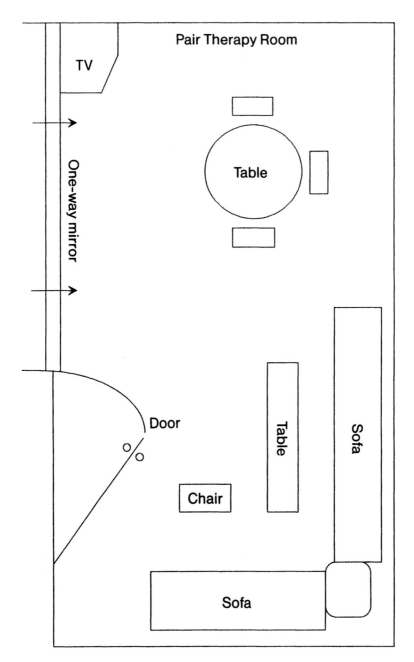

Figure 1

check on verbalized cognitive processes, attending to pacing encourages the observer to develop a more refined social-psychological profile of each pair member. After all, words can be used to keep others at bay as well as to invite them toward shared meanings.

Mood. Friends influence each other's emotions. We adopted the index social mood to acknowledge the emotional range, variation, and relatedness of the expressed affect of a pair. In observing Arnie and Mitchell, for example, we wanted to be alert to any way that either boy's feelings modified the interpersonal context. Obviously, strong feelings can be expressed in any number of powerful or exaggerated ways. By the same token, feelings might not get expressed directly or articulated in revealing words. Arnie might show up feeling angry but indicate his mood only through body language or more-stinging-than-usual sarcasm; Mitchell, hurt at some perceived slight, might say nothing at all but withdraw and shut down instead of expressing his feelings.

Shared History. As a pair progresses through the course of treatment, the partners develop a common history and shared memories within the therapeutic context. Often some common background exists as a result of experiences in the general culture outside of pair therapy. Arnie and Mitchell, for example, both brought to their therapy a similar awareness of G.I. Joe toys and various cartoons and movies. However trivial this kind of common knowledge seems to adults, it is the stuff of which many early adolescent friendships are built—at least we believe many would not be initiated without this essential ingredient. Of course, at more sophisticated levels of development, friends evolve their own personal shared recollections. The shared history index was used to point out any instance—sophisticated or naive, stereotyped or idiosyncratic—of such mutual recollection. In particular, we were interested in understanding the extent to which these troubled children had more difficulty in recalling and using previously shared moments or meanings than less beleaguered children do.

Personal Themes. With this index, we looked for individual concerns, (unspoken) interests, or wishes that seemed to be shaping events. So we decided, in effect, to interpret each boy's on-going preoccupations, sustained interests, fears, or desires. In Arnie's case, for example, much of his time had previously been devoted to elaborating a fantasy world of great destructive power. Occasionally, during the course of treatment, he let the therapist and Mitchell glimpse aspects of this world, where people can be torn apart limb by limb, and there are mutants and monsters and a "bomb of peace" so devastating it can destroy a galaxy. Mitchell, too, used pair therapy to disclose pressing concerns, including an increasingly intense curiosity about sexuality, a strong wish for a friend to pal around with, and, like Arnie, a fantasy life that threatened him with fearful forces. As in the case of mood, we were able to compare our interpretations of certain salient themes—Mitchell's expressed interest in having a friend, for example—to the observations of teachers, counselors, and individual therapists.

Therapist's Acts. This index enabled us to bring into focus what the therapist did to compensate for the boys' poorly developed social skills and regulation processes. There were countless moments in which Arnie and Mitchell clearly lacked the means for mutual social regulation or translation. At these critical moments, the therapist provided bridging structures so that the boys' friendship could continue to develop, noting mutual interests or orchestrating otherwise parallel, exclusive discussions with the therapist into mutual conversations. (Note that "therapist's acts" is more of an "action" index than an "interaction" index because it does not describe the children's interaction, and therefore in some contexts we will refer to five rather than six interaction indices.)

Integrating the Three Perspectives

The interaction indices are necessary but not by themselves sufficient to track the (developmental) trajectory of pair therapy. This analytic task is analogous to that of a navigator on a ship at sea trying to plot its course. The navigator is on a ship that is moving on an earth that is turning on its axis and revolving around the sun. Charting the ship's course involves plotting over time a series of positions representing an intersection of latitude and longitude, both of which are triangulated dimensions. Like plotting a ship's course in moving three-dimensional space, describing the trajectory of pair therapy requires triangulation in horizontal and vertical dimensions. There are simultaneous movements (potentially developmental) within and between all three individuals involved, including each boy's and the therapist's individual selves, the pair's relationship, and each boy's relationship with the therapist. Therefore, we need complex methodological tools to track the social interactions of pair therapy in *three* dimensions over time.

To more fully describe the path of the pair's relationship, we have integrated the interaction indices into our existing empirical methodology. Figure 2 shows how we combined the interaction indices with our two previously developed perspectives of developmental level and social regulation processes using a metaphor of "dimensions" of social interaction. We retained our developmental levels (0-3) as the Y axis of a graph and the continuum of social regulation as the Z axis (from interpersonal negotiation at one extreme to shared experience on the other). We then added the five interaction indices along the horizontal X axis to provide a third dimension for charting the course of pair therapy. As we have arranged them along the X axis, the interaction indices allow for an articulation or specification of interpersonal mes-

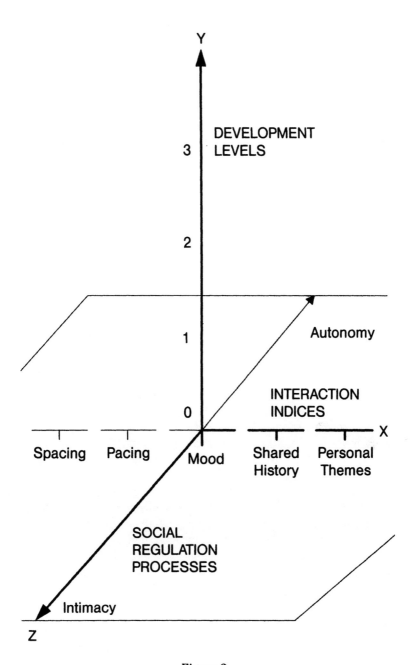

Figure 2

sages or behaviors on two planes. One plane is formed with the Y axis, where the relationships among the interaction indices range from the disconnected, alienated and remote (low on the Y axis) to the proximate, integrated and highly involved (high on the Y axis). A second plane is formed with the Z axis, where specific configurations of the interaction indices profile specific points on the social regulation continuum, ranging from extreme forms of intimacy (forward on the Z axis) to extreme manifestations of autonomy (backward on the Z axis).

In the next section we will use concrete case material from the first year of Arnie's and Mitchell's pair therapy to illustrate the use of this three-fold perspective. The tracking of their pair therapy with the three perspectives yields an interpretive developmental analysis of interpersonal relationship building over time.

II. The Case

Overview

Arnie and Mitchell met together with their pair therapist from the fall of 1985 to the spring of 1988. The narratives that follow are selected from sessions in the first eight months of their therapy.

The course of Arnie's and Mitchell's pair therapy followed a pattern of five predictable phases identified in other pair therapy cases we have analyzed (Selman & Schultz 1988). We have found that each of these phases of pair therapy tends to be characterized by a different relation between interpersonal negotiation and shared experience. In the early phases of pair therapy ("sizing each other up" and "establishing a dominance pattern"), negotiation tends to be in ascendance, that is, conflictual and territorial themes predominate and the pair's interpersonal orientations tend to be polarized, with one child assuming the self-transforming (submissive) role and the other child assuming the other-transforming (dominant) role. Themes of intimacy begin to emerge in the next, "stable imbalance of power" phase, when the dominance pattern established in the previous phase becomes the status quo. Intimacy interactions then take center stage in the "restructuring" phase, when the pair's interaction shifts upward in predominant developmental level and tends to become more balanced in interpersonal orientation. In the "consolidation" phase, the relation between negotiation and shared experience reaches a new state of balance, as the new level and style of interaction and a closer relationship among the triad consolidate.

In the following narrative, period one covers the first three months, from late September until just before the Christmas vacation, when the trio—the pair and the therapist—got to know each other and the two boys demonstrated their habitual patterns of relating, one that we would summarize as "unilateral" in level (1). In the first three sessions, Arnie and Mitchell sized each other up and established a dominance pattern. Their interpersonal orientations were polarized—Arnie was the other-transforming partner and Mitchell, the self-transforming one. A period of "stable imbalance of power" reigned until the middle of December.

Period two marks a transition to greater reciprocity (level 2) in the boys' interactions in a restructuring phase that lasted until almost the end of the first year. At the point we leave off their narrative, the pair were just entering a consolidation phase in which their relationship was stabilizing at the higher level and they were achieving greater degrees of closeness.

During each of these periods, our three perspectives showed the therapist hard at work, providing links between Arnie and Mitchell. In fact, the *therapist's acts* was the one index we could count on to be consistently relevant to the ongoing social interaction throughout the course of the pair therapy.

Period One: Phases of "Sizing Up," "Establishing Dominance," and "Stable Imbalance of Power"

Arnie's and Mitchell's first session constituted the first developmental phase of pair therapy—getting to know each other in the context of the pair.

> In the first meeting (10/22), the therapist acted to define the room in which they were meeting as a safe place. He offered lots of permission to both boys to decide on activities. At the same time, he placed clear limits on hurtful or dangerous possibilities: "I will make sure our time together is safe and that no one gets hurt." He actually provided a physical location for the pair by placing himself at a round table and asking them to join him.

> By the middle of the session there was an activity going on, an explanation of "Dungeons and Dragons," carried out at the therapist's suggestion by Arnie, who had brought a tote (a paper bag) full of personal theme items with him. Notably, though, this was only superficially a shared activity. Mitchell's slumped body position, a wall of D and D books rising between the boys as Arnie lectured first from one and then from another, and the brisk unresponsive pace of his explanations, all showed that the boys were occupying the same table but not the same "space."

In this session the boys were in one place together but neither their speech—as shown by Arnie's obscure "Dungeons and Dragons" vocabulary—nor their timing were in any sort of synchrony. Arnie was talking *at* Mitchell, in a one-way (level 1) fashion. Mitchell had the wilted appearance of someone who was being lectured. Arnie, in turn, looked like a boy who had little experience talking to peers, anxiously raising himself vertically in his chair or rocking back and forth as he dictated instructions.

In sessions two and three, which constituted the phase of "establishing a dominance pattern," there were signs of a different orientation in space, as the pair began to allow itself more of the room.

> Mitchell started the 10/29 session by walking about the space. Arnie occupied the table and began building a card house of his own: a place "to live and have a family." The TV set, located in a corner cabinet in the pair therapy room and used for showing videotapes, became an object of Mitchell's interest. The therapist explained how the set operated and who got to use it—and also took the opportunity to say aloud that Arnie and Mitchell "are a pair."

> The round table had been their initial spot, their point of introduction. Arnie went on to change the spatial balance of the triad by taking over a large area of this table to build his card house. And just as he affected the geographical balance by his physical position, so he also exerted an uncentering effect on the course of attempted conversation. His pacing was eccentric, fast-paced, jabbing—consisting of one-sided wordplay and quips. Invited by the therapist to join Mitchell in a game of "Sorry," he suggested playing "Unhappy" or "Apologize" instead. In this session, the pace was far too quick and the medium too wordy for Mitchell, who, with the therapist's encouragement, went about setting up a game board. Eventually, a shared game of "Sorry" began, but Arnie only agreed to play from a social and physical distance maintained by his move to the far sofa. Arnie's eccentricity, spatial and conceptual, ensured there would be no closeness.

Here Arnie, by distancing himself from, yet still playing, the board game was using space to help establish his other-transforming role.

The third session (11/15) continued this configuration. The therapist provided essential bridging and interpretive interventions. He had to, since neither the boys' placement nor the pacing of their activity showed much coordination.

> Although the boys began this session at the TV together, they rapidly headed off in opposite directions. At the therapist's request, Mitchell dutifully turned off the set and joined him at the round table. Arnie reacted with exaggerated, playful anger to Mitchell's switching off the TV: "Touch it and you die!" Arnie then chose to settle in far across the room on the sofa, while at the table the therapist and Mitchell set up a game of Trivial Pursuit. Like a high-to-low current transformer, the therapist managed to absorb Arnie's fast-paced remarks and reissue them as communications of a sort that Mitchell could handle. Without the therapist's help, communication evidently would have been at a standstill because the boys' pacing was so dissimilar. When,

for example, Arnie seemed ready to try a conversational gambit ("You seen 'The Terminator,' Mitchell?"), MItchell failed to grasp the question rapidly enough and so, before he could respond, Arnie delivered the sarcastic follow-up, "Oh yes, you're too young."

Not in *pacing, spacing, mood,* or *personal themes* were these boys ready to address one another reciprocally. At all times they required the therapist to foster two-way communication. Arnie's spatial orientation (keeping himself at a distance yet making some conversational overtures to Mitchell) and his sarcastic unilateral negotiation style (ordering Mitchell not to touch the TV) suggest that, with his level one, *other-transforming role* well-established, he was able to respond to the therapist's efforts to connect the boys. And Mitchell's dislike of Arnie's jibes and insults found a new voice through the therapist, as Mitchell turned to the therapist (with Arnie in hearing range) and said, "Tell him to shut up!", to which the therapist responded, "Mitchell, can you tell Arnie his insults hurt your feelings?" Here the therapist not only delivers a message to Arnie that Mitchell was unable to communicate directly, he translates Mitchell's unilateral (level 1) order into a reciprocal and reflective (level 2) communication.

Against this background, well into the session, there were signs that these two boys had gained (or perhaps were finally able to use) the capacity for coordinated interchange and sharing of experience when the therapist succeeded in linking them.

> First, Arnie was admiringly impressed by Mitchell's answering a "Trivial Pursuit" question about the location of the Galapagos Islands ("Oh, my God! How did he know that?"), then together the boys—along with the therapist— joined in a surreptitious giggle and shared banter over the meaning of the word "amazia" (a woman without breasts).

By the session of 11/19 Arnie's and Mitchell's relationship was entering the "stable (im)balance" phase. They began to be able to adopt more central positions instead of the previously described off-balance, wide-spaced configurations.

> Arnie began the hour by choosing his now familiar location, the far sofa, but Mitchell joined Arnie on the sofa, although at the opposite end. And while Arnie read a science fiction book from his omnipresent cache (now in a totebag), Mitchell looked in the bag, found a catalogue of practical joke items, and began to leaf through it.

Clearly, spatial barriers and distance were being tentatively reduced. However, it was still highly uncertain whether the boys would be able to coordinate their *pacing.*

Directing his voice toward the therapist, Mitchell began to read aloud the one-liner gags from a series of joke-buttons that could be ordered from the catalogue. As he read, his performance seemed divorced from an understanding of the words he pronounced. It was as though the process of reading to others felt pleasurable to him, but the jokes themselves passed him by. They caught Arnie's attention, though, and therefore allowed all three participants a chance to share information. In fact, the therapist took advantage of this opportunity to attune communicative competence by explaining to Mitchell the meaning of the button, "I AM NOT GOING TO ARGUE WITH YOU. I WON'T HAVE A BATTLE OF WITS WITH AN UNARMED MAN."

The shared learning and the jokes themselves in this session would be recalled in a more consolidated reciprocal form of shared experience at a later date. But at this point, Mitchell's reading and Arnie's reaction had the feel of a tentative transition from unidirectional (level 1) to reciprocal (level 2) forms of connecting. As Mitchell sat on the sofa, facing outward and reading, Arnie did not seek a further distance. Instead, he continued to sit parallel to his pair partner, ostensibly reading his sci-fi book but actually tuned in and able to respond, or at least to editorialize.

A few weeks later (12/11), it was as if Mitchell had taken on some of Arnie's earlier eccentricity and other-transforming style of interacting. In turn, Arnie assumed the cooperative, task-oriented position Mitchell had held until now. This meeting shows both the highest level of social regulation achieved by the pair to that date—and the speed with which it disintegrated when the therapist was no longer available to bridge, modulate, and structure the boys' interaction.

The session began with Mitchell at the TV. (It was also disrupted later on by the nearly irresistible draw the TV-watching had for him.) At the outset, though, while looking over a catalogue the therapist had begun a discussion individually with each boy that soon became an easy exchange of shopping lists. As Mitchell got more involved in the discussion, he moved from one side of the couch nearer to Arnie. The therapist, in turn, drew closer into a right angled position vis-a-vis both boys. The three formed an intimate trio, aligned in space and matched in tempo throughout the length of their discussion.

But then the therapist had reason to be out of the room for approximately five minutes, and he decided to risk leaving in order to see what would unfold. The boys were charged with the responsibility of setting up a Monopoly game. It turned out to be a responsibility they could not yet handle cooperatively. Arnie, now more interested in social interaction, did begin to unpack the pieces and the board. Mitchell, however, raced immediately for the TV.

When Mitchell charged for the TV set, Arnie was actually initiating a conversational gambit ("Do you play Monopoly at home?"). That interpersonal offering was lost on a Mitchell intensely fixed on the isolating activity of TV watching. He tried to tune in a specific program and had trouble with the reception. At that point, he called upon Arnie for assistance. This was a purely functional request, however. It was followed by Arnie's making a quick feint at turning off the TV ("This is silly!") in an awkward attempt to indicate that he wanted Mitchell to come over and play Monopoly. He received in reply to this way of asking Mitchell to join him, a threatening, angry reaction ("Cut it out!"). When Arnie approached the TV again ("This is dumb!"), Mitchell spit out angrily, "No! Don't change it, Arnie!" and under the force of his vehemence Arnie retreated.

Once again, their timing and use of space and language left each boy isolated (level 0 interaction). In what was for Arnie a significant move toward a higher form of intimacy, he offered Mitchell an opportunity to talk about their private lives away from school ("Do you play Monopoly at home?"). Had Mitchell been able to respond to it, or had Arnie been able to be a gentler persuader, this move might have brought the boys to a pattern of reciprocal interchange. Instead of continuing their level 1 style of unilateral negotiation, they might have shared individual experiences of the same activity with one another. In other words, this was an opportunity for the kind of chumship that Harry Stack Sullivan (1953) identified as growth-enhancing. Their earlier coordinated use of *pacing* and *spacing* suggested they were heading in precisely this direction, but at this point it seems that reciprocity could only be achieved with the centralizing presence of the therapist.

Period Two: "Restructuring" from Unilateral to Reciprocal Interaction

In the second group of sessions (from 12/18 to 4/10), we saw the boys becoming more engaged with each other and with the therapist. In this restructuring phase of their therapy, Arnie's and Mitchell's use of space became more settled as the right-angled sofas became the usual site for pair activities. Sometimes they shared the space; sometimes, it was the site of their conflicts. But their predictable use of the furniture and their physical ease within this chosen corner of the room suggested that the space in some sense belonged to both of them rather than to one or the other. Apparently, Arnie no longer felt he had to protect himself from Mitchell and the therapist by peppering them from afar with unrelenting, rapid-paced verbal salvos that would both keep them at bay and keep the interaction under Arnie's control. Similarly, Mitchell no longer seemed trapped in an inflexible "good-boy" dependent position by the therapist's side. Because both boys widened their area of activity, the interaction indices of *spacing* and *pacing* began to show new, more coordinated patterns. But, of course, without the *therapist's acts* Arnie and Mitchell could not or would not have sustained a short conversation, much less an hour of unstructured companionship (q.v. 12/11).

The 2/13 session began with a lot of movement through the room. Eventually, the therapist and Arnie sat adjacent to one another, with Arnie on the sofa at the end of the room and the therapist in a side chair at a ninety degree angle to him. It required the therapist's repeated appeals to Mitchell, however, to get him to stop watching the TV and join the pair. Mitchell did join them, but not fully. He chose a seat facing the therapist across the coffee table, a position that put him at some distance from Arnie. Arnie, in turn, sat leafing through a fantasy horror book. In a visible demonstration of openness, his tote (now a wooden wine box strapped with rubberbands) was with him and in view. Mitchell proceeded to pick the Trivial Pursuit gamebook up from the coffee table and begin his own leafing-through. Although the pacing of the pair looked similar, it was in fact not congruent. Mitchell soon expressed this directly, complaining that Arnie never wanted to do what he wanted—say, to play basketball—but only "to sit and read that stuff." The therapist then posed questions about their differing interests in a way that suggested both boys might find compromise possible. At that point, the attention shifted to what Arnie was reading.

Mitchell had changed his position. In effect, he moved into the trio, adopting a chair he placed in front of the side sofa as his perch. In the Trivial Pursuit game they were playing, the therapist supplied clues, cues, and prototypes for answers. He was, indeed, a storehouse of word resources. Mitchell then freely used this resource. As the therapist sounded out a hint, "Ma-chi..." (syllables in "International Business Machines"), Mitchell picked up the sound with delight, Mushies!" When Arnie did not attend immediately to his joke, Mitchell, with heretofore unobserved force—active but controlled and legitimate—purposefully claimed Arnie's attention by calling his name and repeating the joke. Arnie then responded positively.

Further along in the session, Mitchell offered another sally ("Mr. Fried Egg Day" for "Friday"), and Arnie hazarded a joke at the expense of the therapist ("If the question is famous jerks, who played Dr. _____?") Through this humorous put-down, which may have been motivated by anger over the therapist's recent vacation, the boys achieved a shared instant of fun and a moment of verbal triumph over the relied-upon but dominant adult.

Mitchell's jokes were clearly presented with Arnie in mind. Although at first Arnie was unresponsive, Mitchell neither wilted nor raged. Instead, he proved persistent in a modulated way that soon captured Arnie's attention and interest. Not only did Arnie attend, he actually wound up reciprocating with a form of humor that matched him and Mitchell against the therapist, who willingly served as a foil. As a result, the boys had comfortable grounds for agreement, and Mitchell gained some equality in the relationship.

The session of 4/10 began with both boys in a bad mood and moved to a crisis point when they got too close for comfort.

> At the outset, the three participants took their usual positions, with Arnie on the sofa that faced the door, Mitchell joining him to his right, and the therapist across the coffee table from them in an easy chair. Arnie placed his tote on the table, lifted the lid, and left the contents available. The therapist inquired about whether Arnie was "feeling the effects" of his birthday, as Arnie's teacher had reported earlier in the day. Mitchell reached into Arnie's box and pulled out a hand-held miniature synthesizer, apparently interested in it yet contemptuous in his comments ("idiotic asshole organ"). Everyone's *pacing* was off. When Arnie repossessed the synthesizer, Mitchell turned again to the Arnie's box and started rifling through its contents, "looking for a movie." (Probably this was an indirect way of saying that what he wanted to do that day was watch a video movie on the VCR.) Finally, he settled on a pack of seeds. He jerked them from the box, yelling "Watermelon!" in an attention grabbing, annoying, almost assaultive way.

> Meanwhile, Arnie had started playing the synthesizer, an instrument that not only has intriguing features (it can mimic a violin, a flute, etc., and will play two pre-programmed tunes in a variety of ways), but also has annoying, if not infuriating, features: in any of its modes the synthesizer produces an edgy, harsh quality of sound. Its volume can be pulsingly loud, and when one of its automatic tunes is repeated again and again and again, the effect on an unwilling listener is that of a faucet constantly drip, drip, dripping through the night. Arnie's *timing* was syncopated to take full advantage of the irritating possibilities of the synthesizer. He used it to entertain himself in isolation, to drown out Mitchell or the therapist when he didn't want to listen to them, and to tease Mitchell with a provocative and unreachable toy.

> As Mitchell wnet through Arnie's box looking for a movie and complaining there wasn't one, Arnie was playing away on the ever more attractive synthesizer. Then, with a "Let's see," Mitchell grabbed for it. The therapist responded by advising Mitchell to ask for what he wanted ("Try to use words"). But when Mitchell did indeed ask, Arnie blankly refused. Mitchell headed off for the TV in frustrated defeat, and the therapist acknowledged that "walking away" might feel like the only available option.

Clearly, in this situation words were not building an interpersonal system of exchange. At least for Arnie, they amounted to no more than tools to frustrate Mitchell's agenda. Like *spacing, pacing* was being used to act out angry feelings.

The boys continued a parallel struggle. Mitchell created noise with the TV while Arnie created noise with the synthesizer. Arnie engaged the therapist in a guessing game over what instrument the synthesizer was imitating; Mitchell tossed out a question about TV. The question, however, had no clearly intended target since Mitchell did not look at either of the two possible recipients. Only the therapist's efforts to recall Mitchell from the TV set brought the pair into its initial spatial relation again. Once settled in, their ostensible topic was Arnie's birthday. At that point, Mitchell unhelpfully elaborated on the idea of a birthday party in order to suggest that Arnie was the boyfriend of the most socially disparaged girl in their class: "Arnie invited Angela to a sleepover," he teased.

Arnie largely ignored Mitchell and allowed the synthesizer to play automatically on and on. But the sexual theme Mitchell had initiated continued to play itself out in his actions. At one point he provocatively yelled out, "Boner!" And when the therapist remarked that Mitchell seemed to have some thoughts about sex on his mind, Mitchell shouted loudly, "SEX!" All along Mitchell's pace seemed that of a much younger boy, with few attention-getting social gambits other than loud, abrupt moves and shock-value words. Certainly Arnie's unyielding combination of needling and ignoring thwarted Mitchell's quieter, more uncertain ploys. Although undoubtedly Mitchell was contending with both aggressive and sexual impulses, *personal themes* alone did not account for his behavior. His frustrations were clearly exacerbated by Arnie, who maintained focused attention just below or just beyond anywhere Mitchell appeared. When, for example, Mitchell tried to tie into the topic of the synthesizer ("My brother has a big one of those"), and thus take part in a conversation between Arnie and the therapist, Arnie ended the exchange with a quip at Mitchell's expense, the sort of fast-paced joking Mitchell could not sustain. In this exchange Arnie hazarded that Mitchell would only get to bring the synthesizer to school if he "threatened his brother." When the therapist asked, "He'd threaten him?" Arnie snapped back, "With his looks!"

It seems understandable, then, that Mitchell resorted (regressed) to the loud, slapstick style of teasing that was his baseline response. At the same level of indirect, boisterous defense, he went on to imitate the sound of the unshared synthesizer. It was as if to say, if I can't *have* the synthesizer, I'll *be* the synthesizer. "He's got the sound down," noted the therapist. But Arnie feigned no interest, insisting on the therapist's continuing a separate conversation with him.

Again, Mitchell approached, asking if he could borrow the "Field and Stream" magazine he had drawn from Arnie's box ("If you're not going to use it, I want to show it to my mother"). Arnie, in response, took the magazine and held it in his hand, in clear sight but out of reach. The boys were still smiling, as if they were merely teasing one another. First Mitchell risked a grab, but Arnie pulled the magazine away, too quick for him. Still smiling, as if this was all just teasing, they began to feint blows with their fists and forearms. Then Arnie hit Mitchell in the eye, not hard, but hard enough to injure Mitchell's pride at least. For a moment neither moved, both boys taken aback and frightened by what had occurred. Then Mitchell kicked Arnie. Again, it was not so hard as to do serious damage, yet too hard to be a joke. At that point, the therapist separated the boys, and both withdrew.

Paradoxically, during this exchange most of the categories we use to track the interaction showed synchronous activity. The boys were coordinated and reciprocal in their *pacing, spacing,* and *mood.* However, the interaction was conflictual rather than harmonious: the jokes here were made at each other's expense. Even so, to get to this point of overt conflict they had to show characteristics of a level above power-oriented control (level 1), the kind of acknowledgement of the other person we have called self-reflective reciprocity (level 2). In a kind of inspired pattern of mutual irritation, Arnie and Mitchell proceeded to rub and rasp on each other's nerves. They worked on each other until too much closeness produced an overheated state and striking out. They soon reached a point where, if allowed to proceed, they were likely to either hurt one another or flee the situation entirely.

Immediately after Mitchell was struck, the therapist moved to intervene. (But as we noted he was not quick enough to prevent Mitchell from achieving a retaliatory strike, so Arnie too got hurt.) After inflicting some mutual pain, both boys retreated. Arnie sat stooped over—almost into—his box of personal materials, whereas Mitchell headed for the TV. (If the therapist had permitted it, he would have proceeded to tune in a program and tune out the situation.) The therapist, therefore, moved decisively, changing his own location within the room, shifting to a midpoint between the now far-spaced boys. He began a therapeutic attempt to convert angry and perhaps guilty affect into words.

"Mitchell, are you feeling upset now? Arnie, how are you feeling?" Notably, in their responses to the therapist's invitation to talk, Mitchell's answers were unelaborated and muted ("No"), whereas Arnie's were filigreed with sarcasm ("No, I'm having a rainbow day!"). These boys were locked into a counterpoint of struggle, and their *pacing* and chosen *spacing,* although parallel, remained identifiably characteristic in orientation.

Mitchell, as we have seen, could not ask clearly and persistently for what he wanted. Arnie was terrified by the movement of aggression from the inner world of fantasy to the interpersonal world of reality. At this critical moment, the therapist had to draw on eight months of therapeutic capital: he had the boys move closer together, at right angles on separate couches. Their arousal remained too high, however, for them to tolerate this spatial arrangement. Arnie took advantage of his clear view of Mitchell to target him and shoot off a rubber band. (This ambiguous action probably both meant "Let's get back to business as usual" and signaled the potential for re-igniting highly flammable, disorganized feelings.)

The therapist physically rose to intervene: "I'm going to call this pair session to an end if we can't get back to normal and figure out what happened." His tone was neither angered nor panicked, but authoritative and definite. In a sequence of moves that changed their configuration in space and altered the trio's timing, the therapist effectively insisted on becoming the center of activity—the gravitational point around which conflict continued, but in a diminishing, increasingly redefined fashion.

First, he took a position by Arnie on the sofa, which placed him between the feuding boys. Second, he did not end the session post-haste, despite his uttered threat, and he did not insist on an I'm-going-to-get-to-the-bottom-of-this approach to resolving the situation. As the therapist sat down, Arnie initiated banter with him in an exaggerated, aggrieved tone: "Don't sit on my books!" The therapist responded lightly, then proceeded to test each boy's capacity to tolerate looking back at what had happened: "This conflict started when Mitchell asked to borrow Arnie's "Field and Stream." Mitchell interjected, "I just wanted to show my mother an ad for an inflatable boat." At that moment, neither boy had sufficient emotional flexibility to process the disagreement in depth—for each it remained a (level 1) matter of who started it, who should be blamed, and who should feel guilty. "We do not need to *blame* anyone," said the therapist, translating the reasoning to level 2. But he allowed the subject to simply fade from view. Sensing tension and the need for an easier transition he picked up the disputed "Field and Stream" and leafed through it, thus signaling his willingness to drop the matter as long as he was in control. And indeed he was the central figure at the moment. Things quieted down, almost as if everyone had taken a time out.

When conversation resumed, it was on a different tack, with the boys taking turns at grilling the therapist on contemporary politics. (Neither of them was healed enough to interact civilly with the other, but they were no longer in such pain that they could not accept the therapist's serving as intermediary.) Arnie asked, "Do you think Clint Eastwood will become President?" And Mitchell followed with, "Did you vote for President Reagan?"

Gently but repeatedly throughout the remainder of the session the therapist tried to help the boys negotiate their differences. Although too powerful to be ignored, his influence was gravitational rather than coercive. At one point Mitchell began to take apart the intercom phone, and the therapist considered whether to set limits on this behavior but decided, under the circumstances, not to intervene. While Mitchell was absorbed in that activity, the therapist, somewhat on his behalf, asked Arnie if it was possible for Mitchell to examine the "Field and Stream." "No!" he replied.

"And what's your reason?" "Because he made me mad," Arnie explained. "So you feel like punishing him?" the therapist confirmed. "Is there any way you two could bargain or negotiate about Mitchell's desire to look at the magazine?" Mitchell then turned not to Arnie but to the therapist and asked,

"Could I Xerox this advertisement?" "You need to ask Arnie," said the therapist, "but maybe the three of us could go downstairs to use the machine."
Because Arnie also wanted to photocopy some material, a compromise began
to get worked out. At this juncture, with compromise in the air, the therapist
no longer needed to position himself between the boys. He shifted to a chair
across from the sofa on which both Arnie and Mitchell were now seated—a
move that signified the fight was over and "re-pair" had begun. Although the
details of resolution remained to be worked out, the pair had experienced an
intense conflict and experienced surviving it.

Because there was so much activity during this session, all the interaction indices, except *shared history* were in the foreground. Much of this activity, however, was conflictual in tone. The boys were using the medium of
closeness, but not in ways that promoted mutuality. *Pacing* charted idiosyn-
crasies in each boy's verbal presentation, and throughout most of this session
it was apparent that Arnie and Mitchell were widely separated in *personal
themes*, even though they were sharing a negative desire to thwart one another.
Although the interaction indices showed no regression back to the utterly
unbridgeable private vocabularies of the fall sessions, neither seemed really
interested in conversation. Words and timing were used to provoke, with the
utterly oppositional boys alternately enticing, teasing, and ignoring each other.

Their *moods* were at a high intensity. Anger and frustration seemed to
underlie most of their interactions, which generally had an abrupt, sharp-
edged quality. Finally, the anger took direct form when Arnie struck and then
was struck by Mitchell; at that point, the slow simmer of the session boiled
over. The translation of angry feeling into action did not, however, get rid of
it. Instead, the burner merely was turned down once again to simmer, and the
boys continued to struggle and snipe. For boys like Mitchell and Arnie—or
any individuals for whom social regulation is so much unfamiliar, untuned
machinery—there are bound to be times in the process of moving closer
together when the mark is overshot and discomfort at a "too-closeness" for
comfort is the outcome. Only the therapist's presence allowed Mitchell and
Arnie to stay in the room with one another, and in the end to feel to some
degree that they had come through together.

During the latter part of the spring, Mitchell and Arnie once again took
up the search for a consistent activity to which they could comfortably turn
session after session. After spending a number of sessions viewing VCR movies together, the therapist encouraged them to try something more active—a
fantasy-superheroes board game—as their "home base" activity. Because they
had begun their first session with "Dungeons and Dragons," it was as if they
had traveled full circle during the school year. In the session of 5/6 and in the
weeks that followed, the therapist deliberately took on the function of educational facilitator, hoping the boys could increase their capacity for interaction

and collaboration if they gained equality in their practical game-playing skills. In these sessions Arnie continually grew impatient with Mitchell's much slower pace of acquiring new information, and the boys' disparity in *pacing* led to conflicts and breakdowns in communication. Mitchell, however, was becoming noticeably more verbal and several times took the risk of expressing his desires and emotions, complaining, for example, that in pairs "We use only Arnie's toys." And Arnie's antagonism and disdain was becoming less hostile and demanding (level 1) and more controlled and teasing (level 2). Conflict now had a different outcome than in the session of their fight a month before.

> Again the accusatory words flew back and forth, even toward the therapist in the session of 5/6. But this time, the word play engendered laughter at one another, with both boys falling into silly states. Arnie started to rock back and forth, and Mitchell imitated Arnie. At that point, the therapist tried to redirect conversation, but Mitchell interrupted. He grabbed Arnie's box, flipped it open flamboyantly, and declared in talk-show style, "Okay, now for the Battle of Wits!"

This *shared history* contribution referred to the interchange far back in the winter, when the therapist had tried to explain the meaning of the joke button. Now Mitchell was reintroducing the phrase, enhanced by his sense of humor and control. The result was that what began as a personal memory became transformed into a social idiom; "battle of wits" became for the triad a symbolic and shared verbal indicator of their collective abilities and mutual history.

Mitchell showed the others he had come a long way. Apparently, Arnie agreed. When at the end of the session the therapist complimented the pair on the way they had played the game, Arnie added his own typically cynical version of mutual congratulations—"Yeah, better than usual." Was it the case, perhaps, that Arnie's retreat afforded Mitchell needed time and space to redefine his status in pairs? Although the session was fraught with discord between the boys, both left it having taken a necessary step toward a higher level of autonomy, a step also necessary for gaining a higher level of intimacy. At the end of period two, it looked as though, however uneven the process, reciprocal persistence was replacing unilateral insistence.

III. Interpreting the Case

Developmental Levels of Interaction Indices

Before developing the interaction indices, we used a "critical incident" methodology. That is, we picked out specific social interactions fitting the definition of either interpersonal negotiation or shared experience, then coded and interpreted them by developmental level. We still omitted, however, much of the stream of social interaction, dichotomizing some of it (into the two extremes at each end of the intimacy/autonomy continuum from negotiation to shared experience) and ignoring the rest (behavior in the middle fitting neither definition). This method is nevertheless an advance over one in which interactions are coded merely in terms of their developmental level: behaviors are examined from two complementary perspectives (level and type of social regulation).

Our current methodology, informed by all three perspectives, seems more adequate for describing the social interaction between the members of the triad in the pair therapy sessions than relying solely on the analysis of developmental level and social regulation processes. It is our view that structural-developmental models of the sort we have employed through much of the pair therapy project are basic because they provide a sense of the increasing adequacy and complexity of social development. We are well aware, however, that they have drawbacks. It has been of concern to us, for example, that such models connote an overly orderly and unidirectional picture of the growth of interpersonal maturity. Also there is a tendency when guided solely by hierarchical assumptions to see social interactions—which occur in a continuous stream of mutually influenced events—as discrete, individualized units (Gergen & Gergen 1982, Packer 1985). Long ago in our pair therapy project we reached the point where it was less helpful only to identify, classify, and aggregate instances of shared experience or interpersonal negotiation as though we were bird watchers compiling a life list. ("See, there's a zero, and there's a two, and here's a couple of one's.") Our revised model maintains the traditional developmental vision of increasing psychological complexity without restricting the rich interplay of a therapeutic triad to a uniform, step-like progression. What we try to do, in effect, is to bring our previously established arrangement of levels into conjunction with a continuum of social regulation processes and a set of interaction indices. The result is a loosely worked matrix, an expanded model of development, with less clearcut boundaries but, we believe, greater depth and texture. In this integration we combine levels of the structural approach with the five interaction indices in the following way that is respectful of both developmental and contextual factors.

Spacing. In primitive (low-level) forms of spacing, persons act without cognizance of each other's physical boundaries or their own physical relations to others. At the next level, participants divide space into what's mine and what's yours. Arnie and Mitchell used space in this fashion at the beginning of their pair therapy, with the other-transforming Arnie using extreme distancing and the self-transforming Mitchell using extreme encroachment, not as overt intrusiveness, but simply an unaware "hovering," an unconscious equation of close physical proximity with psychological acceptance by the other. With further development, space is not just divided but coordinated, and the orientation of the self in space is toward the other (face to face, or at least side by side), with a tacitly negotiated distance between persons. At the most advanced level in our system, space is experienced as shared; it is an integrated unit (this is *our* room) the ownership and use of which is continually attended to and renegotiated by the pair.

Pacing. At the most primitive level, pacing is totally out of synchrony. There is a naive solipsism involving privitized speech on the one hand and a nonmalicious non-attendance to the other's utterances on the other. At the next level, communication is one-way, be it an attempt to share the self's thoughts or negotiate the self's interests. The other is expected to get into synchrony (step) with the self. Little attention is paid to others' timing or content or reactions. At a higher level pacing involves processes of clarification and explanation in an attempt to make sure the other "gets it" or the self comprehends. Active self and other regulation is evident in the form of the communication (asking questions, clarifying, etc.), and pacing is modified in response to others. A still higher level is manifest in conscious efforts to establish patterns of feedback and response to the other's concerns as well as asserting one's own needs. Fairly well elaborated synchrony is seen between patterns and paces of talking and acting as well as meanings of talking.

Mood. In charting development in social mood, we were looking for instances of consensual validation, self-revelation, and affect expressed unambiguously in words or gestures rather than in veiled, self-protective, ultimately isolating ways. Most primitive is indirect expression of affect or a lack of any reaction to the feelings of the other. Somewhat less isolating is the sense that only one mood is allowed in the room at one time, with no room for other or conflicting feelings. Acknowledgement of the other's feelings is viewed as higher-level, and even more advanced development is evident in the motivation to work directly on the feelings of the pair in the room, to see the feelings of one as related to and affecting the feelings of the other, and to see the emotions generated in the therapeutic context as processes that need "tending to."

Shared History. In a pair with a poorly developed shared history or with individuals who cannot use their history, actions take place in a "continual present." There is no historical reference to the past or future. Each session is not only a new interaction but virtually a new relationship. All is up for grabs and negotiation begins again each session. At a more advanced but still time-bound level, we find continuity manifest as the reference to or repetition of past activities ("Can we play that again?" "He got to go first last time!"). This level is followed developmentally by a much more conscious relating of (pointing to) past and present in the service of the continuity of the pair.

A sense that "we are a pair because we have done things together" is established. At the most advanced level we see the pair weaving the past, present, and future together. Part of the actual activity of the pair *is* to be historical—to reminisce, recollect, and plan for the future.

Personal Themes. This index can be ranged along a developmental continuum from primitve fears about body integrity and the physical safety of the self, to concerns for total power and control, to concerns about simple social interactions, to social relationship concerns. Thus, the self moves developmentally from asking who can destroy or save whom; to who has the power to tell what to whom; to who is doing what to or with whom and who do we like or don't like; to how are we getting along, perhaps voiced as, why am I the way I am, or why do I do what I do as compared to others?

In contrast to our previous "critical incident" method, which is analogous to looking for a certain kind of fish and pulling it out of the stream with a net (our definitions of incidents of social regulation), then classifying it within the zoological fish taxonomy (classifying by level), in our current method, we do not "catch" the fish. Instead, we look for shifting patterns of relationships among the fish as they swim past (leveling by interaction indices), at the same time as we make a note of what kind of fish they are (type of social regulation). Both methods then interpret the "fish's" place within the ecosystem of the stream (in our case, within the microgenetic and macrogenetic course of pair therapy). With the earlier "critical incident" method, despite our best hermeneutic intentions, we in a sense de-contextualized (typed) an interaction in order to determine its developmental meaning (leveling it) before interpreting it in relation to previous and subsequent interactions (re-contextualizing it temporally). With the current method, we come closer to fully contextualizing and including each moment of interaction, by attending to the three perspectives simultaneously. Then we contextualize each moment again in another (temporal) dimension, interpreting it in its microgenetic and macrogenetic context, to yield a *developmental* analysis of social regulation as process rather than product. In effect the interaction indices give us a way to look at the relation between the two types of social regulaion that eliminates the false dichotomy between them, reflecting the nature of social regulation as a continuum.

Phases in the Closeness of the Boys' Relationship

Let us look now at how the three perspectives of interaction indices, developmental levels, and social regulation processes can be used to make sense of Arnie and Mitchell's first year of pair therapy. Because the interaction indices describe the continuous stream of the triad's interaction, it begins to include more of the whole continuum of social regulation. The perspective provided by the interaction indices illuminates the "middle" ground of social regulation, not just the extremes of negotiation (autonomy) and sharing (intimacy). In so doing, it reveals the progression of the boys' relationship along all three perspectives. As the pair therapy progressed through the phases outlined earlier, the way each boy related changed in *level* (from level 1 to level 2), the relative balance of *social regulation processes* in the pair's interaction shifted (from predominantly negotiation to predominantly shared experience to a fluidity in terms of how one type of social regulation fades into the other, i.e., fluidity of movement along the continuum), and the triadic system showed greater synchrony among the *interaction indices.*

Negotiation was the major theme of the early sessions of Arnie's and Mitchell's therapy. Arnie assumed the dominant role in the dyad early on, partly because of his faster *pacing* and partly by virtue of the primitive power of his *personal themes,* embodied in his everpresent cache. Arnie was (over)controlling in the first session, dictating his fast-paced Dungeons and Dragons lecture without any apparent consideration of whether Mitchell was comprehending the instructions. Mitchell did not venture to communicate the degree of his (mis)understanding or interest in the game; he simply went along. In the next two sessions, Arnie used *spacing* to establish his dominance. By physically distancing himself from the Sorry, Life, and Trivial Pursuit game boards and the other two game players, he forced them to play the games on his terms, which meant having Mitchell and the therapist physically participate in the games for him (moving his piece, reading all the questions, etc.).

In the "stable imbalance of power" phase of their relationship (e.g., 11/19), their unilateral interpersonal negotiations continued to be salient, either dictatorial, or flowing through the perceived authority of the therapist. However, shared experience, albeit at level 1, began to emerge as a significant aspect of their interactions. These shared interactions were still focused on the present moment, on overt behavior rather than on thoughts or feelings, and originated in the expressions or interests of one of the parties. The physical distance between the boys was reduced in these sessions, and at times they formed an "intimate trio" with the therapist. But when the therapist left the room for a short time (12/11), their interaction disintegrated from triadic sharing into low-level, hostile negotiation, showing that the therapist's involvement was necessary for the maintenance of a level 2 structure.

During this phase Arnie slowly yielded some control, moving both physically and psychologically closer and tolerating occasions when Mitchell set the pace. As with many of the pairs with whom we have worked, once an initial dominance pattern was set (here, Arnie in the ascendant position) and a negotiation style established (mostly level 1 orders and commands), the pair began to feel safe enough to explore the less familiar and hence more frightening waters of closeness and intimacy.

The next (restructuring) phase of the treatment (e.g., 2/13) marked the emergence of shared experience as the major theme of the boys' relationship, as a new ease with reciprocity allowed a more sophisticated synchrony. Changes in both *spacing* and *pacing* brought greater opportunities for shared experience. The pair sat in closer proximity, in arrangements that made them more of a reciprocal unit. For instance, Arnie and Mitchell became able to occupy a single sofa, to read together, and to turn directly toward one another when making comments. As Mitchell felt more comfortable in the relationship, he speeded up his jokes and quips, while Arnie in turn slowed his down, showing greater patience with his partner and greater interest in having Mitchell understand what he had to say. With this new interest in exchange on Arnie's part and new skill in engaging someone else on Mitchell's part, interactions that previously would have veered toward conflict veered toward sharing instead. For example, we saw Mitchell's word play during a Trivial Pursuit game evoke Arnie's laughter, with the results that Arnie became engaged voluntarily and went on to make several puns of his own.

Negotiation and consensus still seemed difficult for the boys. Clashes during this period, however, had a more focused, detailed, and specific (less globally undifferentiated) quality than those of the introductory period. Then, defense or disguise of the whole self had seemed to be necessary. Now, in contrast, conflicts occurred when a particular desire or expectation was thwarted. For example, Mitchell became mad at Arnie because Arnie didn't want to play Trivial Pursuit or basketball, rather than being outraged at an undifferentiated, oppressive environment of which Arnie was just a nearby feature or convenient symbol. In other words, during these pair sessions *mood* was less diffuse and had more immediacy, specificity, and situation-groundedness than in the preceding period. Emotionally, the boys were more fully present and more willingly self-revealing.

We could not help but notice the tentative nature of Arnie and Mitchell's growth toward friendship, and its oscillating, to-and-fro pattern of development. Although some sessions in this restructuring phase demonstrated to us how the boys came to try out new forms of ease, others reminded us how new and unconsolidated these interactions were.

The session of 4/10 was a major crisis of the restructuring phase. The structure of the session was that of intense negotiations—a fight—but the content or theme of the session was that of (attempts at but thwarting of) intimacy and connection. The session ended in a physical configuration much like that at the beginning with both boys sitting close together on a sofa and the therapist facing them across the coffee table from an easy chair. The presumed meaning of their spatial set-up—that a degree of interpersonal comfort could be counted on by all three participants—was challenged in this session, as Mitchell and Arnie learned that the danger of intimacy and closeness is a too-closeness that can feel like intrusion. The boys arrived at blows after thwarted attempts at connection, and the physical pain each inflicted on the other came as somewhat of a surprise.

Until the boys' shocked reaction to the semi-unintentional physical blows, the essence of their teasing was the kind of horseplay that most children engage in all the time. However, these boys were too vulnerable to tolerate the semi-accidental physical conflict. Mitchell and Arnie showed themselves as virtually without options in their anger and frustration with one another. They alternated between passive-aggressive strategies (not listening, not responding, handing a requested article over in a way that caused it to break or tear) and outright aggressive maneuvers. They displaced their original conflict onto a new set of issues or tried forms of withdrawal.

However, through the therapist's careful and caring efforts to "repair" the relationship, both boys showed a willingness to stay and work it out even when enduring some inner turmoil. This was a far cry from those early sessions when Arnie set up physical and psychological barriers to any connection with others and Mitchell was too undifferentiated, disorganized, and diffident to risk venturing out of himself. The pair ended on a note of continuity—physically where it had begun but psychologically a bit beyond: knowing their relationship was close enough to tolerate direct conflict.

After experiencing the crisis of the fight, the pair was less vulnerable to the disorganizing effects of disharmony in a close peer relationship. Although their *pacing* was often still at odds, they were able to "play" with their discord, turning an exchange of accusatory words a month after the fight into an experience of laughter and sharing. An important sign of change for Arnie and Mitchell was new-found ability to recall fun they had together in the past with reciprocal *shared history,* notably, Mitchell's recollection of the "battle of wits" joke. Not only did he recall it, he was able to elaborate the memory with a sophistication that gave the experience a new and deeper meaning. As a result of the boys' new (level 2) sophistication in regulating their social interaction, the therapist no longer had to coordinate every meaning-laden interaction; the boys began to do this for themselves.

The Critical Role of the Pair Therapist

By incorporating the continuous stream of interaction, the three-perspective approach illuminates the transformatory role of the pair therapist in the construction of the boys' relationship. The therapeutic process of pair therapy reflects not only the natural course of the pair's relationship, but also the way this course is challenged and changed by the therapist's intervention, that is, how the relationship gets restructured. In picking out interactions of interpersonal negotiation and shared experience ("catching fish") with our previous "critical incident" method, we focused our attention only on those interactions occurring between the two children; although we acknowledged the therapist's crucial role, we did not explicitly analyze it. With the focus on the whole stream of interaction provided by the interaction index approach, we need no longer falsely separate out the dyadic interactions between the boys from what is actually a triadic relationship comprised of three separate dyadic relationships.

The integration of the three perspectives provides a powerful new perspective for both our clinical research and clinical practice. Each of the three perspectives illuminates distinctive aspects of the therapist's role and provides the means to specify concrete therapeutic goals.

The *interaction indices* reveal moment-to-moment aspects of the therapist acts that are effective in facilitating the relationship between the pair. In the case of Arnie and Mitchell the therapist introduced and shared in activities that provide a shared history. He tried to modify, match, and clarify moods ("How do you feel when . . ."). He acted as a pacesetter, slowing Arnie down to Mitchell's less rapid pacing. He articulated and interpreted personal themes ("You seem to have some thoughts of sex on your mind"). He tried to maintain a communal spacing, at times asking one partner to join the other, or placing himself between the boys or in a triangle. By attending to these interaction indices, a therapist can formulate *immediate goals,* mapping aspects of the social interaction to take advantage of moment-to-moment opportunities for intervention.

The *social regulation processes* perspective shows that the therapist often targeted his efforts at the extreme ends of the continuum. He facilitated the boys' interpersonal negotiation by interpreting and translating communications to make them more understandable and appropriate, and taking control when conflict became physical or verbally abusive. He similarly fostered shared experience by linking, re-pairing, and initiating and managing the three-way conversations and activities that are critical sources of sharing. By focusing on the interaction between the regulation processes, a pair therapist can generate the kind of interplay between them that consolidates functioning at a given level and readies the pair for movement to the next level. In this way, the social regulation process perspective can provide the therapist with *short-term goals* for a pair.

Finally, the third, *developemental level* perspective reveals how the *long-term goal* of developmental change in the pair's interaction is reflected in the therapist's acts. Arnie's and Mitchell's pair therapist serves as an interpreter for each of their level 1 negotiations (Mitchell to therapist: "Tell him to shut up") but translates them to level 2 communications (therapist to Mitchell: "Can you tell Arnie his insults hurt your feelings?").

It is somewhat artificial, however, to separate the three perspectives when describing the therapist's role. It is really the integration of the three perspectives that provides the power of our analysis of the therapist's role in the construction of Mitchell's and Arnie's relationship. As the therapist continued to untangle the idiosyncratic twists of each boy's speech and interpret the strategies routed through him into higher-level communication, noticeable changes occurred in the capacity of the pair to pace itself and to choose a mutually recognizable vocabulary. For instance, in the middle of a situation Mitchell seemed to experience as an absolute, irremediable clash of wills (over who got to choose the next movie the boys would watch together), the therapist interpolated a buffering mid-point: "Do we always do what Arnie wants and never what you want? Should we always do what you want and never what he wants—or are there possibilities for compromise?" The therapist continued in this way to serve as translator and pace-setter, presenting opportunities for ease, synchrony, and maturity these boys had rarely, if ever, experienced. The three perspectives together index the shifting relationship among specific aspects of the triad's social interaction to help us understand what drives growth (maturity and closeness) in the boys' relationship: the development of a triadic system supported by an adult who develops too.

IV. Conclusion

What have we learned from this enterprise, this narrative analysis of almost a year's worth of interactions among Arnie, Mitchell, and their pair therapist? When we began to study this case, we chafed at the limitations of our developmental language of levels of negotiation and shared experience. There is no doubt that a hierarchical arrangement of levels, however flexibly interpreted, tends to pull our thinking about relationships toward the vertical, toward the more adequate but not necessarily the more intimate. Yet what we also wanted to record in the case of Arnie and Mitchell was the closeness dimension—the modifications and nuances of aspects of the physical and interpersonal context that make experience in retrospect solid, synchronous, and fully realized. Our interaction indices, we believe, serve this function, balancing out the abstracting tendency of a universal developmental schema with information that is irreducibly specific and particular. What the method captures, in integrating the interaction indices with developmental levels and social regulation processes, is both the specificity of the interactions emerging moment to moment and their developmental trajectory over time.

We have learned something, we believe, about closeness in interpersonal relationships with the new access to and developmental understanding of interaction along the whole continuum of social regulation provided by the interaction indices. Closeness at any level involves a balance of intimacy and autonomy processes. A relationship without intimacy would have no closeness regardless of the developmental level of the autonomy processes. Conversely, a relationship, at any level, based on intimacy processes alone would be a kind of bizarre enmeshment. Closeness, marked by a balance of—or, more precisely, a fluidity of movement between—the two poles of social regulation in close relationships, is possible at any level. Six-year-olds, for example, can be balanced and close even at level 1. However, when a relationship is just beginning to develop, i.e., before closeness develops, the intimacy and autonomy processes are not in balance, at any level. One process tends to dominate the other successively in the early phases of a relationship. Moreover, at least in the pair therapy cases we have observed thus far, the two processes seem to attain ascendancy in a specific order, with concerns around autonomy preceding those of intimacy. We have speculated that in the therapeutic process of relationship building, when autonomy structures and boundaries at a given level are established, the mechanisms for the development of new structures at a higher level may involve the "interpenetrating" of these boundaries and the commingling of affect, which can best be brought about through processes of intimacy and sharing (Selman & Schultz 1988). However, we suspect that not all close relationships develop this way, with autonomy process dominating first. Although defining boundaries may come first and intimacy follows in many close relationships, in others (e.g., boy meets girl) intimacy processes seem to predominate first, followed by boundary-oriented interactions.

We also hope that this now completed phase of the pair therapy project has a practical contribution to make. If, as we believe, our indexical system of interpretation provides a more complete language for discussing therapeutic processes in work with dyads, it may give clinicians a conscious and reflective perspective on their work. What we believe we've done here, in charting small-scale shifts and movements in various aspects of the therapeutic interaction, is to take the practical wisdom of the therapist ("know how") and make it explicit "knowing that," so that it can become a consciously available tool for the therapist. Of course, long before we finished our analysis, this pair therapist had moved "gravitationally" to resolve conflicts, paid attention to the mutual history of the pair to promote a shared identity, and functioned as a "transformer," reworking communications so both children could understand them. Our interaction index method of interpretation doesn't disclose some new, previously unknown therapeutic ploy, but it does offer a new way of thinking about moves that may until now have been made intuitively, and therefore without the surety of self-reflection. With the interaction indices, developmental levels, and social regulations continuum in hand, the therapist can walk into subsequent therapeutic situations with a more detailed and powerful way of looking at and understanding what happens.

CHAPTER 3

Tracing the Hermeneutic Circle:
Articulating an Ontical Study of Moral Conflicts

Martin J. Packer

Introduction

In this chapter I shall lay out an approach to interpretive investigation that follows Heidegger's lead in the hermeneutic phenomenology of *Being and Time* (1927/1962). My aim is to explicate a specific interpretive research project and thereby address both the particular course of interpretation and the broader concerns of interpretive method. The following topics will be addressed: the character of interpretation; the relationship between interpretation and practical understanding; preparing a starting place for interpretation; the articulation that interpretation involves; ways to foster this articulation; and the outcome of interpretation.

The Focus of the Study: Moral Action

The study I shall discuss was an investigation of practical moral conflicts: conflicts that arose and were dealt with in ongoing social interaction. I chose this topic to make a break with interview discussions of morality, especially interviews about hypothetical dilemmas, such as Kohlberg's well-known work with the Heinz dilemma (e.g., Kohlberg, Levine & Hewer, 1983). The use of interviews as a method of access to the psychology of morality makes sense only as long as one accepts there is a kind of engagement common to situations of both speculative thought and practical action. From the hermeneutic perspective this is a questionable assumption (cf. Packer 1985c). My interest was in the way conflicts are recognized and dealt with as and when they arise, since I suspected that immediate responses to moral discord would show characteristics absent from their subsequent discussion and review.

The conflicts took place among college students playing a zero-sum competitive game for points worth a penny each. Ten of these analogue task sessions, each with a different group of eight young adults, comprised the corpus for analysis.[1] The young men and women were friends, generally living in proximity in college dorms, but they were divided into two teams for the game. The setting of their interaction was, then, an artificial analogue rather than naturally occurring. The reasons for this were pragmatic rather than methodological or theoretical: in particular a need to satisfy the unwritten requirement of a traditional psychology doctoral program that research be manipulative, which precluded studying "found" conflicts. Certainly the setting was somewhat contrived, nonetheless it satisfied the needs of the project. In particular, those involved seemed to take the sessions seriously.

Video recordings of the students' exchanges were the records of interaction with which interpretation began. My inquiry centered on a particular kind of event that occurred in four of the sessions: one where the team that was winning cheated on their friends soon after making an agreement to cooperate with them.

A detailed report of this inquiry has been published elsewhere (Packer 1985b). Rather than simply summarize the project I want to re-examine the course of interpretation, to explain what motivated the inquiry and determined its direction. The interpretation in this study involved a praxis that was not made fully explicit at the time. The various traces left by that praxis— notes, drafts of written reports—provide material for an explication of method that moves between a theory of what interpretation involves and the examination of a particular inquiry. This aim may at first glance seem an egotistic one, but my intention is not to demonstrate possession of any special interpretive ability or skill, but to lay out for critical examination efforts made in a process of inquiry that anyone can engage in.

The Character of Interpretation

In *Being and Time* Heidegger undertook a kind of investigation that can provide guidance to interpretive research in psychology and the other social and human sciences. The investigation was a hermeneutic phenomenological one, addressed to the question of the meaning of human being ("Dasein") and of Being in general. Heidegger argued that interpretation is the necessary kind of inquiry for a being that always has an understanding, albeit unarticulated, of the kind of being it is.

Heidegger's analysis was an "ontological" one: describing fundamental structures of human being. A hermeneutic research project in psychology will be what Heidegger terms "ontical": examining specific ways of being in a particular setting or settings, but it will nonetheless share certain simi larities of approach with the investigation carried out in *Being and Time*. As Heidegger stated:[2]

> ... this hermeneutic [i.e., *Being and Time*] contains the roots of what can be called 'hermeneutic' only in a derivative sense: the methodology of those humane sciences which are historiological in character (Heidegger 1927/ 1962, 62).

A "historiological" science is one that deals with the course of particular human events rather than with the fundamental ontological structures of human being.

Before we can consider the details of the moral conflict study, we must consider two preliminaries. The first concerns the relationship between interpretation and understanding, the second the work necessary to reach the appropriate starting point for an interpretive analysis.

The Relationship between Interpretation and Understanding

Interpretation has a close internal connection with engaged practical activity, and with the practical understanding that is involved in such activity. The point that deserves emphasis here is that interpretation always starts in, and is an articulation of, the interpreter's everyday, common-sense understanding of what is going on (cf. Packer 1985b, 1985c.)

> Any interpretation which is to contribute understanding, must already have understood what is to be interpreted. This is a fact that has always been remarked, even if only in the area of derivative ways of understanding and interpretation, such as philological Interpretation (Heidegger 1927/1962, 94).

When we conduct an interpretation of an interaction that we have either participated in or witnessed, we are bringing about a "development" of our practical understanding of that interaction:

> This development of the understanding we call interpretation. In it the understanding appropriates understandingly that which is understood by it. In interpretation, understanding does not become something different. It becomes itself. Such interpretation is grounded existentially in understanding; the latter does not arise from the former. Nor is interpretation the acquiring of information about what is understood; it is rather the working-out of possibilities projected in understanding (Heidegger 1927/1962, 188-9).

The development of understanding into interpretation involves a change in mode of engagement.[3] With this change in engagement we can now talk *about* our action and situation, whereas before any talk was part *of* that action and situation. Such an account is an interpretation (albeit a preliminary one) because it lays out the organization of events in a way that is more articulated and thematized. Although interpretation is always organized and directed by a preliminary understanding, corrections to this understanding will, indeed must, be made in the course of inquiry.

An understanding of how practical activity provides the basis for interpretation of that activity contributed two things to the investigation of moral conflict. The first contribution was an appreciation of the role of the researcher in traditional forms of psychological inquiry. Heidegger's account carries the implication that our traditional training to be detached and disinterested in our study and analysis of people and their behavior, so far as such a stance is possible at all, provides us with only a distorted kind of understanding. If we are to form psychological theories that do justice to humankind, we must start from our *practical* understanding of people and practices, the understanding we have by virtue of being members of our society, instead of attempting to be neutral and objective. Heidegger argues that we can make any sense at all of things when we try to become detached only because of this fundamental concerned involvement, this "primordial familiarity" with the world.

The second contribution made to the study of moral conflict by an understanding of the relationship between interpretation and understanding was a perspective on the young adults' interactions, one that I shall expand upon shortly. What was the mode of their engagement in different activities? What kinds of problem, barrier and challenge did their activity run up against, and how and when did they articulate it?

It was possible, for example, to contrast discourse that was part of the activity of seeking retribution after the broken agreement to cooperate[4]:

> B:413   LM2   [Interrupting] No! We *want* . . . [He raises his index finger, to emphasize his point.]
> 414   WM2   You *want?* [His tone is incredulous. WF2 and WM2 laugh.]
> 415   LM2   No, listen. . . .
> 416   WM2   [Interrupting] You're not in much of a position to *demand* . . .

. . . with discourse that talked *about* engaged activity:

> B:1350   LM2   And, once we. . . . And you guys said you weren't out to make money I mean it was this trust thing, but from the very beginning, every time you guys made money and we *lost,* you guys were real *pleased* about it.

Even the second example is not of course one of completely disinterested observation; it involves concerns and interests. But at line 413 LM2's words are an enacted rejection of the other team and a curtailing of intimacy. LM2 looks down on his friends, interrupting them and demanding recompense for the wrong they have done. Concerns over broken trust and deviant responsibility are not talked about, but they clearly organize *how* LM2 acts and speaks. At line 1350, in contrast, an explicit "issue" is made of the winning team's glee and hypocrisy; he talks *about* these as elements of their interaction together that now stand out.

A Starting Place for Interpretation

We have still not yet reached the point where we can begin to interpret the moral conflicts: we need first to reach an appropriate starting place for this interpretive inquiry. Addison and I described in chapter 1 some of the reasons why interpretive inquiry does not try to ensure that knowledge is built upon a "foundation," but instead places emphasis on recognizing and appropriating a "starting place" for hermeneutic inquiry in practical understanding.

There are two tasks to be carried out in establishing this starting place: "choosing the right entity for our example," and "work[ing] out the genuine way of access to it" (Heidegger 1927/1962, 26). We must select the text appropriate for our inquiry or, since we are dealing here with interaction rather than a written text, we must fix the pertinent interactions. We shall deal with this selection and fixing first, and then consider how to achieve suitable access.

Selecting and Preparing the Entity for Interpretation. "Choosing the right entity" is the first task in establishing the starting point for an interpretive inquiry. In the case of the moral conflict study this was a matter of selecting a kind of event for detailed study, and then preparing the video-recordings for interpretive analysis by transcribing them.

The tapes were viewed repeatedly with a view to the selection of an analytical focus for the inquiry. It became apparent that in four of the ten sessions a similar kind of occurrence took place: I have already referred to the way that the winning team broke an agreement they had made to cooperate with their friends on the other team. After the two teams had talked together and agreed to act so that both would gain points, the team which had been ahead in points very soon played competitively instead, selecting their move in the game so that their friends lost points. "Burning" was the term used in one session by the victims of this betrayal; I came to adopt it too.

The occurrence of burning seemed to be the "right entity" for several reasons. The burning marked the beginning of conflicts between the teams in which moral concerns were enacted and moral issues raised. And since burning was carried out in four of the sessions it was possible to compare and contrast the occurrences, and to compare these four occasions with sessions that were similar in several other respects (a difference in points between the teams; an agreement to cooperate) but in which no burning took place.

Preparing Action for Interpretation. Interpretive research does not deal with action as and when it occurs. Social action, like speech (which of course is itself a kind of action) is located at a particular time and place. It is temporally situated and organized, and intimately tied to its location. These essential characteristics raise problems for any systematic study of action: the original temporality and setting are lost to the researcher. But, just as discourse can be recorded as written text (". . . words do flye, but writing doth remain" Anglo, 1969, cited in Geertz 1983, 127), action leaves "traces" that can be "fixed" in various ways so that it can be studied. Ricoeur has given the most detailed analysis of the fixation of action:

> My claim is that action itself, action as meaningful, may become an object of science, without losing its character of meaningfulness, through a kind of objectification similar to the fixation which occurs in writing (Ricoeur 1979, 81).

Ricoeur discusses the several changes that fixation brings about in action. Changes come about in the act's temporal characteristics, in the relationship of act to agent and of act to recipient, and in the forms of reference and indexicality (more later on this last point). Fixation differs from structuralist abstraction and decontextualization, and the organization of fixed action differs from the purely internal structural relations that constitute a system of competence. In his more recent writing on textuality Ricoeur (1981) emphasizes additional characteristics of narrative texts and of fixed action, in particular the unfolding chronology of plot, which moves from predicament through response to resolution in such a way as to reveal hidden aspects of character and situation.

Fixation can take several forms. In our everyday dealings we fix action in memory, historical records, myths and reputations. Action is often fixed in written narrative accounts, but it can also be fixed by making a video recording. While video taping is often promoted on the grounds that it provides an objective record of events, in actuality social interaction that has been fixed through video taping shows all the characteristics of a text analogue. Taping necessarily transforms the action, rather than neutrally documenting it. First, the tape provides a "record," both visual and auditory, an "inscription" of action, that permits dislodging the action from the time of its production while both preserving and surmounting the temporal organization of sequence and succession. Second, the recorded action retains a meaning that is distinct and detached from both the agent's intention and the recipient's response at the time. "Our deeds escape us," writes Ricoeur, "and have effects which we did not intend" (1979, 83). Third, recorded action "transcends the social conditions of its production" (1979, 85) in so far as the recording possesses meaning and import for viewers who were not originally present.

I have said that a video recording both preserves and surmounts the original temporal organization of social action. The temporality of fixed action is especially important to interpretive inquiry. Our experience of "live" action is one of projection into a future of necessary and possible alternatives: we get caught up in action, with hopes, fears and concerns about what we can accomplish and what may happen to us, faced with intrinsic uncertainties about outcome. Unanticipated consequences are continually evolving, and novel contingencies must always be dealt with. At the same time we are caught up in customary practices and institutions whose existence seems totally independent of our own. Temporality here has a complex, non-linear character, that Heidegger interpreted as the "meaning" of care and existence: we are "thrown" into a social world, where we "project" ourselves toward our existential possibilities, and either come to understand ourselves authentically or fail to do so.

In contrast, the temporality of action that has been fixed becomes more linear and clear-cut. Once action is fixed we are free to move to and fro within it. When viewed for the first time, a video-recording preserves much of the surprise and discovery that characterized the original action. But on subsequent viewings the sequence of acts and experiences, the episodic dimension of the interaction, starts to seem a configuration with an existence of its own. Just as we can skip forward and back in a narrative account, with a video-recording we can jump to the end to see the outcome, or rewind to review something that is now understood as having a fresh significance. The fast-forward and rewind buttons on any hermeneutic researcher's VCR will be the first to need repair.

This new perspective is both revealing and misleading. We must be careful not to become drunk with our elevated perspective as researchers, able as we are to review the entire progress of an interaction, as though from above it, after it has run its course. This perspective appears a privileged one, but it has its hazards. The shift in perspective is like the difference between reading a new book and writing a review of it after finishing, when the movement from beginning to ending has come to seem inevitable. If we are unaware of the shift it can lead to a misreading of praxis as inevitable process: of spontaneous and creative action as a mere unfolding sequence of events that were laid out in advance. What now may seem to have been a determinate course through the exchange was, at the time, secured from a sweep of possibilities that the young adults found facing them. To lose sight of the ambiguity and open-endedness inherent in their situation is to ignore their creative shaping of conduct. It is because it attends only to this detached, elevated perspective, intent on removing narrative and action entirely from their context and setting, that structuralist analysis tends to "de-chronologise" both narrative and action, reducing their temporal aspects to underlying formal properties. When we talk, for instance, of conflicts as involving a "process of resolution" we are misled into thinking that appropriate procedures will lead inevitably to a happy outcome. But there are no such guarantees. In practice, from the perspective we have when engaged, we can never be sure whether a conflict will be resolved or not.

A perspective that provides an overview on action has advantages as well as disadvantages. Nagel (1986) argues that the "problem of excess objectivity" is one of false reductions and a refusal to recognize part of what is real. But he also argues (p. 4) that "appearance and perspective are essential parts of what there is, and in some respects they are best understood from a less detached viewpoint." For interpretive inquiry the danger in fixing action is that we lose sight of the agent's perspective; we need to find a way of holding onto a temporal perspective akin to that of the engaged agent. We can do this by working to become engaged ourselves in our record of fixed action, be it recording, notes or transcript. We must read it as an unfolding drama, regaining a sense of its openness and surprises. We must hold onto the awareness that we know things the participants did not discover until later, if at all.

A further step of fixation takes place when video-recordings are transcribed. A transcript bears a complex relation to its parent video-tape. Conventional symbols replace audible speech; gestures and movements are ignored or "described" (i.e., interpreted); intonation is lost or categorized ("question," "command," "statement") so as to exclude ambiguity. Detailed phonetic transcriptions try to resist some of these changes but instead produce records that generally resist the reader. There is a temptation to consider a transcript as, again, an objective description, where in actuality it is always a reading.

In the study of moral conflicts my practice was to keep transcription devices to a minimum and to use transcripts primarily to serve as reminders, or mementos, of the video recordings. The audio track of each video-recorded session was dubbed onto an audio-cassette to facilitate repeated rewinding on a transcribing machine, and transcribed. Transcripts ranged in length from 650 to 1700 turns of speech; each was checked for questionable readings, first against the corresponding audio-recording, then against the video-recording. At this time speaker identity was noted on the transcript, along with such information as to whom utterances were directed and non-verbal features such as gestures and movements. Once these tasks had been completed the interpreter had an extensive commonsensical familiarity with the episodes.

The audio-recordings served a further function: they could be replayed in more convenient circumstances than the video tapes could, facilitating recall of what had been seen on the videos. Soon there came a point where, when reading the transcripts, I could hear the manner in which words were exchanged and recall what people were doing as they spoke.

Securing Access to the Entity. We can turn now to consider the second task in preparing a starting place for interpretation. This is working out a way of access to the entity we have chosen that seems fitting: securing an appropriate perspective from which to read the text. We are always involved in a hermeneutic circle in so far as a preliminary understanding of the phenomenon provides the terms within which interpretation proceeds, but this circle need not be a vicious one where interpretation is just a restatement of our preconceptions. Heidegger argued that "what is decisive is not to get out of the circle but to come into it in the right way" (Heidegger 1927/1962, 195). "We must rather endeavour to leap into the 'circle', primordially and wholly" (Heidegger 1927/1962, 363). We can never be sure at the outset that we have found the best access to the circle of understanding and interpretation, and the test of the access we chose will come only as an interpretation is worked out, but we can at least avoid, so far as possible, understanding what we are studying in terms of either subjective fancies or commonly accepted misconceptions.

> In the circle is hidden a positive possibility of the most primordial kind of knowing. To be sure, we genuinely take hold of this possibility only when, in our interpretation, we have understood that our first, last, and constant task is never to allow our fore-having, foresight, and fore-conception to be presented to us by fancies and popular conceptions, but rather to make the scientific theme secure by working out these fore-structures in terms of the things themselves (Heidegger 1927/1962, 195).[5]

A legitimate access to the entity being investigated is one that is worked out by adopting an appropriate perspective, and this can be possible only if we try to identify and escape from common misconceptions and personal prejudices. To repeat, shunning what seem to be misconceptions cannot guarantee that our access is a legitimate one; but if we fail to examine our preconceptions critically our access will almost certainly be inappropriate. Our starting point in the hermeneutic circle should be an informed and aware one, but even so, in the course of interpretation our understanding will most likely require reshaping. The effort to adopt an informed starting point and to keep interpretation open to correction are hermeneutic alternatives to the procedures that supposedly guarantee the validity and reliability of so-called objective measurement in empiricist research.

Adopting an appropriate perspective on the moral conflicts required both negative and positive movements. The negative move was one of recognizing that I had to consider both behaviorist and cognitive-developmental accounts of moral action and moral development as misconceptions from which it might prove tricky to escape. The task here was to get distance from these, especially the cognitivist position, which for many psychologists has come to seem the commonsensical way of thinking and talking about morality. A struggle was necessary to give an explanatory account that didn't make reference to schemes and stages, principles, procedures and the other structural and computational terms. It was fortunate that there are articulate and thorough expositions of the cognitive-developmental approach in the writings of Kohlberg, Blasi (1980), Habermas (1979, 1983) and others. To call these works misconceptions is not to say that their proponents are victims of faulty reasoning or poor observation, but that these authors have worked with commitment and consistency within broad metatheoretical frameworks (rationalism, in the case of these three) that, from a Heideggerian perspective, systematically misinterpret the character and relationship of human action and thought.

One way to establish and maintain distance from these two perspectives on moral conflict was to shuttle between them. Merleau-Ponty, who adopts a dialectical tacking between formalist and behaviorist philosophy and psychology to great effect in two of his major works (1942/1963; 1945/1962) provided a model here. Shuttling between these two perspectives on the interaction opened up space for a third more appropriate perspective. Consideration of what the conflicts would look like viewed from the traditional perspectives continued throughout the investigation. (Recall that working to get the forestructures right is "our first, last, and constant task.")

The positive movement in adopting an appropriate perspective was a matter of struggling to understand, in a preliminary way, what action might be if neither formal nor mechanical. This positive perspective was a matter of reading on the topics of action, rhetoric, and emotion. Heidegger's analysis of the structures of practical activity, especially his discussion of the three modes of engagement, was the main reading on action (along with Blasi 1980; Habermas 1979; Hampshire 1959; James 1890/1950; Kenny 1963; Locke 1983; Mackenzie 1977; Merleau-Ponty 1945/1962; Mischel, 1974; Searle 1969; Staub 1978; Thalberg 1971; and Weiner 1980). Rhetoric was of interest as the study of ways in which people influence one another; Aristotle's (1954) analysis of rhetoric (which Heidegger calls "the first systematic hermeneutic of the everydayness of Being with one another," 1927/1962, 178), along with more recent works on rhetoric (e.g., Booth 1974; Kinneavy 1971) and related work on speech (e.g., Searle 1969). The literature on emotions included de Rivera (1977), along with Heidegger's analysis of "Befindlichkeit": the involvement of emotion and mood in understanding, and others (e.g., Arnold 1968; Bailey 1983; Guignon 1984; Hall and Cobey 1976; Hoffman 1979; Hume 1888/1978;

Lange & James 1922; Langer 1967; MacMurray 1962/1972; Mandler 1975; MacCarthy 1978; Rorty 1980; Sartre 1948; Solomon 1983; Zajonc 1980).

This reading led me to sketch a three-fold perspective on social action: as a mode of engagement in the world; as an influence on others; and as structured by emotion and mood. It also pointed out three cross-cutting interpretive foci: the interpersonal distance or "intimacy" people maintained or changed; individuals' relative moral "status"; and the "mythology" of what was talked about (this last term was chosen to emphasize that such talk was interpretation, not neutral description).

So the search for the right kind of access to the burning, one that avoided both cognitivist and behaviorist misunderstandings, led to a tripartite perspective from which to consider action: as mode of engagement, as persuasive rhetoric, and as emotion; and to three aspects of action to be examined: intimacy, status, and mythology. Each portion of the sessions, each exchange between the young adults, could be read as an example of a kind of engagement (unreflectively involved, circumspective, detached), as structured by an emotion (e.g., contempt, anger, remorse), and as presenting the world in persuasive terms (e.g., as a competition, as the "trust game," in phrases of accusation or assuagement). Each portion could also, in a complementary fashion, be seen as bringing about a change in the intimacy and closeness between people; a change in their standing vis a vis each other in credibility, culpability, and capability; and a change in the world they found themselves acting in.

The perspective that provided a starting place for interpretation was made up of three interrelated aspects, selected to complement rather than confuse. To employ a spatial analogy, this was like deliberately viewing a house from several vantages in order to better understand its layout. Separate accounts of an episode given in terms of its intimacy, moral status and mythology would throw light on each other and facilitate articulation and correction. For instance, when the teams in one session distanced each other and continued after the burning to play the "game" only randomly, when they moved far from one another in terms of intimacy but sustained rough equality in status and engaged unreflectively in their joint activity, it was no surprise that they talked of their situation solely in terms of "fun," unable to give voice to the moral concerns that animated their action. Here intimacy, status, and mythology were interrelated in a manner that seems complex, but becomes clearer when each aspect can be considered in turn, then the three brought together again.

Interpretation as Articulation

We have examined the twin preparations for interpretation: choosing the right entity and working out a genuine way of access to it. I have explained that occasions of burning (together with the context of the events preceding them and the conflicts following them) were the kind of entity chosen in the investigation of moral conflict, while access was provided by a three-fold perspective on intimacy, status, and mythology. We can now consider how interpretation proceeds from this starting point.

Recall that an interpretive inquiry taps into our engaged practical understanding of an entity or phenomenon by adopting what seems an appropriate perspective. Interpretation is a matter of articulating this anticipatory sketch, letting an account of the phenomenon emerge gradually and become more explicit. An interpretive account opens up, lays out and articulates the perspective from which an event or interaction has been understood, at the same time as it puts the perspective to test. When we examine it more closely, this articulation of practical understanding into a thematic narrative turns out to have two sides: one negative, the other positive.

The Negative Side of Articulation. Many of the entities and events we understand in an engaged manner have the peculiar property of "withdrawing" from focal awareness, and this places special difficulties in the way of interpretation.

> The peculiarity of what is proximally ready-to-hand is that, in its readiness-to-hand it must, as it were, withdraw in order to be ready-to-hand quite authentically (Heidegger 1927/1962, 99).

Precisely because we are so familiar with everyday phenomena and events, we are able to take most of what we understand about them for granted. Because they are familiar and unexceptional we consider them in only a cursory and perfunctory fashion. In our everyday dealings with the world most of our action is disregarded, ignored and glossed over. The interpretive researcher's practical, everyday understanding, although it provides the necessary access from which interpretation proceeds, is an understanding within which events and entities are "withdrawn."

How can we make the activities and events of which we have a practical understanding become more evident and apparent? The negative side of articulation involves uncovering what has withdrawn by attending to things that are "conspicious (Heidegger 1927/1962, 102) as disturbances. As we try to interpret a narrative or a fixed interaction we are struck first by oddities, anomalies, things that *don't* make sense. These gaps, barriers, and blocks in practical understanding can foster interpretation; by focusing on them we can bring about changes in perspective that can enlarge the scope of our interpretation. In a disturbance our understanding becomes "lit up" so that its organization is more apparent. When practical understanding breaks down, when it meets with interference, with a block or barrier, our engagement in the world changes to one of circumspection (from the ready-to-hand to the unready-to-hand mode). This brings about transformations in our awareness of ourselves, of our activity, and of the people and setting we are dealing with. Each of these becomes thematized: where previously they formed an opaque totality that was the background or context to our action, now they become laid out with a transparent discernible organization.

> The context . . . is lit up, not as something never seen before, but as a totality constantly sighted beforehand in circumspection (Heidegger 1927/1962, 105, original emphasis removed).

Kuhn has elevated this emphasis on attending to disturbances of understanding to the status of hermeneutic maxim: "When reading the works of an important thinker, look first for the apparent absurdities in the text and ask yourself how a sensible person could have written them. When you find an answer, I continue, when those passages make sense, then you may find that more central passages, ones you previously thought you understood, have changed their meaning" (Kuhn 1977, xii).

A central example is provided by the event of burning itself. One motivation, in addition to those already mentioned, for selecting this event as the focus of interpretation was its puzzling character. Who should the participants break their newly made agreement to cooperate? In particular, why should the winning team cheat, since their superiority in points was already assured? The occasion in each session when the burning took place was just after the moment when the theoretically rational solution to the game had been reached. Burning was a course of activity that seemed in direct contradiction with accounts of behavior as rational goal-seeking, or as cognitive appraisal of costs and benefits. At best, one would have to impute goals or benefits whose appearance would be somewhat perverse in what was, as the participants knew, a study of morality. Burning represented, then, a point of breakdown in my own understanding of what went on in the sessions. It also seemed to be an occasion of breakdown in the teams' interaction together; a disturbance *they* had to struggle to deal with, and make new sense of.

As a practical disturbance for the participants themselves, the burning opened up a new and perplexing perspective on their interaction together, especially for the losing team. The losing team's response to the burning showed two new concerns—over trust and responsibility. Their actions suggested they understood the burning as a painful violation of trust, and that they were now confused about the winning team's responsibility for the burning: what exactly had happened? What had they been trying to do? For example:

A:319   LM1   I don't *believe* it! [He turns to LM2, with a shocked
              expression.]
323   LM1   Well, that shows a lack of ... eh ... [He points at the
              winning team.]
328   LM1   I don't believe it.
329   SL   The winning team wants to negotiate; does the los-
              ing team?
330   LF2   No more, no more.
331   LF1   We don't trust them.
337   LF2   We're not playing anymore.

As an interpretive disturbance for the investigator, the burning suggested
the presence of a way of understanding the competitive game, and a form of
engagement between the teams, that had little to do with optimizing winnings. One line of interpretation took the form of an exploration of the winners' satisfaction at beating the other team even if it meant losing points.

Disturbances in our initial understanding of an interaction are not always
occasions of apparent absurdity or puzzlement. A disturbance of understanding can also be something that "stands in the way" of interpretation, something disturbing and offensive. In such a case interpretation meets with
resistances and emotional blocks:

> That to which our concern refuses to turn, that for which it has 'no time,' is
> something *un*-ready-to-hand in the manner of what does not belong here, of
> what has not as yet been attended to. Anything which is un-ready-to-hand in
> this way is disturbing to us, and enables us to see the *obstinacy* of that with
> which we must concern ourselves in the first instance before we do anything
> else (Heidegger 1927/1962, 103).

Even these blocks can be turned to good purpose and used to foster
interpretation. I found myself, for example, avoiding viewing the video of one
group's session (group B); I had "no time" for it. I came to realize that I was
disturbed by the cold, controlled contempt and disdain with which one
team regarded the other after the burning. The exchange has been cited
briefly above:

B:407   LM2   Okay, here, we came up with a new option (since) you
              guys violated the trust (   ). [Laughter from the
              other members of both teams.]
409   WM1   What's your option? Ah, okay, wait ... let me, you
              wanna ... okay, because you violated our trust on the
              last option, (but) we're willing to give you this. ...

413   LM2   [Interrupting.] No! We *want* ... [He raises his index
                finger, to emphasize his point.]
414   WM2   You *want?* [His tone is incredulous. WF2 and WM2
                laugh.]
415   LM2   No, listen. ...
416   WM2   [Interrupting] You're not in much of a position to
                demand ...

My first response to this episode was, then, an avoidance of it much as I might avoid someone who expressed contempt toward me. When I came to consider this reaction as a way of understanding the episode I was able to give a preliminary interpretation of the group's interactions, as movements of contempt and disdain. This in turn led to a new and widening interpretive access to the session. An interpreter's emotions must not be shrugged off as a personal and subjective attitude, but acknowledged as a helpful way of understanding an interaction. Details of this understanding may need correcting later, but it provides an essential opening access to the text-analogue.

Heidegger's use in the quotation above of the term "obstinacy" aptly points out the fact that a text or interaction can resist interpretation. Critics of interpretive inquiry sometimes talk as though there are no constraints on subjectivity or whim in interpretation. Phenomenologically this is inaccurate: a text has its own terms, to which one must accommodate if interpretation is to proceed. (See the discussion on validity of interpretation in Seung 1982, 174ff.)

The Positive Side of Articulation. The second side to the articulation by which interpretation proceeds deals with entities of an interaction that are very different from those that withdraw. Consequently this aspect of articulation does not proceed through attending to disturbances. The phenomena that do not withdraw from our awareness in our everyday practical understanding of action are those to which the action makes *reference.* In everyday activity we have constant dealings with references and signs that show or indicate something to us, or that direct us to do something.

> Such phenomena as references, signs [and] significations. ... let some context of it [the ready-to-hand] become accessible in such a way that our concernful dealings take on an orientation and hold it secure. ... [A sign] raises a totality of equipment into our circumspection so that together with it the worldly character of the ready-to-hand announces itself. ... Signs always indicate primarily 'wherein' one lives, where one's concern dwells, what sort of involvement there is with something (Heidegger 1927/1962, 110-111).

The scope of reference extends far beyond literal signs. Heidegger talks of "signposts, boundary-stones ... , signals, banners, signs of mourning and the like" (Heidegger 1927/1962, 108), but even this list gives scant attention to reference in social interaction. Virtually all of our everyday action "indexes" its setting, in a manner that exhibits the phenomenon of reference. Indexical expressions are those that refer to the speaker, or to the time or place of utterance. "I am happy" is an indexical expression because the personal pronoun refers to the speaker. "It is not raining" is indexical since its truth value depends on the particular weather conditions at the time and location of utterance. Indexicality is, then, a familiar phenomenon, but its importance and scope are underestimated (Garfinkel 1967). Most significantly, indexing and reference are generally conceived of as involving a formal relationship between signifier and signified, between "thing" and "sentence." But our everyday interactions are indexical in a non-formal way: they continuously point out to others "what we are 'at' at any time," not by being "a Thing which stands to another Thing in the relationship of indicating" (Heidegger 1927/ 1962, 110), but by raising into our circumspection the kind of involvement we have in a situation. What action points out are not objectively definable objects and features but aspects of context that are *constituted* by the participants' involvement and concerns.

The speech and action that make up a social interaction continuously index entities and aspects of the setting we are involved in. Understanding what is said and done is in large part a matter of appreciating these entities and aspects. This is not to say that people explicitly talk about such entities and aspects, for it is often the case that concerns and involvements become "lit up" not through *what* is talked about but through *how* things are said and done. I mentioned earlier how, after the burning, concerns over trust and responsibility became lit up as acts of withdrawal and derision. Interrupting and demanding pointed out the demeaned position the other party was now in; this was their role in establishing the winning team's new status.

Let's consider a brief exchange to see how aspects of the situation are pointed out and illuminate the kind of situation the participants find themselves in:

A:522	WF1	They're catching up on us.
523	LF1	Well, it's not a contest.
525	WM1	Oh, no, sorry, sorry.
526	LM2	(He wants more money.) [Laughs.]

The phrases "catching up" and "contest" used here reveal one way of understanding what is going on: as a competitive game. Such an understanding would, one presumes, make reference to "winners" and "losers," "strategy" and "fun," "rivalry" and "struggle." Activity commensurate with this understanding would index certain aspects of the setting: differences in points won, or ways to increase ones own winnings, for instance. At the same time that the winning team talks of catching up, LF1's disavowal of their way of understanding things ("Well, it's not a contest") exposes a divergence between the two teams' concerns and actions. Furthermore, the sarcasm and irony evident in this exchange suggest their conflict is being both enacted and denied. We might say it is enacted *by* being denied: "... Sorry, sorry" is an apology that cancels itself with irony.

Such interpretations are of course only preliminary; an account of divergent perspectives that lead to a conflict that is denied and covered over can hardly be sustained by a transcript a mere four lines long. In the course of placing this excerpt in its larger context, and comparing events with those of other sessions, such an account must be modified and elaborated. But even so, this brief exchange provides several foci for reading and interpreting the remainder of the session: it draws our attention to words and actions of competition; to differences in the teams' understanding of their common activity; and to the dissembling of hostility. If these are not found elsewhere, our preliminary interpretation needs modification; if they are found, it receives support. And, to reiterate, these interpretive foci are arrived at by attending to what is indexed in the talk between the teams: the elements of their situation to which they orient each other.

I have argued that to the extent we understand a conversation we recognize the kind of situation people are acting in and the concerns and involvements their activities embody. The interpretive focus on "mythology" in the moral conflict study was tied most closely to this phenomenon, since it involved close examination of the terms and expressions used by the young adults. Immediately after the burning, for instance, talk of something "broken" was a common image. Then, in the subsequent phase of accusation, a central issue of "points lost" was an explicit topic of talk between the teams. This provided a clear example of indexicality: the participants talked to one another as though the number of points lost was a simple, objective factual matter. But this was not a simple "fact"; it was the product of a particular, highly evaluative way of viewing the agreement and the betrayal (including seeing it *as* betrayal). The issue of "points lost" was motivated by, and at the same time served to cover up, the concerns over trust and responsibility, and for this reason I called it a "pseudo-issue" (cf. Packer 1985a). Images ("broken trust") and issues ("You give us the four you burned us!") pointed to the participants' concerns and involvements, and so these were among those aspects of an interaction the interpreter was first aware of. (We can also see that what is pointed out may be disavowed at other levels of engagement that become evident only as interpretation proceeds.)

Fostering Articulation

Interpretation develops, then, through an articulation that attends to both disturbances of understanding and to reference and indexing. These provide two ways in which what is understood becomes "lit up." Something along the lines of an "expansion" is going on here, but what is being expanded is not something that lies "behind" the action, as an underlying set of rules or an abstract competence, but instead something "inside" the action (cf. Nussbaum 1986). Here my description of the hermeneutic project diverges from Shweder and Much's (1987) position that hermeneutics is an unpacking of "propositions" that constitute what is implicit and "unsaid" in speech. This would seem to imply that action embodies knowledge, and so to reintroduce the rationalist assumption that epistemology has priority over ontology; that knowing comes before acting. Interpretation is better viewed, I think, as an articulation of the ends and concerns that action embodies and expresses, of the possible directions a course of activity can take.

Articulation is fostered in several ways. One of these is through writing *"simple descriptions"* of what is happening. "What are they doing?" is the question guiding such an account. Such a description draws upon the two sides of articulation we have considered: it will include what is pointed out in the action, and it will begin to expose gaps and disturbances in understanding.

Once a simple descriptive account has been made (and often while it is being made) it is possible to ask *why* things seem as they have been described. Such a question is necessary because we still have only a preliminary and provisional account. How do we know this person was demanding retribution? What does "retribution" mean, anyway? How was the demand made? With such questions we can call a simple description into doubt, forcing ourselves to justify or modify it, and so begin to tie elements of the interaction together and discover their interrelationships.

As an interpretation develops we will need to tolerate and sometimes sustain ambiguity. Parts of the account being written may appear contradictory. This must be acknowledged if we are to avoid premature interpretive closure. Utterances may make little sense when considered individually because at first we lack the familiarity with the whole that confers significance on the parts. The consequence can be a dominating sense of confusion. It is important to respect this sense, and not retreat into reporting only what *does* make sense. We must proceed with the assumption that the interaction is itself ambiguous and open to different perspectives. If this is so, an account that has room only for what is undeniable and incontrovertible will be limited to the obvious, and will ignore the very openness and uncertainties that make social interaction interesting:

> Ambiguity is not a popular topic. Because ambiguity is the very milieu out of which meaning is born it is one of the antagonists of everyday life. Ambiguity is an openness into which each of us is thrown each time we converse with a stranger. It is the very nature of a conversation to be undetermined at the outset; and as a conversation proceeds, somehow the parties to it begin to take up a position in a world of meanings (Liberman, 1980, 66).

If there is unavoidable ambiguity to a text or text-analogue, there can be no single correct interpretation. A good interpretation will be one that exposes this ambiguity, but no single account can include all the different forms understanding may take. Any text or interaction can be read in a multitude of ways. To give an interpretive account covering all of them would require the impossible task of anticipating all the questions new readers could pose, all the concerns they might bring. The best we can do is grant that a better interpretation is one that uncovers more of the perspectives from which an interaction can be viewed. At no point can an interpretation be fully complete. It always possible that a little more work will uncover a hitherto unsuspected perspective on things. In this way interpretive inquiry resembles the rest of life.

The Outcome of Interpretive Inquiry

What is the outcome of all this? What do we have when our understanding has been developed as an interpretation? The primary outcome of the interpretive study I have been using as an example was an account of one kind of moral conflict: occasions of minor betrayal where people hurt their friends. The interpretation of these conflicts showed that burning was understood as mean-spirited cheating by its victims, while those who did it took it as harmless fun misunderstood. The conflict over burning began to make sense only when I took into account both these ways of understanding it, and so recognized its openness to alternative interpretations.

Phases of Conflict. My interpretation of burning included an account of "phases" to the conflict. Three main phases were distinguished. The first was an initial response to the burning with moral outrage, surprise, and shock. At this point, the losing team members "Don't know what's going on!" Engagement with the other team was suspended, and the losing team adopted a moral stance of superiority and indignation as concern over trust and responsibility structured the mode of its engagement.

In the second phase, a heated exchange took place as accounts were given of what had occurred. These accounts were progressively articulated; they developed from global, undifferentiated emotive reports ("screwing off," "playing around") to differentiated, relatively articulated statements of the relevant aspects of the situation. They didn't, notably, move toward a statement of abstract moral principles; the most fully articulated accounts were still structured by practical concerns and interests.

Throughout this second phase accounts were given as though they were objective and incontrovertible descriptions of factual events. Each team took it for granted that the others understood things as they did themselves. And talk centered on the pseudo-issue, described above, of how many points were lost; the moral concerns (trust and responsibility) remained unarticulated.

In the third phase conflict either progressed to further articulation or else ended in a standoff between the teams. In two of the sessions (B and D) articulation of accounts developed to a point where the underlying concerns were addressed and the two teams finally appreciated that they understood events differently. They came to accept the others' account as an alternative, valid perspective on an ambiguous interaction. Accounts of events were now given in conditional form, and moves were made toward resuming play in the game.

This has been a much abbreviated version of the narrative account in which I tried to convey what I found out about burning and, on a bigger stage, betrayal. The phases were an attempt to represent, to present again, the dramatic plot of the burning, the circumstances of its occurrence, and its aftermath. I wanted to show how involvement in joint action gave practical moral conflict a character unlike that of disengaged reflection on moral issues.

And I wanted to do this in a way that "rang a bell" for the reader. One task of hermeneutic inquiry is to bring to words experiences we find we have understood all along but have been unable to give voice to. Experiences of moral conflict are perhaps particularly likely to have a side that cannot be spoken but that can be recognized once it is described. Accordingly, another role for the description of phases of conflict was to uncover aspects of moral conflict that tend to be covered over. This included aspects of the interaction among the young adults that were, at least initially, covered up in their conflicts and it also included, at a more general level, aspects of morality and moral conflict typically ignored or suppressed in our psychological theories.

Uncovering What Was Covered Over. Three things were covered over in the conflicts themselves. Each of these three was hidden, at least initially, because it provided a context or background within which action took place, and within which the young adults' interpretations advanced. First were the concerns that arose in response to the burning: concerns over responsibility and trust. These concerns were evident to the interpreter as movements organizing action by the losing team in the first phases. But the young people themselves were not reflectively aware of their own concerns, at least initially, and didn't refer to them in their conversation. Only in the final phase of conflict were the concerns talked about as explicit issues.

A second topic, one that was never talked about explicitly although its influence can be discerned throughout the conflicts, was the friendship among the students. Their friendship provided the ground from which their conflict grew. In a sense, it was friendship that made the burning possible: betrayal can take place only where loyalty and equality have become customary.

The last item whose influence was continual but covert was the task setting in which the young adults were put. The trivial competitive game, and the research environment, placed bounds on the extent to which resolution could be achieved. The two teams became "winners" and "losers" in the game, and this pitted the young people against each other as factions with incompatible goals and viewpoints.

As I suggested, the interpretive account of burning also pointed out several aspects of moral conflict typically covered up in our psychological accounts. First is the part that emotions play in setting up the context within which conflict proceeds. The involvement of emotions is misunderstood if they are considered merely subjective mental states that disrupt or weight moral reasoning and action. Emotions are transformations in social relationships, interpersonal movements (de Rivera 1977), and transmutations of the situation in which action takes place (Hall & Cobey 1976). As such, they provide the grist which any moral deliberation must have to grind upon if it is to lead to action of any consequence. Correlative to this are the limitations inherent in reason as a tool with which to resolve conflict. Reason works with the "facts," but people who are enmeshed in a moral conflict have divergent understandings of what the facts are.

The third thing covered up in research reports is the genuine ambiguity of conduct and events in an interaction or a relationship. Only when this ambiguity is recognized can we appreciate that there will be at least provisional justification for all parties' perspectives on a conflict; from a researcher's perspective there is never an unequivocal indication of who acted properly, or an obvious choice of who gave a correct account of events. We talk of moral *dilemmas* with good reason: they have two facets, each of which has a claim to validity. Contrary to claims by cognitive-developmentalists (e.g., Kohlberg, Levine and Hewer 1983, 49), there appears to be little justification for maintaining that advanced moral functioning permits facile resolution of such dilemmas.

The final aspect of moral conflict whose importance and influence has been minimized is the engaged, temporalized perspective that participants have on their own action, and which was discussed above. The objective, detached perspective that has been lauded as morally superior is in actuality a "view from nowhere" (Nagel 1986) that is powerless unless informed by an involved, engaged viewpoint.

Anomalies and Reinterpretations

In the concluding section of this book Richard Addison and I entertain the notion that accounts of interpretive research should report anomalies and flaws in an interpretation, and point out what remains incomprehensible. I want briefly to address some doubts of my own. First, the situation I studied was an artificial one, raising questions about the typicality of these conflicts. Use of analogue tasks in moral development research stems in part from the ethical and practical problems of studying real-life conflicts, but also in part from a deep-rooted assumption that we must control and manipulate people in order to explain what they do. So I am sympathetic with those (e.g., Barratt & Sloan 1988, Danner 1986) who consider the conflicts I was able to study trivial ones (cf. Packer 1988). But I also think that one strength of this research was demonstrating that even "planned" conflicts are not as rational as we might assume. Real-life moral conflicts are quite likely to show characteristics like those I have described.

Second, alternative interpretations of the motivation of burning have been proposed to me. One is that the winning team was able to indulge in a hostile and aggressive act because it was excused by the simulated game setting and they knew it would be controlled by the experimental situation. A second interpretation is that the winning team knew the burning was harmful but saw harm-doing as an inherent part of competition. Their pleasure came not from the pain they inflicted, but from the increased intimacy and cohesion within their team that came with achieving the status of "winners." Each of these accounts could be compared with my own, and its merit and demerits assessed.

Third, I think that I confused and confounded two different kinds of withdrawal. The first is the withdrawal from ongoing projects that induces the detachment of deliberation (and, if the withdrawal is thorough, of abstract reflection). This withdrawal involves a shift from the ready-to-hand mode of engagement to the unready-to-hand mode (and sometimes to the present-at-hand). The second kind of withdrawal is a rejection of others and a backing away from them, as the losing team does when it is burned. I interpreted the losing team's move of withdrawal as leading to a breakdown in the game that led to deliberation on what had happened. It seemed to me that this deliberation in turn fostered the articulation necessary for the conflict to be resolved. But the teams' argument may have accomplished something else: a decline in the withdrawal and rejection. De Rivera (1986) proposes that the conflict was the result of continuing fear and distrust between the teams, and that trust and acceptance, not disengagement, are the precondition of conflict's end. My tendency not to discriminate between disengagement and rejection is also reflected in the fact that although the fore-structure I developed included de Rivera's "intimacy" and "status" movements, I found no place for his third kind of movement, namely "acceptance" (whose counterpart is "rejection"). In my current research I am careful to attend to all three kinds of movement.

Conclusions

It was no accident that the topic and method of this inquiry were conjoined: that this was a hermeneutic study of moral conflict. Ethical issues are in several respects closely tied to interpretive inquiry, and I want to conclude with a brief examination of their connection. First, interpretive inquiry denies that facts and values can be clearly distinguished and that only the former are worthy of or amenable to scientific study (the familiar position taken by positivism). Evaluations can be, and often are, validly based on assessments of circumstances that positivism would consider factual. Furthermore, the hermeneutic perspective has ethical implications; a partial appreciation of these is the reason hermeneutics is often erroneously associated with a relativist ethics. These ethical implications go beyond the scope of this chapter.

Next, the goal to which interpretive inquiry is ultimately directed is not just one of mirroring reality in a descriptive account, but of changing it for the better in some way. Hermeneutic research is tied to an appreciation that a "better" account is one that at the very least fosters our understanding and clarifies our action. This kind of inquiry, I believe, does not simply provide means to realize ends whose selection lies elsewhere (the technical conception of science), but instead calls for a clarification of ends and values and a recognition that they are often in competition. My study of moral conflict included no effort to communicate the products of interpretation to the young adults, though such a component might well have been an improvement. Lather (1986) discusses some of the complex implications of this aspect of interpretive inquiry.

The final tie between interpretive inquiry and morality is a fundamental one: that any systematic inquiry is an attempt to answer the question "Why?" Why did the conflicts among the young adults take the form they did? We are accustomed to trying to answer this question in causal or formal terms, with expressions of either mechanical or logical necessity, but in human affairs the question often has a moral force. The question itself generally has a moral tone, since the things that we question are those that shock us, and the answer has a moral quality because courses of action involve an understanding of what is right and wrong, and emotions of shame, guilt, or pride. If this is so, then interpretive inquiry will uncover the various moral concerns that run through our relationships with one another, and will provide forms of explanation that make reference to cultural and practical values.

CHAPTER 4

Good and Ill Will:
War Resistance as a Context
for the Study of Moral Action

JOHN R. MERGENDOLLER

*Truly good research means that one allows the investiga-
tion to be guided by the experiences of the investigation.
And this cannot be predicted. If it can be predicted, then
there is little information to be obtained from the research;
and considerably less reason to do the research.*

—David Bakan

*Art is the solving of problems that cannot be expressed until
they are solved.*

—Piet Hein

I first confronted questions of moral commitment and war resistance in
1967 as a college senior. My student deferment was to expire. I assumed I
would soon be summoned to join the army, trained as a murderer, and sent
to sweaty Vietnam where I would mow down "gooks" from a jungle trench.
This vision made me sick.

I wondered if I were a Conscientious Objector or whether the aversion I
felt toward taking life was an expedient way to save my skin. What did it mean
to object to war on religious grounds? What was the litmus test of sincerity?
As I struggled with these questions, I approached a fearful conclusion: someone sincerely opposed to war would be willing to go to prison to avoid induction in the army. Although revolted by war, I was terrified by prison. I continued
to wrestle with the alternatives.

In time my practical problem—avoiding induction—was resolved: I spent
the duration of the Vietnam War teaching high school English. My encounter
with the Vietnam War and the draft, however, left me curious about the experience of men who refused to accept induction and were imprisoned as a
result of this refusal, and confused about the sincerity of my own moral stance.

I wanted to know how others experienced and expressed their resistance to war? How did they decide to submit (or not submit) CO Claims? From what source of strength did they summon the courage to face incarceration? Were there relationships among their actions of war resistance and their thinking about moral issues?

Ten years later, a graduate student in psychology, I returned to questions about the relationship between moral thought and action. I was infatuated with the claims of Lawrence Kohlberg, especially those advanced in his seminal essay "From is to Ought." Here he states:

> To summarize, I have found a no more recent summary statement of the implications of our studies than that made by Socrates:
>
>> First, virtue is ultimately one, not many, and it is always the same ideal form regardless of climate or culture.
>> Second, the name of this ideal form is justice.
>> Third, not only is the good one, but virtue is knowledge of the good. *He who knows the good chooses the good.*
>> Fourth, the kind of knowledge of the good which is virtue is philosophical knowledge or intuition of the ideal form of the good, not correct opinion or acceptance of conventional beliefs. (1971, 232, emphasis added)

Kohlberg argued eloquently that individuals employing higher levels of moral reasoning as measured by his moral judgment interview were typically more willing to resist situational pressures to obey authority or defy the conventions of society in order to express their own personal moral commitment. Empirical studies conducted at that time provided conflicting evidence. Studies conducted by Kohlberg (1970), McNamee (1972), Rothman (1971), and Rothman and Turiel (1972) reported positive associations between individuals' disobedience of authority and higher levels of moral reasoning. On the other hand, Haan, Block, and Smith (1968) reported that individuals reasoning at both low and high levels of moral reasoning participated in the same actions of civil disobedience. It appeared that Kohlberg's contention that "knowledge of the good"—as indicated by higher scores on the Kohlberg Moral Judgment Interview—leads individuals "to choose the good" was open to question.

Putting together personal curiosities and questions of psychological theory, I set out to study the interpenetration of moral thought and action (Mergendoller 1981). I wanted to understand the moral significance of the Vietnam War for those willing to risk and accept hardship and deprivation to live consistently with their moral beliefs. I believed the study of these individuals would enable me to generate a more complex and realistic theory about the relationships among moral thought and action, thereby propelling the psychological study of morality beyond the austerity of Kohlbergian structuralism. I wanted to present the accounts of men who had resisted the war, and examine their CO Claims, Sentencing Statements, letters and other relevant documents. From their recollections and documents I would identify their moral concerns as well as the nature and level of the moral reasoning they employed at that time. I would also assess their current level of moral reasoning within the Kohlbergian paradigm. I believed such a combination of research strategies would flesh out the structuralist account of moral reasoning and behavior and provide the basis for a theoretical account of moral behavior that was recognizably human.

In the pages that follow I describe an interpretive journey that has taken me from my original Platonic, deontological conceptions of moral thought and experience toward a naturalism congenial to Aristotle and Dewey. In light of the Piet Hein quote at the beginning of this chapter, I have organized the first part of my account around a series of interrelated problems which were simultaneously discovered and addressed: problems of method, problems of meaning, and problems of veracity. The separation of these problems is somewhat artificial in that they appeared together, and work on one set of problems influenced the definition and determination of others. Method can not be isolated from meaning, and worries about the veracity of the entire interpretive enterprise linger stubbornly. I then sketch briefly a model of moral action drawing on the words of the men who participated in the study.

Problems of Method

The Selection of Participants. To a large degree, the success of the study I was attempting rested on the selection of participants. I sought to understand the nature and relationship of moral thought and action within the context of war resistance. I thus needed to find men whose resistance reflected a sincere moral stance and was not merely a product of political ideology, unthinking rebelliousness, fear, or a tendency to conform. In more positivistic forms of psychological research, the identification of subjects is straightforward: a study of the impact of divorce on women's status attainment will begin by identifying a population of divorced women. In contrast, I was not exactly sure what criteria could be used to identify someone who should be in the study. Was the avowal of principled moral resistance to the Vietnam War sufficient? If so, then any number of male university students who retained their deferments while protesting the immorality of war should be included in the study. Did one have to prove one's commitment to moral behavior by serving time in prison? If so, then what about men who violated Selective Service Regulations, but were never prosecuted? Incarceration, surely, could not be the only indication of sincere moral commitment.

My problem, simply put, was that one cannot identify moral behavior on the basis of behavioral categories, a problem also recognized by Kohlberg (1971) and resolved with questionable success by others who have studied war resisters (Gaylin 1970; Merklin, Jr. 1974; Mantell 1974). Still, I clung to the idea of a behaviorally anchored sampling frame, not yet realizing its inadequacy. I determined to identify three groups of war resisters: 1) Conscientious Objectors who performed alternative service; 2) war resisters whose protest required direct, confrontative action in the form of non-cooperation with the draft regulations, refusal of deferments, or dramatic self-incarceration; and 3) resisters who exiled themselves to Canada. I assumed similarities among the men found in each group, and that comparisons between each group's characteristic profile would throw light on the significant moral and experiential dimensions of war resistance.

I began interviewing informally anyone who told me he had been a Conscientious Objector or war resister, and whose actions initially appeared to fit within one of my categories. As my tape recorder chronicled the subtleties of resister's stories, I watched my a priori, category-based sampling scheme crumble. The elusive qualities that define sincere moral commitment—integrity, seriousness of purpose, willingness to endure privation in order to remain consistent to one's beliefs, a single-minded devotion to one's own sense of right and wrong—were qualities that had no univocal correlates in behavior or prison sentences. The stories I was told demonstrated that moral resistance was not a dogmatic response to the world. The men with whom I talked did not resist at every opportunity; sometimes they temporized or went along with what was requested of them by the state or by their parents. They acted in unique ways based on their own circumstances and sense of options. As one participant told me regarding his selective actions, "A person in rebellion against all things at all times [is] probably not capable of maintaining that long without losing some perspectives." Finding participants whose lives reflected the thoughtful moral commitment I sought to understand was going to demand that I use my judgment, not an objective-appearing categorization scheme.

I conceived a two-stage sampling strategy in which I would conduct initial interviews with all those who called themselves resisters, and select men whose stories I found more compelling and indicative of their moral commitment. This sub-sample would then receive major emphasis in the research. I was especially interested in men whose experience was documented in letters, diaries or transcripts of court proceedings.

Ten men participated in the study. Three grew up in the Northeast, three were Midwesterners, three were born in the West, and another grew up on different Army bases around the world. Three were from metropolitan areas, two from small towns, and four called small- or moderate-sized cities home.

While this information suggests variation in the background of these men, it cannot indicate their true diversity or the variety found in their experiences with the draft, a finding also reported by Gaylin (1970) and Merklin, Jr. (1974).

Interview Procedures. I interviewed participants during 1978 and 1979, roughly ten years after they turned 18, registered for the draft, and eventually resisted the Vietnam War. Initial interviews began with the Kohlberg Moral Judgment Interview and concluded with an unstructured, open-ended discussion of their experience with the war and the draft.

When I reviewed the transcripts of the first several interviews, I found the accounts of men's experience thin and lacking in detail. The temporal distance between the Vietnam War and their current recollections seemed unbridgeable. I reconsidered my interview strategy. The procedures of the Selective Service System defined a common sequence of events for all participants. Men had registered for the draft, received a classification, resisted in some fashion, and, in some cases, were prosecuted and incarcerated. I decided to refocus the interview around this temporal sequence. Subsequently, I asked interviewees to "tell me something about your background, your high school experience, and then move on to your experience registering for the draft, being classified, and so on. . . ." After making this request, I allowed the resisters to tell their stories as they pleased.

My goal was to understand the general outlines of men's experiences with the Vietnam War and the draft as well as the sense they made of those experiences. I made notes of questions as they arose in my mind, and asked these questions at times when they did not intrude upon the participants' recollections. I asked occasionally for clarification and probed when memories seemed emotionally salient to the interviewees. In general I said little, and sought to minimize my own presence. Although my interests became more focused during the study, there was always room for interviewees to weave their individual ways through my questions.

Initial interviews lasted from 1 to 7½ hours, depending upon my and the participant's interest in the material discussed. The average interview lasted 3 hours. All interviews were tape recorded with the participant's permission and transcribed. Interviews that lasted longer than two hours were generally conducted over several days. Whenever possible, I reviewed the previous interview before beginning a new one with the same individual.

On the basis of these initial interviews I selected five men for portraiture. I judged these individuals to have expressed and acted upon a personal moral vision that was courageous and compelling. Moreover, these men were articulate in their recollections and four (of the five) had documents pertaining to their resistance actions. Using information from the documents and interviews I drafted narrative portraits describing the experience of each man. I then arranged for a follow-up interview. I provided each resister with a copy of the transcript from the initial interview, and asked him to review it before we talked. The follow-up interviews lasted from 2½ to 3½ hours, and allowed me to fill gaps in my understanding of each resister's experience and perceptions. I incorporated new information from the interview into the portrait, gave a copy to each resister, and asked him to review it. We then met or talked by telephone; these final interviews lasted from ½ hour to 2½ hours and focused on inaccuracies in the portraits (these generally concerned minor details such as dates and names) as well as the participant's reactions to reading his story. Following the interview, I made final changes in the portraits, and added a section describing the participant's current reflections on his experience.

Because words provided the fundamental data on which all analysis would be based, it was absolutely essential to verify the accuracy of the interview transcript by comparing it with the tape-recorded record. In the laborious process of checking and emending the transcripts, I discovered the prodigious distance between spoken words and written transcriptions. The stark black words of an interview transcript are devoid of the vocal qualities which subtly affect their significance. The meaning of an interview is not fixed by words alone, but by words in conjunction with an interviewee's inflections, pauses, and emotional tone—qualities of expression largely missing from the textual record. Although initially concerned with the accuracy of the transcription, I found the verification process invaluable for reacquainting me with subtleties of meaning.

Problems of Meaning

Optical metaphors may illuminate the two analytic approaches I employed in this study, although they differ more in degree than in structure. First, I constructed portraits of the experiences of five participants. These were refractory in that they sought to focus attention on the parts of their accounts I selected as important. Second, I compared the experiences and events chronicled in the portraits to magnify similarities and differences and generate a theory of moral thought and action.

Portraiture. A portrait, according to the Latin root, seeks to reveal, expose and draw forth its subject. My subject was the individual experience of war resistance, and I sought to summarize the accounts I had been told. I began by reading and rereading the initial interviews and documents. As I read, I made several types of marginal comments on the text. I summarized and labeled the events that defined the general plot of an individual's account (e.g., registering for the draft, returning one's draft card, etc.), noted aspects of the account I found surprising or salient to questions of moral import (e.g.,

BT doesn't speak about the draft as a moral issue), and highlighted passages the participant or others in the account recognized as being important or significant (e.g., "I thought it important to make the statement", "My friend B couldn't believe what I was going to do"). I also highlighted passages because they expressed especially well the interviewee's state of mind or mood at the time. I did not set out with a distinct intent to "code" the transcripts, but rather to discern the contours and characteristics of one individual's experience. My marginal notations were notes to myself, and in this preliminary scan I was not concerned with the precision and replicability of my categories. I proceeded in a more or less theoretically uninhibited manner, guided primarily by my own curiosity and intuition. Sometimes a passage seemed important, but I could neither attach a marginal label nor identify why it was significant; I highlighted it anyway.

Once I felt thoroughly familiar with an individual's account, I used scissors and paste to assemble from the interview transcripts and documents all accounts of a single event as well as all labels and comments suggesting its significance to the participant, to others in the participant's account, and to me. If a resister, for example, returned at the end of the final interview to comment again upon registering for the draft—something first mentioned in the initial interview—I placed the two accounts together noting on each excerpt the interview from which it was taken. Excerpts were also marked with page numbers so I could return to an undefiled transcript and examine the account in the context and flow of the entire interview. I organized chronologically the events and comments I had excerpted.

I assumed the task of writing portraits would progress rapidly since I was merely recounting what I had been told. My naivete was quickly humbled as I kept encountering situations that required editorial judgment and would affect the actuality of the story being told and its meaning for future readers. If an event, for example, was described slightly differently in two interviews, which description should I use? How much of an interviewee's account of an event should be included in the portrait? How much should be paraphrased? How long should an excerpt be? What words could be omitted? Should a particular excerpt be left alone to speak for itself or should I provide further elucidation? Should I include a tangential anecdote because it buoyed up the story and made it more colorful? Should I excise or include mannerisms such as "You know" or the ever present "Um. . . ."

I resolved these questions by some combination of intuition and judgment, selecting, paraphrasing, or omitting phrases from the interviews by considering whether these actions enabled or disabled the portrait's ability to capture the most significant qualities of person and occasion as resisters' sought to understand and act in accord with their own moral sensibilities. What was *most significant*, of course, was based on my own appraisal and varied somewhat from portrait to portrait. Each portrait represented the reduction of several hundred interview pages into 40 or 50 pages of narrative and expressed my understanding of the core events, thoughts, and actions experienced by each man.

Comparative Analysis. The noun, analysis, as used by the Greeks, means the breaking up or loosening of a complex whole into constituent parts in order to understand better. My purpose was the same: I sought to compare the accounts of all I had interviewed in order to define and understand the relationship between moral thought and action within the context of war resistance.

I began this stage of analysis by re-reading all the portraits. I also reviewed interviews with men I had not portrayed. I was immediately challenged by the diversity of the accounts. Resisters had done different things, gave ostensibly different reasons for their actions, spoke in different terms of the importance of what they had done, and were noticeably inarticulate when probed directly about the morality of their decisions and actions. I sought to establish a common set of theoretical constructs that would delineate the commonalties of participants' experiences. I distinguished three levels of description. First there was a participant's account of his actions: "Five days after I turned 18 I registered for the draft at the local post office." The second level contained the participant's analysis of his actions: "I registered for the draft because I didn't know better." Finally, there was my own interpretation of the participant's actions: "BT was not aware of the moral implications of his actions." These interpretations evolved into more general theoretical constructs that were applied to different events within and across accounts.

As I compared accounts, I examined how men explained what they did at each stage of their draft experience, their past and current feelings about these actions, their explicit and implicit definitions of moral issues, the concerns they expressed about themselves and about others, and the manner in which they spoke of their religious training and practice. I made note of participants' turns of phrase and reflected on their words and deeds as I jogged or washed dishes. I moved in and out of their accounts, jumping from their experiences to my interpretations and back again. Although I fought to distinguish *my* categories of explanation from *their own,* there was often commingling and confusion.

Throughout this process I found it helpful to diagram the experience and perceptions of different participants. I moved from the diagrams to the portraits and returned to the diagrams, modifying and subsuming analytic ideas, moving from conceptual figure to ground and back. I would identify theoretical constructs and posit relationships among them only to reread an interview, understand a comment in a new light, and determine that my interpretation did not quite hang together. Identifying and connecting categories was like climbing a glacier in July; for each conceptual foothold remaining solid, two others had already liquefied.

Eventually, the changes in my thinking and schematic representations became incremental rather than paradigmatic. I moved closer to accepting a set of key constructs that enabled me to describe both the common and the individual within resisters' stories. I had a sense of relief; I had finally figured out what they—and I—were doing.

Problems of Veracity

When I began writing the portraits, I was concerned about the veracity of my representations. I wanted my words to mirror men's experiences. Unaware at the time, I had implicitly adopted a correspondence theory of truth. I noted painstakingly from which interview in a series different excerpts were taken and verified scrupulously that the transcription matched the tape recorded interview. In looking back, I now realize I was confusing the veracity of the portrait with the faithfulness with which its words matched those spoken in the interview. I did not understand portraiture calls for distillation rather than reflection. Its veracity cannot be founded on the accuracy with which words are assembled. The point here is a subtle one, for I am not suggesting that analysts play fast and loose with an interviewee's words, or be nonchalant about the fidelity of text. Textual fidelity, however, does not guarantee that a portrait will convey the more important characteristics of the phenomena under study or will enable a sensible and illuminating analysis.

In contrast to a correspondence theory of truth, I believe the veracity of interpretive research emanates from debate and consensual agreement. The truth of interpretive research is—and should be—questioned by both its author and its audience. Intra- and intersubjective agreement that a portrait or theoretical model is logical, plausible, and supported by the evidence presented is, I believe, the standard by which the veracity of interpretive research must be judged. One must approach one's own writing (and thinking) with a critical eye. Does the narrative support the points being made? Is the selection of material balanced? Are there significant exceptions that need discussion? Is enough information presented so others may judge and respond? Do the theoretical constructs make sense? Are they parsimonious? Elegant? Do they illuminate the phenomena under study? The anthropologist Clifford Geertz (1973) has commented upon the "essentially contestable" nature of interpretive studies.

> It is a strange science whose most telling assertions are its most tremulously based, in which to get somewhere with the matter at hand is to intensify the suspicion, both your own and that of others, that you are not quite getting it right ... there are a number of ways to escape this ... But they are *escapes*.

> The fact is that to commit oneself to a semiotic concept of culture and an interpretive approach to the study of it is to commit oneself to a view of ethnographic assertion as, to borrow W.B. Gallie's by now famous phrase, "essentially contestable." (p. 29, emphasis in text)

The results of an interpretive study careen out of a crazy quilt of perspectives. The reflexive, multi-perspectival nature of interpretive work allows different analysts to consider the same information and reach different conclusions. Or, as was the case with the research discussed here, the same analyst, returning to the same material over the course of several years, draws somewhat different conclusions each time. This process is comforting: with each new conceptualization comes the belief that the data are better understood, their significance better construed. At the same time there is a lingering anxiety the final model may not provide the best fit to the phenomena under study. Perhaps I quit too soon, compromised by article deadlines and other commitments. Or perhaps I persevered too long, fussing with inessentials and distorting centralities? I do not have ready answers to these questions.

A Model of Moral Action

The psychological study of moral issues has been conducted in a variety of contexts with individuals of different ages using an assortment of methodologies. Each context, population, and research strategy influences the findings resulting from each research venture. The study reported here has several distinctive features, and it is worth reviewing these before sketching a model of moral action. Although one must be cautious when suggesting the replicability of this study, I do believe some generalizations may be warranted, depending upon the degree to which other situations are similar in context and participants.

The context in which participants learned of and contemplated the Vietnam War was noteworthy because of the manner in which the reality of war invaded American homes. The nightly news showed repetitive pictures of burned villages and homeless people and toted up the body count of Americans and Vietnamese. The newspapers reported the cat-and-mouse movements of troops and summarized battles for terrain known only by geographical coordinates. The seemingly unending malevolence of the war and the powerful and symbolic images it evoked of American military might gone mad was the backdrop against which participants struggled to understand and resolve the moral implications of their own actions. They felt their decisions mattered; lives were at stake. At the same time, the unrelenting procedures of the Selective Service System confronted men with a succession of situations that made salient the actuality of their own participation in war and provided specific opportunities for resistance.

Most of the participants in this study entered adolescence at roughly the same time they became involved with the Selective Service System and the War. As a consequence, their struggles to recognize and solidify their own identity took place against the backdrop of the War. Numerous historical examples demonstrate that war resistance is not an adolescent preoccupation. Nevertheless, the concurrence of developmental stage and historical circumstance may explain, in part, the considerable psychic energy and personal commitment participants invested in resolving the moral issues the war placed before them.

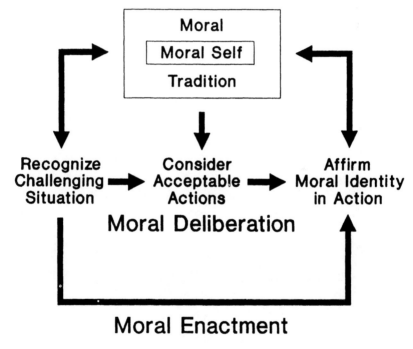

Figure 1
Two Processes of Moral Action

Figure 1 displays the model of moral action that emerged from the study. It is built around two processes: *Moral Deliberation* and *Moral Enactment.* These processes are contingent upon and contribute to an individual's sense of *Moral Identity.* Drawing upon the words of the participants I outline below the essential features of this model.

Moral Identity. The idea of moral identity, a construct both powerful and difficult to pin down, is central to moral action. This concept locates the crux of moral phenomena with the essential character—MacIntyre (1981) would probably say virtue—of the individual in question. Blasi (1984) expresses this idea succinctly:

> Morality is more a characteristic of the agent than of either action or thinking; the ultimate source of goodness lies in good will, and good will is at the core of what a person is. (p. 130)

In drawing attention to the "core" of an individual, Blasi, following Erikson (1968) and McDougall (1936), invokes the concept of identity, or:

> the set of those aspects without which the individual would see himself or herself to be radically different; those so central that one could not even imagine being deprived of them; those whose loss would be considered and felt as irreparable. (p. 131)

The Latin root of the word, identity, means "the same as." An individual's sense of moral identity expresses and delimits what a person of good will does. Beyond the bounds of good will lie deeds of ill will which cause harm to others. Although the distinction of specific acts associated with good and ill will is not without subtleties, the demarcation of benevolent or hurtful intentions is a fundamental one, intuitively appreciable and logically sound. Two components may contribute to an individual's moral identity, although the first is both necessary and sufficient. First, the *moral self* represents an elastic catalogue of contextualized actions and envisioned possibilities associated with deeds of good will. Second, there are the collective aspirations and actions recorded within a *moral tradition*.

Moral Self. Perhaps it is William James who describes the recognition of self most eloquently:

> A man's character is discernible in the mental or moral attitude in which, when it came upon him, he felt himself most deeply and intensely active and alive. At such moments there is a voice inside which speaks and says: "*This* is the real me!" (quoted by Erikson 1968, 19)

Such a recognition—or expression—of self was at the heart of resisters' sense of what was right and wrong for them to do and to shun. The moral self, then, is prescriptive; it expresses and defines good will, enabling individuals to conceive good behavior, and to experience guilt and remorse. Specific rules for living, however, are not its mainstay. Instead there are feelings of satisfaction and accomplishment in living according to one's understanding of good will, and occasional incredulity that life could be any other way. Here is Tony Mancino[1] discussing his Claim for Conscientious Objector Status, a claim that draws upon his Catholic upbringing and training.

> [Tony reads his CO Claim aloud]: My religious beliefs shaped by my Catholic training and Catholic encyclicals cause me to view war in the same light. It is not the case that I will not, it is the case where I cannot serve. But that's exactly what happened. It was not a case that I'd decided not to. I really didn't feel like I had a choice. I just cannot do that. I cannot do that.
>
> This is very much the Friend [Quaker] in me speaking. Or the Self in me speaking, there. [Sarcastically] That's how the church encyclicals compel me. *They* don't compel me, it's just that I cannot serve. That's what compelled me.
>
> What had happened was that I had made promises to follow the example of [St.] Francis ... And I felt bound to do that. Now, it wasn't simply coming from Francis that I was—still or had to follow or live up to St. Francis as in a vow. The vow was made to myself. It came from myself to myself.
>
> [I was] bound, yes. That's the best word to use. But I really didn't feel choice. I did not choose it, I mean it just made sense. It was the only path that was open.

Another example of the power of a personal moral vision of good acts to influence and constrain behavior is seen in the case of Tim Southwood. During Tim's trial, the judge asked him why he could not accept alternative service. He responded:

> I feel the CO status is a question of whether violence is right or wrong, but that is not a question I feel I can answer in yes or no terms. I don't think violence can be judged outside the context in which it is used. Violence in itself is not right or wrong, it is the way in which it is used that we have to judge. And I personally feel that it is being used the wrong way and for the wrong reasons in Vietnam.
>
> So I don't feel that I can tell my draft board that I'm against all wars. I must admit that at times I've been very tempted to be a CO and to adjust my views so that I would be one, but if I did that, what would *I really be?* (emphasis added)

Resisters often compared their own actions and decisions to those of others. Such comparisons helped them to recognize the outlines of their own moral sense and actions of good will in contrast to that of others. In the excerpt below, Robert Perry speaks of his experiences as a draft counselor.

I draft counseled a lot of CO's, all of which confirmed my impression about what the CO route entailed. I was happy to counsel people who were CO's, and if they asked me, I told them what I was going to do [refuse induction]. And I also think that there were a lot of people that it's a real good thing that they got CO's. And I don't regret any of that. But it did sort of confirm in me what I was feeling.

They were essentially taking an easy way out ... and I saw them creeping around it without seeing myself as creeping around it. I sort of saw their procrastination in not succumbing to the logic of their conclusions. And saw my thing as harder, as entailing more sacrifice and somehow making a stronger voice.

Similarly, Tim Southwood watched the commitment of Fred, a fellow war resister, erode inside prison until he finally volunteered for induction to avoid the monotony and degradation of prison life. When Tim learned that Fred had failed his Army physical through trickery and was now "on the streets," he was incensed.

I learned today that Fred failed his physical. I don't know whether it was legitimate or not, but it reminds me of all the simple ways I could have gotten out of being here; all of the ways many men in this country have avoided both going to prison and going to the service; failing physicals, false doctor's reports, false psychiatric reports, lying to their draft boards, continually appealing draft board decisions, etc., etc.

I could have made a little lie to my draft board and become a CO. But I refused to lie, and for that I am in prison while many men are free. It doesn't seem fair.

I know how the people who lie justify their lies. They see all the ambiguity of our leaders, they see our president violating international borders and justifying it on the grounds that the enemy violated them too. They have no respect for our government; it's easy to justify lying to immoral people. I too see our government as immoral; it's the basis for my refusing induction. But at the same time I refuse to use immoral means to avoid an immoral act. I had to use the only moral means available to me; deliberate and outspoken refusal to commit that immoral act ... morality has to start with me ... I cannot live by a double set of values. I cannot criticize my government and at the same time lie to avoid serving that government.

Through comparison with the moral failings and integrity of others, and the recognition of their own vision of themselves as honorable individuals, resisters were able to solidify their own sense of moral identity and strengthen the resolve to be themselves.

Moral Tradition. At times, resisters saw themselves as members or even exemplars of a moral tradition. This often gave a sense of additional depth and breadth to their moral identity and provided a larger context for their acts. It sometimes made it easier to make choices from a set of conflicting alternatives since certain alternatives were seen as antithetical to the moral tradition. Bill Towne was a Quaker. In the statement he made at the time of his sentencing he identified with individuals in several traditions of pacifism and political rebellion.

> My great-great-grandfather came to this country from Prussia with a price on his head for leading student, anti-militarism demonstrations at his university. The Prussians didn't understand the heavy price militarism exacts from a society that would call itself free.
>
> ... Thousands in The Resistance have stopped dodging the draft with all the deferments available to us. Across the country in public squares and college halls and houses of worship we have publicly refused to go to Vietnam or sanction with our cooperation the conscription system that would send others in our place—a public commitment by free citizens to their fellow citizens to begin with their own lives to reconstruct our society. We won't allow militarism to drive us out as my ancestors were driven from Germany.
>
> Before the Civil War, many Quakers broke the law of the land to operate an underground railway to Canada. Many Americans preferred the slow, but legal and orderly, festering of the cancer of slavery in our society to this breach of legal order. It was these people who laid the foundations for the Civil War, not those who acted in affirmation of life.

Just as resisters compared the outlines of their moral selves to others, they sometimes encountered and questioned moral traditions that seemed foreign and placed their own in greater relief. Bill Towne described his meeting with a group considering the wholesale destruction of Philadelphia draft boards.

> We came away from it, rejecting it, not from the principle that destroying property was wrong, because we were pretty open to the idea at that point. We came away from it just because we thought the people involved were kind of crazy. Crazy in a sense that there was a sort of bravado. It didn't feel psychologically sound.
>
> I mean our impression was that half of these people were somehow getting back at the Catholic Church for a lifetime of frustration with the hierarchy. There was a dynamic there which we couldn't understand or deal with. Partly as Quakers; partly as just—I don't think that this is self-serving—but it was kind of a *macho* thing. And the men and women involved in it [were] sort of *partisans*.

Although Bill Towne—and others—found sustenance in thinking of themselves as the current exemplars of the pacifist tradition, he had to construct the personal meaning of that moral tradition and his own place within it. When I asked Bill about the sentencing statement quoted above, he replied:

> Well, first of all, I discovered that tradition. I didn't grow up in that tradition. In fact, my mother told me about this character [who was a war resister] after I turned back my draft cards. He's on my mother's side of the family. She said, "Well, I guess this fits a pattern." So it's not as if that was a conscious part of my sense of myself before I did it. But I rather liked the idea. I was delighted to find out about the old bird. And I had another grandfather who hid slaves in Western Pennsylvania.
>
> I can't say that those were critical factors that led me to where I am now, but it was nice to know. I'm glad I know now. It has its effect. (laugh)

Recognizing a Challenge to Moral Identity. Moral deliberation and moral enactment were initiated when resisters defined a situation as requiring them to commit acts expressing ill will; this challenged their moral identity. Different situations were salient to different participants. Sometimes relatively slight variations on the same situation were perceived entirely differently. During basic training, Pete Ward was required to clean rifles after they were used in target practice. He recalled:

> There was nothing about cleaning a rifle that bothered [me] all that much. In fact, one of the jobs during that first three months was cleaning rifles when they came back from training. There were things to be unoiled. I'd sit there and clean rifles . . . It may have helped the war effort, you know (laugh), I don't know . . . But it didn't occur to me not to do it . . . Maybe if I thought it all through. . . . It was just sort of a mindless thing I could do.

Pete's reaction, however, was quite different when ordered to participate in bayonet drill.

> Yet to be given a gun with a bayonet on it and to be asked to get in a line and do postures with it, thrust it forward and yell, "Kill! Kill!" as you do it—that bothered me. Yet wiping the oil off part of a rifle didn't . . . Bayonet drill did something. Somehow *I felt it would do something to me. It represented something.* I didn't want to do it anyway. But just the same idea of standing there, thrusting it [the bayonet] forward and yelling, "Kill!" *It just went against me and it stood for something.*

> And wiping the screw off wouldn't stand for something. But if you're thrust-
> ing the gun forward it's like you're stabbing somebody. You're not stabbing
> somebody—no problem there—but it's learning to do it and I didn't want to
> know how. Basically, I just didn't want to know how. It's easy enough to do.
> It looked like fun (laugh). But I didn't want to do it. (emphasis added)

Resistance actions of noncooperation were consistently triggered when participants were required to perform actions that violated their moral identity.
Sometimes, because the outlines of their identity were fuzzy, they were uncertain when resistance was required. Tony Mancino, who enlisted as a Navy
medic, was able to spend three years as a soldier by making informal arrangements with his superior officers to avoid duty that compromised his moral
identity. When his orders came to go to Vietnam, all that changed.

> I was going to be a Fleet Marine [sic], a combatant in Vietnam. (pause) I was
> transferred to be a combat medic. I mean [it was] the worst thing that could
> be. Absolutely the worst. Any chance that I could have played around and
> sidestepped being actively involved was now taken away .... I would be
> expected to support the battle by keeping as many men firing as possible as a
> primary concern, and then treat those who would have to be sent to the rear
> because of severe wounds. I would not be there to help wounded men prima-
> rily, but to contribute to the success of the battle by sending the men back to
> the front, and thus endanger their lives again.

For Pete and Tony the boundaries of their moral identities were made
visible as a result of dramatic events: bayonet practice and combat duty. For
Bill Towne, however, maintaining his own sense of moral identity required
more scrupulous consideration of the potential effects of his actions. Concerned about the government's use of tax revenues for defense, Bill made it a
point of principle to never earn enough money so that he would be taxed. As
he put it, "taxes and conscription, it seems to me, are very clear places where
[the line] ought to be drawn." It is worth noting that all participants in this
study registered for the draft with hardly a second thought at the time; it was
not an act that challenged their sense of themselves as moral individuals.

Considering a Range of Acceptable Actions. After resisters recognized
they could not take certain actions, they faced the problem of what they could
do. The ease with which this problem could be resolved depended largely on
the clarity with which each participant saw the outlines of his moral identity
and the strength of conflicting identities that impelled him to *not* resist. Participants considered a range of actions and questioned whether these violated their sense of themselves as moral individuals. They were, by and large,
concerned about being good sons, and not hurting or shaming their parents
by their actions, and these other expressions of good will constrained the
actions they found acceptable. Robert Perry described one such dilemma:

> We started talking about it [e.g., violating prison regulations] in terms of our families and its effect on them . . . Steve [another imprisoned resister] decided that he couldn't do it and I had decided that I was going to do it, but I wanted to talk to my family about it to make sure they understood what was going on. And this was another situation where I regret my decision now, because I feel like I made a mistake in terms of what other people were telling me. My family was totally freaked out at the consequences to me of another three years in prison. So I decided not to do that.

Affirming Moral Identity in Action. Self-definition as a moral being was achieved through simultaneous rejection and affirmation, a point discussed lucidly by Camus (1956). When men's actions witnessed their identity as individuals of good will, the physical consequences to themselves and to others receded. Their attention was on the personal meaning of moral action, and the person it defined. Here is Robert Perry:

> [I was thinking] in very personal terms . . . in terms of what was the moral stance . . . rather than what could I do about the war. . . . I based [my decision] on the existential thing that this was something that was important for me to do. That was why I was doing it. That even if it had no effect at all, that it needed to be done. The analogy to me at the time was to being silent in a way that people were silent about Hitler. That was the way I thought about it. And that's the way I still think about it.

Affirming the moral boundary of one's inner being could be tremendously gratifying. Consider, for example, the words of Tony Mancino after he had presented a Claim for Conscientious Objector Status to his commanding officer:

> I was exhilarated! It was the most wonderful day of freedom of my life. I had something in my hand to say who I was. I could prove who I was.

Robert Perry was both thoughtful and sardonic about his motivation to resist the war.

> If you did the right things then you defined yourself. In part, the things I decided to do were important because they were going to decide this great, (chuckle) good person.

Even Pete Ward, the least analytic of the participants, experienced the satisfaction that accompanies the dramatic expression of one's own morality. In a letter to a friend, Pete recounted his bullying by "one drill sergeant who thought he could force me to do something." After describing the incident, Pete noted:

He didn't seriously hurt me, and I did absolutely nothing to provoke him or defend myself. I have finally proven to myself that I can remain totally nonviolent even when assaulted.

As these excerpts suggest, the question, *What shall I do?*, was fused with, *What will I be if I do it?* John Dewey (1922) recognized the same phenomena:

> the thing actually at stake in any [moral] deliberation is . . . what kind of person one is to become, what sort of self is in the making. (pp. 216-217)

From Knowledge of the Good to Good Will

I began this research seeking to ground Kohlberg's structuralist account of moral judgment in the reality of human experience and concluded his conceptualization of moral behavior was theoretically appealing but empirically false. Among the men in my study, deductive moral reasoning that progressed from consideration of the implications of a priori moral principles to the determination of specific actions was noteworthy by its absence. Pete Ward, to return to a previous example, was not reflecting upon the Vietnamese people's right to a useful and productive life or examining the consequence of this principle when he refused to participate in bayonet practice. Nor did Pete weigh the right of the drill sergeant to order him to participate in bayonet drill versus his right to be a non-combatant. His attention was upon his own actions and their consequence for his moral identity.

Bill Towne, arguably the most thoughtful and articulate of the participants, was mindful of the philosophical foundation of pacifism and the ethical issues raised by the Vietnam War. At the same time he was adamant his actions were based not on philosophical analysis but upon his human response to a situation and his sense of moral identity. A warm and friendly man, philosophical questions tried his patience.

> You know, at some point, those questions have got to stop because somebody's going to say, "OK, we've gone through three of these questions asking, What do you mean by that and all I can reply is, Well, it's just not right."... I guess I'm not very analytical or even all that philosophical about it . . . I don't know how to describe justice, but I know what's not right. *I think you have to develop some emotional response to it. It's not a cold, calculating thing.*

> I think one of the reasons that I've been doing what I've been doing for the last ten or fifteen years is . . . *I just found it harder to think of myself not doing something* . . . I found it harder and harder for myself, even if the war were to end, not being involved somehow or other in social movements and activities trying to do something. (emphasis added)

In the process of completing this study I moved away from Plato and toward people, struggling to describe a vision of moral action rooted in a sense of self rather than a knowledge of rights. This vision is not without problems, but it has the virtue of moving research on moral action out of the cognitive closet and toward the complexities of character and situation that define daily experience. Although I began by seeking the abstract and theoretical, I concluded by finding the concrete and personal. Dewey (1922), of course, had been there before:

> morality is connected with the actualities of existence, not with ideals, ends and obligations independent of concrete actualities. The facts upon which it depends are those which arise out of active connections of human beings with one another, the consequences of their mutually intertwined activities in the life of desire, belief, judgment, satisfaction, and dissatisfaction. (p. 329)

PART TWO

Interpreting from an Adopted Perspective

CHAPTER 5

Reading for Self and Moral Voice:
A Method for Interpreting Narratives
of Real-Life Moral Conflict and Choice

Lyn M. Brown, Mark B. Tappan, Carol Gilligan, Barbara A. Miller, and Dianne E. Argyris[1]

Our aim in this chapter is to describe an interpretive method that we have developed as a guide to reading interview narratives of moral conflict and choice. Central to this effort is our belief in the possibility of different perspectives on moral problems, and the potential for conflict among them. In fact, we believe that tension between differing moral voices, and conflict between opposing values, is essential to the moral life; that, as Martha Nussbaum (1986) states "a conflict-free life would be lacking in value and beauty next to a life in which it is possible for conflict to arise" (p. 81). We embrace, then, both the possibility of creative resolutions to moral conflict, and the potential for tragedy. We chose to examine narratives of moral conflict that people have experienced because we believe this method illuminates the complexity of moral voice, while not overlooking the power of silence.

We claim a place from which to stand, to look, and to listen; hence we struggle with questions of interpretation. The method we will describe in this chapter represents our attempt to bring an explicitly hermeneutic approach to the psychological study of morality and moral development. As such it also provides an alternative approach to more traditional methods that have been used in research on moral development (see Colby & Kohlberg 1987; Gibbs & Widaman 1982; Rest 1979).

Our presentation will unfold as follows: We will turn first to a brief consideration of the theoretical and methodological foundations on which we base our present work. We will discuss: 1) our ongoing work (Gilligan 1977, 1982, 1983, 1986, 1987; Gilligan & Wiggins 1987) on distinguishing two moral voices and the description of differences between a "justice" and a "care" orientation or ethic; 2) recent work on narrative analysis, specifically that of Mishler (1986); and 3) classic work on both hermeneutic theory and interpretive method, specifically that of Dilthey (1900/1976) and Ricoeur (1979). Second, we will outline our "Guide to Reading Narratives of Real-Life Moral Conflict and Choice for Self and Moral Voice" (see Brown, Argyris, Attanucci, Bardige, Gilligan, Johnston, Miller, Osborne, Ward, Wiggins, & Wilcox 1987) which describes our interpretive method. Third, we will present one way we have devised to summarize our reading of narratives of moral conflict, using what we have called "Narrative Types" or "Narrative Strategies." Fourth, we will present and discuss the initial data we have gathered concerning the reliability and validity of this approach. And finally, we will conclude by briefly reflecting on some of the implications, for both theory and research, that stem from our work on this method.

Theoretical and Methodological Foundations

The work we report in this chapter grew out of our efforts to create a theoretical framework that would encompass both equality and attachment as dimensions of human relationship and thus explain the recurrence in life history and history of two moral "voices" or "orientations": "justice" and "care" (see Gilligan, 1977, 1982, 1983, 1986, 1987; Gilligan & Wiggins 1987). The distinction between justice and care as different moral voices and relational perspectives is empirically based, following from the observation that when people shift the focus of their attention from concerns about justice to concerns about care, their definition of what constitutes a moral problem changes; and, consequently, a situation may be seen in a different way. Theoretically, our distinction between justice and care cuts across the familiar divisions between thinking and feeling, egoism and altruism, and theoretical and practical reasoning by reconstructing the meaning of these terms. The moral voices of justice and care call attention to the fact that *all* human relationships, public and private, can be spoken of *both* in terms of equality and in terms of attachment, and that both inequality and detachment constitute grounds for moral concern. We believe that since everyone, by virtue of being human, is vulnerable both to oppression and to abandonment, two moral visions—one of justice and one of care—will always characterize human culture.

Our distinction between justice and care as moral voices thus pertains to the ways in which people conceive and/or define moral problems, and it reflects two different dimensions of human relationships that give rise to moral concern. A justice perspective draws attention to problems of inequality and oppression by holding up an ideal of reciprocity and equal respect between persons. A care perspective draws attention to problems of attachment and abandonment by holding up an ideal of attention and responsiveness in relationships. Two moral injunctions—not to treat others unfairly and not to turn away from someone in need—capture these different concerns.

This theoretical foundation forms the basis from which we have been working to develop a method that can be used by researchers interested in studying the moral voices of justice and care and understanding the experience of self in relation to others. Because the data source for our ongoing work has been open-ended, semi-clinical interviews, we found support for our effort in the similar work of Elliot Mishler (1986).

Mishler helped us clarify a number of crucial aspects of the method we present below. Most importantly, his work on interview narratives helped us see clearly the narrative structure of our data: In our effort to discover and describe peoples' moral voices, when we ask an individual, in an open-ended interview, to talk about a situation of real-life moral conflict and choice that she or he has recently faced, what she or he frequently responds with is a narrative—i.e., a story. Mishler observes that:

> Telling stories is far from unusual in everyday conversation and it is apparently no more unusual for interviewees to respond to questions with narratives if they are given some room to speak. ... In general, researchers in the mainstream tradition either have not recognized the pervasiveness of stories because, as I have already remarked, the standard survey interview "suppresses" them, or have treated stories as a problem because they are difficult to code and quantify. We are more likely to find stories reported in studies using relatively unstructured interviews where respondents are invited to speak in their own voices, allowed to control the introduction and flow of topics, and encouraged to extend their responses. Nonetheless respondents may also tell stories in response to direct, specific questions if they are not interrupted by interviewers trying to keep them to the "point." (Mishler 1986, 69)

A second aspect of our approach to which Mishler's (1986) work has brought clarity is the crucial role that context plays in the interpretation of any interview narrative (see also Mishler 1979). Meaning, argues Mishler, is always "contextually grounded—inherently and irremediably" (p. 3). It follows that in order to understand the meaning of an individual's response to an interview question (let alone the full narrative that he or she provides) the researcher must have some understanding of the context from which both the interview and the interviewee have come, as well as the context of their encounter—i.e., the interview relationship itself and the setting in which it occurs. We have tried to remain sensitive to such contextual issues in developing the method we describe below.

In our effort to clarify the interpretive (or hermeneutic) nature of our "Reading Guide," we also found the work of Wilhelm Dilthey (1900/1976) and Paul Ricoeur (1979) to be quite helpful.

Dilthey's concept of the hermeneutic circle points to the fact that complex human phenomena (e.g., interview narratives) can only be understood in a somewhat paradoxical fashion that involves a circular consideration of both the whole and its parts:

> Here we encounter the general difficulty of all interpretation. The whole of a work must be understood from individual words and their combination but full understanding of an individual part presupposes understanding of the whole. ... [Thus] the whole must be understood in terms of its individual parts, individual parts in terms of the whole. ... Such a comparative procedure allows one to understand every individual work, indeed, every individual sentence, more profoundly than we did before. So understanding of the whole, and of the parts, are interdependent. (Dilthey 1900/1976, 259, 262)

Our Reading Guide offers one way of operationalizing, in a systematic and deliberate manner, the paradoxical hermeneutic circle. As we will describe in detail below, the method involves "building" an interpretation of a whole interview narrative out of its constituent parts. The difficulty is, however, that an understanding of those parts is not possible without some understanding of the whole narrative. Thus the interpretive procedure is a fundamentally circular one, because while the whole can only be understood in terms of its parts, by the same token the parts only acquire their proper meaning within the context of the whole.[2]

Finally, the work of Ricoeur (1979) helped us extend the insights of Dilthey. Ricoeur argues for what he calls the "paradigm of the text," and then shows how "meaningful human action" as the object of the human (social) sciences conforms to the paradigm of the text:

> The human sciences may be said to be hermeneutical (1) inasmuch as their *object* displays some of the features constitutive of a text as text, and (2) inasmuch as their *methodology* develops the same kind of procedures as those of *Auslegung* or text-interpretation. (p. 73)

Ricoeur (1979) proposes that the process of reading represents the appropriate analogy to the interpretive methodology employed by the human sciences. This is because, says Ricoeur, reading manifests the dialectical relationship between *Verstehen* (understanding, comprehension) and *Erklaren* (explanation) that perplexed and preoccupied Dilthey. Dilthey ultimately argued that understanding was the only interpretive method appropriate for the human studies, and that explanation was inappropriate because it was imported from the natural sciences. Ricoeur, however, rejects this view, and instead sees the dialectic between understanding and explanation, as it is manifest in the process of reading a text, as the key to contemporary methodological problems in the human studies.[3] As such, he argues that it is the "balance between the genius of *guessing* and the scientific character of *validation* which constitutes the modern complement of the dialectic between *Verstehen* and *Erklaren*" (p. 91).

Unfortunately, our purposes here do not allow us to discuss all the complex and complicated issues that stem from Ricoeur's argument. Instead, we simply want to acknowledge Ricoeur's analogy between the procedures employed in reading and interpreting texts, and the procedures employed in interpreting meaningful human action in the social sciences. In the method we describe below we have attempted to make that connection explicit—that is, we have developed a method of interpreting human action (i.e., engaging in social scientific research) that involves reading texts of interview narratives in which such action is represented and described.[4]

The Reading Guide

An Overview

As we have said above, our purpose in creating this method was to develop a way of reading and interpreting complex narratives of real-life moral conflict and choice. We have come to see through reading such interviews that how a person constructs a moral conflict—how she or he defines or interprets the situation, and what she or he focuses on as relevant to the problem—is related to what actions she or he describes and the thoughts and feelings that follow from or accompany this description. In a given situation, people differ in what they consider to be the central *moral* problem, and what they consider to be the best (or better) way to respond to that problem.

The way in which a moral problem is constructed, however, also depends on the context, e.g., who is involved, the relationships between the persons involved—their relative power vis-a-vis each other as well as the strength of the connection between them—where the situation takes place, what role the narrator plays in the conflict, and the personal and cultural history of the narrator. We have observed that when different elements of context and different aspects or qualities of relationship are defined and represented as salient in similar conflicts, what is seen as the central moral issue in a situation may shift, and different actions may be defined as moral and immoral, as right or wrong (see Gilligan 1987; Johnston 1985).

The two moral voices of justice and care can be distinguished in part by a shift in the conception of what is relevant to the moral domain. The method presented here picks up on that shift and is designed for use in interpreting narratives of moral conflict and choice, including narratives systematically collected in the course of formal research.

As an interpretive enterprise, then, this method is not a "Coding Manual" that allows a "coder" to match responses to a predetermined set of criteria (see, for example, Colby and Kohlberg 1987). Instead, it is a way of reading— a Reader's Guide. As such, it is a procedure for teaching others to read a text of a real-life moral conflict to identify what we consider "voice-relevant" aspects of a person's narrative.

The distinction between a Coding Manual and a Reading Guide is an important one. It has to do with both our methodological premises and the nature of our data. Our choice of an open-ended clinical interview method (see Table 1 for a copy of our interview questions) yields complex real-life narratives. Such narratives reflect situational, personal, and cultural factors, including issues of language, perspective, and the relationship between the reader's and the narrator's language and perspective. To develop a method that highlights the interpretive nature of the reading process we have tried to create and describe a way of working where we claim both a theoretical and a methodological stance.

Table 1

Real-Life Moral Conflict and Choice Interview

All people have had the experience of being in a situation where they had to make a decision, but weren't sure of what they should do. Would you describe a situation when you faced a moral conflict and you had to make a decision, but weren't sure what you should do?

1. What was the situation? (Be sure you get a full elaboration of the story).

2. What was the conflict for you in that situation? Why was it a conflict?

3. In thinking about what to do, what did you consider? Why? Anything else you considered?

4. What did you decide to do? What happened?

5. Do you think it was the right thing to do? Why/why not?

6. What was at stake for you in this dilemma? What was at stake for others? In general, what was at stake?

7. How did you feel about it? How did you feel about it for the other(s) involved?

8. Is there another way to see the problem (other than the way you described it?)

9. When you think back over the conflict you described, do you think you learned anything from it?

10. Do you consider the situation you described a moral problem? Why/why not?

11. What does morality mean to you? What makes something a moral problem for you?

**Note to Interviewers:* Questions should follow references to judgments about the, situation. Follow any references to feelings that are mentioned—e.g., Why did you feel mad or angry? Also follow moral language, i.e., should, ought. Questions should focus on: In whose terms judgments are made. Try to understand the terms of the self and the self's perspective on the terms of the other.

Reading an interview text in this way, we enter the hermeneutic circle and build an interpretation of that text—an interpretation that moves from the words on the page, toward an understanding of how, and an explanation of why, a narrator structures his/her experience of relationships and how s/he organizes or "frames" the moral conflict, and back again—in terms of self and the two moral voices of justice and care. These voices are not identified by any key code words or phrases, but rather by the framework or perspective provided by the narrator, and illuminated by the reader.

In constructing this Reading Guide we proceeded from evidence that persons know (and can represent) two moral voices or perspectives in discussing moral conflicts, even though they may indicate a preference for one over the other (see, for example, Johnston 1985). From evidence of the ability to switch perspectives, we assume that the "narrative self" is, in some sense, involved in choice. In reading texts, therefore, we view persons as "moral agents" with respect to the standpoint they take and the concerns they voice or keep silent.

Tracking the "voice" of the narrative self draws our attention to the narrator's perspective (both expressed and preferred) in a particular story of moral conflict. This approach has made it possible for us to investigate empirically what understanding of justice and care a person brings to bear on a particular problem, and also what relationship exists between these two moral voices or perspectives in a particular narrative.

Perhaps it is important to emphasize here that we do not conceive of the moral voices of justice and care as either dichotomous or mutually exclusive. Rather, we consider justice and care as visions of relationship that reflect the vulnerabilities of people in relationships—their liability to oppression and to abandonment, indifference, and neglect. These two perspectives on moral problems may shift over time, but each voice is defined in its own terms. In other words, although some of the criteria used to identify a care idea may have counterparts that may identify a justice idea, others will not. Each voice has as its central tenet a dimension of relationship that gives rise to moral concern, from which certain assumptions about self and other are made, and from which a certain view of the moral world is constructed. Thus, each voice has its own psychological "logic," its own psychic legitimacy and organization that can be followed in narratives of moral conflict and choice. We are ultimately most interested in the narrative strategies people use in describing the realm of moral conflict—the choice of moral orientations and the orchestration of moral voices telling human stories.

This way of reading, therefore, takes as its starting point the premise that a person, represented in the interview text by a speaking voice telling a narrative or story, experiences relationships both in terms of attachment and in terms of equality. We are interested in how a person tells a story about his or her experiences of conflict in relationship. Justice and care voices are characterized by the telling of different narratives about relationship. A care voice describes relationships in terms of attachment/detachment, connection or disconnection. *Care narratives*, consequently, focus on the vulnerability of people to isolation and abandonment, and are concerned with the complexities of creating and sustaining human connection. A justice voice describes relationship in terms of inequality/equality, reciprocity, or lack of respect. *Justice narratives* thus focus on the vulnerability of people to oppression, and are centrally concerned with standards or principles of fairness. Reading in this way we track these two relational "voices" and seek to specify the way in which a person orchestrates or chooses between them.

Interpretive Procedures

As a guide to interpreting texts of real-life moral conflict and choice the goal of the Reading Guide is to present a theoretical perspective and to teach those interested to read interview texts using a specific set of referents defined by this perspective. Thus the interpreter (i.e., reader) is first helped to locate a narrative of real-life moral conflict in a larger interview text and then to read this story a total of *four* different times. Each reading serves to identify a different aspect of the narrative deemed relevant in locating self and ascertaining moral voice.

The multiple readings are necessary because each reading approaches the narrative from a different standpoint. The first reading is designed simply to establish the story told by the narrator. Once this is done, the narrative is read using three different interpretive lenses to locate self and the moral voices of care and justice. In the second reading ("Locating Self") the interpreter reads for the active "self", the narrator (the speaking voice) as an agent telling a story in which he or she appears as an actor in a drama of moral conflict and choice. In the third reading ("Reading for Care") the interpreter reads to track the "care voice." And finally, in the fourth reading ("Reading for Justice") the interpreter reads to track the "justice voice."

To extend the metaphor, each lens brings into focus different aspects of the narrative; to switch metaphors, each reading amplifies different voices. A given statement may have different meanings depending on the lens, and a meaning may become apparent with one lens that is hidden from view by another. Again, our goal is to be able to identify when justice and care, as we have described them, are articulated, and to understand the experience of self in relationship as filtered through each of these moral perspectives.

The first time the interpreter reads through the conflict his or her attention is focused on the narrator's story as he or she presents it. The goal is to understand the context, the drama (the who, what, where, when, and why of the story); to listen, to attempt to "hear" as clearly as possible the narrator's voice in the story about him/herself, and about morality and moral conflict, that he or she is telling.

The next three readings entail a two step process. First, the reader uses colored pencils to mark passages that represent self (green), care (red), and justice (blue) in the interview text. We have found that this visual technique attunes the reader to the specific languages or voices of the narrator without losing sight of the larger story and context of the conflict.

Second, after reading (and underlining) for self, care, and justice, the reader is asked to fill in summary Worksheets (see Table 2). While the Reading Guide explains the interpretive procedure, the Worksheets provide a place for the reader to document relevant pieces of the text and to make observations and interpretive remarks. The Worksheets are designed to highlight the critical move from the narrator's actual words to a reader's interpretation or summary of them, since they require the reader to substantiate his or her interpretation with quotes from the interview text itself. As such, the Worksheets stand between the Reading Guide (and the reader) and the interview text; hence they provide the tool with which the hermeneutic circle is built.

Table 2

Excerpts from Summary Worksheets

III. <u>THIRD READING—CARE</u>   Summary/Interpretation

    A. <u>Is the Care Orientation articulated?</u>
       How would you characterize care?

    B. <u>If Care is not (clearly) articulated?</u>
       What would constitute care in this conflict?

    C. <u>Does self align with Care? How do you know?</u>
       Is the alignment explicit or implicit?

IV. FOURTH READING—JUSTICE   Summary/Interpretation

   A. Is the Justice Orientation articulated?
      How would you characterize justice?

   B. If Justice is not (clearly) articulated?
      What would constitute justice in this conflict?

   C. Does self align with Justice? How do you know?
      Is the alignment explicit or implicit?

The final step in the reading process requires the reader to answer a series of summary Coding Questions about his or her understanding of self and the two moral voices in the interview narrative (see Table 3). These questions are used in the summary determination of what we have called "Narrative Types" or "Narrative Strategies," which are described in detail below.

Table 3

Summary Coding Questions

I. The two moral orientations and how they are represented: (check two)

    1. Is the justice orientation articulated? yes _____ no _____

    2. Is the care orientation articulated? yes _____ no _____

II. The relationship between the two moral orientations: (check one)

    1. Justice predominates _____

    2. Care predominates _____

    3. Both justice and care present, neither predominates _____

III. The Narrative Self:

    1. Does the narrative self express an "alignment" in the conflict? (Consider whether or not the narrator comes down on one side of his or her own values. Does the narrator perceive the values of justice or care in relation to his or her own integrity—so that compromising that set of values would be seen as losing a basic or central sense of self? Finally, this "alignment" can be determined by the narrative self rejecting the values of another.)
       yes _____ no _____

    2. What terms/orientation does the narrator use to frame this "alignment" in the conflict?
       justice _____ care _____ both _____

This Reading Guide assumes that the story of a real-life conflict told by the interviewee can be heard and understood by a careful reader. In our open-ended interview format we have partially assured the coherence of the story by training interviewers to ask the narrator clarifying or activating questions, in addition to standard interview questions about his or her construction of the dilemma, resolution of the problem, and evaluation of his or her decision (see Table 1). We *assume* the possibility of understanding the narrator's story because each person has access to experiences of justice and injustice, care and carelessness. We also assume the importance of these experiences in structuring the experience of self (including self-esteem, self-concept, identity) and the ways people act in relation to one another.

An Illustrative Example

In this section we want to briefly illustrate this method using an excerpt of a narrative from an adolescent girl, Tanya. That interview is reproduced in Table 4; in order to approximate the effect of the three color-coded readings (and markings) we have used CAPITAL LETTERING to indicate "self" (green), underlining to indicate "care" (red), and boldface to indicate "justice" (blue).

Table 4

Excerpt from Sample Interview Narrative

I: Can you tell me about a situation where you faced a moral conflict, you had to make a decision, but you weren't sure what was the right thing to do?

R: .... when we were at camp, I went to camp with my sister and my cousin, and he was really young, he was like maybe seven, and he got really, really homesick. It was overnight. And he was like, always crying at night and stuff. And we had this camp guide who was really tough and I WAS REALLY AFRAID OF HIM, it was like two years ago and I WAS REALLY AFRAID OF HIM. **And he said, "nobody is allowed to use the phone,"** and so my cousin really wanted to call his parents, (Yeah) and it was kind of up to me to go ask the guy if he could. So, EITHER LIKE I GOT BAWLED OUT BY THIS GUY AND ASKED, OR I DIDN'T DO ANYTHING ABOUT IT, AND HE WAS MY COUSIN, SO I HAD TO HELP HIM, SO I WENT AND ASKED THE GUY IF HE COULD USE THE PHONE and he started giving me this lecture about **how there shouldn't be homesickness in the camp.** AND I SAID, "SORRY BUT HE'S ONLY SEVEN." (Yeah!) And he was really young and so he finally got to use the phone, so he used the phone. And then we had a camp meeting, and um, and the guy started saying, **"Any kid here who gets homesick shouldn't be here,"** and he didn't say my cousin's name, but like, he was like, almost in tears.

I: Oh, and your cousin was there when he said that? Oh, that wasn't very nice.

R: Yah. It was really mean.

I: When you were in this situation .... what kinds of things did you consider in thinking about what to do?

R: WELL, MOSTLY, FIRST OF ALL, WHAT WAS RIGHT AND WRONG. AND THE RIGHT THING TO DO WAS TO GO BECAUSE IT WAS MY COUSIN'S GOOD YOU KNOW. (um, hum) And he wasn't going to die or anything, but, you know, he's afraid to go to camp now, because he's like 9 now (yah), and he doesn't want to go back, and SO I SAID, "THIS GUY CAN INTIMIDATE ME, BUT HE CAN'T BEAT ME UP OR ANYTHING." (Yah) I'LL REALIZE THAT THAT'S JUST THE WAY HE IS, BUT I HAVE TO DO THIS, SO. I mean, he might say no, but it can't hurt asking.

Key:

CAPS = "self"
underline = "care"
bold = "justice"

Tanya, a seventh grader, tells a story about being at camp with her younger cousin who becomes homesick and wishes to talk to his mother.[5] Tanya, struggling with her fear of the counselor and her felt sense of responsibility to act on behalf of her cousin, decides to approach the counselor. In response to the interviewer's question about what she considered when thinking about what to do, she shares what appears to be an internal dialogue about the limits to the counselor's actions. These considerations, feelings, actions, and spoken or internalized thoughts, highlighted by green underlining (here by capitalization) help the reader to locate the "narrative self"; that is, the person as actor in the story of conflict she tells.

After locating self in the narrative, the reader moves through the interview a third time attending to the care voice only. Having read the interview twice already at this point, the reader is aware of the drama and the intentions, thoughts, feelings, and actions of the narrator. Reading for care is not meant to blind the interpreter to these aspects of the drama, but to attune him or her to any evidence that the story told may be one in which care concerns play an active part. That is, the reader actively looks for any evidence that will allow him or her to build an interpretation of the story as one concerned with care.

In this example, Tanya describes the distress suffered by her cousin. From a care perspective this perceived suffering on the part of her cousin explains the imperative Tanya felt to respond—in this case to talk with a counselor regardless of her own fear which she expresses twice, as though for emphasis. She is able to place her cousin's response in perspective ("He wasn't going to die or anything") but remains concerned, and justifies her concern with the fact that he remains afraid of camp a full two years later. The focus on her own fears and the concern for her cousin are gathered as evidence that a care orientation is present in her story.

Finally, the reader moves through the interview a fourth time in an attempt to trace the justice voice. The reader seeks evidence that justice concerns are understood and used. This means that she or he must begin again, since the goal is to gather evidence for a different interpretation of the text.

In this example, Tanya expresses difficulty with the counselor's belief that there should be no homesickness in the camp—clearly an inadequate belief given her cousin's situation. In addition, she is not willing to accept without question the rule that "nobody is allowed to use the phone." Her dismissal of the counselor's rules and beliefs because they do not account for her cousin's particular situation provides evidence for an understanding of justice, but also for its rejection in this form. Tanya's alignment with care becomes more explicit later in the interview, when she states why she felt her choice to act was the right one: "It might not be for you or somebody else, but it's helping out my cousin. And that camp director, it was a rule, but people are more important than rules, you know."

This process—reading with one interpretive lens and then another, rather than with both simultaneously—is a key element of the procedure employed when using the Reading Guide. It reflects evidence that the two moral voices are distinct moral perspectives and that what a reader uses as evidence depends in part on the lens he or she takes to the story. Thus, the same idea may be used as evidence for both a justice reading and a care reading; that is, it may reflect both justice and care concerns. A case in point are Tanya's statements "he was my cousin, so I had to help him," and, "I said, 'Sorry, he's only 7!'" Reading for care, one could assume that these statements reflect her observation of her cousin's pain, and the necessity she felt to respond given the nature of their relationship (in fact, later in the interview she talks about their closeness), or a belief that he was too young to control his fear. On the other hand, reading for justice, Tanya's statements may indicate that she feels she has an obligation, either because she is a cousin or because she is older, to watch over her cousin. Both interpretations are viable and make sense within the parameters of the story told. Yet, since much of the story focuses on Tanya's closeness to her cousin and her understanding of his fear, the care interpretation appears to be a more adequate representation of her experience.[6]

Narrative Types

In attempting to move from a reading of a particular interview narrative of moral conflict and choice, to an extensive summary of that reading recorded on the summary Worksheets, to a final representation of the way in which self and moral voice are manifest and articulated in that narrative, we have developed a coding typology that we have called Narrative Types. These categorical types distinguish between narratives with respect to the ways in which the moral voices of justice and care are represented.

Narrative Types are determined as follows: The Summary Coding Questions sheet (see Table 3) is clearly divided into three sections. A one-digit numerical code[7] is assigned to each of the three sections, depending upon how the reader answers the series of questions in that section. In Section I, which identifies the "Presence" of the two moral voices in the narrative, the reader is asked to answer both questions 1 and 2; hence there are four possible responses that a reader could make to that section, and four corresponding numerical codes:

1 = Both justice and care are present in the narrative.
2 = Care is present in the narrative; justice is not.
3 = Justice is present in the narrative; care is not.
4 = Neither justice nor care is present in the narrative; i.e., the narrative is "uncodable."

In Section II, the reader is asked to answer one of the three questions asked regarding the "Predominance" of the two moral voices in the narrative. "Predominance" in this sense refers to the voice that is most salient in the interview narrative—i.e., the voice that is most fully elaborated. Consequently, three codes are possible for Section II:

1 = The justice voice predominates in the narrative.
2 = The care voice predominates in the narrative.
3 = Neither voice predominates in the narrative, although both are present.

And finally, in Section III, the reader is asked to answer questions relating to the "Alignment" that the "narrative self" expresses vis-à-vis the two moral voices in the interview. "Alignment" in this sense refers to the voice that is most central to self as it is represented in the narrative. The reader is asked to answer question 1 first and, if the answer is "yes," then to go on to question 2. Consequently, four codes are possible for Section III:

1 = Self aligns with justice.
2 = Self aligns with care.
3 = Self aligns with both justice and care.
4 = Self does not express an alignment with either voice in the narrative (i.e., the answer to question 1 is "no").

Table 5 presents the numerical codes associated with each of the three sections on the Summary Coding Questions sheet.

Table 5

The Three Coding Dimensions

I. PRESENCE

	JY	JN
CY	1	2
CN	3	4

II. PREDOMINANCE

1. Justice Predominant	1
2. Care Predominant	2
3. Neither Predominant	3

III. ALIGNMENT

1. Justice Alignment	1
2. Care Alignment	2
3. Align. with both	3
4. No Alignment	4

Thus the overall Narrative Type that summarizes a particular narrative of moral conflict and choice is actually composed of three separate but related dimensions: Presence, Predominance, and Alignment. Each narrative receives a one-digit code for each dimension; hence the overall narrative type is a three-digit code composed of the individual codes for each dimension. There are 17 possible Narrative Types, listed and identified in Table 6.

In sum, then, these Narrative Types provide a simplified tool for data description and analysis. They allow us to represent, in the form of a categorical typology, some of the aspects of narratives of moral conflict and choice relevant to self and the two moral voices, justice and care. As such they allow us to compare groups of narratives—comparisons that would be unwieldy at best, and impossible at worst, using only the summary Worksheets obtained from a reader's use of the Reading Guide. We want to stress, however, that these types are by no means the only way to move from the Worksheets to a representation of the data captured by the reader. But they do provide a useful way to generate and explore interesting hypotheses regarding the ways in which self and moral voice are manifest in narratives of moral conflict and choice.

Table 6

Narrative Types

Both Justice and Care Present	"Pure" Care	"Pure" Justice	Uncodable
111	222	311	400
112	224	314	
113			
114			
121			
122			
123			
124			
131			
132			
133			
134			

Reliability and Validity

Our interest in this method has led us to begin to explore both the reliability and the validity of the Reading Guide and the Narrative Types. However, traditional psychometric conceptions of the reliability and validity of psychological tests and measures (see Anastasi 1976; Chronbach 1949) are based on assumptions which render them inappropriate for interpretive approaches such as the one we outline in this chapter (see also Mishler 1986; Packer 1985). The interest in interpretive methodologies among psychologists at present calls for a redefinition, in hermeneutic terms, of these basic notions of research practice—a rethinking of what reliability and validity mean and what concerns these concepts address (see Rogers 1987; Tappan 1987). We can not claim to offer such a redefinition here. We do hope, however, that our preliminary struggles with these issues will be of interest to others doing similar work, and that they represent a helpful step in the right direction.

The determination of *reliability*, meaning here the ability of two or more different interpreters to agree on their interpretation and understanding of a particular interview narrative, is obviously crucial if an interpretive method such as the one we have described above is to be useful to other researchers and practitioners. The establishment of such agreement among interpreters (i.e., "interpretive agreement") creates a common ground for conversing about the data in question; it assumes that, within acceptable limits, both are reading the text in the same way, or interpreting the same text (see Hirsch 1967).

With respect to the method we have developed, we have thought about such interpretive agreement in two related ways. The first, and most general, focuses on agreement in "reading" (cf. Ricoeur 1979). At this level we feel it is important to determine if two readers (i.e., interpreters), using the Reading Guide, do in fact read the same interview narrative of real-life moral conflict and choice in more or less the same way.

Such agreement can be determined by considering three different pieces of information: 1) the degree to which both readers *underline* the same parts of the interview text for self, justice, and care as they read through the narrative of moral conflict and choice; 2) the degree to which both readers agree in their respective *summaries* of that narrative, as those summaries are captured by the Worksheets; and 3) the degree to which both readers express a similar *interpretation* of the narrative, specifically with respect to how self and the two moral voices are orchestrated or represented, as they discuss their readings of that narrative in conference.

In practice, the first and second kinds of agreement, above, provide specific procedures and techniques that facilitate the attainment of the third kind of agreement. And, in fact, while we have not "measured" levels of agreement in each of these three ways, our experience indicates that among the research team that has developed and used the Reading Guide such agreement is consistently high.

The second, and more precise way in which we have determined interpretive agreement among readers using this method is based on the Narrative Types described above. Because the determination of Narrative Type yields categorical representations on several different dimensions of interest, simple percent agreement figures can be computed between readers with respect to the codes that each records for a given set of interviews. Thus, traditional "inter-judge" reliability assessments can be made.

We have ascertained such percent agreement figures for several different readers, based on a set of "reliability cases"—interviews with adolescents, both males and females, taken from both private suburban high schools and public inner-city high schools. Table 7 presents these figures. Readers 1 (Brown), 2 (Miller), and 3 (Argyris) are all considered "expert" readers (all are authors of the Reading Guide); their reliability figures are based on a set of 14 interviews. Readers 4 and 5 are two female graduate students who were trained to use the Reading Guide over the course of a six-week training session conducted by Miller; their reliability figures are based on a set of 10 interviews. As Table 7 indicates, all of the percent agreement figures, when adjusted for chance using Cohen's (1960) *Kappa* statistic, represent levels of "fair" to "almost perfect" agreement beyond chance (Landis & Koch 1977).

Table 7

Agreement between Readers on Coding Dimensions and Narrative Types (%)

Readers	Presence	Predominance	Alignment	Narrative Type
Expert				
1 and 2	.86	.93	.79	.71
	(.62)	(.88)	(.71)	(.67)
1 and 3	.64	.79	.86	.64
	(.33)	(.65)	(.81)	(.55)
2 and 3	.79	.79	.79	.64
	(.63)	(.76)	(.58)	(.58)
Trained				
4 and 5	.90	.70	.80	.50
	(0.0)*	(.42)	(.73)	(.42)
1 and 4	.80	.90	.70	.60
	(0.0)*	(.83)	(.59)	(.53)
1 and 5	.90	.70	.80	.70
	(.63)	(.52)	(.73)	(.63)

Note: Figures in parentheses are Cohen's (1960) *Kappa* coefficients.
*when $p_o = p_e$, *kappa* = 0.0

Given these figures, we are confident that the method we have described can be used "reliably" by different readers using the Narrative Typologies to summarize their interpretations of the same set of narratives. It must be stressed, however, that such reliability figures are of a very different sort than those obtained by using other ostensibly interpretive coding manuals (e.g., Colby & Kohlberg, 1987, Loevinger & Wessler 1970). As we have described above, in the Reading Guide there are no prototypical statements that can be "matched" to statements from the interview text (cf. the "Criterion Judgments" employed by Colby & Kohlberg 1987). Rather, the Reading Guide simply provides a framework that the reader uses to guide him or herself through four different readings of a narrative, as he or she enters the hermeneutic circle by "building" an interpretation of that narrative. The Narrative Types on which the above reliability figures are based entail the most basic and simplified summary of that interpretation—a summary that we believe captures important aspects of the way self and the two moral voices are represented in the narrative, but which clearly can not represent the full complexity of the reader's interpretation and understanding of that narrative.

Turning now to a brief consideration of the *validity* of the interpretive method we have described above, again we are faced with the difficulty of both using traditional terms and categories, and using them in new ways. For example, *construct validity* (see Chronbach & Meehl 1955/1973) is crucial if we are to claim that the information our method yields about a narrative and its narrator is germane to the constructs of self and moral voice, and if differences in Narrative Types make any difference with respect to the way individuals feel, think, and act in real life. Thus our validation efforts have focused exclusively on gathering preliminary information about the construct validity of the Reading Guide.

Chronbach and Meehl (1955/1973) argue that the process of construct valdiation is essentially the same as the general scientific procedure used for developing and confirming (or disconfirming) theories. Thus "a construct is defined implicitly by a network of associations or propositions in which it occurs," (the "nomological net") and "construct validation is possible only when some of the statements in the network lead to predicted relations among variables" (p. 30). One of the central validation procedures for testing hypotheses relating to such constructs is the examination of group differences: "If our understanding of a construct leads us to expect two groups to differ on the test [sic], this expectation may be tested directly" (p. 12).

Thus the first source to which we have turned in assessing the construct validity of our method is a comparison of group differences between adolescent males and females with respect to self and moral voice. While Gilligan has been clear to argue that the justice and care voices are not gender specific, she does hypothesize that they are gender related (Gilligan & Wiggins 1987; see also Gilligan 1977, 1982). Hence our hypothesis was that while a majority of both males and females would show evidence of using and understanding both justice and care in their interview narratives, the justice orientation would predominate among males and the care orientation would predominate among females.

Subjects for this study came from the freshman and sophomore classes of a private independent high school in the Northeast (see Gilligan, Johnston, & Miller 1988). The sample consisted of 37 male and 43 female adolescents, aged 14-16. While data on IQ and SES were not obtained for this sample it is reasonable to assume that the two groups were evenly matched on such variables, since the school is characterized by a high degree of selectivity and status, and hence it draws from a very homogeneous population.

The real-life moral conflict and choice interview narratives from this sample were read by Miller and Argyris. The frequency and percentage of

Narrative Types for both males and females are presented in Table 8. The comparison based on the Presence dimension suggests that, as we expected, the majority of both males and females articulate both the justice and care voices in their narratives, and hence there is no significant difference between males and females vis-à-vis this dimension. There is a significant difference, however, with respect to the Predominance dimension, in support of our initial hypothesis.

Finally, we find the virtually identical distribution in the Alignment dimension particularly interesting. Recall that Alignment indicates the voice that is most central to self as it is represented in the narrative of moral conflict. Thus, the fact that both males and females in the sample align similarly—despite differences in predominance—suggests to us that context may play an important role in determining at least one aspect of moral voice.

The school from which this sample was drawn was, until 10 years ago, all male. It has not, however, changed significantly in philosophy or environment since the decision to admit female students. Consequently, we would characterize the atmosphere of the school as primarily "justice focused," and we would suggest that it may be the power of this kind of context that leads to the similarity in Alignment that these data indicate.[8]

Admittedly these are very preliminary findings and interpretations. They do suggest, however, that the Reading Guide and the Narrative Types illuminate both a gender difference, and a context effect, in the representation of self, justice, and care in these adolescent narratives of real-life moral conflict and choice. Consequently, we would argue that these data provide one piece of evidence that we can use in building our case for the construct validity of the Reading Guide.

Before we conclude this discussion we want to take the opportunity to raise an issue related to the validity of this method that, while related to concerns about construct validity, actually comes *prior* to any such concern. This issue is best captured by the term "interpretive validity." In short, we believe that the information that this method yields is not so much focused on a specific construct (although self and the justice and care voices do, to a certain extent, function as constructs) as it is focused on the construction of a particular interpretation of a narrative—an interpretation that is built on the reader's view of how self and the two moral voices are represented in that narrative.

The issue of validity in interpretation has always been of major concern to both hermeneutic theorists and practitioners (see, for example, Bleicher 1980; Hirsch 1967, 1978; Juhl 1980; Palmer 1969; Spence 1982). It is again the work of Ricoeur (1979), however, that has been of most help to us in thinking through these difficult issues.

Table 8

Frequency of Presence, Predominance, and Alignment Scores for Adolescent Co-ed Sample (Age 13-16)

I. PRESENCE

	1	2	3	
Males	24 (.65)	2 (.05)	11 (.30)	37
Females	32 (.74)	6 (.14)	5 (.12)	43
	56	8	16	80

Note: $X^2 (2, N = 80) = 4.97, p$ .10

II. PREDOMINANCE

	1	2	3	
Males	26 (.70)	10 (.27)	1 (.03)	37
Females	17 (.40)	17 (.40)	9 (.20)	43
	43	27	10	80

Note: $X^2 (2, N = 80) = 9.69, p$ .01

III. ALIGNMENT

	1	2	3	4	
Males	11 (.30)	6 (.16)	2 (.05)	18 (.49)	37
Females	11 (.26)	10 (.23)	2 (.04)	20 (.47)	43
	22	16	4	38	80

Note: $X^2 (2, N = 80) = 0.66, p$ .90

Recall that Ricoeur (1979) argues that the modern-day synonym for *Verstehen* is "guessing," and for *Erklaren* it is "validation": both are involved, he claims, in the process of reading. Hence striving for validity in interpretation necessarily involves taking seriously the dialectic between guessing and validation. In fact, argues Ricoeur, this is precisely what the "hermeneutic circle" entails from the start:

> We are [now] prepared to give an acceptable meaning to the famous concept of a *hermeneutical circle*. Guess and validation are in a sense circularly related as subjective and objective approaches to the text. But this circle is not a vicious circularity. It would be a cage if we were unable to escape the kind of "self-confirmability" which, according to Hirsch (1967), threatens this relation between guess and validation. To the procedures of validation also belong procedures of invalidation similar to the criteria of falsifiability emphasized by Karl Popper (1959) . . . The role of falsification is played here by the conflict between competing interpretations. An interpretation must not only be probable, but more probable than another. There are criteria of relative superiority which may easily be derived from the logic of subjective probability.
>
> In conclusion, if it is true that there is always more than one way of construing a text, it is not that all interpretations are equal and may be assimilated to so-called "rules of thumb." The text is a limited field of possible constructions. The logic of validation allows us to move between the two limits of dogmatism and skepticism. It is always possible to argue for or against an interpretation, to confront interpretations, to arbitrate between them, and to seek for an agreement, even if this agreement remains beyond our reach. (Ricoeur 1979, 91)

In practice, the "logic of validation" is operationalized most clearly when readers are able to discuss their respective interpretations of the same interview text. Ample opportunity exists at that point for alternative interpretations to be entertained, and for the relative probabilities of each to be considered. In fact, we would recommend that whenever the Reading Guide is used in empirical research at least two readers should read each narrative. Once each has read the interview then it can be discussed between them and differences in interpretation can be addressed. At this point, ways of choosing between them or reconciling them in terms of a new interpretation can be considered or created. Only in this way can the dialectic between guess and validation that Ricoeur (1979) emphasizes be fully maintained.

Discussion and Conclusion

The goal of this chapter has been to outline the interpretive method we have developed for reading complex narratives of moral conflict and choice; a method that represents both equality and attachment as dimensions of human relationship. Given that we continue to face the challenge of developing and refining such a method, we will conclude by discussing some of the implications that we believe flow from this effort—some of which will provide the direction for our ongoing work.

First, our interest in questions of interpretive validity suggests to us the need to create a format for synthesizing the interpretations recorded on the Worksheets in order that more of the richness and complexity of the narrative can be included, while at the same time allowing for a comparison of both different narratives and different interpretations of the same narrative. We are exploring the idea that readers would write a "narrative paragraph" summarizing a given interview, the construction of which might be guided by a set of questions that would be both theoretically derived, and informed by our experience in discovering what questions facilitate "better" (i.e., more valid) interpretations.

A second implication is related to this issue. As we have indicated, it is in practice, and in dialogue, that we make judgments about valid and invalid interpretations. One way for us to further develop our methodology is to reflect on that practice itself by, for example, taping our conference discussions about individual interviews. This would allow us to make our validity *criteria* not only more explicit, but also to subject them to the same kind of scrutiny to which we subject our *interpretations*.[9]

A third implication of this method, as we have argued, is that it allows us to avoid the confining and confusing dualities of traditional theory and research on moral development. Thus, for example, we have tried to avoid the rigid opposition of egoism to altruism, thought to feeling, and justice to care. In addition, we believe that this method allows us to avoid the traditional distinction between moral judgment and moral action.

When we first began interviewing people about their real-life moral conflicts, we obtained more information about how interviewees reasoned about their conflicts than we did about the unfolding narrative of the conflict itself. We found those interviews to be long on interviewees' interpretations but short on the descriptions of the events they were interpreting. In turn, we found it difficult to build interpretations that we could connect to the interviewees' real-life experience. It was as though we had asked the interviewee to perform a monologue, with only very lightly sketched supporting characters, and very little information about what they, or any one else, actually *did*.

Consequently, we redesigned our interview questions (see Table 1). We now ask interviewees to be more specific about the situation in which they experienced themselves in conflict and the actions they took when faced with that situation. In short, we have asked our interviewees to become more elaborate storytellers—to draw richer portraits of both themselves and the other characters in the conflict and—this is crucial—to recount *actual dialogue* from the situation. In a sense we are asking interviewees to *reenact* their conflict in the interview setting.

This has led us to a number of important insights regarding the nature of moral action. First, the stories and dialogues we have obtained vividly illustrate that very few people face or solve moral conflicts in a vacuum. Rather, the person appears to function in an everyday, ongoing context of relationships.

Second, moral action and interaction is much more complex than it has been portrayed in the literature on moral judgment and moral action (see, for example, Kohlberg 1984). We find that people act in at least two contexts that are crucial to our understanding of their moral conflicts, and hence to our interpretation of their moral voice. One is an information-gathering context— moral voice is often revealed by what people feel they need to know from others to solve a conflict and how they go about obtaining that information.

The other is the context in which people implement their decisions in the face of a moral conflict. Both contexts involve a complex series of actions. At times we find that the dialogues people have with themselves and with each other are highly skilled, yet paradoxical and contradictory. For example, people facing difficult, complex moral choices often act in ways that produce the very consequences they wished to avoid in the first place (Argyris 1987).

These findings challenge us to create frameworks that can be used to describe the complex, frequently paradoxical and ironic, nature of moral action. They also challenge us to produce knowledge that is of use to other human beings, not only in generating new insight, but also in helping people to *act* differently. For, as John Macmurray (1957) argues, "we should substitute the 'I do' for the 'I think' as our starting-point and centre of reference; and do our thinking from the standpoint of action" (p. 84).

Thus, in the last analysis, our hope for this method is that it enables and facilitates research that does not sacrifice complexity to duality, usefulness to precision, and action to judgment.

CHAPTER 6

Comprehensive Process Analysis: Understanding the Change Process in Significant Therapy Events

ROBERT ELLIOTT[1]

The analysis of significant psychotherapy events is difficult but exciting work. Moments in therapy that clients point to as helpful or important are rarely exactly what therapists expect and are sometimes quite surprising. Understanding even a single event in therapy can be as complex as surveying an entire river, first mapping its diverse tributaries (prior factors in and out of therapy); then following its sometimes circuitous windings or disappearances underground (indirect and covert processes); and finally evaluating its affect on the land it flows through and the sea it eventually reaches (immediate impacts and treatment outcome). For such a research task, a natural-history approach emphasizing discovery and description must certainly be the best way to begin.

Significant therapy events consist of sequences of client and therapist actions which facilitate specific psychological impacts in clients. For example, if a client requests help in understanding something about self and the therapist offers an interpretation involving the client's core conflicts, delivered in a warm, collaborative manner, the client may experience helpful insight into self (Elliott 1984). The existence of such key, critical or significant events in psychotherapy has been documented by a variety of researchers and scholars (e.g., Elliott, James, Reimschuessel & Sack 1985; Kelman 1969; Mahrer & Nadler 1986) and is at the heart of the "Events Paradigm" for psychotherapy research, illustrated by this chapter, the work of Rice and Greenberg (1984), and others (e.g., Sampson & Weiss 1986).

Psychotherapy process research is a field of investigation whose twin goals are (a) theoretical understanding of effective processes in psychotherapy (e.g., Frank 1974, Goldfried 1982), and (b) applied knowledge for guiding the actions of practicing psychotherapists (Elliott 1983a, Orlinsky & Howard 1978). Research focusing on significant change events can facilitate both of these goals. Whatever change processes operate within therapy are likely to appear in "purer" form during significant therapy events. Further, studying significant events can yield practical information useful to therapists for fostering specific types of helpful events and avoiding or ameliorating specific types of hindering events; this information is beginning to provide a set of "roadmaps" showing ideal and alternate routes as well as dead ends and road hazards (cf. Rice & Greenberg 1984).

Approaches to the study of significant therapy events vary in the degree to which they emphasize theory-testing vs. discovery. Psychoanalytic events researchers (e.g., Sampson & Weiss 1986) represent the more traditional confirmatory end of the continuum. Rice and Greenberg's (1984) Task Analytic approach occupies a middle, "rational-empirical" position, while the Comprehensive Process Analysis method described here represents the qualitative, discovery-oriented end of the scale.

Having given some background on the study of significant therapy events, I will next present a personal account of the origin of Comprehensive Process Analysis, using this to make a case for the greater use of discovery-oriented research methods by psychotherapy researchers. This will be followed by a description of the general principles and steps used in CPA, along with examples from a study of significant events in which clients' self-awareness was enhanced.

A Personal Account of the Development of Comprehensive Process Analysis

Comprehensive Process Analysis did not emerge directly from either the sociological Grounded Theory tradition (Glaser & Strauss 1967, Taylor & Bogdan 1984) or the philosophical Interpretive-Hermeneutical traditions of qualitative phenomenological research, (Giorgi 1983, Packer 1985, Wertz 1983) although it does reflect their influence. Therefore, a brief account of its context seems in order.

In all my therapy research, I have relied on a phenomenological (in the American, small "p," sense) research method, tape-assisted recall (Interpersonal Process Recall, Kagan 1975; Elliott 1986). In this procedure, the client listens to a tape of his or her therapy session and is asked to rate or describe experiences that occurred at particular moments. Since I had been trained in traditional quantitative methods, in my early work I attempted to predict client experiences of being helped from ratings of therapist in-session behavior.

However, over the course of a series of studies using increasingly sophisticated statistical methods, my coworkers and I failed to generate any clinically or theoretically meaningful results. After I had first failed to find useful results with single types of therapist behavior (Elliott, Barker, Caskey & Pistrang 1982), I attempted to measure the therapeutic process in as thorough and complete a fashion as possible, resulting in an earlier quantitative version of Comprehensive Process Analysis (Elliott 1983b, 1984). This culminated in a study (Elliott, Cline & Shulman 1983) in which some 40 client and therapist process variables were measured immediately prior to, during and following significant events; these ratings were then subjected to a range of multivariate analyses. This investigation also failed to produce any clinically meaningful results.

In contrast, it became clear to me that, whenever in the course of my quantitative analyses, I had immersed myself clinically in particular significant therapy events, I had gained a much richer understanding of what had brought change about (e.g., Elliott 1983b, 1984; Elliott, Barker et al. 1982).

Based on this experience, I felt compelled to develop a systematic qualitative method for analyzing significant therapy events. Starting from Labov and Fanshel's (1977) method of textual expansion, and logical distinctions (a) among content, action and stylistic variables (Russell & Stiles 1979) and (b) among context, intervention and impact (cf. Rice & Greenberg 1984) in therapy process research, I began developing a heuristic framework whose purpose was to sensitize qualitative observers to the range of possible factors that might be important in understanding significant therapy events. The rubrics of the framework gradually emerged between 1982 and 1985 in the course of analyzing four sets of significant therapy events. At the same time, the other aspects of the procedure (e.g., methods for combining qualitative judgments) evolved into the systematic research strategy described here.

As I sought to understand why my quantitative investigations seemed so unproductive, I realized my methods had forced me to make a number of simplifying assumptions that disregarded the natural complexity of therapy. Pursuing this farther, I assembled a set of seven common simplifying assumptions typically found in therapy process research. In Table 1, these are contrasted with a set of clinically obvious facts about the complex nature of psychotherapeutic process.

The Potential of Discovery-Oriented Research. Greater clinical relevance is likely to result from therapy research that corresponds more closely to the qualitative clinical approach of skilled practitioners. This approach consists of close attention to what is happening between client and therapist; careful focus on the perceptual worlds of therapist and client; and integration of complex sets of information (cf. Elliott 1983a). Historically, the most clinically useful therapy research has evolved from qualitative exploration of therapy process and has developed theory and measures in a grounded fashion (e.g., Luborsky 1976, Rice & Greenberg 1984, Rogers 1957).

Table 1

Contrasting Assumptions and Properties of Therapy Events

Common Simplifying Assumption	*Property of Therapy Events*
1. All events are equally important; therefore, events may be sampled randomly or averaged (=equal weighting of events).	1. Some therapy events are more important than others (=significant events).
2. Ratings of therapy events are more valid if done out of context or rated in random order (=context independence).	2. Therapy events take their meaning from the contexts in which they are imbedded (=context dependence).
3. Descriptions of therapy process are more valid if rated by trained, objective raters (=objective measurement).	3. The effects of therapeutic events are mediated through the perceptions of their recipient-client (phenomenological measurement).
4. Single or simple combinations of variables are adequate for describing therapy process (=simple main effects).	4. Therapeutic events consist of complex configurations of contextual and process features (=interaction effects).
5. The same process variables can be applied usefully to all types of therapy event (=uniformity).	5. Different sets of contextual and process features are relevant to different types of therapy or therapeutic task (=specificity).
6. Therapy events can be classified as containing only one type of action or impact (=nominal scale measurement).	6. Therapy events usually carry multiple actions and impacts (=dimensional measurement).
7. Process is related to outcome in a linear unidirectional fashion (dose-effect curve: "drug metaphor").	7. Process variables have optimal levels; process and outcome interact (curvilinear, bidirectional effects).
8. Associations between process and impact/outcome reflect direct causal links which are stable over time (=directness, stability).	8. Links between process and impact/outcome involve complex sequential processes; impacts are often unexpected or evolve over time (=mediation, delayed effects).

The Comprehensive Process Analysis method presented in this chapter is an attempt to strike a balance between clinical understanding and methodological rigor. Premature reliance on over-quantified, confirmatory research strategies has forced therapy process research beyond its data base, reducing its clinical and scientific usefulness. What we need is more description of the change process in therapy, of what factors contribute to this process, and of how these factors and processes unfold. Description is an exploratory research task, which calls for more extensive use of open-ended, qualitative research methods. At the same time, quantitative research methods may be used to probe such specific questions ("hypotheses") as the possibility of observer bias or the generalizability of results to other events.

General Principles of Comprehensive Process Analysis

Comprehensive Process Analysis attempts to identify three aspects of significant therapy events: (a) the *contributing factors* involved in significant change events (e.g., good working alliance, therapist interpretation); (b) the observed and experienced *impacts* of significant events (e.g., self-exploration; insight); and (c) the *sequence* of contributing factors and impacts (the "pathway"). The Comprehensive Process Analysis method is best introduced by describing the six operating principles on which it is based.

1. Focus on Specific Classes of Change Event. The process of psychotherapy is too complex and its events too heterogeneous to be meaningfully combined for analysis. In contrast to the simplification strategies typically used in other forms of therapy process research (see Table 1; cf. Bordin 1974), Rice and Greenberg (1984) recommend a different way of making process research manageable: focusing investigations on specific, well-defined classes of change event (e.g., resolution of intrapsychic conflicts using the Two-Chair technique).

However, this strategy of working with clearly defined classes raises the tactical issue of how significant events should be classified. If events are too dissimilar, clinically meaningful commonalities are unlikely to emerge. There are three useful bases for classifying significant events. First, events can be classified by the therapeutic *task* presented by the client (e.g., clarify a problematic, unclear felt sense, Gendlin 1978). Second, events can be classified on the basis of therapist *technique* (e.g., transference interpretation; Luborsky et al. 1979). Third, events can be classified on the basis of the type of *impact* the event had on the client (e.g., insight, feeling understood; Elliott et al. 1985). It may also be useful to combine these classification criteria (e.g., interpretations leading to client insight).

Table 2

Framework for Comprehensive Process Analysis (1986)

I. *Expansion of implicit and explicit propositions in event:* (What is said "between the lines," including key propositions in event and derived by client.)

II. *Contextual Factors:*

A. *Background* (Relevant features of client and therapist which preceded and were brought to treatment, including Client Basic Interpersonal Conflicts, Client Style/Symptoms, Client Situation, Therapist Personal Characteristics, Therapist Treatment Principles.)

B. *Presession Context* (Important events that have occurred since treatment began, in or out of treatment, including Extratherapy Events, Previous Sessions.)

C. *Session Context* (Important events or features of the session in which the significant event occurs, including Client and Therapist Tasks, Alliance, Relevant Events.

D. *Episode Context* (What has been happening in the current episode leading up to the event, including Client and Therapist Tasks, Relevant Events, Local Cue.)

III. *Event Factors:* (Characteristics of the client and therapist responses within the event that explain its significance.)

A. *Action* (Tasks and response modes within the event)

B. *Content* (What is being talked *about* that is relevant to the impact.)

C. *Style/State* (E.g., friendly, long, vivid.)

D. *Quality* (Extent to which client and therapist are working skillfully or well at the relevant therapeutic tasks.)

IV. *Impact on Client:*

A. *Process Impact Pathway* (The sequence of observable responses by client and therapist during and immediately following the event.)

B. *Client Experience Pathway* (The sequence of internal experienced responses by the client during and immediately following the event.)

C. *Delayed Impact of Event* (Subsequent therapeutic impacts and changes in client apparently due to Event.)

D. *Effectiveness of Event* (Quantitative measures bearing on the effectiveness of the Event, including Immediate Impact [within session], Session Outcome, Delayed Effectiveness [e.g., one-month follow-up], Treatment Outcome.)

---

2. Comprehensive Framework. In analyzing events, observers are guided by an outline of potential contributing factors and impacts. The outline is actually a list of sensitizing topics whose purpose is to remind observers to consider specific issues (e.g., Is some aspect of the client's life situation relevant to understanding this event?). This outline represents a "generic" theory or framework of types of factors that may figure in specific significant events (cf. Orlinsky & Howard 1987). The CPA framework is grounded in previous analyses of significant events but contains useful distinctions drawn from the work of Kiesler (1973), Labov and Fanshel (1977), Luborsky, Crits-Christoph, and Mellon (1986), Orlinsky and Howard (1978), and Russell and Stiles (1979). While the method does reflect these influences, its organizing and sensitizing concepts were not imposed on the data but were added as they became necessary in order to understand particular significant events.

The CPA framework is summarized in Table 2 and consists of four major sections. First is the expansion of the important explicit and implicit meanings in the event (see below). The second, most complex, section covers the context of the event. Factors which may have possibly contributed to the event and its impact are described and organized into the four levels of Background, Presession Context, Session Context, and Episode Context, with numerous subheadings within each.

Next come the relevant characteristics of the identified significant event itself, organized by person (client, therapist) and aspect of process (action, content, style/state, and quality; see Russell & Stiles 1979, Elliott 1984). Thus, the effects of an event are likely to reflect the contributions of both client and therapist. They may also derive from what is said (content), what is done (action or task), how it is said or done (style/state) or how well (i.e., skillfully) it is done.

Finally, the impact of the event is organized into three aspects: Process Impact (observable), Experienced Impact, and Effectiveness (quantitative). While the first three sections of the framework involve the factors that contributed to the event's importance for the client, the impact section deals with (a) how change unfolds from the significant event, and (b) what additional evidence is available to evaluate the clinical significance of the event.

3. Multiple Qualitative Observers. Other qualitative researchers (Taylor & Bogdan 1984, Huberman & Miles 1983) have recommended using more than one observer or analyst. Relying on a single qualitative observer raises issues of generalizability to other observers. For example, a particular observer may miss an important contributing factor while making several unwarranted inferences elsewhere in her analysis. When confronted with the analyses of three other observers, she may readily see both the omission and the inferences as "errors" (i.e., not reflective of the data).

CPA uses groups of three to five qualitative observers. The multiple observers resemble the groups of quantitative raters used in traditional therapy process analysis, except that their observations are not constrained by a set of a priori categories or rating scales; nor are their observations pooled statistically by averaging or "two-of-three" rules. Qualitative observers should have clinical experience and training, although carefully selected advanced undergraduates and pre-internship graduate students have also been used successfully. While it is desirable to use observers with differing backgrounds and orientations to increase generalizability, it is also important to include observers familiar both with the treatment approach used in the events and with the cultural and language community of client and therapist. Observers work independently to develop initial analyses of each unit, then meet together as a group to develop a consensual version. (This procedure is described below.)

4. Verification of Clinical Significance of Events. Significant events can be identified using a variety of methods (see below); each method involves evaluating therapy process by means of imperfect measures. The use of imperfect methods creates the need to verify the significance of events by asking a series of questions about them. For example, do Patient Experiencing ratings (Klein, Mathieu-Coughlan & Kiesler 1986) show positive shifts during or following the event? Do session ratings, weekly behavior change measures, or outcome data indicate that something important has happened in the session or treatment? The verification of significant events by using other criteria supports the claim that the events under analysis are what they purport to be—a collection of significant events. Note that since specific "hypotheses" are implicit in these questions, quantification is appropriate in this part of the analysis; however, quantitative data are treated qualitatively, as potential signs of significance.

5. Recording and Testing Expectations. Comprehensive Process Analysis, as a discovery-oriented approach to understanding significant therapy events, is concerned with letting the data "speak for themselves." The central analyses of contributing factors and impacts are not carried out in order to test specific hypotheses. Nevertheless, the danger remains that, in spite of conscious attempts to "bracket" their expectations for the data, the observers' implicit assumptions or preunderstandings may "contaminate" the results. Therefore, in CPA, it is important that observer expectations be assessed and later compared to the actual findings. (This process will be detailed later.)

6. Construction of Tentative Process Models or "Pathways." At each stage in the process, observers tie themes together into process models or sequential "pathways." Models of individual events are first constructed. Common themes are then used to construct higher-order models describing the collection of similar events. It is also possible to derive themes that distinguish between different subtypes of events (e.g., insight events in Cognitive vs. Interpersonal therapies). Higher-order models provide tentative clinical "microtheories" (Rice & Greenberg 1984) for further investigation.

Stages in Comprehensive Process Analysis

The operating principles presented for Comprehensive Process Analysis are implemented through a series of stages, beginning with the collection of suitable events for analysis and ending with the generation of tentative process models or microtheories for testing with comparable collections. The presentation will be divided into four sections: collecting events, analyzing single events, analyzing collections of events, and recording and evaluating observer expectations. The discussion will be illustrated with data from a study of "awareness events" (Elliott, Underwood, Cislo & Sack 1985).

1. Collecting Significant Events

Comprehensive Process Analysis requires a collection of 6-10 similar significant therapy events and descriptive information. As mentioned earlier, a number of alternatives are available for identifying significant events. However, an important issue not touched on earlier is the size of the events identified. This varies widely, from single therapist interventions to 15-40 minute segments of therapy sessions.[2] The awareness events (Elliott Underwood et al., 1985), to be used as a running example in this chapter, are each a single therapist speaking turn, for example,

Ther.: Yeah, The truth is [client's name], you are really, you are left out of a lot of [lover's name]'s life.

In the process of collecting significant events, it is also important to obtain certain other data, in order to facilitate the CPA. These data include demographic background information on client and therapist (e.g., age, orientation, presenting problem); self-report data from client or therapist especially on the impact the event had on the client); and outcome data on the effectiveness of the therapy session (and, if possible, on the outcome of the treatment as a whole).

In the study of awareness events, eight significant therapist interventions involving increased client awareness were selected from 216 responses randomly sampled and rated from 16 sessions of ongoing therapy (each with a different client-therapist pair). Using tape-assisted recall, clients gave 35 therapist responses the highest possible helpfulness ratings ("extremely" helpful). Client's free-response descriptions of the therapeutic impacts of these events were content analyzed (Elliott, James et al. 1985), resulting in eight events with a predominant impact on awareness.

Table 3

Awareness Event Transcript

T1: 'Hh It's being confronted, r- really h (1.5) with the reality 'h (that) [lover] has a
wi*fe*:, 'h with whom he ((said deliberately:)) *does these things* (.5)

C1: *De*finitely!, because when [lover] came in and saw I was crying, I (T: mhm) said,
"*What* am I *doing* here?" (T: mhm) 'n he said, "Well, (1.5) we're being *friends*, we're
friends, we're keeping each other *com*pany." (T: mhm) 'n I said, "But rea:lly, what
am I doing ·here·" (T:Mhm) 'n I told him I had the feeling I didn't used to have
that this was [lover's wife's] (house), *her* place, 'h (1.0), his home was, his and, share
it with *he:r,* I just didn't feel *pa:rt* of it, as I used to feel, 'h ((sniff)) and I said, "I
used to feel things would *some*how work out 'h=Now I just don't think they *will*
the way I want them to." and, "What are we *doing* here?" 'hh (1.6) I told him I just
couldn't *do* it anymore. (3.8) Then another customer came in and they were talking
Ge:rman, and I felt *rea:lly* left out. hh 'hh (4.0) She, was taking a trip and (T:
mhm) she was a stranger and they discovered they both ca(h)me from Ge(h)ermany,
and they started talking German. =It reminded me of [lover] talking with his wife
on the phone in Ger//man ((sniff)) so-

T2: ·Yeah·, the truth] is, [client's name], you are really, you are left out of a lot of
[lover's] life. (.5)

C2: Then I told him, "You know, I'm *tired* of little bits and *pieces*= It isn't *enough.*" 'h
(1.0) While he was talking Ge(heh)rma(h)n in the other part of the store, I picked
up my stuff and I just *left* 'hh (1.5), and I called him up, and I said, h "I just don't
think (that) there's any, good reason to suffer like this anymore, and this is *about*
how I felt toward the end of my *ma*(h)rriage. 'h This is *ter*rible" an' I said, "It isn't
like my marriage because there was a lot of *lo:ve* in this 'hh But I'm beginning to
feel, uhh, ((voice wavers:)) trapped and hopeless." 'hh So: (1.5) t It was really
strange= I went to school, saw my patient. (1.0) He was getting along *fine.* 'hh I got
a *lot* of positive feeling about *all* of my work in, in partials an' he, he was just
de*light*ed with his an' he was wearing it all the time an' it was *work*ing 'hh (T: mm)
an' he said, "You know, I- I started brushing my *teeth*" . . .

Note: Transcription symbols from Sacks, Schegloff & Jefferson 1974) are as follows:
"H" "h", out-breaths; " 'Hh", " 'h", in-breaths; ":" prolongation of sound; "·   ·" softer than
expected; "(T: Mhm)" backchannel utterances; "(   )" or e.g., "(house)", inaudible or
unclear; "=" absence of expected pause ("latching"); "(he)", "(h)", laughter within a word;
"//" "]" beginning and end of interruption; "t", tongue click; numbers in parentheses are
timings of internal and interresponse pauses; double parentheses are used for anno-
tations: "((said deliberately:))"

2. Analysis of Single Events

The heart of Comprehensive Process Analysis is the thorough analysis of single events, a process that involves five steps:

a. Transcription of Event. The analysis of each event begins with the transcription of the significant event, including its episode context. The transcribed segment should reflect the natural episode structure of the session (i.e., coincide with major changes of topic or task); it should also include enough client talk to allow meaningful "pre-post" or "beginning-to-end" comparisons of how well the client is working. Transcripts should be as exact and detailed as possible. The transcription conventions developed for Conversational Analysis (Sacks, Schegloff, & Jefferson 1974) are useful because of their precision. Table 3 contains a transcript from the study of awareness events.

b. Process Notes. Observers begin their analysis by taking process notes on the entire session in which the event occurs. Process notes include major therapist and client statements and repeating client and therapist themes. Client themes typically involve interpersonal wishes and fears (e.g., seeks belonging, fear rejection; see Luborsky et al. 1986); therapist themes are generally treatment principles e.g., expression of feelings is therapeutic; cf. Labov & Fanshel 1977). Observers also identify and demarcate the major naturally occurring conversational episodes in the session. Listening to the entire session is important because what happens after the significant event often reveals further impacts of the event as well as its implicit meanings.

c. Expansion of Meanings in Event. Each observer next focuses on the event itself by developing an account of (a) what client or therapist were "really" saying and (b) the key meanings (propositions, ideas) the client derived from the event.

Like all conversation, therapeutic discourse contains both explicit statements and implicit meanings. The observer must use the contextual information he or she has obtained from listening to the entire session to determine what is being implied or said "between the lines. " This process is referred to as "expansion" (Labov & Fanshel 1977) and includes supplying taken-for-granted knowledge or beliefs, references to previously described or shared events, omitted logical steps in chains of reasoning, and what client and therapist are each indirectly suggesting to the other via stylistic cues. The result of performing an expansion is a series of *propositions* or logical statements.

The same method of analysis can be carried out on client accounts of the key ideas derived from the event. Such client descriptions may be offered spontaneously in the event, described later in the session, elicited on a post-session questionnaire (Llewelyn, in press), or assessed using an Interpersonal Process Recall method (Elliott & Shapiro, in press). Observers state the key meanings as a series of propositions.

Observers each do their own expansions, then meet to develop a consensual version. (See below for a discussion of the consensualizing process.) The agreed-upon expansion provides the basis for the qualitative judgments of possible contributing factors. For example, a properly done expansion makes the speaker's speech acts apparent. In the awareness event we have been using as an example, the pivotal therapist response consisted of:

"Yeah, The truth is [client's name], you are really, you are left out of a lot of [lover's name]'s life.

The following expansion was developed for this response:

1. I agree with what you're saying about being left out of L.'s life. (=agreement)
2. You have told me many things about your relationship with L., both previously and just now. (=implied reflection)
3. And all of the things you've told me point to the fact that you are left out of most aspects of L.'s life. (=reflection)

In addition, based on all the available data, the observers agreed that the key ideas derived by the client were:

1. I really am left out of L.'s life; and
2. That is painful

d. *Draft "Pathways" of Important Contributing Factors and Client Impacts.* In the next step, each observer applies the outline of possible contributing factors and client impacts (see Table 2) to the event, using transcript, tape, process notes and self-report data. In describing relevant elements in the pathway, observers must justify how the element helps explain the event. This is done by having observers specify what a contributing factor is believed to influence further down the pathway. The sequence of contributing factors, processes, and experiences comprises the event "pathway." (See below for an example.) Several observers may also rate the event on several quantitative process variables (e.g., therapist response modes, client experiencing). Observers make copies of their draft pathways for each other.

e. *Consensual Pathways.* Next, the observers meet to agree upon a single version of the expansion of the event and its pathway. The consensualizing process is time-consuming and may require several meetings for each event; it is helpful to have observers work between meetings to integrate elements from each other's pathways. Consensualizing is best achieved by analyzing one part of the pathway at a time (i.e., by agreeing on client conflicts, then going on to client style, etc.). Observers present arguments for and against the importance of particular elements in order to resolve disagreements. In rare instances where disagreements cannot be completely resolved, the judgment of the majority of observers is used. Two aspects that require consensualizing: (a) which specific elements should be included, and (b) how these elements should be worded or labeled. It is helpful to agree on a factor before developing the proper wording. (This also works with expansions.) A useful test for deciding to include an element in the pathway is provided by the following three criteria: (a) whether it is present or true of the event; (b) whether it is nonredundant with other elements; and (c) whether it appears to be relevant or important in bringing about or explaining the event or its impact.

For example, in their initial pathways for the awareness event given above, the four observers described the therapist's task for the pivotal response as follows:

Dave: 1. Focus C. on source of distress
        2. Move C. toward resolving that source

Linda: 1. Reinforce C.'s line of thinking about having no major part in L.'s life

Laura: 1. Verify C's perception that she is left out

Robert: 1. Confront C. with feeling of being left out
        2. Evoke C. feelings

The following is a reconstruction of how these six possible themes were consensualized: First, the observers agreed that two of the initial themes were in fact *not present* in the pivotal therapist response: the response was not intended to move the client toward problem solution (Dave, theme 2), nor specifically to evoke the client's already stirred-up feelings (Robert, theme 2). In addition, they agreed that the themes of verifying or reinforcing the client's views (Linda, theme 1; Laura, theme 1) were present but only in a minor way (in "Yeah" with which the therapist began her response), and therefore *not relevant* to the event's impact. Finally, the two themes of focusing or confronting the client (Dave, theme 1; Robert, theme 1) were present but really referred to the same thing (i.e., were *redundant* with each other). Having agreed upon the content of the theme, a consensus on its exact wording had to be developed. The verb "confront" was chosen over "focus" because of its consistency with the psychodynamic treatment model used by the therapist; however, the observers felt it was important to specify the sense in which the word "confront" was being used here, so they added a parenthetical "get client to look at." Finally, "feelings of being left out" seemed more precise than the alternate wording "the source of the distress"; they also connected to the client conflict theme higher up in the pathway ("Seeks belonging, fears rejection"). Thus, the consensus for the therapist event task element of the pathway was:

Confront C. with (get C. to look at) feelings of being left out.

The result of the preceding steps is a complete analysis of an individual significant event following the outline presented in Table 2. The consensual pathway for our event (not presented due to space limitations) contained thirty-five qualitative and ten quantitative elements. The large number and complexity of the relationships among the elements in pathways such as this make it difficult to grasp their flow; however, one can readily follow particular threads (called "subpathways"). For example,

Background: Client Conflict: "Seeks belonging, fears rejection",

is relevant to,

Presession: "Client has recently had a painful interaction with L,"

because this presession life event was a playing out of the conflict. This recent painful life event in turn led to,

Session: Therapist task: "Get client to confront avoided feelings regarding L,"

and,

Episode: Client task: "Explore painful interaction."

Then, leading up to the significant event, the client pursues her episode task with:

Event: "Client describes visit to L. and feeling left out,"

which leads to the immediate stimulus for the pivotal therapist utterance:

Local Cue: "Client describes being reminded of being left out of L's life by L's speaking to someone else in a foreign language.

The task of the therapist's response (confront client) and its content (current relationship as example of basic conflict) account in part for the emotional pain that the client feels immediately following this response (Experienced Impact) and the fact that she later moves to a description of a positive work experience (Process Impact). On the other hand, by picking up another thread, we can see that the strength of the therapeutic alliance (Session Context) and therapist's style in the event (expert, warm) enable the client to transmute her pain into fruitful exploration (Process Impact) and self-awareness (Experienced Impact).

3. Analysis of Collections of Significant Events

The process described above is applied to all events in the collection, resulting in a complete set of event pathways. The next stage in Comprehensive Process Analysis centers on an analysis of themes similar to that used in grounded theory. This analysis proceeds in four steps:

a. Identification of Possible Themes. Themes are identified separately for each section of the pathways (i.e., each heading in the CPA framework; e.g., episode task). Each observer studies the consensual themes listed under a given heading in the pathways for all events in the collection. The observers describe any themes they see in at least two events, using the constant comparative method (Glaser & Strauss 1967).

b. Consensual Themes. Observers then meet to develop a consensus on the themes generated for each part of the pathway. This process resembles that used to develop consensual pathways for individual events. That is, themes generated by all observers are evaluated for correspondence to the data and nonredundancy; after agreeing on the content of the themes, their wording is worked out. In addition, at this point observers also determine whether each event fits each theme: these judgments are consensualized and used to assess the rate of occurrence of the theme in the collection. For example, the therapist event tasks (and eventual scoring for themes) for each of the eight awareness events studied were as follows:

Event 1: Keep C. talking productively (consensual theme 1)
Event 2: Support C. (residual: theme only occurred once)
Event 3: Repair misunderstanding (residual)
Foster examination of self-criticism (theme 1)
Event 4: Probe uncomfortable feelings (theme 1)
Event 5: Get C. to confront other (theme 2)
Disclaim responsibility for (previous) advisement (residual)
Event 6: Educate C (re: cost of openness) (residual)
Support C. action (openness) (theme 2)
Event 7: Refocus C. on exploration of feelings (theme 1)
Encourage expression of feelings (theme 1)
Event 8: Confront C. with (get C. to look at) feelings (being left out) (theme 1)

The consensual themes that occurred in at least two events were identified and labeled as follows:

1. Facilitate exploration/expression of feelings, conflicts (5 out of 8 events)
2. Get client to take some action (2/8)

In the study of awareness events, roughly ninety consensual themes were identified. Twenty-seven of these appeared in at least three-quarters of the units. These may be thought of as the predominant or "general" themes for the awareness events represented in the collection. (Space limitations prevent listing them, but some are described below.)

c. Evaluation of Clinical Significance of Events. The last general heading in the CPA framework deals with the clinical significance or effectiveness of the event as assessed by variety of measures. The available effectiveness data for the awareness events indicates the following: (a) Clients also felt moderately or greatly understood and cognitively stimulated by them, but often also felt worse (client perceptions of event). (b) Therapists typically saw these events as not at all or only slightly helpful or cognitively stimulating to clients, and often felt they made the client feel worse, although they did feel at least moderate empathy for the client (therapist perceptions of event). (c) Client Experiencing ratings following the awareness events showed limited disclosure of feelings, indicating either a decrease or no change (impact on client process). (d) Clients rated the sessions in which these events occurred between moderately and greatly helpful, while therapists rated the sessions as slightly to moderately helpful (session outcome).

By these criteria, the awareness events examined were rather circumscribed in their clinical significance. Thus, the events studied appeared not to be as strongly therapeutic as the insight events studied by Elliott (1984) using an earlier, more quantitative form of CPA. Perhaps the important thing is that clients found them helpful at all, given how painful they were. In the event presented earlier as an example, the client said

> Those things [that my therapist says] stick in my mind and they kind of wrench me into reality, when I'm willing for it, although it hurts. It makes me feel terrible, but at the same time it's constructive, . . . so you could also feel better while you're feeling sad.

These events document the existence of an important clinical phenomenon—clients sharing the therapist belief that painful emotional experiencing can be therapeutic.

d. Integration of Themes into Models. The final step in the CPA of a collection of significant events is organizing the themes into pathways or models of how a given type of event might unfold. Because of the complexity and number of themes it is impossible to include all in a single model. There are three ways of reducing this complexity.

General Models. First, one can set stringent standards for which themes to include in the model, allowing only themes that characterize all or almost all of the events. The general model for awareness events shows that contextual factors—especially what the client brings to therapy—are more important than features of the event itself.

Thematic Models. Second, one can select elements related to a particular theme for the model. An example of a thematic model is given in Figure 1, which depicts the "task subpathway" in awareness events. This model centers on the elements which influenced and were influenced by the predominant client and therapist tasks evident in awareness events. It illustrates the importance of client and therapist tasks in significant events (cf. Rice & Greenberg 1984) and the way in which tasks form a bridge between background characteristics (e.g., therapist psychodynamic orientation) and the impacts significant events have on clients (e.g., in-session self-exploration and avoidance).

Micromodels of Alternative Paths. Third, one can focus on a small section of the pathway in order to map the alternate paths the events suggest are possible. A useful section of pathway to model in this way is the transition between the type of therapist speech act involved in key therapist responses and the immediate therapeutic impacts reported or displayed by the client. Figure 2 shows how awareness events are linked to a variety of therapist speech acts, establishing the fact that even advisement and acknowledgement

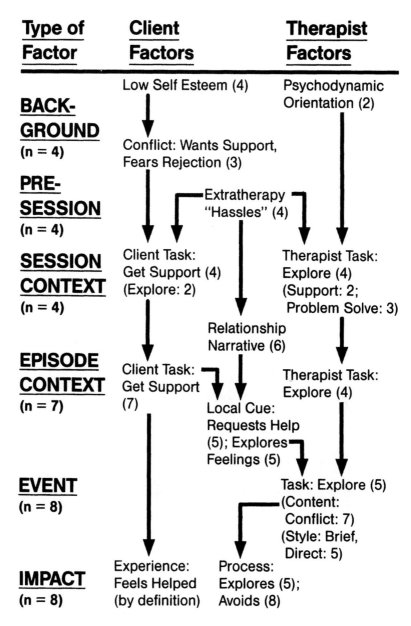

Type of Factor	Client Factors	Therapist Factors

BACK-GROUND (n = 4)

Low Self Esteem (4)

Psychodynamic Orientation (2)

Conflict: Wants Support, Fears Rejection (3)

PRE-SESSION (n = 4)

Extratherapy "Hassles" (4)

SESSION CONTEXT (n = 4)

Client Task: Get Support (4) (Explore: 2)

Therapist Task: Explore (4) (Support: 2; Problem Solve: 3)

EPISODE CONTEXT (n = 7)

Relationship Narrative (6)

Client Task: Get Support (7)

Therapist Task: Explore (4)

Local Cue: Requests Help (5); Explores Feelings (5)

EVENT (n = 8)

Task: Explore (5) (Content: Conflict: 7) (Style: Brief, Direct: 5)

IMPACT (n = 8)

Experience: Feels Helped (by definition)

Process: Explores (5); Avoids (8)

Figure 1

Task Subpathway for Awareness Events. Frequencies of themes given in parentheses. Number of units for each section is given in left column. Minor elements or elements not directly relevant to the pathway given in parentheses.

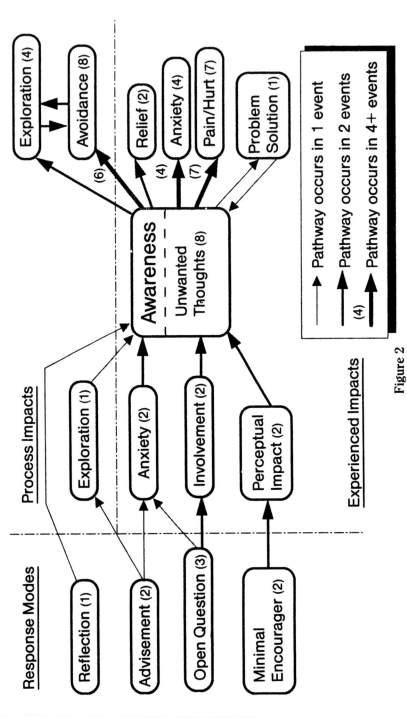

Figure 2

Composite of Response Mode-Impact Pathways. Numbers in parentheses indicate number of events in which element or pathway occurred.

("Uh-huhs") can lead to enhanced self-awareness. The figure also portrays how clients cope with the pain that accompanies the awareness, alternating between exploration and avoidance.

4. *Recording and Evaluating Expectations for Events*

In order to examine the possibility of observer expectancy bias systematically, the following procedure is used: Before beginning analysis of a collection of events, the observers are given a general description of the nature of the events. The observers use the CPA framework to record their expectations regarding the major contributing factors and impacts for events in the collection. Later, at the conclusion of the analysis, the observers rate the obtained themes for the degree to which each was expected. These post-hoc expectancy ratings are used in order to pick up "emergent expectations." Finally, the expectancy ratings are compared to the actual occurrence of themes in the collection and can be used to define expected and unexpected findings, as well as to point to disconfirmed expectations.

In the study of awareness events, 77 themes (effectiveness data themes were excluded from this analysis) were evaluated for the degree to which they were expected. A theme was counted as expected if at least half the observers expected it; it was counted as "obtained" if it was found to be present in at least half the units. These analyses show a modest tendency for expectations to be confirmed by the data. However, a third of the expectations were *not* confirmed, including expectations regarding specific therapist speech acts (e.g., interpretation, reflection) and the mediation of awareness by client involvement and exploration impacts. Further, over a quarter of the themes found to be present had not been expected, including:

Client previous therapy experience

Client divorced

Client session and episode tasks: get support, relief

Therapist session task: support client

Local cue: Client indirectly requests therapist intervention

The presence of unexpected findings makes observer bias less likely as an explanation for the results, both expected and unexpected.

Discussion

Clinical Implications. The methods described in this paper, and similar ones used by Rice & Greenberg (1984), offer the promise of allowing the development of sequential microtheories analogous to the metabolic pathways that are the foundation of modern biochemistry (e.g., the Krebs cycle or the protein synthesis pathways). Formulation of valid, specific "psychotherapeutic pathways" would greatly aid in the "synthesis" of psychological change in therapy. In fact, the analysis of awareness events has directly affected my own practice and supervision of therapy in the following ways: (a) When my main therapeutic task is to foster client awareness of painful experience, I am more likely to allow clients to alternate between avoidance and exploration. (b) Having found that therapist advice-giving is one pathway to client awareness, I have begun to experiment with giving clients advice and then helping them to explore the fears stimulated by contemplating new ways of acting toward others. The results also support the views of dynamic and experiential therapists that the exploration of painful content can be helpful under certain circumstances. The results of the awareness event study offer some hints about these circumstances, the further explication of which is an exciting task for future CPA work.

Methodological Implications. Based on our experience in the awareness-events study, I recommend the following for future Comprehensive Process Analyses: (a) Drawing more than one event from a single session and dyad complicated the analyses by requiring differing numbers of units. I recommend that no more than one event from a particular treatment be used in a given analysis. (b) In order to improve clinical significance, analyses should focus on the most helpful event in a given therapy session, and a wider range of measures of clinical significance should be used for events. (c) The themes obtained in the awareness events study can be used as a set of initial expectations for another collection of awareness events. I am particularly looking forward to comparing these events to awareness events that occur in Experiential Therapy, a treatment that gives central theoretical status to enhancing client awareness.

A point of general importance for therapy-process researchers is the powerful role of contextual factors in significant events. Process researchers should devote greater attention to defining and measuring contextual factors, including general characteristics of client and therapist. The Comprehensive Process Analysis method is one way of doing so. On the other hand, qualitative researchers may find value in the methods described here for using multiple qualitative observers and assessing observer expectations.

CHAPTER 7

Emotions as
Narrative Emplotments

THEODORE R. SARBIN[1]

Introduction

Over the past few years, I have asked more than 30 adults, most of them psychologists, to define the term 'emotion.' After each respondent formulated a definition, I asked him or her to give me an instance, an illustration, of emotion drawn from observation of self or others. Little uniformity characterized the off-the-cuff definitions save for one feature. Almost all the respondents included in their definitions a locus for emotion: *inside the body*. The psychologists in my sample phrased their definitions with the language of psychophysiology, sometimes elegantly. The agreement on bodily locus is not surprising: all of us have been exposed to the writings of several generations of textbook authors who composed chapters on emotion with the vocabulary of psychophysiology. These authors were indebted to the work of earlier exponents of this paradigm, William James and Walter B. Cannon, who, each in his own way, focused research and theory on emotion as internal happenings. An examination of current textbooks shows no break with this tradition.

The responses to the second part of my informal survey covered a large territory of human action. The content of the instances of 'emotion' differed one from another. Most focused on anger, a few on fear, and one on caring.[2] In one respect, however, all instances were alike: they were recounted as narratives without reference to happenings inside the body.

The non-overlapping domains of meaning emerging from this survey are clearly illustrated in the following protocol.

A professor of drama who is also a part-time playwright offered the following definition of emotion: "It is something that I feel inside of me. I know when I'm having an emotion because I feel it." When asked for a concrete illustration, he responded with the following account (slightly edited):

185

I'll tell you about anger. I had written a one-act play for a competition. The play had been accepted and was to be produced at the Somerset Theater. The director had been engaged, the cast selected, and rehearsals were under way. A good deal of the play's action centered around a prop, a life-size bust of Shakespeare. This prop had been ordered three weeks before opening night from a New York supply house. The order-taker at the supply house assured me that the bust would be delivered to my office within ten days. About a week before opening night, I phoned the supply house to inquire about the bust, which had not yet arrived. Several long-distance phone calls later, I learned that the Shakespeare bust, the only one in stock, had been dispatched as promised. I had repeatedly notified the secretaries, mail clerks, and my colleagues to be on the alert for the tardy bust. A great deal of hectic and desperate action followed in an effort to find a substitute bust, without success. The play could not go on without this essential prop—many of the lines and the action centered on the bust of Shakespeare. There was talk of cancelling the show. Two days before the dress rehearsal, inadvertently, I noticed a box behind a wastebasket in the departmental steno pool. It was the long awaited bust. I asked the secretary how long the box had been in the mail room, she said, "About a week", and then as an innocent afterthought, "Oh, is that the box you've been waiting for?" My immediate emotional response was anger, maybe rage. I blew my stack. It was her stupidity and incompetence that angered me.

The observation of interest is the unbridgeable gap between the definition and the exemplification of 'emotion.' The playwright's definition reflects the entrenched position of psychophysiological symbolism in our thought-ways (Averill 1974). The example ignores the implications of the definition, and instead reveals the readiness to emplot (or organize) human actions in narrative form.

This anecdote and the results of my informal survey announce the direction of my essay. First, I attempt to show why reports or measurements of inside-the-body happenings have little utility for understanding the complexities of human action. Second, I advance the argument that for those human events sometimes labeled 'emotions' or 'passions,' the narrative provides a more satisfying and more ecologically valid explanatory model.

To support my choice of the narrative as the basis for interpreting human conduct, I have argued for the wisdom of recognizing that a narratory principle guides thought and action (Sarbin 1986). Any slice of life reveals the operation of the narratory principle. Our dreams are experienced as stories, as dramatic encounters, sometimes interpretable as exemplars of ancient myths. Fantasies and daydreams are constructed along story lines. A close look at the rituals of daily life reveals unvoiced stories. The pageantry of rites of passage and rites of intensification are dramatized narratives. Stories guide the plans we make, the rememberings we construct, even our loving and hating. Making sense of the random movements of small geometric figures on a screen is guided by conventional narrative plots (Michotte 1963/1946, Heider & Simmel 1944). It is reasonable to advance the claim that the narratory principle facilitates survival. In a world of meanings, survival is problematic in the absence of the talent for making up and interpreting stories about interweaving lives.

I advance the thesis that those aspects of human action sometimes identified as 'emotions' can be illuminated through the use of the narratory principle.

Making 'Emotion' Less Ambiguous

The word 'emotion' has become opaque as a result of indifferent and casual use by generations of psychologists and physiologists, not to mention popular writers of advice to the lovelorn. The imagery varies from one person to another, from one theory to another, creating difficulties in communication. A glance at the etymology of emotion tells us that it is derived from a root that signified outer-directed movement, as in mass migrations. Along the way, the term was metaphorically transferred to the outward expression of perceived or imagined internal motions.

In most prevailing theories, psychophysiological symbolism encourages the detachment of phenomena identified as 'emotions' from social contexts. Traditional psychological writings about anger, grief, love, shame, guilt, etc., illicitly import an implication that the events of interest are detachable from the context of action, not unlike discourses on digestion, liver function, or vision. This detachability is traceable in the first instance to the ontological status assigned to such historically treasured substantives as mind, soul, psyche, and consciousness. The readiness to take emotional phenomena out of context can be traced also to the long forgotten reification of an old metaphor: *the body is a container,* and to the extended reification that emotion is a fluid-like substance located in the bodily container. The extended metaphor created the conditions for incorporating Boyle's law into the meaning: the container and its contents are subject to certain vicissitudes under conditions of metaphorical heat and pressure. (Lakoff and Kövecses 1983). Freud, among others, made liberal use of reified metaphors. In fact, he was partly responsible for the reification of a number of nineteenth-century metaphors. Some have attained mythic status, among them, repression, the unconscious, and psychic energy.

In psychophysiological symbolism, emotion is a *happening,* not an intentional *doing.* This fundamental characteristic can be traced to emotion being adopted as a technical term to replace 'passion.' In the literature of the eighteenth and nineteenth centuries (and probably before) the person is a passive victim who suffers the passion—like the passive victim of vapors, miasma, witchcraft, or humoral distemper. The assumption that the person was only a vehicle for bodily or mental happenings facilitated the adoption of the mechanistic credo for the study of human action. This credo supported the search for *causes* of behavior in the somatic machinery or in the psychic apparatus.

The uncritical acceptance of the reified metaphor, "the body is a container" has led to some interesting debates. An exchange in *American Psychologist* between two highly visible psychologists, Richard Lazarus (1984) and Robert Zajonc (1984) is illustrative. Neither questioned the ontological status of emotion—the debate centered on whether emotion was a happening unmediated by cognition (Zajonc's position), or a happening mediated by perception and cognition (Lazarus' position). The arguments put forth by Zajonc led me to infer that emotion, as exemplified by such phenomena as pain and taste preferences, belonged to a category that would include knee-jerks, eye-blinks, sneezes, and the startle pattern. Lazarus' contrary arguments led to the inference that purported 'emotional states' as measured by physiological indicators, facial or bodily movements, and reported fantasies, are influenced by 'cognitive appraisals.' In my judgment, the debate failed to advance our understanding of human behavior because the proponents of the two views were both asking the wrong question: namely, *what is emotion?* Sir Karl Popper cautioned us that such questions are footless. They belong to the discredited methods of the Scholastics whose answers to such questions were couched in increasingly abstract verbalizations.

Interpreting the Nexus Between Action and Emotion

Instead of joining in the futile effort to answer the footless question, what is emotion, it would be more fruitful to begin our inquiry from specific observations. Who are the actors? What is the setting? When did the action take place? What did the actors do or say? What were the features of the ecological setting that instigated or maintained certain actions?[3] In seeking answers to these questions I suppress the academic appetite for abstract generalizations. Instead, I focus on people with proper names or, for illustrative purposes, fictional people.

A case taken from police files is instructive. Albert Jones, a steamfitter, was engaged in a heated quarrel with Donald Miller, a co-worker, over responsibility for a botched-up job. Employing Anglo-Saxon expletives, Miller pointedly insulted Jones with a well-recognized digital gesture. Without hesitation, Jones struck Miller on the head with a fourteen-inch pipe wrench. When Jones subsequently explained his actions to a police officer, he said, "I just felt the anger surging up in me and I exploded."

This little slice of life contains an abundance of text for hermeneutical analysis. Jones had been acculturated to the concept 'insult.' Both he and his antagonist held shared meanings of the insulting words and accompanying gesture. His perception that he was the object of insult called for action to maintain self-respect. (The concept of insult contains in its meaning a challenge to one's self-respect.) It is important to note that at the same time Jones acquired the meaning of insult, he also acquired knowledge about appropriate adversarial response, i.e., that retaliation was an integral part of the concept, and that the initial appropriate conduct was the adoption of an anger role. In the fast-moving scenario, the form of retaliation chosen by Jones was direct assault. The protocol is silent whether Jones entertained attenuated forms of retaliation such as verbal put-down, reciprocal insult, or challenge to a duel.

It is not the case that 'insult' stands alone, or that 'retaliation' stands alone, or that the observations identified as anger are detachable from insult and retaliation. All these features are integral to the emplotment of an anger narrative. They are learned as a unity and perceived as a unity.

Jones' causal attribution is an important feature of the plot. His explanation, "the anger surged up in me and I exploded," is not problematic to adherents of the myth of the passions as represented in the widespread use of psychophysiological symbolism. However, to interpreters committed to a constructivist position, Jones' explanation is problematic. It would be foolish to accept his openly metaphorical description as literal.

The explanation was consistent with a belief common in our culture, namely, that emotions or passions are mechanically triggered, like reflexes, by biological or *unconscious* processes. This entrenched belief served as the premise for Jones' implied claim that the feelings of anger were *happenings*. The origin of this belief is organically related to the reified metaphor to which I have already referred: the body is a container and the fluid-like contents respond to pressure and heat. With this metaphor, Jones could transfigure a dramatic encounter—a complex plot in which he was an agent, a doer, a performer—to 'feelings of anger.' In this transfiguration, Jones assigned causality to a semantically ambiguous internal state, concomitantly removing himself as the causal agent.

The two reference cases, the frustrated playwright and the insulted steamfitter, are concrete instances of the penchant of human beings to account for multi-dimensional human actions by invoking unidimensional internal forces. The steamfitter reduced a dramatic narrative to "feelings of anger." The playwright reversed the order, he accounted for his feelings of anger with a dramatic narrative. In both cases, the ambiguous concept 'feelings' was at the center of the causal network. (In the penultimate section of this essay, I return to a discussion of feelings.)

Narrative and Conceptual Thinking

The two reference cases and the informal survey reflect a confusion in the use of two problem-solving strategies, two styles of thinking. Bruner referred to these mutually exclusive patterns of thinking as propositional (paradigmatic) and narrative (1986). I employed a similar distinction in contrasting the metaphysical underpinnings of statistical and clinical approaches to understanding a person: conceptual thinking and narrative thinking (Sarbin 1986b).

The two modes reflect two world views: mechanism and contextualism (Pepper 1942). In the mechanistic world view, the root metaphor is the transmittal of force—a metaphor that underlies the search for causality. The conceptual or propositional mode guides the effort to explain human action by intensively searching for decontextualized causes, a method that was successful for 19th-century practitioners of natural science. In the contextualist world view, the underlying metaphor is the historical act in all its complexity. The recognition of the influence of context is the bridge that connects historical acts and narrative thinking. To understand any human phenomenon, one must be able to construct a coherent narrative, a narrative that tries to account for the reasons that historical figures chose one rather than another mode of conduct. The language of reasons is patently different from the language of causes. Reasons make sense only in identifiable contexts, often moral contexts. Causes are intended to be context-free.

The Passions Interpreted as Rhetorical Acts

Before further developing my theme, I want to delimit the range of observations for which my claim for the usefulness of narrative understanding is intended. For some writers, the word 'emotion' includes one or more of the following: feelings, affects, moods, sentiments, aesthetic experience, taste preferences, visceral reactions, pain, passions, and sundry other classes of conduct and experience. I intend my remarks to be applied to phenomena that in the past have been denoted by the term 'passions.' This class of phenomena would include anger, fear, love, joy, caring, exultation, shame, guilt, jealousy, and envy (among others). Two features distinguish the passions from other forms of conduct: first, they are intimately bound to the process of communicating a moral position, and second, the participants in passionate encounters are highly involved in the action.[4]

To make this characterization of the passions more imageful, I refer again to the frustrated playwright and the insulted steamfitter. Both engaged in rhetorical action to communicate their respective moral postures, the one verbally, the other instrumentally. The playwright made known his moral position on secretarial stupidity; the steamfitter made known the value he placed on challenges to his moral identity. Both were enacting roles demanded by an anger script—such roles are enacted with high degrees of organismic involvement. The degree of involvement is not always obvious to casual observation. For example, for the person who reports "suffering the pangs of conscience," i.e., guilt, the high degree of involvement may not be visible to an outsider.

The expression, 'rhetorical action' has an alien quality to psychologists schooled in positivist science. Traditionally, psychologists have borrowed their descriptive and causal metaphors from the sciences dealing with energy, spatial, mathematical, and geological dimensions. For the social scientist, rhetoric, a humanistic discipline, is a rich source of metaphors. The use of rhetoric as a source of metaphors is consistent with the ongoing "refiguration" in the social sciences (Geertz 1980). The potential contribution of rhetoric parallels that of the theater which has provided metaphorical enrichment to symbolic interaction theory and role theory. In fact, everyday vocabulary reflects the widespread diffusion of dramaturgical terms such as roles, scenarios, role models, scripts, role-conflict, upstaged, etc.

Rhetoric is the disciplined use of oral and gestural behavior for the purpose of persuading and convincing others of the propriety of the speaker's values and conduct. Classical rhetoricians define rhetorical acts as confrontations of human beings to resolve exigencies or urgencies. Rhetorical acts could be categorized as problem-solving behavior, with the proviso that the problem to be solved is in the realm of interpersonal action. In face-to-face rhetoric, the speaker and the listener invite, sometimes extort, involved actions from each other.

The rhetorician's exigencies have their counterparts in psychological theories, among them, epistemic strain, identity crisis, anxiety, threat, uncertainty, and conflict. Survival as a social being depends on successfully resolving the exigencies and strains that are endemic to social life. Human beings have invented a variety of adaptive acts to facilitate social survival; i.e., to facilitate enhancement of the self or reduce potential damage to the self. Not all adaptive acts are instances of rhetorical action. Exigencies may be resolved in other ways, where rhetoric is absent or only incidental. Three additional classes of adaptive acts may be identified: dialectical, such as changing beliefs through inductive and deductive reasoning; attention deployment, such as observed in the operation of classical defense mechanisms; and tranquilizing and releasing tactics, such as chemically modifying physiological arousal sometimes associated with highly involved commitments.

A moment's reflection about the variety of adaptive acts available to human beings will lead to the inference that rhetorical acts—the organized use of verbal and gestural conduct to bring about changes in the relationship between self and other—are the most powerful means of resolving and/or creating the exigencies and uncertainties that characterize social life.[5]

To recapitulate before proceeding with the argument, my thesis is that the passions, phenomena sometimes labeled 'emotions,' can be profitably viewed as narrative emplotments. Standing in the way of a ready acceptance of this thesis is the entrenched belief that passions are reflex-like happenings located within the body. I take an alternate position: the actions that lead to our describing an event as a passion are agentic. They are intentional acts performed in the course of dealing with the strains of social living. In the next section, I develop more fully the theme of rhetorical acts as intentional action. This theme is preparatory to the conclusion that the passions are *storied.*

Dramaturgic and Dramatistic Rhetorical Action

Earlier I noted that the passions are patterned actions in the service of resolving value-laden problems. Anger, grief, shame, exultation, and jealousy are rhetorical acts intended to convince others or self of one's moral claims. When located in a narrative context, rhetorical acts are the stuff out of which personal drama is created. At this point a critic might declare that I have taken the passion out of the passions when I assert that they are intentional acts designed to persuade. In monitoring one's own behavior in problematic situations, the critic is likely to focus on the apparent automaticity, the apparent unmediated quality, of his or her actions, especially if attention is directed to interoceptive sensations rather than to social contexts. The criticism would have merit if we were to regard rhetorical acts exclusively as tricks and moves of eloquent public speakers. The criticism is blunted when we examine closely the nature of two forms of rhetorical action: *dramaturgic* and *dramatistic.*

Dramaturgic rhetoric includes all the patterned oral and gestural behavior created and employed by the actor in the interest of impression formation. A catalog of such rhetorical devices would include the many forms of pretense, deception, withholding or restricting the flow of information, and selective feedback (Scheibe 1979). The actor is the author of these strategic interaction roles, making them up in the course of interacting with other actors. The late Erving Goffman (1959) sensitized us to the universality of strategic action in the service of maintaining and enhancing a moral identity. The intention of strategic action is parallel to that of classical rhetoric: to persuade and to convince an audience (sometimes the self) of the validity of the actor's claims. The imagery of the debater creating eloquent arguments is applicable to dramaturgical action. Like debaters and professional stage actors, the actors in personal dramas monitor their rhetoric, when necessary modulating the amplitude, shifting from one tactic to another, and alert to feedback from the audience. Hardly any example of social conduct is free of deception, disguise, plotting, pretending, secrets, and some degree of differential emphasis. Courtship behavior, poker playing, warfare, and political campaigns exemplify dramaturgical action. It is important to emphasize that the actor is the *author* of the unwritten script, not only in preparing for interaction, but also in creating on-the-spot tactical maneuvers.

Rhetorical acts of the dramatistic kind are different in terms of their authorship. Unlike dramaturgical roles that are enacted to follow a self-made contemporaneous script, dramatistic roles are enacted according to cultural prescriptions. Some prescriptions are in the form of codified rules, but most are contained in half-remembered folktales, myths, legends, fables, morality plays, parables, songs, poems, bedtime stories, novels, scenarios, and other narrative forms. A narrative that qualifies as a well-formed story will have a theme, a subtext. "What's the point?" guides the interpreter in the search for the theme or subtext, whether that interpreter is a biblical scholar, a theater-goer, a reader of fairy tales, or the audience for a raconteur. The point is to be found in the narrative's development or solution of a moral problem. The protagonists in these narratives are models for solving moral problems generated in connection with the upward or downward valuation of one's identity. The plots of these stories address, sometimes obliquely, the moral features of human relations, such as, duty and obligation, wisdom and folly, pride and shame, and honor and dishonor.

In the course of enculturation, children of all ages absorb the plots of these value-laden tales. Not necessarily taught nor learned in a systematic way, the plots of these stories are guides to sense-making in problematic human situations. The actions of persons in grief, joy, jealousy, anger, and so on, are recognizable patterns of conduct. Along with James Averill (1982), I find it useful to describe these patterns of conduct as social roles.

Role-Taking in Dramatistic Rhetoric. My shift from rhetorical acts to the language of roles is not accidental. A moment's reflection will support the claim that the passions are logical, organized acts, not disorganized responses. The thesis that the passions are disorganized and illogical has been supported by the assertions of laboratory scientists who assumed a continuity between the behavior of experimentally enraged cats and the highly involved conduct of people in problematic social situations.

The vocabulary of roles requires some refinement. Of the many usages, two are pertinent to the present analysis. As used in social analysis, role is the abbreviated form of social role. It is etymologically related to the 'part' in a theatrical script. It stands for the expected conduct of a person, given his/her position or status in a collectivity. Tied to social structure, social roles prescribe performances that maintain the stability of the collectivity. The criteria for judging the appropriateness and convincingness of the enactments are public. In enacting social roles, the participants acquire information to provide answers to the unvoiced and recurring question: who am I? The composite of answers comprises a person's *social identity* (Sarbin and Scheibe 1983).

The second usage emerged from the first. Related to, but not identical with social identity, is the concept *moral identity*. The achievement of a moral identity is dependent upon the performance of 'identity roles'. The content of these roles are also patterned actions but qualitatively different from the contents of social roles. Enactments of identity roles provide the means to evaluate oneself as a moral agent. The rhetorical acts in anger, grief, jealousy, joy, and so on, are in the service of preserving or enhancing one's moral identity. Always present in parallel with the social identity question is the unvoiced and persistent moral identity question: what am I in relation to the Good? to my moral codes? to my ethical standards? Whatever the source of an actor's moral rules, the construction and maintenance of his or her self-narrative requires justification for action in the name of the Good. Post hoc rationalization, illustrated by Aesop's fable of the fox and the grapes, is one such justification. The actor also makes use of a priori justifications to keep intact his ongoing self-narrative.

Moral identity roles are always enacted in a context of social roles. As an aid in differentiating social roles from identity roles, we can benefit from the use of literary stereotypes. Othello is an example of such a literary stereotype. Othello occupied the social status of a successful general. His uncritical acceptance of the contrived evidence of his wife's infidelity challenged his moral identity—not his social identity. The jealous-husband plot served to organize his actions in the light of culturally supported morality tales about faithless wives. In punishing his wife, he enacted the role of moral avenger, supported for a brief and terrible moment by the implied morality contained in the text of the faithless-wife story. Othello's a priori justification was framed in the language of honor.

In the course of our enculturation, we acquire many such literary stereotypes. From a wide variety of sources, we have Cinderella, Pagliacci, Sleeping Beauty, Hamlet, Robin Hood, George Washington, Nathan Hale, Faust, Scrooge, the Good Samaritan, as well as Wyatt Earp, Billy the Kid, and other cowboy heroes and villians in the fictional stories of the Old West. Announcing the names of these familiar stereotyped figures is a sufficient stimulus for the reader to call up prototypical plots. It would be extremely difficult imaginatively to construct these figures without at the same time recalling the plots of the stories in which they are central actors.

It requires no elaborate argument to declare that stories help to create order in human affairs. Well-formed narratives have immediate or remote moral messages, solutions for human problems. The narratives provide guidelines for dramaturgical and dramatistic role enactments to persons who are living out their own self-narratives. As the narrative figure (the self as actor) in one's own self-narrative confronts problematic moral situations, the self-as-author of the ongoing self-narrative, as agent, chooses a role enactment that fits the perceived requirements of his/her moral career.

A reminder is necessary to ward off a possible misinterpretation that the protagonists of my stories operate in a solipsistic universe. I underscore the postulate that the task of maintaining a moral identity is carried out in social contexts. Co-actors, and their representations in the form of imaginary actors, are always involved. These co-actors are also engaged in living out their own self-narratives. A constantly restructured self-narrative is thus the product of an enforced collaboration between a protagonist's self-as-author and a reciprocal actor's self-as-author. The performances of co-actors constrain the direction and amplitude of each other's rhetorical acts. It is thus inevitable that the self-narratives of interactants in a social encounter become commingled. Pirandello brought this phenomenon home to us in his brilliant play, *Six Characters in Search of an Author.* The plot centers on the moral complications that follow the protagonist's entry into a dramatic context begun by other authors and players, on a stage prepared without his knowledge or participation.

The Embodiment of the Passions

When I introduced this paper, I pointed to some concrete illustrations of the separation between traditional definitions of emotion and concrete examples. The definitions centered on internal states or happenings. The examples were storied accounts of highly involved action. The focus of my essay to this point has been on the exemplifications. My essay has attempted to show that the passions are dramatistic rhetorical acts performed in the interest of maintaining or enhancing a moral identity. The sources of the dramatistic performances are the reconstructed plots of narratives heard, seen, and read in the process of enculturation. The narrative is the overarching metaphor for my arguments.

I devote the remainder of this essay to interpreting the embodiment of the passions. The interpretation, to be credible, must be congruent with my previous arguments that the passions are intentional acts performed under the guidance of the narratory principle.

The embodiment claims of the two reference cases cited earlier are typical. The frustrated playwright said, "It is something I feel inside of me. I know when I'm having an emotion because I feel it." The insulted steamfitter said, "I just felt the anger surging up in me and I exploded." Add to these self-reports the frequently-appearing autobiographical accounts that contain such expressions as, "I was overwhelmed by grief," "I was caught in the grip of the emotion and I could not escape," "I was seized by envy and it wouldn't go away." Phenomenological reports of this kind are cited in support of the claim that emotions are autonomous happenings.

In addition, the conclusions of psychophysiologists about the universality of certain internal bodily reactions are cited to give credibility to the autonomy argument. The twin emphasis on self-perceived internal happenings and autonomous bodily reactions has been instrumental in giving unquestioned ontological status to emotions as internal happenings. Not without significance is James Averill's observation that the association of physiology with emotions has a long history in which bodily reactions were taken to symbolize "animal-like" behavior (1974). He traced psychophysiological symbolism from the Greeks to modern physiologists and concluded that, in an unbroken chain, certain emotions have been associated with bodily actions, both internal and external. The history shows that the theological antinomy of Flesh and Spirit, later translated to passions and reason, has had a profound influence on psychological theory, jurisprudence, and public policy.

It is not that bodily reactions are absent from psychological events. In fact, psychological events not identified as "emotional" are accompanied by increases in measurable physiological activity. Laboratory studies and common observation confirm the notion that physiological activity occurs in connection with fantasy and dreaming and with intellectual work.

The purported association between physiology and emotions has been asserted on the basis of selected pairings. Physiologists, in their efforts to demonstrate the evolutionary significance of emotions, addressed their studies to such highly involving emotions as fear, rage, and lust. The fact of heightened arousal in both humans and cats was taken as support for physiological substrate theories of emotion. The generalization from, let us say, anger, to the more quiet emotions, such as envy and contentment, was gratuitous. It is unproductive to maintain the separation of human activity into arbitrary categories invented to support certain theological doctrines. We can stipulate that *all* human action is grounded in biology. The premise needs no justification that the varieties of human experience are embodied. Acknowledging this premise carries no implication that complex conduct can be reduced to the interplay of biological forces. More productive are attempts to answer questions of this sort: How do human beings make use of sensory inputs arising within the body to attribute causality to their actions? Or, alternately, how do human beings interpret such sensory inputs so as to assign control of their conduct to agencies other than the self? What are the metaphoric and metonymic reifications that make possible the transformation of an intentional act into a happening? How are specific bodily acts, e.g., tears, recruited into rhetorical acts in dramaturgic and dramatistic roles?

As a starting point, I would adapt a dimension, "levels of organismic involvement," that has proven useful in assessing the quality of social role enactment (Sarbin 1954, Sarbin and Allen 1968). I have identified reference cases at different points on the dimension. At the low end is casual role enactment, such as an interchange between a motorist and a toll collector. Next is uninvolved ritual acting, "going through the motions." A higher degree is heated or engrossed acting, as in the professional theater. Ecstasy, as in religious excitement, is near the upper end of the dimension. When a person calls upon his dramaturgical skills to convince an audience of the legitimacy of his claims to a social status, he/she monitors the action in the interest of presenting just the right level of involvement. Goffman (1961) reported observations to confirm the hypothesis that unvoiced rules govern the optimal degree of involvement for any particular role enactment. These rules are of the same order as the well-recognized unspoken rules regarding optimal interpersonal distance. For the passions, the degree of organismic involvement would be at the upper end of the dimension. In anger, for example, the actor performs with increased vigor. Essential to the anger role is vigorous action. The anger narrative demands a form of communication to convey that the actor is responding to insult or perceived injustice. In this connection, I point out that *emphasis* is one of the categories of classical rhetoric. To achieve emphasis, that is, to imply more than is actually stated, the actor increases the vigor of his enactments. The rhetorical acts in typical anger scripts could include such vigorous motoric actions as clenching of fists, shouting, posturing, gesticulating, controlling uninhibited aggression through antagonistic muscle contraction, pacing, grimacing, and so on. As in any vigorous action, the organismic involvement in enacting the role stimulates vegetative functions served by the autonomic nervous system. Such functions are not agentic. Heart rate, respiratory rate, glandular secretions, and other internal processes have a semi-autonomous life. The physiology of recovery takes time—increased cardiac and respiratory rates continue after the termination of the highly involved rhetorical act. Some of the internal changes produce somaesthetic inputs. These are vague and not easily localizable. Nevertheless, they can be assigned cue properties by the actor in search of an explanation for his/her conduct. If pushed to describe his/her behavior, in the absence of communicable dimensions such as those characteristic of vision and audition, the actor invokes the vague concept of feelings. Parenthetically, some writers regard feelings and emotions as equivalents, others see feelings as constitutive of emotions.

Not only the actor, but the scientist as well, make use of autonomous internal processes in describing the passions. These internal happenings are but a small part of a complex whole that includes the emplotment of action that has connections with the past and the future. The scientist, in perceiving internally generated bodily effects as emotions, unwittingly performs a synecdochic transformation, assimilating the part to the whole. The extensive use of devices for monitoring bodily functions served by the autonomic nervous system reflects this illicit synecdochic transformation. The diffusion of scientific lore, in the light of the unexamined part-to-whole transformation, has encouraged quasi-scientific self-reports such as that of a victorious boxer: "I hit harder in the third round after I got my adrenalin up."

On Feelings. In interpreting a person's report about his or her feelings, we need to consider the certainty with which he or she holds the belief that non-agentic feelings are part of the human condition and that they arise not from clearly defined intentions, but from biological mechanisms or from equally mysterious psychic forces. Not open to public inspection, feelings (when they refer specifically to the perception of somaesthetic inputs) require an unusual skill to be able to articulate a description understandable to others. Since our language is impoverished in regard to somaesthetic events, we must rely on metaphors. Only a few stock metaphors relate to interior events, e.g., butterflies in the stomach, a lump in the throat. Skilled poets interested in communicating about feelings create metaphors to convey the intricacies of the relations of persons to other persons, nature, the Divinity, etc. Metaphors about feelings make little sense unless embedded in narrative accounts.

I have collected spontaneous verbal expressions that purport to describe feelings. Many of the expressions are non-informative, such as, "it feels great, "incredible," "wow," "the most wonderful feeling." These are examples of responses to the TV reporter's stock question, "How does it feel?" to winners of lottery sweepstakes, to successful round-the-world aviators, and to victors in tennis championships. The reporter places the instant celebrity in the unenviable position of rendering an *opinion* about a supposed happening. If the reporter persists in his effort to extract an account of "feelings," the respondent will usually tell an emplotted story about the event. The tennis champion's story might exemplify pride, exultation, gratitude, and include generous remarks about the skill of the opponent, and the frustrations of wind and weather conditions, and so on. The aviator's story might focus on features of the flight, the reliability of the aircraft, and problems of navigation. The lottery winner might tell of the events that led him into the supermarket from which he purchased the ticket. It is of interest to note that the reporters continue to ask for an opinion about feelings despite the fact that their respondents hardly ever give a satisfactory answer. The popularity of this journalistic practice helps to reinforce the belief that in fact, there must be feelings somewhere to be reported.

It is clear that phenomenal experience is ordered through the use of metaphors and the implied connections between metaphors. When we take a close look at the metaphoric ordering of experience, we can see the workings of the narratory principle, the tendency to frame bits and pieces of experience into a coherent story. When a person describes "feeling ashamed and hoping that the floor would open up and swallow me," the description can be interpreted as shorthand for a story emplotted as shame. The subtext of such a story would involve the uncovering of the protagonist in public nakedness or in the disclosure of an unshareable secret, and the predictable effort to hide, to seek cover, to render the self as small as possible to escape moral judgment by the "eye of the other."

My conclusion about feelings is that the term has only metaphoric utility for communicating one's involvement in a personal story. It is a linguistic device, devoid of meaning unless located in a narrative context.

The Reciprocity of Doings and Happenings. A critic might accept the foregoing as plausible, but remain unconvinced. When reconstructing a scenario involving one of the passions, he remembers experiencing the "feeling of guilt" as something that happened to him, not something he did to himself. In considering a response to this critic, I recognize that I have not emphasized sufficiently the social nature of narrative nor the correlative social construction of the passions. I have unduly focused on the protagonist in the personal drama, in most cases merely implying the co-presence of reciprocal or complementary role players. At this point, I want to revive the imagery of one person constructing a self-narrative in the same symbolic space as other actors. The protagonist cannot avoid all the actions of other players, all of whom are creating their own narratives. The figures in the self-narratives often collide with each other. When the protagonist is the agent, the antagonist is on the receiving end of the protagonist's actions. Recall the encounter between the two steamfitters. Miller's verbal and gestural insult—clearly an intentional act—preceded Jones's assault. Jones suffered the insult, he was the object of Miller's act. From Jones's perspective, the insult was a happening. At the moment he struck Miller on the head, Miller was the recipient. He suffered the blow. From Miller's perspective, the blow on the head was a happening. From the perspective of a disinterested observer, Jones was clearly the agent of the aggressive act. Yet Jones without hesitation attributed causality to mysterious inner forces, his feelings. Observers who accepted this attribution would have to be subscribers to the same epistemology as Jones, to wit, that the assault was caused by forces outside his control. Observers who rejected Jones's attribution would be faced with the problem of deciding if Jones was self-deceived when he declared that the apparent intentional act was a happening.

The claim that the aggressive act was caused by inner forces may be no more than a reflection of a metonymous connection between the "feeling" that supposedly caused the act and the immediately preceding state of affairs—Miller's offensive behavior in the context of a heated quarrel. When Miller uttered the insult, he was the agent and for a moment Jones was the passive receiver. Jones suffered the insult—from his perspective, a happening. At the moment he perceived Miller's act as insult, he initiated retaliation, including the bodily involvement in vigorous action. In attributing causality to feelings, presumably an interpretation of somaesthetic inputs, Jones employed the rhetorical device of metonymy, where the observation of interest is denoted by one of its adjuncts, as in identifying an effect as a cause. Instead of attributing causality to Miller's insult and to the storied guidance for maintaining his moral identity, Jones metonymously assigned causality to the adjunct, that vague entity, his feelings.

Metonymy, like metaphor, is a figure of speech. It is one of a family of terms to denote a rhetorical technique to influence meaning. Metaphor as the ground for myth-making has been studied extensively. Ample evidence can be adduced to support the proposition that metaphors can be reified. The history of science, for example, is full of instances where a metaphor assumed mythic status. Phlogiston, the luminiferous ether, and the humors were first coined as metaphors to help describe puzzling phenomena. For identifiable reasons, the metaphors were transfigured to myths (Chun and Sarbin 1970; Sarbin 1968; Turbayne 1962).

As in the case of metaphor, metonymy, too, can be reified. Under the influence of theological doctrines that supported psychophysiological symbolism, internal happenings—the effects of involved action—were treated as causes of behavior. Of course, the reader of one of Shakespeare's sonnets is not likely to reify metaphors or metonymies. But in constructing and maintaining a world view, the figurative function of a particular metonymy may give way to a literal interpretation. An earlier generation of psychoanalysts produced a parallel metonymic transformation when they transfigured anxiety to a cause from its original use as the effects of interpersonal actions.

Social beings cannot help but be involved in reciprocal interaction. Therefore, the interpreter of human action must operate from the premise that at one moment people are agents, at another moment they are sufferers of the intentional acts performed by co-actors. Such reciprocal interaction of necessity brings about an enforced collaboration with others in living out their self-narratives. With practice in reciprocal interaction, and with skill in transfiguring metonymies, social beings can take a complex narrative that includes both happenings and doings, and assign responsibility for some of their agentic acts to vague and incommunicable "feelings" rather than to the storied acts that test or threaten their moral identities.

Coda

I began this essay by noting the disjunction between definitions and exemplifications of emotion. Definitions are couched in the language of psychophysiology, examples are rendered in narrative form without reference to the content of the definitions. I have tried to make the case that the passions are rhetorical acts intentionally performed in the service of maintaining or enhancing a person's moral identity. Rhetorical acts are of two kinds: dramaturgic and dramatistic. The former acts are authored by the actor (impression management), the latter are drawn from cultural narratives. Dramatistic rhetorical acts serve to maintain the actor's self-narrative. To emphasize the social construction of the passions, I point to the observation that, strictly speaking, self-narratives are co-authored, they are the result of enforced collaboration between an actor and reciprocal actors.

My discussion has focused on interpreting an account of highly involved action as narrative emplotment. My interpretations of the reference cases are storied accounts of rhetorical acts.

Narrative emplotment as the ground for interpretation is far removed from the usual basis for construing the passions. Psychophysiological symbolism is the conventional ground; the concept of feelings as quasi-sensations guides the interpreter. The common claim that a person is "gripped" by an emotion is often used to support the theory that feelings are autonomous happenings. Employing a semiotic strategy, I have tried to show that the actor who attributes causality to feelings is unwittingly engaging in a metonymic transformation. The actor has taken one of the effects of a complex act—the perception of somaesthetic inputs associated with involved action—and assigned a causal status to it rather than to the plots that guide the intentional acts of the participants. This metonymy has been reified in the writings of traditional practitioners of the normal science of psychology so that feelings have unquestioned ontological status.

A final observation. Metaphoric descriptors, such as "madly in love," "livid with rage," and "overcome by jealousy" are textual items for interpreters of conduct. The metaphors have influenced many interpreters to regard the autonomous "feelings" connoted by the descriptors as having causal properties. The burden of my arguments is that the metaphors have a different ground, namely, that the actions connoted by the descriptors are highly involving rhetorical performances guided by the requirements of dramatistic plots. The interpreter of human actions has a choice: to perceive Romeo and Juliet as pawns *in the grip* of their feelings, or to regard the star-cross'd lovers as agents *gripping* a narrative plot.

PART THREE

Critiquing the Perspective
of an Interpretation

CHAPTER 8

Rhetoric vs. Evidence as a Source of Persuasion: A Critique of the Case Study Genre

Donald P. Spence

To speak of the role of evidence in bringing about persuasion is to identify one of the key features of our current conception of science. Evidence forms the basis for reasoned argument and the drawing up of lawful conclusions, and the evidence, by common understanding, is available to all. From its earliest beginnings, science has prided itself on being fanatically democratic. Data belong to the public domain and are open to inspection or re-analysis by any interested party. Procedures are publicly available. Public procedures combined with public data make it possible for anyone with the proper training and apparatus to carry out standard experiments and thus determine whether a given finding can or cannot be replicated. "Old beliefs," writes Campbell (1986), "are to be doubted until they have been reconfirmed by the methods of the new science. Persuasion is to be limited to egalitarian means, potentially accessible to all, that is, to visual and logical demonstrations (note how much of proof in Euclid is based on dependably shareable visual judgments)" (p. 119).

As science developed, replication became more and more the road to persuasion and it can be seen that replication depends to a very great extent on the model of participatory democracy. Campbell tells us that "a crucial part of the egalitarian, anti-authoritarian ideology of the seventeenth-century 'new science' was the ideal that each member of the scientific community could replicate a demonstration for himself. . . . Each scientist was to be allowed to inspect the apparatus and try out the shared recipe" (p. 122). Restrict such open access and truth suffers. "A healthy community of truth seekers can flourish where such replication is possible. It becomes precarious where it is not" (p. 122).

For an account of what may happen when these principles are not observed, we need look no further than the history of alchemy during the Renaissance. Although the distinction between alchemy and science is less sharp than popular stereotypes would suggest (see Vickers 1984), there is no question that alchemy relied heavily on secrecy and magic, in clear violation of the egalitarian ethic of traditional science. "The occult [of which alchemy was a part] has always been secretive, restricting knowledge to adepts or initiates, communicating only in hermetic forms or in messages designed to sabotage themselves (such as alchemical recipes in cipher or exotic foreign languages—Ethiopian, say—or with names of crucial substances or quantities omitted). Where scientific experiments are repeatable and ublic, occult experiments, or experiences, are personal and notoriously not repeatable (above all not in alchemy, where the absence of any established criteria for determining the purity or concentration of substances, solid or liquid, or of standardizing temperature, made for insuperable difficulties in emulation)" (Vickers 1984, 41-42). Once secrecy obtains a footing in the enterprise, it tends to elevate argument by authority and other rhetorical figures over the careful sifting of archival evidence. As rhetoric displaces evidence, we lose the ability to reach what Habermas has called an "uncompelled consensus." Replication loses much of its leverage as a test of persuasion because failures of replication can be put down to poor technique, to lack of access to the proper ingredients, to a misreading of the recipe, or—in the last resort—to the principle that occult experiments are non-repeatable. If that principle is scrupulously observed, then replication failure merely confirms the axiom and thus supports the general system. What Campbell calls "mutual monitoring" fails because procedures and data are no longer in the public domain.

Protected by its use of secrecy and arcane language from the challenges of the disbelievers, alchemy and the occult in general became even more of a closed system in which all beliefs were inter-connected. "If a belief in numerology were abandoned, it would destroy the basis for alchemy and astrology; if a belief in astrology were abandoned, it would destroy alchemy, botanical medicine, and much else" (Vickers 1984, 35). It could be argued that the closed system probably encouraged the need for secrecy and increased reliance on arcane ciphers and exotic languages because any challenge would threaten the total web of belief and thus every challenge was potentially destructive.

Not only was the occult system highly interdependent; its practitioners also maintained a protective attitude toward established theory. Truth was largely known and needed only to be embellished. In contrast to traditional science, practitioners of the occult "never threw away anything, and much of the system elaborated in the Hellenistic period survives intact today. Modern astrology has absorbed some later planetary discoveries, and there are some sporadic instances of the application of quantitative techniques to mystical goals (as in Leonhard Thurneisser's use of quantitative analysis of urine to identify the three Paracelsian principles, mixing chemical with analogical and metaphorical procedures), but by and large the occult sciences have gone on unchanged" (Vickers 1984, 38).

As evidence gives way to rhetoric, argument, bolstered by a wide array of rhetorical figures, carries the burden of persuasion. Appeals to authority replace the participatory democracy of peer review; as procedures become exotic, self-destructive or cabalistic, and secrecy becomes the norm, words take over from things. As rhetoric takes over from evidence, we see a clear change in the way alchemists approach language and related language to the world. The contrast with traditional science becomes increasingly sharpened. "In the scientific tradition," writes Vickers, ". . . a clear distinction is made between words and things and between literal and metaphorical language. The occult tradition does not recognize this distinction; words are treated as if they are equivalent to things and can be substituted for them. Manipulate the one and you manipulate the other. Analogies, instead of being . . . explanatory devices subordinate to argument and proof, or heuristic tools to make models that can be tested, corrected, and abandoned if necessary, are, instead, modes of conceiving relationships in the universe that reify, rigidify, and ultimately come to dominate thought" (1884, 95).

Language was also used carelessly. Boyle attacked the language of the occult tradition for its "obscure, ambiguous . . . aenigmatical way of expressing what they pretend to teach . . . of playing with names at pleasure . . . so they will oftentimes give one thing many names" (quoted in Vickers, 114). The same carelessness also applied to the use of figures of speech. Whereas metaphor and simile were recognized by the new sciences as separate from the nonfigurative, normal level of discourse, quite a different position was taken by the occult sciences who might mistake these same figures for representations of reality. The metaphor was treated like the object it represents; analogy was collapsed into identity. What was even more destructive to clear thinking, the use of a given metaphor was not seen as a provisional means of representing a particular happening but as representing its very essence. This form of concrete thinking contributed to the reluctance to change, noted above, and to a belief in words as talismans. "The word is not merely like a quality of the thing it designates, such as its color or weight; it is, or exactly represents, its essence or substance" (Walker 1958; quoted in Vickers, 119).

It can be seen how the fascination with rhetoric, language, and metaphor in particular tended to focus attention away from the real world and back to the intricacies of the occult system. As a result, less and less attention was paid to ways of validating the system or to exceptions to this or that rule; the system was sacred, to be preserved at all costs, and accessible only to those chosen few who understood its secret ways.

Psychoanalysis and Science

Psychoanalysis also prides itself on being a science and belonging to the mainstream of the scientific tradition. Freud was quite clear on this point.

Grünbaum notes that "throughout his long career, Freud insisted that the psychoanalytic enterprise has the status of a natural science. As he told us at the very end of his life, the explanatory gains from positing unconscious mental processes 'enabled psychology to take its place as a natural science like any other'" (1984, 2). "The intellect and the mind [wrote Freud] are objects for scientific research in exactly the same way as any non-human things. Psychoanalysis has a special right to speak for the scientific *Weltanschauung*" (1933, 159). In an earlier statement, he expressed his regret that the scientific standing of psychoanalysis was not obvious to others. "I have always felt it as a gross injustice that people have refused to treat psychoanalysis like any other science" (1925, 58).

Similar support comes from his followers. "Like every other scientist [writes Brenner] a psychoanalyst is an empiricist, who imaginatively infers functional and causal relations among his data" (1982, p. 5). Holt has described the profession as a "fledgling science" which is struggling to become respectable despite the fact that "it is hard to admit how little *proof* there is for any psychoanalytic hypothesis after all these years of use" (1984, p. 26).

These are brave words. At the same time, science is as science does. When we turn from how psychoanalysis is defined to the way it is reported, its scientific status becomes somewhat harder to recognize. A careful inspection of the psychoanalytic literature, as represented by its three major journals, reveals many ways in which it does not conform to the traditional scientific principles outlined above. In the first place, data are largely private and not accessible to the curious scholar who wants to see for himself. Part of this privacy is needed to protect the patient, but it has the effect of ruling out the traditional kinds of replication by participant-observation This kind of secrecy leads directly to persuasion through rhetoric, with heavy reliance on argument by authority. In the second place, concern for the privacy of the patient leads to the dubious tradition of protection through disguise. As a result, many of the details of so-called case reports are actually falsified but the line where truth stops and disguise begins is never made clear. As a result, the vast majority of case reports have little or no archival value. Thirdly, there is no precedent for the kind of open discussion of conflicting findings that is central to the traditional scientific approach. Negative instances are almost never published, and unsuccessful cases are practically never reported.

Further inspection of the case study genre also reveals some disturbing parallels with the occult tradition. There is, first of all, an overriding reliance on metaphor and a tendency to substitute word for thing (see Spencer 1982, 1987). Use of metaphor interferes with careful observation because the true nature of the referent is always falsified by its name. (Think of the "seething cauldron" of the unconscious.) What is more disturbing, metaphor tends to be used in a highly concrete and dogmatic manner; it does not represent a provisional or tentative means of representing the world, but rather, it is accepted as a final statement. Second, there is the tendency to refer to causative agents that can never be made visible and thus examined directly; consider, in this connection, the unconscious, its contents, or the true nature of an unconscious fantasy. They are treated as real objects but they operate largely as metaphors. Jacobsen and Steele (1979) have discussed a parallel tendency of Freud's to push explanatory events further and further back into the past. "He begins with observations of adult pathology and moves from the adult present via psychoanalytic interpretations to the infantile past. This past is then considered to be real and contain within it causes for the present" (p. 353). But because it is set in some earlier time period, the triggering event can never be inspected directly; thus the hypothesis can never be directly tested. Third, critical dialogue is handicapped by the theory-laden nature of many of the facts. Only verbatim samples of clinical happenings make it possible for an outside observer to determine how much of a given statement is observation and how much is theory, but because of the scarcity of clinical data in the public domain, this recourse is essentially ruled out.

As background for these differences we find an approach to the theory and its relation to the evidence which differs significantly from the approach of traditional science, and which places psychoanalysis somewhat closer to the occult tradition. Truth is taken as largely discovered; standard beliefs are to be accepted rather than doubted; the old is given preference over the new. Psychoanalysis is traditionally reluctant to consider new alternatives and revise its theories and models. The prevailing attitude was clearly set by Freud in an early paper. If the reader, he stated, was not inclined to agree with his formulation about a case, then additional data would scarcely change his mind (1912, 114).

With the critical findings largely outside the public domain, traditional forms of replication are ruled out and persuasion relies largely on appeal to authority and narrative persuasion. This kind of appeal depends heavily on the traditional tools of formal rhetoric (of which Freud was a master). We need look no further than the Dora Case to see this mastery in action. Perhaps only Freud would have the narrative skill to turn a clinical failure into a literary masterpiece.

A Specimen Case

To further explore the relative uses of evidence and rhetoric in the standard psychoanalytic case, I decided to take a detailed look at a recent clinical report and examine the form of the argument, the use of different kinds of rhetorical figures, and the interplay of literary and scientific forms of reasoning used in the service of persuasion. I hope to draw your attention to the different kinds of rhetorical influence that the author of a case study can bring to bear on the reader, and how these tools of persuasion compare with the more traditional uses of evidence. To achieve this goal, I have set myself the task of trying to share with you, the reader, the specific thoughts and feelings I experienced while reading a particular article in a particular journal. The article thus becomes the text of the discussion, but the text is actually secondary to the reactions it aroused in me and the implications that followed on their heels. This chapter is, among other things, an experiment in method because I know of no good model for what I am setting out to accomplish. It begins as a traditional *explication de texte*, but because I will pay even more attention to the reactions aroused by the text, it also becomes an experiment in autobiography coupled with an exercise in persuasion.

As I begin to analyze my reactions to the target article, I am struck, first of all, by questions of where to start. My first thought was to cite author and title and thus establish the text as an object of investigation. But such an approach already falsifies what I am trying to accomplish because it turns the text into something "out there," and this object would be something quite different from my changing experience of it as I began reading and reacting. To establish the text as an object also gives you, the reader, the chance to form your own opinion of it and this move could only get in the way of any attempt to persuade you of my reactions. Because it would seem that once you have decided how to "read" the article in question, you will have formed your own image of the argument; this image becomes the referent for all subsequent discussion. Not only have we stopped making references to the article as written but we have substituted for it an unseen collection of meanings that is inside your head and thus unavailable for public inspection or evaluation. For these reasons, I choose to disclose the details of the target text as we go along; in this way, you will have no choice but to experience my reactions in the same order as they occurred to me. The method has already become something new and different; we might call it *explication (de texte)*.

We can distinguish at least two domains of discourse in the target article. On the one hand, there is a series of events in real life concerning a real patient, his upbringing, his memory of this upbringing, and the use made of these memories in two specific periods of psychoanalysis with two different analysts. The two treatments brought about two quite different outcomes and this difference becomes one of the points at issue. There is also, on the other hand, the thoughts and comments of the author *about* the first domain of discourse. Reading the article, I found myself feeling that the second was always getting in the way of the first; that the author was making statements that either did not agree with my perception of the patient's experience or made it clear that she, the author, was not sufficiently curious about gaps or inconsistencies in the original record. It reminded me of the role of Strether, the narrator, in Henry James' *The Ambassadors*, forever getting in the way of a clear view of the events, always filtering what took place through *his* eyes, the eyes of a visiting American who is settled in his ways and uses too much imagination in some respects and too little in others.

As my irritation with the author mounted, I tried to gain access to the material more directly and thus find ways of bypassing her point of view. I began to violate her sequence of presentation by raising my own questions of the patient's experience and trying to answer them directly, jumping around in the text to discover relevant passages. Sections which seemed obscure or ambiguous I put through a second or third reading. These maneuvers produced a heightened awareness of the first domain of discourse—the patient's life and memories—and a diminished awareness of the author's. But I found the struggle frustrating because (quite naturally) it did not actually *change* the author's assertions and overall point of view. Her views were in print; mine were only thoughts. As my stand became firmer, I experienced the author more and more as a kind of scolding voice in the background who always disagreed with my gradually forming conclusion and who had the overwhelming power of print on her side. Of equal importance to the two domains of discourse already described is another voice—Freud's—which is quoted early in the article and which forms a subtext for much of the argument. Because of its importance to the overall argument, it deserves to be quoted in full. With reference to the primal scene of the Wolf Man, Freud makes the following statement:

> Scenes ... which date from such an early period ... and which further lay claim to such an extraordinary significance for the history of the case, are as a rule not reproduced as recollections, but have to be divined—constructed— gradually and laboriously from an aggregate of indications ... It seems to me absolutely equivalent to recollection, if the memories are replaced (as in the present case) by dreams the analysis of which invariably leads back to the same scene and which reproduce every portion of its content in an inexhaustible variety of new shapes. Indeed, dreaming is another kind of remembering, though one that is subject to the conditions that rule at night and to the laws of dream-formation. It is this recurrence in dreams that I regard as the explanation of the fact that the patients themselves gradually acquire a profound conviction of the reality of these primal scenes, a conviction which is in no respect inferior to one based on recollection.
>
> —Williams 1987, 146-47

This statement by the founder of psychoanalysis is clearly intended as an epigraph for the paper. We are being prepared for some kind of validation or corroboration of its main thesis. We are led to believe that 1) dreams are lawful; 2) dreams are equivalent to memories; and 3) that conviction in the dreamer can be used as a form of validation.

Further inspection of the topic paragraph also provided some hints to my growing feeling of restlessness and discomfort as I tried to grapple with the main arguments in the article. It is clear from the outset that the author has no intention of quarreling with any part of Freud's argument; his authority will go unchallenged throughout the paper. But if these assertions are allowed to stand, I began to feel increasingly pessimistic about the clarity or precision of the author's reasoning and about her ability to draw her own conclusions from the clinical material, independent of the teachings of standard theory. If her findings did not, in fact, support these teachings, what would be their fate? It seemed to me that her silent reaction to Freud's argument boded ill for the climate of discussion. If the author was not going to be properly critical of the evidence as it appeared, I realized I would have to assume the role of skeptical listener and this awareness increased my discomfort with her part in the proceedings. She became even more of an obstructive and intrusive observer. Not only was she uncurious and interfering, but she had become Freud's alter ego, protective of his point of view and probably not open to disconfirming or embarassing evidence. I began to feel more pessimistic about the article and what it would teach me, and more determined to find my own answers and raise my own questions.

Turning to the target article, we find that the early childhood of the patient quickly becomes the focus of the discussion. When he was two, his parents were divorced and "immediately following the divorce, the mother left on an extended trip that in some family versions lasted ten months, but according to her only five. The patient was left in the care of an elderly aunt and uncle, who in turn entrusted the boy to the care of a strict nurse and a friendly male servant to whom, according to the patient and family members, the boy was very attached" (Williams 1987, 147-48) The author then turns to the patient's later development in childhood and adolescence, describes his adult adjustment difficulties and his search for relief through psychoanalysis. The first analysis was broken off after some eight years of discontinuous treatment at a time when the patient felt he had made no progress; he was referred to the author for a second analysis. During the course of the first treatment, there were multiple indications that some childhood trauma had taken place, but the details of the event were neither fully reconstructed nor forcefully addressed.

We have now reached the heart of the argument. The author suggests that failure to focus attention on the seduction was responsible for lack of success in the first treatment and that when it became the center of the clinical work (in the second analysis), the patient's symptoms began to diminish and he reached a successful resolution of his problem. But to make this argument, the author must provide convincing evidence that a seduction had actually taken place, and here is where the paper becomes its most unsatisfactory. We are given no direct evidence that the early seduction (by the male servant) had actually taken place; instead, we are given only summaries of repetitive dreams about ugly buildings, overflowing toilets, floating feces, and a bedroom with many beds. Despite the importance of this material to the argument, no single dream is ever reported verbatim. We are also told by the patient, after the reconstruction was made, that he remembers going to the servant's home— not once, but many times—and that relatives had told him how attached he was to the servant and how he followed him around. But such a memory, together with the repetitive dreams, are merely consistent with a possible seduction; they add nothing to its proof. Once again, I was troubled by the author's failure to raise this distinction and show us a skeptical mind at work.

But something else is going on as well. Not only is the seduction hypothesis never examined in a critical manner, but its status changes, over the course of the paper, from hypothesis to fact. On p. 152 we are told once again about the male servant who, "as the first analysis revealed and the second analysis confirmed [sic], had molested his young charge. In a clinical presentation in a circle of analysts, the first analyst reported he had come to this conclusion from a few screen memories and repetitive dreams of the patient; he saw this molestation as a homosexual trauma; it apparently was not pursued further." In the next paragraph, the author describes how she told the patient that she *suspected* he had been seduced and molested by the male servant, based on the evidence of the repetitive dreams (and also influenced, we may assume, by the conviction of the first analyst). But suspicion quickly changes to conviction. On the next page, we are told of the "seduction by Joseph" (no qualification); further references to "the seduction" occur repeatedly throughout the article, in the title, and the abstract. The author (and evidently the patient) are convinced of its factual basis and in the next-to-last paragraph, we are told that "the seduction [now a simple fact] hindered his freedom to develop normally; he lived in shackles until he learned to remove them" (p. 163).

In a general way, the possibility of early seduction by the male servant, at a time when the father had left the home, the mother was away on an extended trip, and the patient was left in the care of elderly relatives, seems a plausible hypothesis which *could* explain the repetitive dreams, the patient's fear of closeness, and other aspects of his symptom picture. It ranks as a *possible* but not a *necessary* cause of the clinical details, but the distinction between the two kinds of cause is not examined in any depth. These questions are all the more relevant because of the ambiguity of the evidence. Here is another case where interpretation seems to masquerade as explanation, an interpretation which receives particular sanction because it agrees with standard theory.

What more is needed in the way of confirming evidence? First, we would expect to find clarification of the memory as its significance was unfolded in the course of the analysis. Additional details might also be recovered, even at an early stage, which would make the happening more clearly a first-person experience that happened to the patient and was remembered by him. No such additional facts are reported. The patient recovers a memory of going home with Joseph not once "but many times," but nothing more emerges in the way of new memories or dreams. The dilapidated buildings in the repetitive dreams are taken to be references to Joseph's home, but their form does not seem to change after the reconstruction is made explicit. Thus the hypothesis of early seduction has about the same evidential standing at the end of the treatment as at the beginning, but it is treated as if confirmed by the clinical data and, by the end of the article, confirmed beyond question. To the author's satisfaction, perhaps, but not to mine.

I was becoming more impatient with the author, with the disparity between my sense of the evidence and hers, and with my position as a captive reader who has no way of entering into a discussion with either the author or the evidence. (Here is where the lack of public data becomes especially telling.) I was also becoming impatient with the standard genre of case reporting that relies largely on a narrative form of presentation and tends to substitute conclusions for facts. This genre effectively prevents the skeptical reader from making contact with the clinical material, from reaching his or her own conclusions from the evidence, or from applying his therapeutic expertise to the material in question. More specifically, it prevents the analyst/reader from applying what Isakower has called his "analyzing instrument" to the full extent of its capacity.

Perhaps if the narrative had been more persuasive, I would have been less impatient. Freud was ruefully aware of the similarity between his case reports and narrative fiction, and in the hands of a master storyteller, the standard genre is highly effective. But if the craft is imperfectly practiced, if the narrative smoothing is perhaps too obvious or if hypothesis slides too quickly into explanation, then we are left feeling dissatisfied and unpersuaded. Rather than suspending whatever disbelief we may bring to the account at the outset, we tend to double our skepticism with each unsupported assertion. In the final reckoning, bad case reports read like bad fiction and leave us feeling unhappy and argued with—certainly not convinced or informed.

But of course the case report is not only bad fiction. It presents itself as a piece of the truth, a sample of clinical reporting that has a bearing on psychoanalytic theory. An uncritical reading of the target article would seem to support the standard assumption that early seduction can have long-term effects on the patient's development and later adjustment; that derivatives of this seduction can be detected in dreams many years later; that dreams do indeed behave like memories and that early experiences are lawfully transformed into dream content; and that the proper reconstruction of an early event can significantly affect the course of psychoanalysis. An uncritical reading of the article would suggest that Freud's formulation was essentially correct and that his hypothesis stands confirmed in all its details—a truly remarkable state of affairs. A more critical reading suggests something quite different. Not only is standard theory *not* being confirmed, but it is being examined in a largely uncritical fashion. As I focused on this strand of the author's argument, I became all the more impatient with the outcome and all the more aware of my own inability to change the author's mind.

At this point my thoughts turn to the vantage point of the author and exactly how she came to see the evidence in the way she did. Where I am unconvinced, she is clearly persuaded and it is this difference between us that accounts for my restless reaction to her line of argument. She was, after all, much closer than I to the clinical material; does that account for our different reactions? Were there one or more clinical happenings which she could have included which would have caused me to change my mind? Was there some quality in the material that she found difficult to put into words and that, if included, would have made a difference? Most alarming of all, were there details that could not be revealed because of reasons of privacy and the need to protect the identity of the patient? I could find no clear answers to these questions, but the doubts remained.

Of particular interest is the relation between the quotation from Freud on the traumatizing effects of early experience and the clinical findings reported in the case study. The statement by Freud gives permission to look for the long-term effects of early trauma in later dreams and associations. The statement, by the first analyst, that he had found evidence for early trauma further reinforces Freud's argument and further prepares the way for its confirmation. Against this background, any evidence that is *consistent* with the formulation tends to be judged sufficient.

The difference in our response to the clinical findings underlines the obvious fact that meanings in the first domain of discourse—the patient's life—are far from transparent. They are always being colored by a) the context of events and b) the author's theoretical assumptions. The theory-laden nature of the facts poses a particular problem for this kind of account because the standard narrative method may be simply unequipped to present the story along with its context of understanding. We can put the point more directly by saying the standard narrative approach disarms the reader into believing that a simple story is being told—but this is clearly not the case. Seen in that light, we can think of the standard case study method as serving a specific kind of rhetorical function designed to tempt the reader into a suspension of disbelief. He is persuaded to put himself into the hands of the author, as opposed to having a conversation with the author concerning the merits of the argument.

Further evidence for the rhetorical function of the case report appears when we ask ourselves what other conclusions could be drawn from it. It would clearly be difficult to arrive at a different formulation because we are not presented with all the evidence, and the selection of some details and the omission of others is almost certainly in the service of the author's rhetorical aim—to persuade us of the rightness of her conclusions. But such persuasion, even if it did occur, could hardly be described as uncompelled. Not only are the relevant facts preselected with the aim of making the best case, but they are presented against the backdrop of the Freudian epigraph which adds authority to anything which seems consistent with it. Far from being an objective account of a clinical happening, the report is carefully scripted to influence our conclusions in a particular way.

Whether or not this particular piece of rhetoric is convincing, it is nevertheless masquerading as supporting evidence for a standard piece of psychoanalytic theory. The masquerade is misleading because, as we have seen, the clinical report is carefully fashioned to persuade the reader of a certain line of argument. It is also misleading because it is immune to alternative formulations; to this extent, it can be distinguished from an archival account that is open to a wide range of interpretations.

Scientific Standing of a Case Report

It may be useful at this point to reconsider the standing of this particular clinical report against the traditional ideology of science. We quote once again from Campbell:

> The ideology of science was and is explicitly antiauthoritarian, antitraditional, antirevelational, and individualistic. Truth is yet to be revealed. Old beliefs are to be doubted until they have been reconfirmed by the methods of the new science. Persuasion is to be limited to egalitarian means, potentially accessible to all, that is, to visual and logical demonstrations (note how much of proof in Euclid is based on dependably shareable visual judgments). The community of scientists is to stay together in focused disputation, monitoring and keeping each other honest until some working consensus emerges (but conformity of belief per se is rejected as an acceptable goal).
> —Campbell 1986, 119

We are immediately struck by a number of vivid contrasts between these assumptions and those made by the author of the target article. She takes Freud's original assertion as the subtext of her presentation; this old belief is honored rather than questioned. Truth, she seems to assume, is already known and needs only to be reconfirmed; the details are unlikely to change. Persuasion, as we have seen, is far from a democratic procedure because the facts surrounding the presumed infantile seduction are incompletely presented; they are certainly not "potentially accessible" to all interested parties. Persuasion, what is more, tends to be arbitrary and authoritarian, depending heavily on prior statements by Freud and other expert witnesses (especially the first analyst). Because the relevant data are not made public, there is no opportunity for open discussion of alternative meanings of the evidence, a dialogue which would lead to the "uncompelled consensus" recommended by Habermas. On the contrary, the conclusion is explicitly compelled and, as a result, quite unsurprising.

It could be argued that the very fact that meanings in clinical material are *not* transparent makes it more necessary that we do not fall back on authoritarian forms of argument. To depend on a single opinion is perilous enough; to depend on it when meanings are frequently ambiguous and context-determined is to confound the problem more. Nor does it follow that the particular confidential nature of clinical material necessarily interferes with a democratic dialogue. While the privacy of the patient is certainly an important issue, there is reason to believe that the shoe is sometimes on the other foot: the use of privacy becomes a defense of the narrative method. It provides a rationale for the use of disguise and arbitrary selection and if these are allowed to stand, there is no possibility for open access to the original data. Disguise and selection are forms of censorship and as such, they support the traditional authoritarian form of argument.

When findings are selected in the service of the argument and presented in a way that suits the narrative thrust of the case report, it is hard to see how theory will ever change. If rhetorical appeal becomes the standard that governs arrangement of the findings, then the new or surprising or unheard-of clinical happening will never be heard of because it spoils the story and interferes with the traditional suspension of disbelief so necessary for the persuasive, spellbinding tale. We are reminded uncomfortably of the alchemists with their faith in closed theory that sees no need for change, and with their fondness for general conclusion over specific detail.

This form of reasoning tends to be conservative in nature and to maintain established doctrine as long as needed—possibly forever. Science too is conservative, but because of the principle of democratic participation, continues to be held accountable as new findings come into view that challenge the received wisdom and propose other explanations for established observations. Its conservatism is maintained at the price of constant argument. Because some arguments are better than others, theory changes albeit slowly. But psychoanalysis defends itself by rhetoric, by ruling certain facts inadmissible, and by taking an implicit position that the grand theory is largely correct and should not be changed. So long as rhetoric holds the upper hand, the role of evidence will always come in second and the scientific standing of psychoanalysis becomes more and more open to serious question.

What conclusions can be drawn from this attempt to look critically at the form and content of a recently published case study? We see, first, that it lends itself more suitably to a rhetorical analysis because the facts are in short supply, are rarely transparent, and are incompletely presented. The rhetoric, on the other hand, is very much on the surface and will inevitably influence the conclusions drawn by the reader. Hence it would appear that a sophisticated awareness of rhetorical method is a first requirement for any intelligent reading of the case report. This awareness begins with the idea that the case study is not a simple report of a clinical happening, even though it may masquerade as such; rather, it is a complicated exercise in persuasion that tries to bring about an overall suspension of disbelief. Put crudely, it is a piece of propaganda in support of established theory that is masquerading as an objective description of a clinical interchange.

The attempt to read between the lines of the case report and discover, by whatever means available, what is not directly presented and what other readings are possible, has obvious similarities with the time-honored method of evenly hovering attention. But we are suggesting—our second recommendation—an orientation that goes beyond the traditional use of the analytic instrument (to borrow Isakower's phrase once again). Bertolt Brecht, not Freud, may be the more appropriate role model. Brecht was continually on guard against ways in which certain meanings were suppressed by convention, and encouraged his readers to practice a form of "interventionist thinking" (*eingreifendes Denken*; see Wright 1987). He was particularly sensitive to the rote repetition of received wisdom and was constantly seeking new procedures, particularly rooted in the theatre, that would open up the text to new forms of understanding. "Where authority aims at memesis, a reproduction of the already established, Brecht wishes to avoid such mimesis, refusing any notions of an expressive realism" (Wright 1987, 96). This description could be applied directly to the way in which the long quotation from Freud is used as the topic sentence of the target article. To the extent that we are urging the reader to beware of such argument by authority and to try, wherever possible, to look at the case report with a more skeptical posture, we are siding with Brecht against Freud.

Up to this point, we have listed suggestions 'for improving the competence and sensitivity of the reader who finds himself exposed to a piece of rhetorical argument. But do we need to stay wedded to this genre? We are beginning to see the development of a new discipline of qualitative research in the social sciences (see the special section in the Summer, 1987 number of *American Educational Research Journal*), and many of its principles apply to the traditional case study method. This method, as we have seen, is characterized by providing a narrative as its final endproduct; by drawing on the teachings of the new field of qualitative research, the significance of this narrative can be more systematically evaluated by means of the following set of criteria:

> First, the story should be true. Second, the story should be the simplest internally consistent account that can be offered. It should emphasize those qualities of the situation that can be translated to broader contexts. Finally, there should be minimal distortion by the ideology of the storyteller, who should have subjected his or her values and work to scrutiny. . . . Without standardized criteria, in other words, the editors must rely on the completeness, coherence, and internal consistency of the account; whether it penetrated and illuminated the subject; its plausibility; and the credibility of the author.
> —Smith 1987, 1978

In presenting (and evaluating) any piece of qualitative research, it is important to be aware of the distinction between two kinds of data: *emic* data, which are expressed in the categories and meanings of the subject being studied (in this case, the patient); and *etic* data, which are expressed in either the researcher's language or the categories of some theory (see Smith 1987, 174). One of the difficulties with the target article was the fact that little of the emic data remained to be evaluated by the reader; on the contrary, it had been too quickly translated into the standard etic formulations of psychoanalytic theory. Not only do such translations prevent the reader from drawing his own conclusions from the original clinical material, as we have noted above; they also violate the principle of context sensitivity. To quote again from Smith: "What sets qualitative research apart most clearly from other forms of research is the belief that the particular physical, historical, material, and social environment in which people find themselves has a great bearing on what they think and how they act. Acts must be interpreted by drawing on those larger contexts. Qualitative researchers reject the notion of universal, context-free generalization" (p. 175).

Closely linked to this assumption is the principle of participant-observation, and this rule has a particular bearing on the role of the analyst/researcher and his relation to the patient.

> Most importantly, the researcher must personally become situated in the subject's natural setting and study, firsthand and over a prolonged time, the object of interest and the various contextual features that influence it.

This introduces notions about the "personhood" of the qualitative researcher and what roles and relationships are formed between researcher and subject. Unlike the model experimenter, the qualitative researcher is not a faceless replicate. Objectivity in the conventional sense is an illusion; the subject's intentions, beliefs, views of the researcher [read transference], and interests must be considered.

—Smith 1987, 175

Because each analysis is unique and because different types of clinical happenings acquire differential significance in the final understanding of the case, it would seem impossible to legislate a particular research method. Again we quote from Smith:

The social scene [and in particular the analytic situation] is thought to be so complex that one cannot anticipate it sufficiently to select a priori a single or even a few meanings for a construct (as one does in operationalization) and adopt a uniform way of measuring it. Standardized methods have little utility, and because preordinant procedures are not used, establishing such things as interobserver agreement and representative sampling become problematic and, in some approaches, irrelevant. Methods are not viewed as guarantors of truth, as they seem to be in the orthodox, textbook model of experimentation. Rather, methods are used inventively and tailored to the situation. . . . Because there is no catalog of qualitative designs or certified methods, thoughtful researchers describe what they did in detail.

—Smith 1987, 175

Both rhetoric and evidence can influence belief, but as we have seen, they function in different ways and according to different assumptions. To the extent that rhetoric leans heavily on argument by authority, on private and partial testimony, and on encouraging the suspension of disbelief, we are in favor of turning to a more egalitarian form of persuasion. We recommend giving up the traditional genre of the case report and replacing it with a form of presentation that is grounded in the principles of the new field of qualitative research. Narrative is still respected but does not stand alone; as a result, the reader is less vulnerable to its particular rhetorical appeal. Rather, the narrative is buttressed by a continuing awareness of the context being considered and by the particular "personhood" of the analyst/ researcher. (It might be necessary to explicitly introduce reflections on countertransference when presenting a clinical account.) A significant proportion of the data is cast in emic formulations; as a result, the reader has access to concrete portions of the original observations and can better evaluate their translation into etic abstractions. And finally, the method used to gather, evaluate, and present the findings is individually tailored to the problem at hand, and the choice of method is explained and defended. No longer is a standard genre deemed adequate. By the same token, the findings are explicitly relative to the particular case being discussed; universal generalizations are to be avoided.

In the final analysis, we are all in favor of narrative appeal, but we also believe that science is not synonymous with literature.

CHAPTER 9

A Critical Hermeneutics for Psychology: Beyond Positivism to an Exploration of the Textual Unconscious

ROBERT S. STEELE

When poetics replaces positivism reading becomes radical. As one moves from the invisibility of scientific prose, which always points past itself to an object, to the recognition that the text, itself, is a place where objects are created and shared then words become worthy of the same scrutiny and analysis as other phenomena. The fact that many objects of science are known to us not from observation but from reading about them or seeing them illustrated in a text makes it plain that the "thing itself" for many scientists is actually a textual representative, a signifier, for some supposed extant entity. However, the critical reader knows that from a strictly textual point of view black holes and angels have a similar ontological status: we know them by word of text.

Poetics brings language alive. It helps us hear the resonance in what we read by making us aware of the multiple meanings in words and by aiding us to see the features of a linguistic landscape that scientists have virtually ignored, especially in their own writings. Science will become truly reflexive, truly self-critical, when it allows the wisdom of a prose poetics—a hermeneutics of the representation of the real—to alter its practice.

Background

Our concern here is to make visible what training and custom has rendered invisible. I want to show you the psychological text in a journal article on psychology, to call to your attention the ways the words are manipulated to reproduce a psychologist's vision of the world. Instead of looking at the objects of the world, the things of the scientific gaze, we will look at what

223

is doing the pointing: the textual signs. This seeing of signs, this hermeneutic gaze, is a type of double vision, because the reader must not only be absolutely conversant in the traditional idiom of expression so that she or he may perform an average expectable reading, but must simultaneously "read between the lines." To accomplish this one needs more than anything else to be aware of the forms of play in texts. These include the flexibility of meaning that words and phrases have, the myriad possibilities for translating an imaginative creation into a symbolic form and yet the absolute determinate significance of choosing one word instead of another, and the fun a reader can have of discovering or making up something the author did not mean to be seen in her or his work.

To read critically one must come to see texts from odd angles, from perspectives that do not square with an authorized reading or a conventional view. Developing and using the hermeneutic gaze—a critically interpretive approach to texts, people, and the world—is a good deal like consciousness raising for women who become feminists: "Women's understandings of our lives are transformed so that we see, understand and feel them in a new and quite different way, at the same time as we see them in the 'old' way" (Stanley and Wise 1983, 54). Such a radical alteration of consciousness produces a renewed vision of reality; "Reality *is* much more complex and multidimensional than we ordinarily suppose it to be, and it *is* contradictory" (Stanley and Wise 1983, 540). For the rational positivist, contradiction is an indication of at best an anomaly and at worst an error; for the critical reader it is a reassurance that she or he is learning to see signs in new ways. Reading with a radical eye means that one should not only be able to immerse oneself in a text and faithfully follow the author's intended argument, but that one is also capable of moving outside the text and viewing it from several different perspectives with an eye to seeing it more completely.

There is a tradition of textual exigesis in psychology. For example much of Freud's and Jung's evidence came from interpreting texts and in America researchers in the thematic tradition like Murray (1941), McClelland (1961), and Winter (1973) have done a good deal of textual interpretation in analyzing fictional works, political speeches, and coding TATs for various motivational themes. However, such readings have looked outward, taking as their subject the traditional object of scientific observation—the other person or thing being closely examined and commented on. Only in rare instances have psychologists turned their gaze upon their own texts and practiced disciplinary reflexivity by analyzing how we as psychologists authoring texts represent our worlds. This paucity of research is perhaps, in part, because the traditions nurturing modern critical inquiry are not those that have fed scientific psychology, which has taken its ways of doing things from the natural and not the human sciences.

Critical hermeneutics is nourished by many forms of inquiry: feminism, marxism, phenomenology, psychoanalysis, structuralism, and deconstruction. Rather than review at length each of these, their relations to each other, and their contributions to post-modern literary criticism, let us simply highlight the textual signs to which each of these alerts a reader.

Feminism

A feminist perspective sensitizes one to the interdependence of gender roles, to how within a text masculine and feminine terms are used in complementary or opposing ways to create differing images of males and females. As deBeauvoir (1961), Irigaray (1980), and many others have shown, woman is the other in male-authored works. In such "phallologocentric" texts the female as a linguistic structural term is held in opposition to the male and is the category against which things considered male—culture, mind, subject status— are compared. Any such comparison is, however, implicit because the female term lies latently in the backround as an unacknowledged other or an unseen context in which man explores the significance of his world. For example Griffin (1978) has shown how both nature and the body are considered female in scientific prose, and Chesler (1972) has demonstrated how women are identified as deviant, crazy objects by medicine. Feminism also alerts us to the near omission of womankind from most scientific texts and the concomitant assumption that generalizations about males hold true for humankind, when at best they only apply to man.

Marxism

A marxist reading brings out how under capitalism we produce ideas as goods and draws attention to the ways our texts are influenced by economic realities. This perspective will help us to see how objectivity, alienation, and class differences make their ways into supposedly unbiased reports.

Phenomenology

For two centuries phenomenology has battled natural scientific attempts to extract the observer from the empiricist context and to operate as if consciousness were an unproblematic medium of comprehension. When a reader is radicalized by phenomenology he or she will be attuned to the methods an author uses to try to absent him or herself from a text, to the tricks of perspective that are used to construct objectively seen objects, and to the ways in which subjects are transformed into objects.

Psychoanalysis

Although often misused, when used with care, psychoanalysis is a continual reminder to the reader that texts manifest all the signs of sexual repression found in dreams, fantasies, and everyday life: displacement, condensation, secondary revision, and symbolic representation.

Structuralism

A structural analysis means the identification of the dialectically coupled interplay of nested binary oppositions throughout a text. Microstructural readings focus on the sub-structures of a work, the linguistic interplay of signifiers that form the molecules of meaning. Macrostructural exigesis identifies the archetypal patterning in a text showing how a work is organized around typical themes of human fantasy.

Deconstruction

Deconstructionism, as one of the leading forms of post-modern literary criticism, is an anarchic amalgam of phenomenological structuralism critiqued by marxism, psychoanalysis, and in some cases, feminism. What a passion for deconstruction means to reading is a suspension of willing disbelief, the refusal to actively collude with a text, its author, and the social order in the production of the illusions of objectivity, authority, neutral and neutered language, facticity, and rationality. All or most of this must be done while maintaining an ironic, self-critical sense that one is somehow being deceived and misdirected in ways that will come clear in time and that the "self" which is being so critical is not the isolated observer with an all-knowing consciousness, but a social construction of cultural, natural, and individual forces which is thoroughly immersed in the very universe it is critiquing. Texts help one to learn all of this because they are the collective consciousness, the relatively stable memory traces of a thoroughly literate and wealthy society. Meditation on them uncovers their and the reader's depths.

In performing a reading that is informed by each of these perspectives one must not only be critically self-conscious, but must also evidence care for the text. One must not misquote or misrepresent it. Care must also be taken with the various analytic perspectives. They must not be used as simple templates to be applied mechanically to the text. Each is a style of seeing which is best used by one whose life has been significantly changed by association with the radical movement that created this new vision of the world. Deconstruction is a vocation, not a job.

The realization that language, like individual consciousness, is "neither thing nor idea" but a metaphysical combination of both is central to phenomenological hermeneutics and it provides an equation that opens up psychology to exploration with many of the insights of post-modern criticism (Merleau-Ponty 1964, 88). Ricouer's (1979) proposition that a person is like a text is metaphorically transitive because a text is also like a person. When the common sense of experience that runs through marxism, psychoanalysis, and feminism is brought to textual deconstruction one quickly sees that consciousness and text have nearly identical structures. Knowing that consciousness can be deceived and that only through the simultaneous analysis of the individual and society can we become disillusioned means that when one reads one is nearly overwhelmed by textual schizions—divisions in a work that signal unresolved but covered-over cultural and personal conflicts, distortions, repressions, and omissions. Such textual self-division has been described by Freud as the difference between the manifest and the latent dream and in the psyche as the difference between the conscious and the unconscious. It is a difference that is described phenomenologically as that between figure and ground, the literal text being the figure while the text out of awareness is the ground. Entering textual territories previously dominated by positivism, deconstruction leads us from the figure to the ground, from the literal in language to the figurative. It leads us into an exploration of the textual unconscious. To a culture that places too high a value on the sober, rational, objective, scientific document, deconstruction brings a sense of the subjective, the playful, poetic, and irrational. Where science operates with a reduced sense of language trying to ape the mathematical formula, deconstruction reminds us that rhetoric, metaphor, persuasion and propaganda are a living, if denied, part of every text.

Method

Reading counter to a text presupposes that the critic is so thoroughly familiar with her or his culture that she or he can easily follow along with and understand an essay or story and while doing so choose to juxtapose with her or his naive, almost reflex, understanding a reflexive, sophisticated critique of the same text. To demonstrate how such a reading is done requires a textual case study, and with the notable exception of studies by Jung (1955-6), Hershberger (1970), Derrida (1976) and a few others, such works are rarely performed with psychological texts as their object of analysis.

In general, textual research offers some definite psychometric advantages to the psychologist. Unlike the anonymous subjects or unreproducible populations of most studies, the text is an easily identifiable object open to any number of investigations because it is continuously renewable and reproducible. It does not change with observation so if someone wishes to replicate or critique a reading, the original text uncontaminated by its first analysis can be subjected to a second, third, or fourth; it meets every observing eye afresh.

In addition to this advantage of reproducibility, texts because they are the product of a confluence of forces—economic, social, individual, and historic—might easily become an important object of study for social psychology. Texts are a paragon of ecological validity: they are one of the material manifestations of the way people represent each other, and within psychology are a prime medium of discourse, so it follows that by analyzing psychological texts we are directly investigating one of the ways our society represents us to ourselves.

In analyzing texts there are a good many signs to look for which move one from the ordinary to the extraordinary text. Some signposts to the unconscious, latent, background or counter text include: inappropriate arguments, postponements in making points or the omission of an important point, displacements, condensations, conventional unthinking dismissals or highly charged emotional attacks, the deceptive use of metaphors, a change in cadence, and startling variations in tone.

The Reading

Because not a great many texts by psychologists have been analyzed, our choice of reading material is nearly unlimited. For this analysis let us take up an important position paper in modern personality theory, Mischel's "Continuity and Change in Personality." Mischel argues that in order to make personology more accountable to quantitative data, and therefore more objective and cognitively oriented, we must respond to the fact that personality inventories show very low retest correlations and we must face the fact that there is little continuity through the years or across situations in people's socio-emotional traits. This is not, however, the case with cognitive styles that show considerable constancy through the years and consistency from situation to situation. Mischel concludes from this that personality research should join what was to become the cognitive revolution in psychology by turning to the more scientifically viable study of the variety of ways in which people cognitively process their environments. However, a deconstruction of Mischel's paper uncovers an entirely different thrust. In our reading we will discover that his text undercuts itself because there lies latent within the background of the manifest work an elaborate sub-text in which one of the oldest personality stereotypes held by man is reproduced: women are dangerously inconsistent creatures and men—when acting truly human—are cognitively consistent, rational, and as predictable as machines. While Mischel is calling for more objectivity, his sub-text clearly shows that objectivity is simply a rationalization of the male point of view, a bias that is seen in Mischel's insistence on his authority, his taking away of other people's autonomy, and his animation of machines. The recognition of this prejudice leads us further into the text, where we will uncover a deeply embedded male perspective on the world. For in the text's denial of emotion, dread of castration, and fear of women's power we find archetypal manifestations of the male imagination. In short, behind the author's positivist argument for cognitive continuity we will discover an emotionally disordered work held together by masculine dread.

Authoring Authority

The initial movement of the text, one which is typical of authoritative works, is the privileging of the author and the discrediting of the subjects being analyzed. Mischel argues that most "subjects" transform "their seemingly discrepant behavior into a constructed continuity, making unified wholes out of almost anything" (1969, p. 1012). There is nothing exceptional in this observation. Any being who exists over time and knows it, (that is, is a subject) must construct a history for her or himself. However, for the scientist there can be no subject, other than himself, because the whole world is the object of his investigations. Mischel quickly assumes the role of scientist by informing the reader that although subjects construct genotypic unities for themselves by which they characterize themselves and others no such uniformities in character traits are seen in the research; "the consistency data on IBM sheets ... probably would account for only a trivial portion of the variance" (p. 1012). In other words, there are very low retest correlations for socioemotional traits. Two strands of Mischel's argument are knotted in the metonomy "IBM sheets." One trope reduces people, subjects, to data on cards. It is as a number that they are represented. "IBM sheets" also stands for the precision and prestige of science. There is for Mischel a tension between what subjects do, (that is, finding consistency in their behaviors,) and what data sheets representing subjects show: no such consistency exists. The tension that creates the unstable IBM trope is eliminated when Mischel chooses the sheets over the subjects, and reduces subjects to datum. He thereby makes them objects of science, invalidates their subjective worlds, and finds they are inconsistent. Even though they claim a continuity in their lives, they are wrong because the scientific data says otherwise.

In the next paragraph he counters this desubjectification of others when he introduces and privileges himself as a subject—the scientist who knows. He says that, "I had" the opportunity to review the "voluminous evidence" on consistency, and that "In my appraisal, the overall evidence ... shows the human mind to function like an extraordinarily effective reducing valve that creates and maintains the perception of continuity even in the face of ...

changes" (p. 1013). Allying his "I," his subjectivity, with the scientific evidence he asserts that the mind functions like a valve. This overworked simile in psychology is used by Mischel to characterize what others do, although he seems to be unaware that he has just explained his own prose and caricatured the scientific enterprise. He has reduced people to data on sheets and decades of research to a simple mechanical metaphor. He, like science, has failed to reflect upon himself, and therefore has projected into the world the structures of his own subjectivity. Ever since Descartes the scientist has looked outward assuming that his thoughts, cognitions, motives, and instruments were pure, unclouded, and not liable to the vicissitudes of worldly perception. But like all subjects and all perceptual perspectives, scientists and science create the worlds they see and describe with their prose by reducing the multiplicity of being into a schematically ordered, often mechanical representation.

Machines Over People

Mischel advances his thesis by saying "Data from many sources converge" to document the finding that cognitive constructions are resistant to change (p. 1012). Notice how the earlier "consistency data on IBM sheets" is here transformed into active agents—data converging. The data has taken on a volition of its own. This type of metaphoric transubstantiation is typical of positivist prose. Data becomes animate for it knows, while people are made mute, inanimate objects.

After a long detour—to which we will return—Mischel completes this transformation of people into machines and machines into animate beings. The closing of his argument rests on the detour he will take because his conclusion depends on a crucial displacement he will navigate in that long aside: the marginalization of women and nature that is essential to scientific discourse. Mischel's final point is triumphantly made when he asserts that over the "last decade" there has been an "exciting growth of research on cognitive styles and many researchers have begun to study the person as an information processing and problem-solving organism" (p. 1016). People, Mischel adds, show remarkable consistency in certain cognitive traits. He asserts that as organisms for information processing—remember the IBM trope—people do possess a continuous and reliable history. By fully turning people into computing machines Mischel reanimates the subjects he made lifeless when he found they knew less about themselves than a computer did. It is as machine organisms, the ultimate object of a mechanistic science of life, that people show consistency. It is in their ways of thinking, their cognitive styles, their Cartesian subjectivity that they are most stable. Machine, science, and man come together historically in possessing consistency over time when scientific problem-solving methods show that people are information processors.

Mischel's metaphoric closure is complete and the fit between his position and the scientism of his society is exact, for "scientism is a particular case of alienation or objectification ... which deprives man of his human reality and makes him confuse himself with things" (Merleau-Ponty 1964, 126). Mischel's art in creating this identity of man and machine must, however, go unseen because the reader as machine or scientist sees only what is printed on the page and misses the textual background of figures of speech and the history of linguistic usage which make it possible to compose such a world. What is missing in this machineman world view is emotion, but we will see how the repressed returns.

Hidden Meanings: Emotions and Women

All texts participate in the culture in which they are composed; they articulate societal structures within the field of language. Structuralism has long studied this, and post-structuralist deconstruction has advanced this program in an attempt to uncover what lies beneath the facade of texts and cultures. In looking at the backround, instead of the foreground, deconstruction, like feminist analysis, draws out what goes unseen. Seeming detours or asides, allusions, and metaphors become central to such an analysis because they form the unconscious of a work. They are what the text is built on, even though the text would rather have us view its facade than its deeper meanings. The climax in Mischel's use of the often repeated, reducing-valve trope is found nearly at the center of his article, and it introduces the detour in which the central displacement of his paper takes place. He writes, "It is essential for the mind to be a reducing valve—if it were not it might literally blow itself!" (p. 1015). "Reducing valve" is no longer a simple simile for the mind, as it was at the beginning. It is now "essential" that the mind *be* a reducing valve. This single sentence will serve nicely to illustrate several keys deconstructionism uses to open up texts that close too neatly on themselves. Mischel intensifies the simile of the reducing valve he began with, by asserting that the mind is a valve. If it were not, then it might "literally blow itself." The threat is implicit. Believe this metaphor is actual description or your mind will self-destruct. Language, like man, is always trying to overcome its limitations with declarations and threats. The word "literal" screams actuality before one's eyes, but if one looks again all one sees is a word trying to point beyond itself. Mischel joins in the excitement of his language by assuming that he is describing something literal, when in fact he has been duped by the magic of a metaphor suddenly and miraculously becoming reality. His compositional composure can hardly be contained as he uses the most ejaculatory of all punctuation, the exclamation point, to emphasize his point.

However, making this metaphor into a reality not only injects emotion into the paper, it also introduces beneath it another metaphor which Mischel must deny creating. If one were to follow Mischel's instructions and read his sentence literally, one would see the brain, the materialist translation of mind, "blowing off steam" like valves do. Mischel, then, would be referring to some sort of brain hemorrhage. Such a literal reading, however, misses Mischel's excitement and the ambiguity of "blow itself," thereby ignoring the latent sexual metaphor that motivates the three denials that follow this textual climax. A mind "blowing itself" suggests the phrase "blow my mind," while the ejaculatory action of a valve gaining relief from pressure suggests the phrase "blow job" with its orgasmic and penile connotations. A mind "blowing itself" is the phallologocentric metaphor par excellence. The penis is the most prominent valve of the male machine and the mind is man's most celebrated tool. This mindpenisvalve, then, must be protected from stimulation by itself, and as Mischel will eventually argue, from women. Is this text worried about the harmful effects of mental masturbation, or perhaps impotence, or maybe just emotion?

Keeping in mind that in the text its position immediately follows the valve threatening to "blow itself," let us read on following Mischel's detour into emotion by exploring the series of denials that serve as unconscious refutations of castration, such denials themselves being a defense against fears of impotence and punishment for masturbation. The first point Mischel takes up is to deny the validity of psychoanalysis. While this is not an unreasonable act, he does it for a rather odd reason. He dismisses the "hydraulic Freudian-derived personality model" which reduces a multiplicity of behaviors to a few central traits (p. 1015). However, Mischel until the reducing valve climax had himself depended on just such a metaphoric structure. Why use it himself to characterize the operations of the mind, but deny its validity in psychoanalytic model building? His illustration of why the analytic paradigm does not work reveals the reason for his inconsistent action. He says, "While a child's fears sometimes may be in the service of an underlying motive" most research "would lead me" to see fears as organized response systems independently maintained by different regulating conditions (p. 1015). According to psychoanalysis the male child's overwhelming fear is of castration because of his sexual lust for the mother. Mischel, here, dismisses such a fear by presenting his reading of the evidence, and he lays them to rest in the next paragraph which brings his detour to an end.

The paragraph's tone, like the rest of the detour's, is emotional. Associated with this affectivity, as is traditional in our culture, are women. The detour in which all the emotional displacements by denial are taking place contains the text's sole references to women. After denying the validity of psychoanalysis and dismissing the belief that there are regnant childhood fears, Mischel produces his third and conclusive denial. He writes, "When we observe a woman who seems hostile and fiercely independent some of the time but passive, dependent, and feminine on other occasions, our reducing valve usually makes us choose between the two syndromes" (p. 1015). Notice the "reducing valve" has become the organ of choice when deciding what a woman is like; the valve is a penismind! Mischel then writes that because multiplicity is reduced to unity by the mind the woman will be seen as one of two things, "She must be a really castrating lady with a facade of passivity—or perhaps she is a warm passive dependent woman with a surface defense of aggressiveness" (p. 1015). This introduction of women into a previously genderless text—or a text assumed to refer to all people because males, masculine experience, and androcentric thought are its subjects—creates a tropic storm. First, there is "castrating lady." The common phrase is "castrating bitch" or "castrating woman." Mischel creates the "facade of passivity" he describes by substituting a genteel signifier for these earlier terms. This oxymoron, "castrating lady," however, serves an important purpose. It denies the imaginary woman the power of being castrating by turning her into a lady. Mischel thereby inverts the feared castration by himself metaphorically castrating women. He makes them ladies instead of powerful fear-provoking bitches, bitches who might breed and have sons whom they might castrate. Once the bitch has been turned into a lady she can then be seen in the second half of the sentence as a "warm, passive-dependent woman."

Mischel continues, "But perhaps nature is bigger than our concepts and it is possible for the lady to be a hostile, fiercely independent, passive, dependent, feminine, aggressive, warm, castrating person all-in-one" (p. 1015). Note here the classic identification of women with nature. Scientific fantasy often personifies nature as "she" and imagines the scientist uncovering her secrets by pulling back her veil or by penetrating her (Griffin 1978, Merchant 1980). For Mischel's sentence to work, the reader must be dimly aware of this tradition because Mischel in turning the lady into nature says it/she might "perhaps" be bigger than "our concepts." It is typical hubris to think that man's conception of the world, that is culture, encompasses all of nature. Mischel is beyond hubris, however. He has so completely accepted this typical masculist view that he now entertains the possibility that just "perhaps" nature has not been entirely encoded by man. Naturelady, he tells us, might be superabundant with traits, she might be a "person." Personhood is granted, by Mischel, as a state of wholeness that is more complete than being a woman.

In this short digression on women, which completes Mischel's detour of denials, he unconsciously recapitulates a narrative that object-relations theory has long maintained is a typical emotional fantasy of little boys. When the infant male comes to fear the threatening aspects of the mother, her aggressiveness, he splits the maternal image into two part objects: the castrating, fear-inspiring witch and the benevolent, loving angel. It is only with the maturation of his cognitive and emotional being that he reunites these images into a whole object—to quote Mischel, a "person all-in-one." However, this whole object is rarely seen as a sexual being, for in making her whole the boy strips his mother imago of her over-exciting sexual and aggressive aspects (Fairbairn 1952, Chodorow 1978). No longer a castrating bitch, mother becomes a lady.

The object relations scenario which Mischel unintentionally recapitulates is itself a recasting in scientific terms of the split image of woman and nature that is a traditional patriarchical mytheme: She is a devouring monster—the Medusa, and a benevolent minister—Athena. Having completed his detour, which he uses to dismiss psychoanalysis but in which we have found he unconsciously recapitulates its most central emotional scenario, Mischel is free to return to science. In concluding he assures us that people are remarkably consistent when they are seen as information-processing machines.

Man's View

Men are consistent because in their language, their fundamental information transforming system, they keep recapitulating gender typical behaviors. When Mischel introduced the passage on the "castrating lady" he wrote "When we observe women" and thereby assumed a male gaze identifying himself and other men as the "we" who observe women (perhaps voyeuristically) and fear their castrating retaliation. Mischel's assumption of the male identity helps us to identify in his prose a typical male fantasy of domination: Women, like nature, are identified by male observation and taken into man's world through his adjectives and nouns of signification. Mischel never considers what the "lady" might think of herself, for she does not have the status of a subject, one who is capable of self-signification. In the end Mischel grants greater humanity to machines in terms of having a reliable history, being agents of action, and being subjects of his text than he does to women. In this he takes his place with the masters of culture who have far more in print on man as a tool-using animal, on the industrial revolution, on the man-machine interface, and on man and computers than women have ever published about themselves and the non-mechanical worlds they create.

Intercourse and discourse between man and machine has been the obsessive affair of science for centuries to the extent that, in man's imagination, it has transformed nature from a living organism into a machine (see, for example, Bronowski 1981). Men have become so enamored with their tools that they have through narcissistic reincorporation come to think of themselves as machines—mindpenisvalves.

In his "Continuity and Change in Personality" we have seen that Mischel has used his psychological science to affirm man's truth: Only thought-cognition-reason—the tools of scienceman—have continuity over time. These alone are historical subjects. All else is inconsistent. At the manifest level of his text he uses personological science to deny the consistency of socio-emotional traits, while at the latent level—in the realm of the textual unconscious of metaphor, allusion, and illusion and situated in a detour in the article—he produces a series of denials that dismiss the possibility of lasting effects from typical male fears associated with masturbation, childhood, castration, and women. In the wider culture the omission of children, women, and sexuality from mankind's official public histories of his past is a similar kind of denial. Both are forms of repression and oppression that reaffirm man's independence by suppressing his initial dependence as a son within women's "private domain," the socio-emotional matrix of the body, the home, mothering, and sensual recreation (Dinnerstein 1977).

Resistance and Reflection

If you have been at all startled by these revelations of the seething undercurrents of overwrought emotion in a seemingly rational text arguing the virtues of cognitive control and if you are thinking, "Steele's gone too far," I invite you to read Mischel's article for yourself and thereby judge the validity of my reading. Such a checking of interpretation against text by a critically sympathetic reader is at the heart of hermeneutical reflection. In making such a comparison the reader should be aware that her or his judgment may be warped by traditional misunderstandings and that such biases need to be analyzed as closely as the text itself. This is self-criticism, the reflection by the reader on her or his own resistance, and it is the complement to the reader's criticism of the text.

To help us analyze our resistances to radical readings in general and my reading of Mischel in particular, let us look at some of the reasons why we might think such textual exigesis odd. It cannot be because such work is not empirical. Textual hermeneutics proceeds by the most exacting empiricism. The interpreter must at all times see what the text says, intimates, and does not say. In many ways an interpreter must be extremely literal, taking the words for what they actually say and not for what most readers take them to mean. Also, as was pointed out earlier, texts can fulfill an observational criterion rarely met by people. They can be re-examined and show no effects of the first reading, although the person doing the second examination might well have been changed by her or his knowledge of the initial critical analysis. A longtime dream of science, replication without the objects having been altered by observation, is then fulfilled by textual hermeneutics.

Why then if readings fulfill so many empirical criteria has hermeneutics only recently made its way into American psychology? Because of the operation of several types of resistance in both the personal and social spheres.

There is resistance on the reader's part because deconstructive analyses are seen as personal attacks on the author by the interpreter. For example, I have used Mischel's name and said his text has emotional problems; am I daring to intimate that he does? We, I feel, all have emotional difficulties and one of the problems men face in coping with emotions is the fact that they think they must deny having problems. Mischel's text, like most of cognitive psychology, colludes in such a denial. Also, the degree to which the Mischel, who published an article in 1969, is like anyone living today with the name Mischel is uncertain, especially if what he argues about the discontinuity of personality is true.

Along with a reader's defense of an author's character comes a concern about his or her own, "If these deconstructors can find this here, then what will they uncover in what I've written?" This is a common wariness that people have of psychologists. When being introduced to another person as a psychologist, many of us have heard, "Oh, so you're a psychologist, I better watch what I say." Deconstruction, being reflexive, brings this fear of exposure to psychologists themselves for it calls upon us to examine ourselves as closely as we look at others.

There is a reservation about intradisciplinary criticism that, based on historical precedent, is well-founded. In its early years the psychoanalytic movement was plagued by infighting. Unfortunately, instead of arguing the merits of each other's theories and observations, the analysts attacked each other's neuroses. All semblance of scientific decorum was often lost in personal attacks, backbiting, and gossip (Steele 1982). The emotional gained ascendancy over the intellectual. Of course, both should play a role in any discourse, and we should be aware that the more we champion the rule of reason the more we ignore the emotional, thereby becoming prey to its unconscious expression (Jung 1931).

There might be resistance to radical readings simply because they are relatively new to psychology. As psychologists most of us were trained to read abstracts, look at the data, and be critical of an argument's logic, not to consider an article's literary merits, its linguistic structure, or poetic diction. We were also trained to accept as given, if not natural, a few basic metaphors; one of these being, "man is a machine." The mere fact that such a statement does not seem bizarre is a tribute to the triumph of scientific ideology. It is an argument for training ourselves to read more critically, so that we are not blinded by scientism, depriving ourselves of human reality in favor of believing that we are machines (Steele in press).

Finally, I think, we resist hermeneutics, marxism, psychoanalysis, and deconstructionism because they are foreign, and it is often difficult to import ideas into a society as ideologically xenophobic as America. Such ideas are also at the heart of the culture of critical discourse, which in the United States is seen to be at odds with the social order of science (Gouldner 1979). While the former produces social discontent, the promise of progress is the most important product of the latter. Mischel's article is in the progressive, all-American, problem-solving tradition of positivist psychology; my reading is feminist, foreign, and from an eclectic otherness. It is not constructive, but de(con)structive.

CHAPTER 10

The Possibility of Psychological Knowledge: A Hermeneutic Inquiry

KENNETH J. GERGEN

The science of psychology has now officially entered its second century. In many respects the growth of the discipline during its first century was little short of spectacular. At the turn of the century there was no official organization of psychologists in the United States, and psychology was scarcely recognized as a discipline of study. Universities sheltered no departments and course offerings were rare. In dramatic contrast, the American Psychological Association alone now boasts a membership of over 65,000. Only a minority of university graduates in the country have not been exposed to psychology. For many the promise of psychology is based in large part on the assumption that objective knowledge of mind is possible. As it is reasoned, through careful research we may discover the nature of thought, emotion, motivation, memory, and the like. As the rigor of our methods improve, so will the quality and sophistication of our knowledge.

Although this is an optimistically compelling outlook, many now recognize clouds of threatening demeanor gathering on the horizon. These ominous vapors are varyingly labeled post-structuralist, post-empiricist, post-modern, interpretive, constructionist, and hermeneutic. And, while these orientations are not identical they do share certain underlying affinities that lend to them a unifying power. This is not an appropriate context for reviewing these various movements and their interlocking dialogues. For the reader who is interested there are many sources available (see, for example, Bernstein 1978; Bleicher 1980; Hollinger 1985; Gergen & Davis 1985; Gauld & Shotter 1977; Rabinow & Sullivan 1979; Sarbin 1987; Suleiman & Crosman 1980; Clifford & Marcus 1986; Knorr-Cetina & Cicourel 1981; Norris 1985). Rather, it is my aim in the present chapter to take but a single line of argument as it emerges within the hermeneutic-interpretive domain and to demonstrate the profundity of its implications for psychological research. For, as the story is played out, it becomes increasingly clear that the model of inquiry shared by the predominance of the profession during the first century of the discipline

239

simply cannot, save through inertia and/or some form of self-contented myopia, remain intact. After demonstrating why this is so, we may turn to ways in which future inquiry may be altered and enriched.

Psychological Inquiry and the Interpetive Fore-structure

For most psychologists the chief focus of inquiry is the mind—its means of representing reality, processing and storing information, intending, feeling, and the like. For others, the behaving person is the chief focus of interest, but primarily as this behavior may be determined by or is dependent on psychological processes. Bodily movements attributed to nonpsychological sources, e.g. (gravity, radiation) are typically of tangential interest. Thus the presumption is generally made that 1) systematic relationships exist between psychological processes (mechanisms, states, etc.) on the one hand and behavioral actions on the other, and 2) through careful assessment of behavioral actions, inferences may be drawn to the domain of mental states. In keeping with these interlocking assumptions, psychologists have variously used behaviors listed in the left-hand column below to furnish information about the mental states indicated in the column to the right:

behavior in a maze	reveals information on	learning
reaction time	"	perception
frequency of word usage	"	motivation
paired associates performance	"	memory
rating scales	"	attitudes
facial configurations	"	emotions
spinach consumption	"	dissonance reduction
button pressing	"	hostility
verbal assent	"	opinions
crawling	"	strength of attachment
language forms	"	moral reasoning
word recognition	"	repression

In all these randomly selected instances, the psychologist essentially employs the exterior behavior as one might a text; in this sense the problem for the researcher is to use the text to determine the nature of the author's intentions. Behavior furnishes a range of textual signifiers, and the challenge for the researcher is to locate the sub-text of the signified.

Much thinking in the hermeneutic domain has shared such assumptions. From the theoretical treatises of Schleirmacher (1959) and Dilthey (1894) through the more recent writings of Betti (1980) and Hirsch (1976), a central task for the hermeneuticist has been to furnish a set of grounding principles or rules that would enable the reader (of a biblical text, a poem, or a nation's constitution, for example) to distinguish a good or accurate interpretation from a misguided or inaccurate one. Yet, in spite of the many attempts to solve the problem of accuracy in interpretation, most scholars now argue that a viable solution has yet to be achieved. Or, in terms closer to the heart of psychology, the attempts of hermeneutic theorists over the centuries to determine psychological states from exterior signs has been singularly unsuccessful.

In light of this impasse, traditional presumptions underlying psychological inquiry are thrown into critical relief. It is part of our common sense belief system to hold that psychological events are related to our behavior, but on what grounds can such a belief be justified? To undertake the task of inferring the covert from the overt would require that we possess rudimentary knowledge of 1) the range of psychological states to which inferences are to be made and 2) the ways in which these states are related to behavioral expressions. However, because all we have as investigators are the expressions themselves, propositions about the character of mental states and their modes of expression must be fully hypothetical. But how are we to select one set of hypotheticals over another? This question becomes particularly vexing when we consider ethnopsychological inquiry. As various ethnographic inquiries indicate, cultures vary considerably in their assumptions concerning the constituents of the internal world. The Western vocabulary of the emotions (Lutz 1982), motivation (Rosaldo 1980), personal dispositions (Kirkpatrick 1985; Shweder & Miller 1985) would border on the nonsensical in other cultural domains. Much the same conclusions are reached from inquiry in historical psychology. Much that we take for granted about the nature of mental states would seem alien or possibly unintelligible (and vice versa) in earlier historical climes. For example, in today's laboratories of psychology a test for the existence of soul would be little short of charlatanism. Yet, even in 1907 it was possible for an investigator, Dr. Duncan MacDougall, to make such a test. By weighing bodies shortly before and soon after death, he was able to demonstrate a loss of approximately one ounce of weight—presumably the result of the departure of the soul. The conclusions seemed all the more compelling when, in subsequent research, this decrement in weight could not be located in the death of 15 dogs.

Both anthropological and historical comparisons pose an arduous question for those who search for validity in interpretation: on what grounds can we presume that the array of mental terms currently taken for granted in Western culture possesses the kind of ontological status that would permit objective exploration. What if we are the mistaken victims of our systems of historically situated beliefs, and our minds actually possess the characteristics attributed to them in other cultures and historical periods? Further, it is unclear how observations of overt behavior could ever serve to correct our contemporary beliefs about mind. If we cannot be certain about the states of mind there are to explore, then it is equally difficult to determine in what manner these states are connected to (or are expressed in) the vocabulary of overt action. And if we cannot determine in any independent fashion how the covert is related to the overt, how the signifiers are related to the signified, then reading the psyche can be none other than an exercise in cultural presuppositions.

It is in this light that we can appreciate one of the most important turns in post-modern debate over interpretation. As has become increasingly clear to interpretation theorists, the manner in which a text is interpreted is vitally dependent on historically located conventions of interpretation. It is these interpretive dispositions, sometimes termed *"fore-structures of understanding,"* that determine how a text is interpreted and not the author's intention (if there is such an entity). In this sense a text or utterance may properly be expected to convey different meanings within various subcultures and across history. From this perspective, the concept of "true meaning" (or authorial intention) is rendered problematic. Thus, for example, Gadamer (1975) argued that the reader does not confront a text in a historical vacuum. Rather, people dwell within a contemporary "horizon of understandings," and these understandings inevitably fashion their interpretation of texts. Or, as Ricoeur (1971) proposed, "with written disourse, the author's intention and the meaning of the text cease to coincide . . . the text's career escapes the finite horizon lived by the author" (p. 532). And as Fish (1980) has argued, the conclusions one draws as to a text's meaning are fundamentally dependent on the shared understandings existing within the community of which the reader is a member.

It follows from these arguments that the chief limitation over interpretation in the psychological sciences (as well as in the culture more generally) lies within the conventions of discourse shared by the community of interpreters. That is, various interpretations of data relevant to psychological processes and mechanisms may be sustained to the extent that conventions of language use within the relevant community of interlocutors are shared. As new forms of discourse are developed, or as one moves to other interpretive communities, alternative interpretations may be favored. Given sufficient flexibility of language use within a culture, it may be possible for virtually any behavior to be considered a reasonable signifier for any given psychological state. Similarly, it may be possible for skilled users of the language to generate reasons linking virtually any psychological state to any given behavioral action. In effect, given the continuous and unsystematic change and growth of language conventions in a culture, the upward limit on interpretation of behavioral action may be indeterminate. It is this possibility and its implications that will be explored within the remainder of this paper.

Interpretive Relativity and the Psychology of Control

One inviting context for exploring the limits of interpretive flexibility within psychology is that of personality measurement. To a greater extent than most other disciplines, research in personality assessment has been concerned with the development of valid indicators of psychological dispositions. For most disciplines, measurement is a *means* to the more general end of understanding the processes of interest; in contrast, for many researchers in the personality domain valid assessment constitutes an end in itself. Whereas most researchers outside the personality domain will employ single measures of unknown reliability and unchecked validity, for a personality researcher such matters are of focal concern. In effect, personality test devices should be among the most resistant to charges of interpretive relativity. With these thoughts in mind, a single personality assessment device was selected on the grounds that it (a) had been subjected to intensive study, (b) continues to be in broad usage, and (c) has elicited generalized agreement regarding proper interpretation. The Rotter (1975) measure of perceived locus of control meets all of these criteria. The test attempts to measure the degree to which individuals see their outcomes in life as resulting from their own actions as opposed to processes, structures or events outside their control. Perceiving oneself as high in personal control is generally held to be a superior life orientation than that of viewing oneself as a victim of circumstance. Evidence regarding predictive validity for the measure has accumulated for almost two decades (cf. Findley & Cooper 1983; Lefcourt 1976, 1981; Phares 1976; Strickland et al. 1976). The measure continues to play a prominent role in wide-ranging research endeavors. Largely because of the high degree of face validity of the 23 items that constitute the measure, minimal question has been raised over what psychological disposition the items enable one to measure. In the present studies, we place into question the warrant for the received view. The specific attempt is to explore what limits may be placed over the options for interpreting the research data on which existing conclusions rest. What limits, if any, may be placed over the range of meanings that may be assigned to scale outcomes and thus the range of existing research in this domain?

Study 1: Can Any Response Express Any Trait?

In contrast to most research in which the ideal is to procure an average sample from the population at large, inquiry into the potentials of language use requires a sample of highly skilled practitioners. The attempt is to challenge sophisticated language users to interpret items ostensibly measuring locus of control in a variety of alternative ways. Initial participants in the research were thus 24 students enrolled in the University of Pennsylvania Graduate School of Education. Each participant was furnished with a small booklet of "Interpretation Puzzles." In the initial section of the booklet they were instructed that they would be presented with a series of opinion statements, each coupled with a single personality trait. It was their task to show how it would make sense to say of someone who agreed with the opinion statement that he or she possessed the trait in question. Or, as it was said, if someone had the trait in question, could an explanation be furnished as to why he or she would agree with the opinion statement. If no sensible explanation could be found, participants were to try to indicate why. The opinion items were drawn from the Rotter I-E measure; all items from the measure were employed. The trait terms were taken from Anderson's (1968) list of 555 common personality-trait terms. Each booklet contained five separate interpretation puzzles; each puzzle was represented by a randomly selected I-E item (without regard to whether the item was scored in the internal or the external direction) along with a randomly selected trait term (e.g. relaxed, moral, cautious). In total, the participants were exposed to 120 separate trait-item combinations.

The results of this inquiry into the flexibility of explanatory conventions were clear-cut. Of the array of 120 combinations only four failed to "make sense" to the participants. Two of the four were found incoherent by the same subject. In most cases, the solutions to the puzzles were achieved with little apparent effort. Typically, only a single sentence was required to demonstrate how agreement with an I-E item served as a plausible indicator of a randomly selected trait. The flavor of the participants' solutions is best demonstrated with several examples:

1. A person who is *shy* says, "There is a direct connection between how hard I study and the grades I get" (scored as *internal* on the Rotter scale) because, "Such a rationale excuses the shy person from too much socializing and allows him (grammatical gender, please do not give me a hard time) to secrete himself in his room."

2. A person who is *impulsive* says, "Unfortunately, an individual's worth often passes unrecognized no matter how hard he tries" (scored as *external*) because, "An impulsive person might very well need to justify his feelings of staying too short a time with one project or another by believing that no matter how persevering or committed he remains, he won't be acknowledged anyway."

3. A person who is *logical* says, "In the long run people get the respect they deserve in this world" (scored as *internal*) because "People don't get respect randomly; some prior events determine how much respect people get. Thus, the logical person can use his logic to make predictions."

It is possible, of course, that under the duress of solving such problems the participants may have furnished answers that were incoherent or nonsensical. Thus, a separate inquiry was made into the plausibility of the various solutions. In this case ratings were made by a panel of seven additional graduate students, each asked independently to judge the plausibility of a series of approximately a dozen interpretations selected at random from the protocols of the twenty-four participants. Judgments were made on a four-point scale ranging from 1 = nonsense, to 4 = highly plausible (with 2 = doubtful rationale and 3 = plausible). The overall mean evaluation of the eighty-four accounts made by the participants proved to be $\overline{X}$ = 3.25 (SD = .84), indicating that the solutions to the challenges were generally quite plausible. Four of the judges were then furnished with additional puzzles to solve, among which were the four cases which members of the original sample were unable to solve. In this case, a solution was readily found to each. These solutions were included in the array to be evaluated by three members of the panel of judges. The mean judgment of plausibility of these items proved to be $\overline{X}$ = 3.11 (SD = .97), indicating that they too were reasonable.

To summarize, the results of this initial study suggest that contemporary language conventions permit virtually any item of the I-E scale to be plausibly interpreted as an expression of virtually any common trait term.

Study 2. Multiple Traits and Responses

Given the high degree of flexibility in interpretation found in the initial study, additional attempts were made to press for possible limits to interpretive flexibility. In the first of these queries, the question was raised as to whether any given item from the I-E measure could be plausibly interpreted as an indicator of a variety of different underlying traits. To explore this possibility a group of seven undergraduate volunteers from Swarthmore College was exposed to a series of interpretation puzzles. Among them were seven items from the I-E scale (four indicating an external orientation and three an internal). For each item, three different trait terms were randomly drawn. Thus, each of the seven items appeared three different times on the protocols, in each instance with a separate trait term. Each participant confronted each item only once but there was no duplication across participants in the trait term associated with the item. The instructions for this task were identical to those for the first study.

The results of this inquiry demonstrated first that there were no trait item pairings for which participants failed to furnish a solution. Thus, for example, the participants could demonstrate that the item "How many friends you have depends upon how nice a person you are" (internal) could serve as a reasonable indicator of *responsibility, loyalty* and *shyness*. And, according to participants the item "Who gets to be boss depends on who was lucky enough to be in the right place first" (external) could sensibly be seen as an expression of a person's *oversensitivity, practicality,* or *boldness*. A later panel of five judges also found these interpretive solutions to be quite plausible. In this case the average plausibility rating was $\overline{X} = 3.04$ (SD $= 1.12$).

To extend this inquiry an attempt was then made to explore whether a variety of items could all serve as signifiers for the same trait, a trait other than locus of control. And, most cogently, are the rules of intelligibility sufficiently flexible, it was asked, to permit various traits to be plausibly expressed in *logically opposing* statements? To explore this possibility eight trait-item pairs were embedded within the booklets to which subjects in the above study were exposed. Four traits (e.g. *broad-minded, optimistic, fearful, jealous*) were randomly selected (two from the positive and two from the negative pole of Anderson's list), and each paired with two I-E items—one traditionally used to assess an internal and the other an external orientation. Each of the eight participants in this sub-study were exposed to all four traits, but to only one of the two pairings (i.e., either an internal or an external pairing).

The results of this exploration revealed that participants were successfully able to develop linking rationales for all pairings. The same trait could successfully be related to expressions of both internally and externally scored items. For example, one participant wrote that a *broad-minded* person would say, "In the case of the well-prepared student there is rarely if ever such a thing as an unfair test," (scored as internal) because "A broad-minded person is willing to admit that if one is well prepared tests will rarely be unfair. A narrow-minded individual would be more suspecting and defensive." On the other hand, wrote another participant, a *broad-minded* person would say, "As far as world affairs are concerned, most of us are the victims of forces we can neither understand or control," (scored as external) because, "A broad-minded person wouldn't try to 'blame' world events on a particular politician or groups." The average plausibility of the explanations proved acceptable ($\overline{X} = 3.21$, SD $= .98$).

To strengthen the case still farther, 12 additional students were furnished with the same task but this time asked if they could demonstrate how opposite traits (i.e. *broad-minded* and *narrow-minded*; *optimistic* and *pessimistic*; *fearful* and *brave*) could be expressed in the same response. In this case half the participants were asked to demonstrate how broad-minded, optimistic and fearful were expressed in a series of internal and external items, while the remaining half were asked to develop rationales for linking narrow-minded, pessimistic and brave to the same statements. The results of the analysis paralleled the above. All pairings were explained by the participants. A flavor of the results may be obtained by comparing the above accounts of how broad-mindedness would be expressed in both internal and external items, with explanations of how narrow-mindedness would be revealed in the same items. In the case of the internal statement concerning the well-prepared student not believing in an unfair test, one student wrote, "A narrow-minded person would say this because he would not take into account all the many reasons a test could be unfair." In the case of the external statement concerning being victims of forces we can't understand or control, another student wrote, "a narrow-minded person is one who doesn't want to look too deeply inside himself to see how he is really responsible for what happens to him." The average plausibility of these various explanations was $\overline{X} = 3.16$ (SD = 1.03).

As these studies indicate, intelligent language users can construct a plausible rationale for interpreting randomly selected items from the I-E scale as indicators of a multiplicity of traits. Further, any single trait may be seen as expressed in multiple items from the I-E scale. Of particular note, the rules of interpretation appear sufficiently flexible that both internal and external statements can both be understood as revealing the same basic trait. And, such statements can be interpreted satisfactorily as indicators of both a given trait and its opposite.

Study 4. Making Sense of Multiple Items

Thus far the results suggest an impressive degree of flexibility in contemporary conventions for linking terms referring to various psychological states with various self-descriptive statements. How might the weight of these results be diminished? What counter arguments may be posed? At least one possibility derives from the logic of personality assessment, namely, the rationale for employing multiple items. As it is reasoned, any given item may be influenced by a variety of psychological factors, and one would thus be ill advised to trust single-item measures of any trait. Rather, it is essential to employ multiple items that have a demonstrated relationship to each other. In this way extraneous factors influencing responses on any single item will be obscured, and the contribution of the focal trait will be maximized in the summary score. Applying this logic to the above results, it may be argued that the flexibility of interpretation has been demonstrated only with single items. While any single item may be multiply interpreted, significant constraints over interpretation may derive from the use of multiple traits.

To explore this possibility two studies were carried out, the first preliminary to the second. The initial study was prompted not only by the present concern, but also by the fact that the I-E scale traditionally demands of respondents that they select between pairs of self-descriptive items, one treated as an expression of an internal and the other an external orientation. Yet, in all studies described thus far, traits have been linked to *either* an internal *or* an external statement. Thus, to explore whether plausible linkages could be constructed when both items appeared simultaneously, eight Swarthmore students were given six pairs of statements randomly selected from the I-E measure. For each pair a trait was randomly drawn from the Anderson list, and the participant asked to explain why a person who possesses that trait (e.g. *insecure, independent, inquisitive*, etc.) would agree with one of the statements (selected at random) rather than the other. In all, twelve different traits were matched with twelve different item-pairs, with subjects challenged to construct half of the linkages to internal and half to external choices.

As it was found, participants were able to construct all linkages with which they were challenged. The addition of the second statement, said to be "not chosen" by the test taker, produced no barrier to the effective exercise of interpretive capacities. Further, when these linkages were given to an additional sample of six students, it was found that the average plausibility rating was $\overline{X} = 3.32$ (SD = .97).

These results furnished a useful prelude to a more stringent assessment of interpretive flexibility. In this case a group of 24 graduate students at the University of Pennsylvania was exposed to a series of "Triple Puzzles." That is, they were asked to explain how an individual who possessed a single trait, selected at random, could agree with three separate statements from the I-E measure (also randomly selected). Thus, for example, a participant might be asked how a *fearful* person could agree with all three of the following statements:

1. In any case getting what I want has little or nothing to do with luck. (Internal)

2. As far as world affairs are concerned, most of us are the victims of forces we can neither understand nor control. (External)

3. Many times we might just as well decide what to do by flipping a coin. (External) Each participant was presented with three triple puzzles. Nine different traits were used with nine corresponding item triads.

As the analysis of these data demonstrated, of the 72 interpretive challenges, 68 were executed. Because the triple puzzles were included in a larger battery of tasks, and required a greater degree of effort than other sections of the questionnaire, the slightly elevated number of failures to complete might be anticipated. However, as these failures could also be viewed as a signal of interpretive inflexibility, it was possible to examine whether any trait-triple item pair was insoluble for the other seven participants exposed to the same pairing. As this analysis revealed, there was no trait-triple item pair for which at least seven of the eight relevant participants could not furnish linkages. Thus, for example, in the above triad, it was said by one participant that the initial statement would express fearfulness because, "The fearful person believes he controls his own situation by watching out for all things he fears." Such a person was said to endorse the second statement because, "A fearful person recognizes the limits of his vigilance." And the third item would be endorsed because "A fearful person gets depressed when confronted with the limits of his vigilance."

To assess the intelligibility of these interpretations a further sample of eight college students was asked to rate, in the same manner reported above, the reasonableness of a selection of rationales from a random group of 18 trait-item pairs. Using the same four-point rating as above, the mean evaluations were $\overline{X} = 3.04$, (SD = 1.11), indicating that the interpretations furnished by participants were well within the bounds of reason.

To summarize, relatively sophisticated language users could make good cultural sense for viewing agreement with randomly selected statements from the I-E battery, in the context of disagreement with a contrasting statement, as indicative of a wide range of underlying traits. Further, randomly selected traits could be seen as intelligibly and simultaneously expressed by as many as three separate I-E items.

Study 5. From Face Validity to Generic Trait

A further argument to be made against the present analysis again issues from an extension of fundamental views of the assessment process. Although it may be possible for sophisticated language users to show how a handful of items may be expressions of traits other than the one initially designated, such interpretive demonstrations might wear thin if applied to the battery of 23 items. In effect, it may be ventured, each of these items possesses face validity. The most obvious interpretation to be made of the claim to seeing oneself as internally controlled is that the individual believes him or herself to be internally controlled. If the various interpretations constructed within these exercises were pitted against the designated interpretation, the latter might well be found the superior in plausibility. Alternative interpretations possess varying degrees of plausibility (as evidenced in the magnitude of the standard deviations), but on the face of it they will be less plausible than the designated interpretation.

Let us inspect this line of defense more carefully. First, such a defense makes the traditional error of assuming that "face validity" reflects the degree to which a response accurately indicates the underlying disposition. In fact, the argument for face validity essentially asks that one accept the most conventional interpretation (typically for a given subculture) rather than the most accurate one. It is true that acceding to convention enables social life (or life within scientific subcultures) to proceed more smoothly. As Garfinkel (1967) has shown, when people are consistently asked to clarify what their utterances "really mean" relationships rapidly deteriorate. However, to capitulate to the demand for smooth relations does not thereby enhance the accuracy of the interpretations. Under many circumstances (e.g. when people wish to create a good impression, avoid attention, seek help) there may be good pragmatic reason for casting aside the convention of "face validity." And should one be concerned with generating "an enlightened view," "fresh insight" or a catalytic conceptualization within the sciences, an appeal to convention may be counterproductive.

Yet, there is a deeper difficulty at stake in the argument for face validity, one that when upacked, favors an indeterminacy of interpretation even more extended than that suggested thus far. The problem is essentially that of locating *the generic source* for item responses. One assumes in the case of face validity that the linguistic expression reflects an immediately underlying intention or disposition. However, this assumption does not warrant the further assertion that the intention or disposition is the generic source of the expression. Such intentions or dispositions may only be superficial vehicles for the expression of deeper or more fundamental motives. In the case of the I-E measure, an individual may indicate as many as 23 times that he or she is not in control of outcomes. Yet, it may be asked, what is the psychological basis for such patterns? The individual may be giving voice to his or her immediate intentions, but what lies behind the intentions? It is at this point that the door is open to myriad possibilities. One may find that many deeper motives or traits could plausibly give rise to the more superficial or proximal intention.

To explore the implications of this argument more concretely, a group of nine Swarthmore undergraduates was first given questionnaires in which they were asked to conjecture about the goals or needs that might underlie a person's saying (in various ways) that he or she either 1) viewed him or herself as in control of outcomes or 2) viewed outcomes as largely a result of circumstances beyond his or her control. As this inquiry demonstrated, most participants could easily furnish many possible generic sources for such statements. For example, it was said of those who generally see outcomes as outside of their control that they are expressing: a need for others to help them succeed (nurturance), a need to excuse their current position, a complacency over their condition, basic cynicism, a state of serenity, pessimism, need for others' reassurance, and so on.

As we see, even if all items on the I-E scale are taken as face valid indicators of what people desire to communicate, multiple assertions that one sees his or her outcomes as under personal or environmental control do not themselves permit one to designate the underlying motivational or dispositional source. Common linguistic conventions will permit such assertions to be interpreted as motivated, driven, stimulated, or otherwise influenced by a wide variety of "deeper" psychological sources. But let us push the analysis a step further. To say that a person's utterances are the result of needs for nurturance, drive for success, basic cynicism and the like, still leaves open the question of psychological basis. What motivates a person to seek nurturance, strive for success, and so on? More generally, this is to say that every candidate for a generic source trait or disposition could be dislodged from such candidacy by inquiring into its genesis. Each generic trait or stimulus becomes an effect or a response when its source is considered.

The implications of this argument were explored in two additional studies. In the preliminary study the free responses generated by participants in the preceding exercise were examined. Four traits or dispositions said to be the cause of people's claims that they were in control of their outcomes were selected on the basis of their frequency. A group of eight undergraudates was then exposed to a set of "psychological speculation puzzles" in which they were asked how it is that a person who characterized themselves as possessing one trait might actually be demonstrating an underlying (or more basic) alternative trait. For example, a participant was asked how a person who expressed a *need to be superior* could actually be demonstrating a more basic *need for control*. Thus each of the four traits (need for *superiority, control, freedom from anxiety,* and *self-esteem*) was featured in both a generic and a surface position, and each related to all others. As the results demonstrated, participants experienced no difficulty in forming intelligible connections among all surface and source traits. For example, as one participant wrote, "A person who indicates his need for superiority may actually be expressing a need for control because those who want control need superior positions in order for them to be able to control." And as another participant indicated, "One who expresses freedom from anxiety is more basically a person who feels good about himself, i.e., has high self-esteem." As this exercise indicates, then, each manifest disposition could be intelligibly interpreted as a result of another more generic psychological disposition. And each of these dispositions could be viewed, in turn, as the surface manifestation of a more basic source. In effect, four layers of explanation could be traversed; and the explanatory base rendered fully circular as the most basic trait could then be viewed as an effect or manifestation of the surface disposition with which the search began. Expressions of internality can be seen as a result of the individual's need for superiority, which is intelligibly viewed as the result of the individual's need for self-esteem, which functions to reduce anxiety. However, the state of reduced anxiety may be viewed as a by-product of the more basic tendency to see one's outcomes as contingent upon one's actions.

These results raise the more general question: Are the linguistic conventions sufficiently flexible that virtually any psychological disposition may be understood as a reasonable cause for any other disposition? To explore this possibility a group of 18 Swarthmore undergraduates was exposed to four different pairs of trait terms drawn randomly from the Anderson list. For each pair the student was asked how a particular characteristic of the person (trait 1) could be motivated or caused by a second attribute (trait 2). Thus, for example, it was asked, how a person's *practicality* might be motivated or caused by his or her *hopefulness*, how being *comical* could be caused by *resentfulness*, how being *foolish* could be caused by the person's desire to be *charming*, and so on. In all, 40 different trait combinations were employed.

The results of this study largely duplicated the previous patterns. Of the 40 different trait combinations, linkages were successfully constructed for all. (Three such linkages were not executed by certain participants, but where one participant failed to make the linkage, another or others successfully did so.) To assess general plausibility, each questionnaire was then evaluated by one other participant in the group. The average plausibility rating for all trait combinations in this case was $\overline{X} = 3.31$ (SD = .74), a mean that closely approximates the pattern revealed in earlier studies and indicates a high degree of plausibility.

As this series of explorations thus suggests, contemporary language conventions are sufficiently flexible to permit many common trait designations to be plausibly understood as surface manifestations of many other traits at a "deeper level." Trait dispositions operating at the deeper level may intelligibly be understood as a manifestation of still more remote generic sources. Is it possible, one may ask, that any pattern of action, such as claims made to see one's outcomes as under chance or personal control, could be compellingly traced to the full range of common trait dispositions extant within the culture?

Study 6. The Negotiability of Predictive Validity

A final means of combatting the implications of the present line of argument must be addressed. Traditional assessment theory holds that the validity of a measure is established in important degree through predictive study (Lanyon & Goodstein 1971; Mischel 1968; Sundberg 1977). In order to achieve validity any given measure should predict to various behaviors to which it is conceptually related (convergent validity) and should not predict to those behaviors from which it is conceptually independent (discriminant validity). Thus far our analysis has chiefly dealt with the indeterminacy of interpretation of personality tests. However, using the argument for predictive validity it may be proposed that such indeterminacy may be constrained by predictive study. Although test items, either individually or collectively, may be subject to an indefinite number of interpretations, many of these interpretations may be rendered untenable as the measure is correlated with or used to predict other patterns of behavior.

This line of argument seems compelling enough until one returns to the fundamental line of reasoning with which the present analysis began. As outlined, from the hermeneutic standpoint all linguistic utterances stand in need of interpretation. What may be said of underlying intention, meaning, or motivation must be framed within contemporary conventions of intelligibility; otherwise it is simply nonsense. Yet various behavioral patterns stand in the same relationship to underlying dispositions as do linguistic utterances. What can be said of their relationship also depends on historically located conventions of making sense. For example, what underlying disposition does "smoking behavior" reveal? It is conventional in some sectors to interpret such behavior as indicating "oral needs;" others see it as an anxiety indicator or reducer; yet, the conventions do not currently permit one to interpret smoking as a sign of "spirituality." To the extent that behavior patterns are considered in a decontextualized manner, and the meanings of such patterns are rendered flexible through usage, then behavioral observations may be subject to the same flexibility of interpretation as personality-test data.

To explore the implications of this reasoning an additional 16 Swarthmore undergraduates were given a fresh set of interpretation puzzles to solve. They were asked to explain how various behavior patterns could indicate that a person possesses a given trait. The behavior patterns in this case were drawn from the annals of research on the I-E test, and in particular those predictive studies demonstrating that the test successfully predicts to joining social movements (Gore & Rotter 1963), social persuasiveness (Phares 1965), assertiveness (Doherty & Ryder 1979), perception of others' friendliness (Holmes & Jackson 1975), task solving (Lefcourt 1976), experience of anger (Holmes & Jackson 1975), and so on. The traits were again drawn at random from Anderson's list. The questionnaires were further arranged so that four of the trait-behavior pattern pairs were repeated, but in this case participants were asked to explain how the trait in question could be expressed in the opposite of the pattern in question. Thus, for example, participants were asked how joining a social movement is a good indicator of a person's underlying *hostility*, and then later, how deciding *against* joining a social movement is a good indicator of the same trait. In this way a more stringent assessment could be made of the flexibility of interpretive conventions: Are the conventions sufficiently flexible that various behavior patterns and their contradictions can be used as "evidence" for a given trait?

As this exploration first revealed, of the 240 trait-behavior pattern combinations, there were none that participants failed to render intelligible. Second, the participants located multiple linkages between trait and pattern. Thus, for example, a person who is *helpful* fails "to be persuasive" because, as one participant put it, "Helpful people are so eager to be accepted that their actions are unnatural and therefore unpersuasive"; or as another wrote, because "helpful people are interested in others' welfare and not in manipulating them through persuasion"; and as a third asserted, because "helpful people are likely to offer a variety of alternatives to people in their effort to help and therefore don't persuade others to take any one position." For the 16 participants the modal number of explanatory rationales generated for each trait-pattern pair was three. As a third finding, a corollary of the preceding, participants were able in each of the four reversals to show how a given trait could account for both a given pattern and its contradiction. Thus, for example, a *hostile* person might join a social movement "as a way of finding an expressive outlet for his emotions" and would decide against joining a social movement because "by nature people who are hostile to others are loners." A *logical* person would "fail to be assertive in a relationship" because "people who are logical spend most of their time trying to figure out what is happening in a relationship rather than taking action," and the same type of person would be "very assertive in a relationship" because "they can see clearly what is going on and would thus want to assert themselves." A further check was made of the general plausibility of the participants' solutions. The mean plausibility ratings assigned by a group of five raters, exposed to 20 randomly selected solutions, was $\overline{X} = 3.32$ (SD $= .86$), on the same 4-point scale employed in earlier studies.

In summary, predictive validity does not appear to offer an objective crucible for interpreting trait measures. Behavior patterns, such as being persuasive or assertive, are, like assertions on personality tests, subject to a high degree of interpretive indeterminacy. Each may be compellingly viewed as the overt result of myriad source dispositions, which may in turn be viewed as the product of an extended range of alternative sources, and so on.

The Fruits of Relativity

As a whole, the findings emerging from these various explorations reveal a remarkable flexibility in the explanatory conventions linking overt conduct, including both verbal utterances and other patterns of behavior, to underlying psychological dispositions. In brief, the findings indicate that among relatively sophisticated users of the language:

1. Most statements from the I-E inventory can be plausibly interpreted as a reflection of an indeterminate number of common psychological trait terms.

2. Single statements from the I-E inventory can be plausibly understood as an indicator of many different trait dispositions, and differing trait dispositions may be revealed in single I-E statements.

3. It can be plausibly demonstrated how logically opposing statements, that is, avowals of both an internal and an external orientation, are expressions of the same underlying trait disposition. Further, logically opposing dispositions may be found revealed in the same I-E item.

4. It can plausibly be demonstrated how as many as three different items from the I-E measure (scored in both the internal and external directions) are reasonable indicators of the same underlying trait.

5. Any internal cause of one's overt activity may also be seen as an effect. Thus, even if it were less taxing to conclude that I-E items were expressing generalized perceptions of control rather than any other disposition, such perceptions may plausibly be viewed as the localized effect of more fundamental trait dispositions. Language users can spontaneously generate a large number of underlying dispositions that may foster a disposition toward control. Further, these dispositions may be traced to still more fundamental dispositions and so on. Ultimately it should be possible to make a plausible case for explaining virtually any psychological trait as an effect of virtually any other kind of psychological disposition.

6. Behavior patterns traditionally correlated with the I-E scale (for purposes of generating construct validity) can be explained as an expression of an indeterminate number of trait dispositions within the common vernacular. In effect, behavioral validation of psychological tests is subject to the same interpretive impasse as the decoding of trait items.

In light of the pattern of results emerging here, how are we to consider the broader range of systematic investigation in psychology? As indicated, personality assessment was selected as a test case for the general class of research strategies directed at tapping psychological processes. It is in the personality domain that most assiduous attention is typically paid to the problem of establishing mensurational validity. However, on what grounds could one argue that other domains of psychology are saved from interpretive relativity? Aren't findings in the domains of social, cognitive, perception, learning, and developmental psychology, for example, equally subject to an indeterminacy of interpretation? Is it not possible that a rationale could be developed to demonstrate how any pattern of action could be intelligibly related to virtually any assumptions about mental life? What, save the flexibility of existing language conventions, would prevent such an outcome?

For many interpretivists, such conclusions militate against the further pursuit of timeless truths about human functioning through the systematic measurement and control of variables. Regardless of the methodological rigour of the research, and regardless of the sophistication of the statistical analyses, one must inevitably draw inferences from what is observed to the world of mind. And, these inferences must inevitably be made intelligible in terms of the conventions of sense-making shared within the interpretive community. Regardless of what they observe, contemporary Western researchers will not discover in their data evidence of soul, demons, or holy spirit. Behavioral research may furnish an excuse for exercising the linguistic forestructure of a given community, but it does not, on this account, furnish a justification or proof of the forestructure.

Research in a Hermeneutic Context

Some readers may locate in this analysis an invitation to return to some form of behaviorism. After all, if the attempt to access mental states is bankrupt, then why not confine the science altogether to that which is publicly observable? Why not restrict ourselves to charting the systematic relationship among environmental antecedents and behavioral consequents? Yet, for many in the interpretive camp it is indeed the impossibility of this project that initially paved the way toward an interpretive orientation. For, as argued by a host of social theorists (cf. Collingwood, Geertz, Peters, Taylor, Winch) a mere charting of behavior provides nothing we would recognize as understanding. To be sure, we might locate the exact relationship between such antecedents as ambient temperature, available light, decibel level, the wave patterns of others' voices, and the like, and such consequents as the velocity and trajectory of limb movements, salivation, rate of eye blinking, and so on. However, such information would be of trivial interest and of practical inconsequence. To understand another depends on knowing what is *meant* by certain actions, and the determination of meaning depends on one's interpretive strategy.

As the route to behaviorism is occluded, many will find the present conclusions all too dolorous. They seem, only too rudely and unsympathetically, to slam the door on a well-developed enterprise with rigorous standards, highly intelligent participants, and rewarded by significant sectors of society. However, for most hermeneuticists arguments for interpretive indeterminacy do not militate against scholarly inquiry. Rather, it is believed, within these various critical appraisals lie buried assumptions that, when fully articulated, lay the groundwork for forms of inquiry of greater promise for the culture. The hope, then, is that work such as that described above will help us to locate viable alternatives to empiricist foundationalism. Let us see how the hermeneutic-interpretive commitment can play itself out in this respect.

At the outset, it is seen that the major concern of scholarly research programs in psychology should not be with generating objective truth about mental states and conditions. On the present account, the various means of generating systematic and replicable data do not, in the final analysis, furnish truth warrants for propositions about mental states. Attempts to accumulate knowledge, "get to the bottom of things," or unlock the true workings of memory, motivation, cognition, emotion, and the like do not, in the present context, seem especially fruitful.

However, to search for incorrigible truths about the mind is to misunderstand the way in which propositions about the mental world function within daily life. As we see, when it is said that "John remembered," "Nancy intended," "Harold believes," or "Rhoda feels sad," such statements do not rest on logical inferences from an observable realm of material to an interior realm of the mind. However, irrespective of their objective indeterminacy, such statements do play a major role in social life. For indeed, such statements are requisite constituents of just those patterns of ongoing interchange that fall under the rubric of "leading meaningful lives." When Harold tells us he *believes* in strong democracy he is not thus reporting on the state of his mental condition; rather, he is informing us of what we can anticipate from him on subsequent occasions when, let us say, an astronomical defense budget is proposed to Congress. Upon the death of a family member, it is virtually incumbent upon the survivors to engage in a series of actions (marked by demeanor, gate, dress, and so on) appropriate to the occasion. This pattern will include reports of sadness, not because family members have examined their neurons to be certain that this is indeed what they are experiencing, but because such a report is a constituent of a pattern that, should it be lacking, would be for us in Western culture something "less than human." In effect, words about mental states operate as Austinian performatives (Austin 1962). They are not reflections on some other world; their significance is achieved in their very doing. In daily life, then, statements about mental conditions operate more like smiles and embraces than mirrors or maps.

In this light, scholarly efforts in psychology acquire potential of considerable moment. For, rather than producing propositional networks of shaky validity, the utility of which must typically await the unlikely application by those outside the professional guild (e.g. various practitioners, business organizations, political parties), the scholar may participate more directly in the cultural dialogue. Scholarly accounts of the mind are, in effect, contributions to the culture's resources for carrying out social life. They are forms of intelligibility that can, if properly crafted, enable people to live more enriched or fully potentiated lives. If effectively rendered, they may open new options for action, point to new ways of living, buttress shaky relations, or furnish languages with which greater social integration can be achieved.

If the major aim of psychological inquiry is the crafting of intelligibilities, then the process of research is both altered and expanded. At the outset, the emphasis shifts dramatically from means of proof to means of discursive rendering. Methods of experimentation, precision measurement, multivariate designs, statistical procedures and all the other accouterments of scientism are reduced in importance. They do not, as long believed, legitimate the scholarly insight—furnishing it genuine authority (and thus power in the marketplace of ideas). Rather, it is the skill of the scholar in the medium of discourse that best enables him/her to contribute to useful systems of intelligibility. It is immersion in the ongoing dialogues of the culture that is critical for the development of such skills. For, it is in such dialogues that problems become identified, issues isolated, concepts developed, and the possibility for intelligible answers derived. To the extent that the traditional armamentarium of methods has a place in such an enterprise, it is to render rhetorical power to emerging intelligibilities.

As we see, the kind of hermeneutic orientation outlined here offers to the scholar an immense latitude in the interpretation of human conduct. He or she may not only employ the available intelligibilities of the culture, but is simultaneously free to create new amalgams, metaphors, or constructions. To be sure, this freedom places an enormous burden of responsibility on the scholar. Previous debates on research ethics are trivial by comparison, for these debates have presumed the possibility of value-free descriptions of human action. Traditionally the ideal scientist is one who holds a mirror to nature; should the scholar also possess passionate interests, they pose problems of potential interference in the process. The good scientist should operate as a rational automoton. In this context, technologically oriented researchers seldom attend to the implicit values championed by their work. However, from the present perspective we find that the intelligibilities of science operate as constituents of social life; they are used by people in the course of their relationships with each other. In this light the scholar confronts a major responsibility for his/her interpretations of the world. From the interpretivist perspective, moral discourse should thus become an integral part of the theoretical enterprise. Scholarly intelligibilities should ideally be suffused with considerations of value, ideology, and the social good.

CHAPTER 11

Hermeneutics as the Undisciplined Child: Hermeneutic and Technical Images of Education

DIETER MISGELD AND DAVID W. JARDINE

Introduction

In a document entitled *Program of Studies for Elementary Schools* (1982) there is a section outlining what is called the unique "mission" of the elementary school. Listed under this mission are "the acquisition of fundamental learning skills, the acquisition of requisite knowledge in the physical, intellectual, and personal functioning areas, the acquisition of requisite social skills and the development of desirable attitudes and commitments toward themselves, their peers and the world as they know it." (p. vi) Each of these general formulations provides the underlying orientation for the development of specific curriculum guides which articulate, grade by grade, how each of these requisite skills is to be achieved.

This document also contains a section entitled "Developing Desirable Personal Characteristics":

> Children inhabit schools for a significant portion of their lives. Each day, in their relationships with fellow students, teachers and other adults who are in the school, children are exposed to a complex combination of influences, some deliberate, and others incidental. In Canada, the common pattern of attitudes derives from many cultural sources, religious, ethnic and legal. Public schools exist within this culture and it is from this culture that schools' dominant values emerge. (p. vi)

A list is then offered that provides a "compilation of the more important attributes which schools ought to foster" (p. vi) respectful, responsible, fair/just, tolerant, honest, kind, forgiving, committed to democratic ideals, loyal, openminded, thinks critically, intellectually curious, creative, pursues excellence, appreciative, cooperative, accepting, conserving, industrious, possesses a strong sense of self-worth, persevering, prompt, neat, attentive, unselfish and mentally and physically fit.

Our purpose here is not to comment specifically about education in Canada, or more specifically about the peculiarities of the basic goals of education as formulated in the province of Alberta. We find, in the above statements, a more pervasive phenomenon, one that underlies the specifications peculiar to these particular documents. Any educational curriculum document, whether it be general, as with the above, or more specifically related to particular curriculum areas, contains an implicit image of what it is that we wish to bring forth *(educare)* in the educational process. Such documents give rise to an image of what it means to be a "competent," "mature," adult, an image that functions as the *telos* for the educational process. Our concern in this paper is to examine two images of adulthood that provide alternative interpretive grounds for understanding what it is we wish to bring forth in the educational process. We will be contrasting a "technical" and an "hermeneutic" conception of "adulthood" or "maturity" and the relation between adult and child that these conceptions imply.

Such a contrast between technical and hermeneutic approaches is applicable across the human sciences. However, this contrast involves unique convolutions when we address the particular area of education. Both technical and hermenoutic approaches are not simply alternative methods for investigating phenomena relevant to the area of educational theory and practice. More than this, in the very act of investigating, in their very conception of the nature of understanding, of "research," of inquiry, they are *exemplifications of images of adulthood.* Thus, hermeneutic inquiry is just as much an example of a notion of adulthood as it is a method for investigating the notion of adulthood. And the same, of course, can be said for a technical approach. Objectivistic, experimentally based research is as much something that adults engage in as it is a method for engaging adulthood as the object of such research. Thus, our paper is not precisely an "empirical" investigation of curricular images based on hermeneutic methodology (as if these were simply our object), but a reflective investigation of the interpretive grounds of phenomena relevant to psychological-educational research: predominant conceptions of adulthood/childhood, and images of development and maturity. We are not so much concerned with adding to or subtracting from the list compiled above or adding to or subtracting elements from the mission of elementary education, but with unearthing alternative ways in which such phenomena can be understood. We see this line of inquiry as relevant to more "concrete" investigations of human behavior precisely because of the character of hermeneutic investigation. Hermeneutics gains its power and relevance to the fields of psychological and educational research precisely because it refuses to separate interpretations of concrete phenomena (e.g., notions of reouisite learning skills, linguistic competence, etc.) from a reflection on the grounds of interpretation, precisely because it does not sever the task of understanding a particular phenomenon from the task of self-under-standing. One can never "settle" on a hermeneutic mode of inquiry as if it can offer itself as just another method that can be taken for granted, allowing us to speak about some entity as if we are not always also giving a voice to our place vis-à-vis that entity. As Hans-Georg Gadamer contends, "The hermeneutic phenomenon is basically not a problem of method at all" (1975, xi). It is not a matter of methodically achieving a relationship to a certain phenomenon, but of reflectively explicating the assumptions, prejudices, or understandings with which we already live. We cannot begin with the pretense that we do not already live in a culture in which adulthood and childhood are already understood.

There is, therefore, a deeper motive to this paper. We live in a culture in which technical knowledge is valued, in which technical knowledge has become a predominant interpretive context that informs educational theory and practice. The relationships and transition between child and adult are slowly becoming understandable as little more than a technical problem requiring a technical solution:

> It is not simply that educational institutions begin to focus on the production and use of knowledge and turn away from issues of communication and personal/social identity. Rather, it is that issues of communication and personal/social identity come surreptitiously to be equated with the production and use of knowledge. (Misgeld, Jardine & Grahame 1985, 204).

We will contend that a technical approach to education gains its predominance because it is a method of domination—method relying on control, prediction, and manipulation as both a research paradigm and as an underlying pedagogical orientation. This leads to a predominant reading of curriculum guidelines and suggestions in which the development of children into adults is recast into a process of methodically replacing one set of objective properties (the competencies typical of childhood) with another (the competencies requisite of adulthood). One of the most disturbing features of this predominance is that alternatives to it become visible only as irresponsible failures to methodologically secure our understanding of educational phenomena on a sure footing. Critiquing behavioral objectives in lesson planning as attempts to gain technical mastery and control over pedagogical activity is taken as an invitation to chaos; pointing out the ways in which teacher accountability has recast actual pedagogical encounters in the image of bureaucratic and administrative rationality is taken as an instance of failing to strive for "excellence."

Under the shadow of a technical image of "adulthood," hermeneutics becomes understandable only as the undisciplined child, as a refusal of the methodological guarantees that a technical understanding of adulthood offers.

And those of us already imbued with commitment to what hermeneutics can offer the human sciences, can all too easily fall victim to this caricature by attempting to promote hermeneutics as an "alternative methodology," as a supplement, complement, or replacement for technical understanding. In the concluding section of this paper, we provide an analogy that attempts to bring out these issues and address the underlying resistance to hermeneutics in the field of education.

We now turn to outlining the contrasting images of education, adulthood, and maturity found in a hermeneutic and technical approach.

The Belonging Together of Adult and Child:
Education as a Process of the Development of Reciprocity

A Technical Approach to Educational Phenomena

In a technical approach to education, "being an adult," has the *telos* of education, is envisaged as a specific, definable "object domain" with specific requisite properties or characteristics: fundamental learning skills, requisite knowledge, requisite social skills, desirable attitudes and the like. These properties are culled from an examination of contemporary cultural requirements and expectations, and are formulated as specifiable "competencies" that can be understood, developed, and possessed independently of the ongoing, contingent, and fluid way in which they actually appear over the course of everyday life. This object domain becomes the normative paradigm against which the steps or stages in the child's development are understood. It is the normative paradigm against which the particular activities of the child are measured and accounted for as "educational" activities. It is, moreover, the normative paradigm against which the teacher's actions, in relation to the child, are assessed as pedagogically significant. "Being an adult" is thus disassembled into specific curriculum areas, sequentially ordered in a way that will ensure ease of inculcation, or, at least will ensure accountability for the relative successes or failures of such inculcation. Testing in schools tracks such inculcation; failure of a child on a test is grounds for more pervasive and strategic intervention in the child's life—an opportunity to "develop special programs" that "serve the child's individual needs." The child's individual needs, in such a case, are *already understood* in light of psychological findings regarding "developmentally appropriate behaviors." The individual child is nothing more than a special case of behaviors. The development of "special programs" is not an occasion to reflect on the original image of children that produced failure. (Failure is either a matter of the child not having requisite skills, the teacher not adopting appropriate strategies, a mismatch between the two, or a lack of concerted effort on the child's part.) "Special programs" are simply a matter of mastering and controlling the specificities of this particular instance. The child's failure is not a reflection of the failure or inappropriateness of a technical approach per se, but a reflection of the need for a technical fix, for more vigilance and vigor in our attempts to "pin down the problem." (cf. Smith, forthcoming; Jardine 1988).

Against this background of envisaging the nature of adulthood and childhood as specific object domains, the task of educational research becomes one of pinning down, as precisely as possible, just what it means to be an adult ("meaning" here being identifiable with objective properties) just what it means to be a child ("meaning" here is identified with locating the child on a developmental sequence that has such properties as its *telos*) and precisely how the transition is made between the two. Ideally research orients to that first articulation of what it means to be a child or an adult about which nothing more needs to be said. No further specification is needed or possible. Every variable has been controlled such that in the end, research dispels the need to say more. Being an adult or a child would, ideally, become exhausted issues, in need of no further consideration. This accounts for the rather manic and hysterical character of some forms of educational research, and the relentless proliferation of "research data" that has disassembled children and adults into the smallest specifiable variables. The impetus of such research seems to be the as-yet-unfixed variable, the discovery of which in and of itself warrants further research. The goal of such research seems to be silence—the end of the need to address such issues. If we can finally pin down the developmental features of linguistic competence and all of the conditions pertaining to its inculcation, we will never have to consider this phenomena again. To become linguistically competent will come to mean the possession of a fixed, univocally specifiable set of competencies, the possession of which has been demonstrated to the extent that such possession is no longer in question. To possess such competencies will come to mean that such competencies are objectively testable. And it is precisely such objectively testable competencies that provide the impetus for curriculum guidelines and thereby the impetus for the development of behavioral objectives in lesson planning: "The children will demonstrate the ability to discriminate between a long and short 'o' by identifying words which contain such sounds." Individual differences and statistical probability demand that we add to such an impetus qualifiers such as "eight out of ten children" and "nine out of ten times." The very anticipatory schemata of the pedagogical act comes to embody within it the principles of statistics. The individual child, developing toward linguistic competence, and the individual teacher, serving such inculcation, will become simply the anonymous and mute instruments of such inculcation. They will become simply *instances* of something already understood (i.e., the specificities of phonemic recognition) and education will become simply a concrete application of pre-scribed normative principles.

In all of this, understanding the world is pictured as a process whereby we methodically secure ahead of time what our place in the world is. Under-standing the world *begins* with the establishment of an objective method which defines ahead of time how we stand vis a vis the world. Once estab-lished, the world becomes the ensemble of states and processes that can be objectively accounted for, controlled, and predicted proceeding from this method. Becoming educated in understanding the world means learning the relevant methods of thought and cognition, the relevant social skills, the desirable personal attributes. It means bringing forth the objective skills and competencies requisite of adulthood. The child is thought to grow toward a stage of cognitive competence, possessing cognitive capacities for engag-ing in formal and argumentative discourse, or having the capacity for moral judgment at a stage in which universal, anonymous principles are operative. Adult maturity is thus based on a developmental sequence constructed by the researcher as the attainment of a state of principled reasoning, judg-ment, and character in which one's self is identical with itself, as if, at the end of development, who one is, is no longer in question. One "has," for example, "requisite social skills" as a property that one can ascribe to one-self, and which one can demonstrate in particular settings. The emergence of such skills in a particular situation becomes simply a matter of the "application" of what one already knows, what one has already become, the competencies one already "has." Such competencies are not brought into question by such settings. They are simply applied or misapplied. One can never fail to be what one objectively "is." In this way, failing to understand a particular situation, becoming speechless in the face of a particular event, are technical problems requiring technical solutions. The self comes into ques-tion only to the extent that it has fallen away from this state or reverted to a developmentally earlier state, both of which are understood to be nothing more than a return to egocentricity or to a self-centered subjectivity. The self that emerges in the educational process is thus identical with itself. Once objectively secured, such identity is not jeopardized through "application," since such application is already understood as simply the particularization of what is already secured. Once I become linguistically competent, becom-ing speechless is merely an abberation, one which does not reflect on my competence itself, but merely on the fact that certain variables in the envi-ronment are not yet fixed. Adult maturity, and the self-understanding it requires, become a form of absolutely uniform self-recognition (Jardine 1987). There is no self to be recognized other than the functioning of this anony-mous subject. Or better, any self recognized other than this self is identifiable as at a lower stage of developmental functioning, and as therefore understood under the auspices of the "fully developed" subject as that which this lower functioning self fails to be.

Mutual understanding, in this view, is not the concrete confrontation of one point of view with another. Rather, "social life is provided with the facade of an objective identity that must be manipulated and mastered" (Murphy 1985, 169). This facade does not appear as such, but appears as rooted in the underlying "processes common to all subjects" (Piaget 1971, 108) which make possible mutual understanding. After all, as Piaget (1970) maintains, mutual understanding would not be possible were there not a "deep natural identity of the 'operations' of individual thought and those that occur in any social 'cooperation'" (p. 110). Mutual understanding is accomplished through the enactment of competencies already secured prior to such enactment. It is thus a mutual deferral of both parties to a common method of operation, a methodology (processes common to all subjects—precisely those requisite competencies that provide the *telos* for the educational process, technically conceived). Mutual understanding is secured through such a methodology and through the subjection of oneself to such a methodology. It is therefore not a dialogue between two points of view, oriented to developing an understanding between them, but a mutual deferral to something akin to the monologue of scientific discourse (cf. Habermas 1971). The concreteness of individual points-of-view is seen as consisting of blockages to a true understanding of oneself. To truly understand oneself, even in one's particularity, that particularity must become the object of scientific discourse: it must become an object equally accessible to all. One's social skill must pass through the norm of requisite social skills typical of adulthood, a norm to which we must all defer in order to truly understand ourselves and our relative place vis-à-vis each other. In the area of curriculum this occurs by understanding the individual child vis-à-vis a predetermined developmental sequence on which the child can be placed. Requisite social skills, for example, are broken down in a sequential order of developmental sub-skills, and instruction orients to the sequential inculcation of such skills and the sequential testing of such inculcation.

Educational research, in such a view, *begins* when the concrete inter-plays between researcher and those studied have been severed. It is precisely such severance that constitutes the objectivity of research. This interplay is methodologically reconstructed through the enactment of the methods of objective science, an enactment that brings with it an image of childhood and adulthood as the objects of such a science. Therefore, Habermas (1971) is correct when he remarks that the predominant forms of empirical research reflect an interest in the control, prediction, and manipulation of objects, a model taken over from our understanding of natural objects (cf. Misgeld 1983, 1985a). The justification for such a technical interest in the area of education is its success in the control of objectifiable and objective processes. This success is due to the separation of inquiry from its "object," to the adoption of a procedure, resting on disembodied, impersonal competence, of a view that looks at the world from everywhere and nowhere at the same time (Merleau-Ponty 1964). And this picture of inquiry not only provides the predominant orientation to educational research. It also reconstructs adulthood into the very sort of object to which such inquiry is appropriate: in the end, adulthood is understood as *precisely the ability to conduct such research, precisely the possession of disembodied, impersonal competencies.* Moreover, *childhood* is understood as precisely the inability to orient to such disembodiedness, such impersonalness (this is how Piaget understands the notion of "egocentricity") It is the availability of such an Archimedean point of disembodied and situation-free knowing that is denied by hermeneutics and requires a contrary articulation of the relation between researcher and researched, between adult and child.

One must notice, however, that objective and objectifying research have great appeal in education. Such research, whether it be one of providing statistical generalizations, inventories of skills and competencies, stage sequences of development, or generalizable methods of testing and tracking children's development, is useful as a policy instrument. It shows considerable resemblance to the impersonal and anonymous procedures that predominate in modern administrative structures. These procedures are tied to notions of accountability in the formal/legal apparatus. Thus, objective research can help document statistically the changes people undergo and the relation between such changes and manipulable variables in the environment that can help or hinder such changes. It seems to facilitate the monitoring of development and, where needed, provides concerted intervention to stay the course of development. Although technical approaches cannot guarantee that children will grow and develop, they can provide an appearance of accuracy and accountability when it comes to specifying why children are taking a particular course. Taken to its extreme, then, education, technically conceived, becomes the inculcation of measurable, objectively testable skills or competencies, and teaching becomes the method whereby such inculcation can be controlled and brought about. In the end, the emerging life of the developing child becomes conceived as a problem to be solved, adults become conceived as those whose lives embody such solutions, and education is the means to such an end.

Interlude

Once adulthood and childhood are reconstructed into objects of scientific/ technical discourse, the alternative to such an approach is already prescribed.

Since childhood is understood to be an object whose course can be sequentially secured under a technical image of adulthood, failure to orient to such securing is a failure to be an adult. It is to opt for unaccountability, for the immaturity of the unmethodical. Hermeneutics becomes understood precisely as such a failure, precisely as an inability or unwillingness to secure that which can be secured. At best, if it is simply unwilling, hermeneutics becomes a sort of adolescent rebelliousness, able but unwilling to operate under the objective norms requisite of adulthood. At worst, if it is unable, hermeneutics becomes formulated as akin to the undisciplined child.

A Hermeneutic Approach to Educational Phenomena

Hermeneutically conceived, adult and child are not taken to be univocal object domains, but are conceived as constantly interpreted and re-interpreted events whose meaning and relation to each other is always yet-to-be-decided. Adulthood is not a fixed set of properties, as if it were never in question. Rather, to be an adult, to be mature, requires the unceasing effort to establish for ourselves courses of action, indicating possibilities of self-understanding, which are not there as a matter of course, simply open for theoretical examination and ascription.

Given this, the process of becoming an adult is a matter, not of increasing methodical self-possession, but a matter of self-transcendence. In this process of self-formation, "understanding involves a moment of 'loss of self'" (Gadamer 1977, 51), of transcending the bounds of the self in the encounter with what is other than myself and, from this encounter, recovering a new sense of myself. Thus, for example, hermeneutically conceived, linguistic competence is not an objective property that I can ascribe to myself. Rather, it is a contingent, dialogical accomplishment that is not accomplished once and for all. I only "have" this character in the dialogical struggle with situations that call for such competence, situations that call for the concrete engagement, the concrete effort to speak with others. Linguistic competence is thus a form of mutual understanding, requiring of me that I transcend or go beyond the self-possessive confidence with which I might ascribe linguistic competence to myself as a property, and risk the possibility of speechlessness in the face of situations that require me to speak. From this movement of self-transcendence, a new possibility arises of interpreting and re-interpreting who I am and what my place is in relation to others. Self-understanding is thus conceived, "not in the sense of a ... self-possession or of one finally and definitively achieved. For self-understanding only realizes itself in the understanding of a subject-matter and does not have the character of a free self-realization. The self that we are does not possess itself; one could say that it 'happens'" (Gadamer

1977, 55). Understanding myself as an adult, understanding the children all around me (Jardine, in press) does not occur, therefore, in a retreat into methodological anonymity. It occurs in the midst of living my life as this particular individual, in community with these particular others, within the particular constraints in which we already find ourselves belonging together. Understanding myself as linguistically competent, or as possessing requisite social skills must thus risk the concrete unfolding and development of such an understanding over the course of the actual engagement with others, with all the contingency that such a pursual contains. Understanding oneself to be an adult, or this other to be a child, is, therefore, a practical matter and the criteria of the curriculum guide are, so to speak, practical indicators, not theoretical properties. To speak well, I must live with the practical possibility of becoming speechless; to understand, I must live with the possibility of no longer understanding. Hermeneutically conceived, such matters are not to be decided in general, once and for all, or alone. Hermeneutic inquiries are meant to develop, risk and accomplish the reciprocity of intersubjective understanding without obliterating the real differences between human beings which call for this effort. Such inquiries are therefore not simply research findings *about* education. Rather, they are part of the process of self-formation (Ricoeur 1984) or education that is uniquely our own and is worked out in concert with others. In light of this, method cannot be first. What is first is dialogue, communication, negotiation, confrontation, and the like. "There would be no hermeneutical task if there were no mutual understanding that has been disturbed and that those involved in a conversation must search to find it again." (Gadamer 1977, 25). There is no impervious method or pregiven standpoint from which such a recovering of mutual understanding proceeds, since it is *precisely the question of where I stand vis-à-vis others that is at issue in such a recovery.* If I am taken aback in a conversation with a child by the insightfulness and power of her questions, I cannot simply retreat into a self-possessed confidence in my ability to understand. Nor can I without hesitation simply banish the child's remark and turn away. Rather, my ability to understand is called into question. The "requisite skills" of adulthood are therefore not an impervious set of objective properties which I possess once and for all and in general, but interpretive possibilities that emerge in the concrete engagement with others.

      In this way, rather than locating children and adults as being at different stages in a developmental sequence, with a fixed end point as an immutable standard available for the appraisal of the sequence, a properly hermeneutic orientation calls into question the definitely locatable identities of adults and children. It is a questioning in which the *community of adult and child,* their *belonging together,* is brought forth. This only comes about in recognizing that as an adult, one is not beyond the movement back to the child and from there, forward to the point where one began the movement. Having been a child is still a possibility one lives with, something one has to return to in order to establish oneself as an adult. And we find in this movement between adult and child that typifies education, that issues of understanding, of desirable attitudes, of requisite skills and competencies are at issue *on both sides.* We are all involved in the process of self-formation in which our understanding of ourselves emerges in the concrete confrontation with others. We find, for example, that tolerance is not straightforwardly a "desirable personal attitude" that adults unequivocally possess and children do not; we may often find, in certain situations, precisely the opposite to be the case. Moreover, we do not define "intolerance" ahead of time as something adults must always and everywhere possess: some things are simply "intolerable," some things I have found that I cannot tolerate, and therefore simply avoid, sometimes my intolerance appears when I least expect it. The situational "bringing forth" of tolerance is a question we all face. Thus, when we read in the above cited curriculum document that "public schools exist within this culture and it is from this culture that schools' dominant values emerge," we find ourselves, as adults, belonging together with children in this very culture, in which, e.g., tolerance is at issue for us all. To define such values and competencies as requisite educational *outcomes,* in the end, banishes all of us from becoming adults. Technically conceived, the curriculum guides turn *all of us* into children, for none of us, practically speaking, can live our lives under their ideals, where competencies and values are given properties which are no longer in question.

Hermeneutically conceived, then, education is not simply the inculcation of technical skills. It is the bringing forth and exploring of possibilities of understanding, possible places the traversing of which brings forth a sense of self, a sense of what is possible for us (of which the instigation of technical skills may be one such possibility). Only in dialogue with such possibilities does the self emerge. Self-understanding thus emerges through the engagement with others who may think differently. These others can be conceived concretely, as classmates, teachers, friends, rivals, etc., or abstractly, as the other one might engage in the understanding of a subject matter that embodies a different point-of-view, a different interpretation of the nature of the world and one's place in it. One does not know where one is, what place one has, unless one develops a sense of the possibility of being elsewhere, of what else is possible. This requires an openness to the world, such that what we are and what we can become returns to us from places other than the ones in which we have already come to exist. This engagement, this traversing, not only brings with it the realization that other possibilities exist. It also brings with it the self-recognition that one's own place is *itself* a possibility among others, and not a fixed actuality (like the property of an object). We are, in other words, participants with others in a play of multiple roles and positions, a play in which one's place is not set once and for all. This further brings with it the possibility of engaging one's place *as* a possibility, as something one has chosen, could have chosen, or must choose, even if who and where we are is what we have "grown up into" without knowing it. I and you are not merely self-identical subjects whose identity is methodically secured behind and before all circumstances that might force us to become someone in particular (cf. Buber 1970). Rather, we are the ones who must stand up for a life-history as it happens to be, a life-history which comes to expression in a sense of who we can be. We can only be ourselves in the recognition of and struggle with a particular history. Here, one's relation to oneself passes through the recognition of others (such as children) as distinct, different, yet also similar (Jardine & Morgan 1987). Those involved in educational research need to admit that children also belong to precisely the same sort of process of recognition and struggle, in which their understanding of themselves passes through the recognition of others (parents, teachers, siblings etc). Even in the act of refusing this struggle and recognition (a refusal requisite of objectivistic research), the researcher places himself/herself vis-à-vis the question of who he or she is and can be as an adult in relation to children. The researcher finds him or herself as the one who stands for the methodological anonymity of objective science, and finds children as the "objects" of such anonymity.

In the end, then, there is a final convolution when we look at the relation between technical and hermeneutic approaches in education. Hermeneutically conceived, researchers and their subjects are thought of as engaging one another as real, actual subjects. One can no longer make a claim for being an adult that preserves itself beyond all circumstances that might call into question such a character. The researchers' own formation is a dialectical process, in which their own childhood, their immaturity or the ability and promise they had as children, is a feature of their situation of inquiry. Similarly, the yet-to-develop child is to be recognized as mature in his or her own right, insofar as even a child can challenge the researcher/adult to develop to a level of maturity not noticed by the adult unless so challenged. When inquiry takes this path, it becomes dialogical. It provides narrative accounts of histories of reciprocal interactions between adult and child, rather than generalizable findings. It does not methodically document the theoretical nature of, say, "requisite social skills," as if we want our children to become adults in theory. Rather, it gives accounts of the formation of real identities, of challenges to such formation, crises, successful resolutions or failures. And here is the final convolution. Hermeneutic studies in the area of education intend to move as much as to inform. They are essentially pedagogical, intending to bring forth understanding rather than to hand over objective information as if it was already understood. (If we only had the vigilance to take up the methods that produced it.) Clearly, it is possible to document in curriculum guidelines the broad theoretical features of social skills, cognitive skills, learning skills, and the like. But such documentation, hermeneutically interpreted, is not fully understood if it is taken to indicate that what we wish to bring forth in children is a set of objective properties one can possess without question if we only have the vigilance. We want to bring up children so they can live a life of their own, and we take that possibility away when we pretend that what we wish them to become is something we are not—an object with properties that are fixed. But again, in all of this, the risk of misunderstanding cannot be methodically remedied. Hermeneutics is willing and able to live with such a risk, since only in the face of such a risk can the process of education occur as something more than simply technical replication orienting to a theoretical adulthood, which is no one's. Perhaps technical approaches, in their methodical avoidance of such risks, display their own version of being a child—the one who fears becoming other than what he or she has already become and secures him or herself against such becoming, the one who fearfully holds back from being brought forth, the one who is uneducable.

Conclusion

Studies have shown that animals under various forms of threat—lack of adequate food, drought, the presence of predators—tend to play less and less. They tend, quite naturally, to revert to those kinds of activities that will secure comparative control over their situation, activities which involve little or no risk. They revert to what is tried and true, what is most familiar, what is already established. When endangered, they turn away from activities that have any "play" in them (Jardine, in press b) for the consequences of lack of control are too high. Clearly, in the act of playing, competencies can be developed, but under threat, the playful development of competencies must be forfeited in favor of that which is already secured.

As an analogue to this, one could say that a predatory job market and adverse economic conditions have turned education more and more toward the development and securing of "marketable skills" and away from a "liberal" education, which has come to be rather vaguely equated with not knowing how to *do* anything. Education has turned away from the risks of self-transcendence (involving the playful, risk-laden exploration of many possibilities of understanding, self-understanding and mutual understanding, risking in all of this that one might come to understand oneself anew) and toward the comparative security of self-possession (involved in the often manic accumulation and securing of specific skills). Education, as a playful bringing forth, has come to collapse into training, where what is to be brought forth is already prescribed. Let us push this analogy one step further, since there is a point at which it fundamentally breaks down.

The increasing specialization of technical knowledge seems to bring with it the perception that one does not really understand the world, oneself and others without it. Because an overwhelming technical knowledge of every conceivable phenomenon is *possible*, this possibility begins to harbor the perception that one is increasingly out of control if one does not *pursue* this possibility. One is increasingly in danger of no longer understanding. Understanding begins to appear possible only to the extent that we have guarded ourselves ahead of time against the possibility of misunderstanding, against the possibility of understanding differently. And, as educators, this manifests itself in the attempt to methodically guard the development of understanding by pinning down both its objective characteristics and its curricular sequence, and pinning down those methods that will allow the inculcation of such a sequence. And this perception of being out of control without technical knowledge, of being left behind, leads to the anxiety that drives us to relentlessly pursue it, since technical knowledge offers us a sense of control. In this way, the mere existence of technical knowledge as a possibility creates the need to pursue it, by creating the anxiety for which it appears to be the solution. In education, once our understanding of issues of childhood, adulthood, and development become estranged from the ongoing interpretive narrative of everyday life and are reconstructed into objects ripe for technical manipulation, technical understanding and the objectivistic research it spawns, take over "guidance for Being-in-the-world" (Heidegger 1962, 90). Technical understanding and objectivistic research appear to provide that form of understanding that offers the possibility of remedying the anxiety produced by such estrangement. Living the life of an adult is seen as a series of problems to be fixed, aided by self-help manuals, parenting manuals, and courses in life-skills education. And hermeneutics, as an interpretive approach to Being-in-the-world, appears as in favor of chaos, as unable or unwilling to secure its inquiry within accountable parameters of evidence, truth and methodological reproducability. It appears, to some objectivistically oriented inquirers, as precisely the sort of predator against which one must be secured. In fact, it seems to make things worse instead of better. It seems to make things even more questionable, more ambiguous.

Hermeneutic research begins at the moment of the belonging together of adult and child, the moment of the belonging together of researcher and researched. It is not oriented toward producing estrangement, but toward remedying it, calling up possibilities of conversation, of mutual understanding, of dialogue. It has to do, not with the anonymous production of information, but with questions of how one lives one's life in interplay with others.

This understanding, therefore, is not a matter of what I know "in theory," but of what I stand for, where I stand, what my place is in practice, that is, in relation to how I conduct myself with others. Thus, "knowledge is always a matter of lived, practical insight, and, understood in this sense, knowledge cannot be separated from questions of responsibility for the conduct of one's life. In the end, none of us know more than what we have learned to live with, what we have learned to use as knowledge relevant to the organization of our relations with others and to the acquisition of self-understanding, which can then orient further actions" (Misgeld, Jardine & Grahame 1986).

In our times, the kind of reflection illustrated in this paper needs to be employed in order to make sense of the widespread use of objective psychology and educational research, and the impact of these in daily life and communication. Childhood and adulthood have become planned-for phenomena, which frequently defy interpretation in terms of the understandings available to people on the background of taken-for-granted cultural traditions. Objective research hands our own childhood and adulthood back to us as unrecognizable objects. Research informs us we know nothing of childhood and adulthood without its service.

We have attempted to evoke images of childhood and adulthood as a play back and forth, between different yet intimately interacting domains of human life. In this interplay, concern for the phenomena of adult and child is not the exclusive province of the adult, let alone the exclusive province of the researcher. Because hermeneutics begins with this interplay, it displays a form of questioning that reflectively explodes the limits of conventional research by making the researcher's embeddedness in the play of life both "object" of research and that to which he or she already belongs with all those not participating in the research. As a "playmate," the researcher does not have a privileged access to the play of life, but addresses precisely those issues, in the sphere of education, with which we are all already involved: childhood, adulthood, maturity, development, and how we are to go about living our lives with an understanding of such issues.

CHAPTER 12

Evaluating an
Interpretive Account

MARTIN J. PACKER AND RICHARD B. ADDISON

Evaluating an Interpretation

In the Introduction we described a persisting concern that has appeared: the concern over evaluation of interpretive accounts. We suggested that this is a reaction to the failure of attempts to identify a foundation that would guarantee our knowledge claims in psychological inquiry. This failure has given people a dim sense of the circularity in understanding, but the circle is misunderstood as a vicious one instead of an essential one. Now that the efforts to build a foundation with formal logic and objective observation have failed, some psychologists fear that scientific inquiry must drop into a swamp of mere opinion and speculation. And it must be agreed that without a foundation of interpretation-free facts, without fundamental principles that are self-evidently basic, it is not immediately apparent what kinds of claim to knowledge we can still make. Without an interpretation-free standard (usually "the facts of the matter") it is not clear how we can evaluate an interpretive account. Are there other criteria that can be applied? How can we apply them to interpretations, if not by assessing correspondence? These are the topics of this chapter.

We have emphasized the importance of appreciating both arcs of the hermeneutic circle: the forward arc of projection, and the return arc which we shall see is a movement of uncovering. The former makes understanding possible, and the latter, we shall see, provides the possibility for evaluating an interpretive account. In this final chapter we want especially to examine this return arc. We shall consider how, in the hermeneutic world-view, an interpretive account can be true or false. Our aim is not to introduce new approaches to evaluation, but become clearer on the approaches that are already used, and to better understand just what evaluation entails. We'll examine four approaches that are representative of those employed, and show that a hidden search for validation—for evaluation in terms of interpretation-free norms and standards

—and a hidden application of the correspondence theory of truth, still run through much of the effort at evaluation of interpretive research.

Interpretation is not Conjecture

Evaluation continues to be subsumed to validation because of a persistent misunderstanding of interpretation. Otherwise acute interpretive thinkers have been seduced by the view that both natural science and interpretive inquiry proceed by "conjectures and refutations" (Popper 1972): by the testing of speculative hypotheses. Here again a positivist model of the natural sciences has been applied uncritically to the human sciences in general, and to interpretive inquiry in particular.

Positivist philosophers developed the hypothesis-testing model of science when they became aware of problems in the view that inductive reasoning was the way scientific and everyday knowledge is formed. Central among these problems was the difficulty that induction, necessarily based on examination of a limited number of cases, can never justify a universal statement such as "All swans are white." Popper, especially, proposed that "the method of science is the method of bold conjectures and ingenious and severe attempts to refute them" (1979, 81). Scientific theories, he argued, framed as universal statements, inevitably go beyond the available evidence without proper logical justification, and the role of logic lay in subjecting these speculative hypotheses to testing and correction. The logic's discipline was needed as a corrective to the fanciful character of hypothesis. The proper focus of the philosopher of science was on this "logic of validation" that operated when the scientist planned and conducted an effort to test, falsify or refute her theory. The "psychology of discovery" that was at play in the making of conjectures was, on the other hand, unsystematic and uninteresting.

Many writers have assumed that this is an appropriate model for interpretation, too. Hirsch, for instance, went perhaps even further than Popper in claiming that "the act of understanding is at first a genial (or a mistaken) guess, and there are no methods for making guesses, no rules for generating insights. The methodical activity of interpretation commences when we begin to test and criticize our guesses" (Hirsch 1967, 203). We must not confuse "the whimsical lawlessness of guessing with the ultimately methodical character of testing (1967, 204). Interpretations must be tested with a "fundamental" hypothetico-deductive process identical, in his opinion, to that of the natural sciences (1967, 264). Here interpretation is seen as unavoidably speculative, in contrast to validation which can and does follow rules. Hirsch outlined a logic of probabilistic judgments operating on "classes" of texts with manifest "traits," by which evidence was to be weighed to select the most probable hypothesized reading.

Ricoeur goes along with Hirsch's view, at least in his middle-period work. "We have to guess the meaning of the text because the author's intention is beyond our reach" (1976, 75), and "if there are no rules for making good guesses, there are methods for validating those guesses we do make" (p. 76). Now, in a sense Ricoeur is correct: we have argued that there are indeed no procedures for interpreting. But this hardly implies that interpretations are "divinatory" (as Schleiermacher put it, and as Ricoeur quotes approvingly). There is room to drive a coach and horses between rule-following and guessing. Yet Ricoeur adopts the most conservative view that interpretation is a matter of guessing, and so needs the corrective of disciplined and rigid validation.

Hirsch and Ricoeur have got off the coach too soon. To see interpretation as conjecture is to misunderstand interpretive inquiry, just as to think that the natural sciences proceed by guess-and-validation is to have a mistaken view of science. Ricoeur and Hirsch missed the significance of projection. Interpretation is the working out of possibilities that have become apparent in a preliminary, dim understanding of events. And this pre-understanding embodies a particular concern, a kind of caring. It provides a way of reading, a preliminary initial accessibility, a stance or perspective (a fore-structure) that opens up the field being investigated. Interpretation operates within this initial way of understanding and reading. Reading for care (Brown et al.) or for plot (Sarbin), or for procedure (Misgeld and Jardine), all occur within the possibilities opened up by the researcher's perspective. And this means that interpretive accounts are not undisciplined guesses, and do not shoot beyond the available evidence in a speculative way. They are ordered and organized by the fore-structure of projection; the fore-structure guides interpretation. The guidance is not automatic, of course; we have a responsibility to prepare so that we "enter the circle" with an appropriate fore-structure, and so conduct our interpretation in a proper manner.

The guidance stems in large part from the fact that a fore-structure is primarily a practical, not a conceptual, organization. Entering the circle in the right way is mostly getting the *manner* of inquiry right. Careful interpretive research is conducted in a manner that can hardly be said to foster unsupported speculation. Lather (1986), for instance, describes it as inquiry that seeks reciprocity; that calls for interactive, dialogic interviews "that require self-disclosure on the part of the researcher"; that involves negotiation of meaning (including the recycling of descriptions, emergent analysis, and conclusions to respondents); and discussions of false-consciousness. If you prefer such a description these are components of validation built into the conduct of the research. We prefer to see them as aspects of a manner of inquiry that is guided by a sense of the complexity of the human relationship between researcher and research participant.

So an interpretation is oriented by the researcher's effort to come into the hermeneutic circle in an appropriate manner. It is guided by the fore-structure that is worked out in this entering. And the interpretation articulates possibilities that are laid out in the researcher's preliminary understanding. All this means that interpretation is far from being an undisciplined guess. And if an interpretation is not a guess, then evaluating it need not be like testing a hypothesis.

Truth is Uncovering

If truth is not a matter of correspondence between a theory or account and the way things "really are," should we dispense with the notion of truth altogether? Or can we get to a new understanding of what truth is, that strips away metaphysical notions? The latter is what Heidegger proposed to do. In *Being and Time* he attempted to demonstrate that the truth of an interpretation, a theory, or even a practical activity, is a matter of *uncovering*. This uncovering of an entity is the return arc of the hermeneutic circle; it is the response to our inquiry.

Because an interpretation . . .

> . . . is a letting-something-be-seen, it can *therefore* be true or false. But here everything depends on our steering clear of any conception of truth which is construed in the sense of 'agreement.' This idea is by no means the primary one in the concept of *aletheia*. . . . [T]he entities *of which* one is talking must be taken out of their hiddenness; one must let them be seen as something unhidden *(alethes)*; that is, they must be *discovered* (Heidegger 1927/1962, 56).

(The Greek word for 'truth,' *aletheia* can be translated as unconcealed, unhidden or uncovered.) Interpretation, working out the possibilities projected in understanding, shows entities explicitly, often for the first time. These entities have been hidden from our awareness. Now what is crucial is, as Heidegger put it (in a rather awkward phrase), "to let that which shows itself be seen from itself in the very way in which it shows itself from itself" (p. 58). We must show the entity or, more precisely, let it show itself, not forcing our perspective on it. And we must do this in a way that respects the *way* it shows itself.

Heidegger was not saying that a good interpretation shows things as they "really are" (even Caputo 1987, seems to suspect this, in an otherwise exemplary interpretation of *Being and Time*). This could hardly be the case, given Heidegger's discussion of projection. What Heidegger describes is neither a simple realism nor a view of truth as coherence. On the contrary, he states explicitly that "an entity can show itself *from* itself in many ways, depending in each case on the kind of access we have to it" (p. 51). To say that a true interpretation lets an entity show itself "as it is in itself," or "shows itself from itself" is not to say that we have a description corresponding to a timeless, universal essence, but that the entity has been uncovered "as it is capable of being dealt with" (Okrent 1988, 163). What is uncovered in an interpretation depends on the access we have developed, the kind of entry into the circle we have achieved. What is uncovered in the course of a true interpretation is a *solution* to the problem, the confusion, the question, the concern, and the breakdown in understanding that motivated our inquiry in the first place.

In Heidegger's view, a good interpretation will not provide validated knowledge, or timeless truth, but instead an answer to the practical or existential concern that motivated our inquiry. This concern may be a simple breakdown in our dealings with objects, or it may be a complex social or psychological trouble, such as conflict, alienation, or clinical disorder.

We can see more clearly now why the circularity of understanding and interpretation is not vicious. If our inquiry is shaped and motivated by a practical concern or difficulty, and if as a consequence of interpretation we uncover a solution to that difficulty, it is not the case that we have found only what we read into things. The truth of an account will be suited to the perspective adopted in the inquiry, but this is not a vicious circularity, it is precisely what we want. It does imply that we have to be careful to adopt an appropriate perspective and become aware of what our practical concern is, but this is only as it should be. A true interpretive account is one that helps us and the people we study, that furthers our concerns. Interpretive inquiry (like other forms of human inquiry) must not be misunderstood as just an effort to describe, or even just understand, human phenomena. Interpretation always begins from concerned engagement. "There is no 'pure truth' that lies outside human engagement in the world" (Polkinghorne 1983, 224).

It is important to note that Heidegger, in interpreting truth as uncovering, has not provided us with a new norm of validation, nor was this his intent. It remains a matter of interpretation whether our interpretive concern has been answered adequately. But Heidegger has indicated *what we are doing* when we evaluate an interpretive account. We are considering whether our concern has been answered. Evaluation of an interpretive account with an eye to uncovering fulfills the suggestion that in interpretive inquiry "any notion of validity must concern itself both with the knower and with what is to be known: valid knowledge is a matter of relationship" (Reason & Rowan 1981, 243).

Approaches to Evaluation

We shall consider four approaches to evaluation, namely requiring that an interpretive account be coherent; examining its relationship to external evidence; seeking consensus among various groups; and assessing the account's relationship to future events. These approaches seem reasonable ones. But, as we shall see, they do not guarantee correctness and so researchers who employ "an ecumenical blend of epistemologies and procedures" (Miles & Huberman 1984b, 20) have tended to view them with ambivalence. These approaches and others like them are frequently proposed as though they are somehow analogous to traditional validation procedures. Then 'flaws' are found in one approach that expose it as an untrustworthy procedure, and another must be used to bolster it.

The problem here is the outmoded view of truth that is tacitly employed. Interpretation-free validation is, as we saw in the Introduction, intimately tied to the view that a true account is one that corresponds to "what really happened," or "the way things really are." Even when "ecumenical" researchers deny that they are applying a correspondence theory of truth they can find no alternative to employ instead, and they slip back unwittingly into the traditional notion. Kirk and Miller (1986, p. 80), for instance, define validity as "the quality of fit between an observation and the basis on which it is made." And although Fischer (1987) asserts that her notion of validity "does not invoke an ideal . . . of approximating an in-itself reality," she asks such questions as "is it a faithful summary of instances? . . . Do citizens recognize the phenomenon from their own experience (the old correspondence criterion)." Similarly, Guba and Lincoln (1982, p. 326) claim that "internal validity is best demonstrated through an isomorphism between the data of an inquiry and the phenomena those data represent." And LeCompte and Goetz (1982, p. 43) maintain that "validity necessitates demonstrating that the propositions generated, refined, or tested match the causal conditions which obtain in human life," and that this should be done by establishing whether there is a "match between scientific categories and participant reality." Miles and Huberman (1984a, p. 230) give their game away when they complain that "the problem . . . is that there are no canons, decision rules, algorithms, or even any agreed-upon heuristics in qualitative research to indicate whether findings are valid and procedures robust. . . . We are doing our best . . . to operationalize ways of testing/confirming findings." On the contrary, the absence of decision rules is a necessary and positive consequence of abandoning the traditional account of inquiry and the untenable correspondence theory of truth. The "problem" that remains is that without working to get a clear understanding of what they are *trying to do* when they evaluate an interpretive account, researchers fall back into the world-view they've struggled to escape. Smith and Heshusius (1986) argue convincingly that this view of evaluation tends to bring to a premature closure the dialogue between the traditional and interpretive world-views. Let us see whether an alternative view can be found.

Coherence. The first approach we consider is that of requiring that an interpretive account have a particular internal character. Coherence (we might also call it plausibility or intelligibility) is a characteristic that a good account should demonstrate. It seems reasonable to require this, but this approach to evaluation has frequently been rejected as inadequate. Miles and Huberman (1984a), for instance, consider plausibility "a last-refuge tactic for drawing conclusions" because "plausibility can easily become the refuge of, if not scoundrels, analysts who are too ready to jump to conclusions. . . . Subject the preliminary conclusions to *other* tactics of conclusion drawing and verification" (216-217).

Appeals to coherence and plausibility are generally rejected on the grounds that such an approach fails to live up to the requirements of a validation procedure. Hirsch (1967) has given the most influential argument for rejecting coherence as an evaluative criterion. He claimed to have identified the "fundamental difficulty" in this approach: because of the projective structure of understanding, the perspective we have on a text shapes readings of that text and so, according to Hirsch, it will tend to point out the evidence that supports it and ignore evidence that runs against it. New material uncovered as we interpret will tend to fit what is known already, because both are viewed through the same lens. To Hirsch this constitutes an inherent "self-confirmability" to interpretive inquiry that means that an interpretation will tend automatically to be coherent.

Hirsch correctly recognizes the projective organization of understanding, but he exaggerates the problem. Interpretation is only weakly self-confirming, in contrast with other kinds of understanding (delusions, for instance) that should be called strongly self-confirming because counter evidence is so threatening that it is totally suppressed. Material that fits an interpretation does indeed tend to be seen first, but counter evidence can certainly appear. In fact, a good interpretive inquiry will employ stratagems to critique an interpretation and so facilitate a change in understanding. For example, Packer (this volume) mentions Thomas Kuhn's suggestion that we should look for *dis*confirming evidence in order to better understand a text. This strategy would be totally impracticable if only corroborative evidence could appear; it works because interpretation focuses on breakdown and misunderstanding to show things (the "negative side of articulation" described by Packer, this volume). Hirsch would be correct if understanding and interpretation went only one way, projecting forward onto a text and violently imposing a perspective on it. Hirsch ignores the return arc, in which the inadequacies of a projective fore-structure become apparent.

Coherence is not, after all, inevitable, and good interpretive inquiry will scrutinize and check an interpretation that appears coherent by searching out and focusing on material that doesn't make sense. Hirsch is correct to the extent that even weak self-confirmability means coherence cannot provide the objective standard that a validation procedure is supposed to use, but we should conclude from this that evaluation is not simply validation, not that coherence, plausibility, or intelligibility is a thoroughly unreliable criterion. Here is another circle to hermeneutics, as Taylor points out.

> Our conviction that the account makes sense is contingent on our reading of action and situation. But these readings cannot be explained or justified except by reference to other such readings, and their relation to the whole. If an interlocutor does not understand this kind of reading, or will not accept it as valid, there is nowhere else the argument can go. Ultimately, a good explanation is one which makes sense of the behavior; but then to appreciate a good explanation, one has to agree on what makes good sense; what makes good sense is a function of one's readings; and these in turn are based on the kind of sense one understands (Taylor 1985b, 24).

External Evidence. Hirsch suggested a different solution to the problem of the self-confirming character of interpretation: a move out of the text. The danger of being "trapped in the hermeneutic circle" (Hirsch 1967, 165) by a self-confirming interpretation could be overcome, he proposed, by seeking external evidence: information that lay outside the text. He argued that an interpretation must be "measured against a genuinely discriminating norm" (p. 26), one that provides an interpretation-free standard. Only by doing this would we be able to decide among competing interpretations, all of which might be quite plausible. And in a similar manner some interpretive methodologists have proposed that an interpretation be tested against various kinds of external evidence.

Hirsch himself suggested a specific norm: "the old-fashioned ideal of rightly understanding what the author meant" (p. 26), by which Hirsch meant "what the author most probably intended." And although Hirsch's reasons for rejecting coherence as a criterion were unnecessarily harsh, it does indeed seem appropriate that we should check with the person whose 'text' we are studying. If we interpret a written text we should consider the author; if we study action we should consider the agent. When we give an interpretive account it is appropriate to ask the author or agent whether we have understood what they meant. And so using an agent's intentions as the norm against which to evaluate an interpretive account has seemed a fruitful move for psychologists to make, too.

Reasonable though it seems, this approach leads into difficulties if we are still looking, as Hirsch was, for a validation procedure. The central difficulty is that it is unclear how the intention can be identified. The intention-in-action no longer exists; it was present only at the time of acting. Ricoeur (1976, p. 100) points out, in explicit disagreement with Hirsch, that "the intention of the author is lost as a psychical event." Lost, it can hardly function as the norm by which to evaluate an interpretation. Ricoeur goes so far as to deny that the author's intention has any existence outside the meaning of the text: "The intention of writing has no other expression than the verbal meaning of the text itself. Hence all information concerning the biography and the psychology of the author constitutes only a part of the total information which the logic of validation has to take into account. This information, as distinct from the text interpretation, is in no way normative as regards the task of interpretation" (1976, p. 100). The same argument holds against using an agent's intention in acting as an evaluative norm. Even if we can talk with the agent and ask her what she meant by acting as she did, she has to recall and interpret her own action. If the agent is not accessible we can only infer intention on the basis of biographical information and knowledge of the circumstances of the action. Either way, the agent's intention is just as open to interpretation as the account we are trying to evaluate by means of that intention.

Hirsch has no convincing solution to this difficulty. He proposed, unconvincingly, that an interpreter can have empathic access to the author's intention: "The interpreter needs to adopt sympathetically the author's stance (his disposition to engage in particular kinds of intentional acts) so that he can 'intend' with some degree of probability the same intentional objects as the author" (p. 238). But how can this empathic response be made in a way that is "external" to a reading of the text? How can our identification of the author's intention be uninformed by the familiarity we have with the text? How shall we resolve the disagreements that are bound to arise over the author's stance? We can only understand an author's intention in terms of our own culture and time, and so the character of that intention will always remain open to reinterpretation.

This is not to deny that biographical information can be helpful, perhaps essential, to an interpretive inquiry. But it is not at all clear how this information provides a "discriminating norm" to distinguish good interpretive accounts from bad. In fact "good" and "bad" seem only to mean correspondence, or its lack, between the interpretation and the participant's intention. A correspondence theory of truth is still at work here. The appeal to the author's or agent's intention as an "external" uninterpreted norm can only fail to provide the validation sought by Hirsch and others. But this suggests they are searching for an impossible kind of evaluation, not that intentions (and other external material) are of no interest. While it remains open to further interpretation, the participants' recollection of their intentions can be valuable material for an interpretive inquiry.

The Participants' Interpretation. Perhaps a better norm could be chosen, though, one that would provide the desired objectivity? A second norm that has often been proposed is the agent's *current* view of their action. This norm avoids the problems of evanescent intentions; we can just ask our research participants what their action means to them right now. Guba and

Lincoln (1982) call for "member checks" to assure "confirmability" of an interpretation. Miles and Huberman (1984a) note that "as careful, plausible, and exhaustive as [an interpretation] may appear to be, parts or most of it could be dead wrong. One way of avoiding that outcome is to feed [it] back to site informants and ask for their corrective responses" (p. 142).

Of course this doesn't provide an objective norm either. At times such suggestions get suspiciously close to the notion that a valid interpretation is one that corresponds to a competent person's intuitions, and this, as we discussed in the Introduction, is at root a rationalist notion that does not hold up under scrutiny. Chomsky and Habermas have appealed to "informants'" intuitions to validate their reconstructions of linguistic and communicative competence. We have argued that intuitions, although interesting, can't provide the degree of certainty that is required of a validity test. What is the "meaning" of a text, or the "reality" of a situation, or the informants' view of the "accuracy" of an account, except another interpretation of it? If our research participants disagree with us we may indeed have made significant errors of interpretation. But we cannot rule out the possibility, perhaps small, that they disagree because they misunderstand their own activity, either because they were unaware of hidden aspects of that activity, or because defenses such as denial are at work.

This isn't at all to say that researchers always know better than research participants, or that talking with people about the way they see things can't be illuminating when one is struggling to make sense of puzzling material. Our point is again that the participants' view of things cannot provide an objective standard against which we can validate an interpretation, although this often seems to be what proponents of this approach are seeking. Significantly, they generally fail to suggest what we should do when genuine disagreements occur. If the researcher and the participants do not see eye to eye, how does evaluation proceed further? Miles and Huberman acknowledge that researchers and informants may disagree: "And we were left sitting on it, trying to think of a satisfactory way of getting resolution. We did find one good way of getting around these problems. It is that of testing the validity of one's findings by predicting what will happen at the site in six months or a year" (1984a, p. 142). But this is no solution. Instead of exploring why the disagreement occurred, the researcher is advised to shift to a different norm: prediction. Unfortunately, this norm is equally unable to provide unambiguous validity. Whose interpretation of events in six months should we consider valid? There are strong reasons (discussed in the Introduction) for thinking that meaningful prediction is impossible in human affairs. And when, on those occasions when the participants disagree with him, should the researcher modify an interpretation, and when should he turn to prediction instead in order to evaluate his account?

Consensus. Seeking consensus among researchers is a third approach to evaluation. An interpretation that can be called convincing should be communicable to others, should make sense to them and enable them to interpret new material in its light. This may be done by discussion among investigators in the same project, consultation with colleagues not involved in the project, and by peer response to published reports. But consensus too is often viewed as equivalent to a traditional evaluation procedure: the assessment of reliability. Agreement among interpretive researchers is seen as analogous to inter-observer or inter-rater reliability. When this is taken to its logical conclusion, agreements are quantified and treated statistically.

But obvious difficulties arise in treating consensus as though it is equivalent to repeated application of a measuring instrument. The most often mentioned difficulty is the possibility of collective delusion. We can easily imagine (or recall) occasions when agreements were reached that turned out to be mistaken. Agreement alone is no guarantee of correctness, and so consensus provides no foolproof criterion for evaluation. And consensus is of several different kinds. There is a difference between consensus among people simply new to the material, and consensus among people committed to a point of view different from our own.

When consensus is sought among people who are coming fresh to the topic of investigation there is a danger that we may simply train them to see things as we do. This kind of "training up" into an interpretive perspective seems a common (but usually hidden) occurrence in traditional research. When this happens it shows that our perspective is a viable one, but not that it is the best perspective, let alone the only one. We would seem to be setting a tougher test of an interpretation if we tried to convince others who have a different perspective. We would then need to show that our interpretation was viable, and also that it acknowledged the possibility of other perspectives (including that of the people we were talking with) and also that it somehow improved on these perspectives. An interpretation that could claim to be better would be one that provided a better account than rival interpretations.

Taylor outlines such a test for his interpretive account of the Enlightenment world view. "What would ultimately carry conviction would be an account of this development [of the modern world view] which illuminated it and made more sense of it than its rivals" (Taylor 1985a, 7). And the better interpretation would also explain how these rivals exist as possible, but mistaken, points of view: "The superiority of one position over another will thus consist in this, that from the more adequate position one can understand one's own stand and that of one's opponent, but not the other way around" (Taylor 1979, 67).

Perhaps instead of seeking consensus among researchers we should promote reasoned disagreement with our peers. Proponents of rival interpretations should each try to explain the other's perspective. Taylor comments with a touch of cynicism on his "superiority" approach that "it goes without saying that this argument can only have weight for those in the superior position." This surely need not be so; one would hope that arguments of this kind, if engaged in constructively, could be convincing even to those they are directed against.

But there is a further difficulty, one that Kuhn has pointed out. Competing perspectives are often incommensurable (Kuhn considers those involved in scientific paradigms, but the same holds for interpretative inquiry). Their proponents may use different terminology, have different cognitive commitments, and see the world so differently that their ability to grasp each other's viewpoints is so limited that reasoned discourse is scarcely possible. Taylor, too, is aware of this difficulty. "Put in forensic terms . . . we can only convince an interlocutor if at some point he shares our understanding of the language concerned. If he does not, there is no further step to take in rational argument; we can try to awaken these intuitions in him or we can simply give up; argument will advance us no further" (Taylor 1979, 28).

Consensus cannot, then, be taken as an interpretive analog to traditional reliability assessment. Even if people reach consensus on an interpretation further material may show it to be false. Conversely, holders of rival interpretations may fail to reach consensus not because the interpretations are flawed but because incommensurable perspectives prevent reasoned disagreement, and people talk past each other. Consensus, like coherence and external evidence, cannot be used as a technique for interpretation-free evaluation. However, some kind of discussion between researchers is clearly an essential aspect of interpretive inquiry.

Practical Implications. The fourth approach to evaluation is that of examining the relationship between an interpretive account and future events. But what should this relationship be? It is sometimes assumed that, just like an explanation in the natural sciences (at least in the positivist picture), an interpretive account should *predict* future events. We have already mentioned how Miles and Huberman talk of "testing the validity of one's findings by predicting what will happen at the site in six months or a year" (1984a, p. 142). But there is actually little reason to agree with these authors that "Presumably, if the [qualitative] analysis is correct, it has implications or consequences. These can be spelled out and operationalized. The real-world results can be checked out in a new contact with the site. The result is the qualitative researcher's version of a predictive validity coefficient that statisticians might use, for example, to see whether academic success predicts later job success" (p. 143-144).

There are several reasons why interpretive accounts don't make testable predictions. MacIntyre (1984) and Taylor (1979) argue strongly that predictive generalization are inadequate explanations in social science and, more strongly, that meaningful prediction is impossible in human affairs. Understanding is essentially retrospective, after the fact. "Really to be able to predict the future would be to have explicated so clearly the human condition that one would already have preempted all cultural innovation and transformation" (Taylor 1979, 70). Granted, Taylor is talking here of major cultural shifts, but the same kind of innovation is perfectly possible, and possibly more frequent, in an individual institution like a school. Interpretive accounts cannot make meaningful predictions, nor is predicting a useful kind of explanation in the human sciences. The implication is that an interpretive account cannot be evaluated on the basis of its success or failure at predicting the future. If an interpretive account has implications for the future, these are not such that give us a version of predictive validity.

What, then, is the nature of these future implications? Fischer (1987, p. 8) provides a useful suggestion when she talks of a "pragmatism criterion" for evaluating interpretation: "does the presentation prove useful for understanding related phenomena and for maneuvering in the everyday world?" We have seen how interpretive inquiry is intrinsically linked to practical activity. The motivation for an interpretive inquiry is a practical concern, and what is uncovered when things go well is an answer to this concern. This answer should have direct implications for practice.

Interpretive research is itself a kind of praxis or practical activity, and its aim is not to describe the world in a detached manner but to act in the world, in an engaged manner. Interpretive inquiry has an emancipatory interest, not an instrumental one (cf., Habermas 1971); an interpretive account has the potential to emancipate people, to free them from practical troubles. (This is presumably why psychotherapy involves narrative interpretation so intimately.) As Lather (1986) puts it, "Emancipatory knowledge increases awareness of the contradictions hidden or distorted by everyday understandings, and in doing so it directs attention to the possibilities for social transformation inherent in the present configuration of social processes" (p. 259).

This indicates that an interpretive account might be evaluated with reference to practical changes that it has brought about, or at the least its usefulness for "maneuvering in the everyday world," as Fischer suggests. In this vein Lather talks of "catalytic validity," where we examine "the degree to which the research process reorients, focuses, and energizes participants toward knowing reality in order to transform it" (p. 272).

The Grail Escapes Again

The four approaches we have discussed do not make possible the kind of interpretation-free validation that traditional inquiry vaunts. Because of this, the interpretive methodologists who propose them often have second thoughts and end up apologizing. Certainly, if we were seeking the grail of validation these approaches should dissatisfy us. But on the contrary, they are reasonable approaches that are used regularly and fruitfully. Approaches such as these should not be abandoned; instead we need a better account of *what kind* of evaluation they provide.

We move closer to this by considering briefly the form that evaluation takes in the natural sciences. For it might seem that our argument merely shows that interpretive inquiry in the human sciences is unable to provide the kind of certainty that can be achieved in the natural sciences. But this is far from the case. Those who seek fixed validity criteria are requiring something of interpretive inquiry that, in actuality, not even natural science can provide. Interpretation-free validation is impossible there too and Kuhn, in an analysis of selection among scientific paradigms, contends that it would stifle science if it were possible.

Kuhn maintains (1977) that while scientists tend to agree on criteria of adequacy such as consistency, scope, fruitfulness, simplicity, accuracy, and others, far from these being meta-paradigmatic criteria that provide interpretation-free decision procedures for theory-choice, they are values that remain imprecise and open to interpretation. Scientists will legitimately differ in their evaluation of a specific theory. Furthermore, these values will often conflict with one another, as when accuracy may only be achieved at the cost of reduced scope, and so on. In Kuhn's view this does not indicate that the criteria are inadequate or poorly defined. They appear incomplete only because the standard is an inappropriate one: logical rules or procedures. On the contrary, as "criteria that influence decisions without specifying what those decisions must be" (p. 330) they serve the crucial roles of permitting rational disagreement and spreading the risks that introducing and supporting a novel view of the world always entail. They serve to point out what is and is not relevant in a choice between theories, not to render the winner obvious and the choice unnecessary.

We propose that the four approaches to evaluation we have considered are reasonable because they direct our attention and our discussions to considerations we value when evaluating an interpretive account. Consistency, relationship to other material, the response of research participants, communicability to both sympathetic and skeptical peers, the responses of these peers, relations to alternative perspectives, practical implications, are all important. Neither together nor separately can they indicate whether an interpretation corresponds to the way things really are; they are not ways of validating. But they are ways we can consider whether what has been uncovered in an interpretive inquiry answers the practical, concernful question that directed that inquiry.

We said that two things needed to be seen in order to understand why these four approaches to evaluation satisfy us, even though they cannot provide interpretation-free validation. The first was that interpretation is not a matter of conjecture and guess, so that stringent validation (refutation) is unnecessary. (This should come as a relief, since we have also seen that validation is impossible!) The second was that a true interpretation is one that uncovers an answer to the concern motivating the inquiry. If an answer has been uncovered by an interpretive account we should find it plausible, it should fit other material that we are aware of, other people should find it convincing, and it should have the power to change practice. These are the four approaches to evaluation. But it will not necessarily be all of these at once. Nor may the account be *any* of these immediately. An interpretation that brings a solution to a practical concern may seem implausible and unconnected at first. Evaluation will never be straightfoward and procedural; a choice among perspectives will be risky and sometimes incorrect. And as Taylor points out:

> The practical and the theoretical are inextricably joined here. It may not just be that to understand a certain explanation one has to sharpen one's intuitions, it may be that one has to change one's orientation—if not in adopting another orientation, at least in living one's own in a way which allows for greater comprehension of others. Thus, in the sciences of man insofar as they are hermeneutical there can be a valid response to "I don't understand" which takes the form, not only "develop your intuitions," but more radically "change yourself." This puts an end to any aspiration to a value-free or 'ideology-free' science of man. A study of the science of man is inseparable from the options between which men must choose (Taylor 1979, 67-68).

One thing more. Even when an interpretation has been evaluated and seems to have uncovered something that answers our interpretive concern, there is yet another difference between this kind of evaluation and objective validation. Not only does interpretive inquiry provide accounts that will not seem true to all people (because their concerns and their perspectives will differ), it provides accounts that will not remain true for all time. This is a phenomenon Heidegger calls "fallenness." Any elucidating account of a phenomenon has a tendency to lose its power and immediacy, to become a slogan and no longer be felt a moving description; to become a mere "assertion"—a hollow claim. Assertions—predicative statements—are the stuff of detached objectivity, and in the traditional approach they have been seen as privileged:

"The swan is white", "Frustration leads to aggression." For Heidegger, knowledge in assertions is subordinated to the more primordial kind of knowing involved in understanding and interpretation. Indeed, the correspondence theory is a consequence of mistakenly granting assertions a privileged position over ordinary practical understanding. (The personality-test items that Gergen exposed in Chapter 10 are assertions.) Stripped of their context, they are open to unbounded, and hence meaningless, interpretation.

> No interpretation is safe. Even after an authentic projection has been drawn from primordial sources, we cannot assume it will be preserved. On the contrary, we must assume that the incessant pull of fallenness will set to work on it, threatening to turn it into something second-hand, derivative, used up (Caputo 1987, 73).

Any interpretation is passed along in the form of derivative assertions, and this means dimming it down. Eventually these assertions lose their power to disclose and no longer uncover anything of value.

Conclusions

We have suggested that a good interpretation, one that gives an account we can call true, is one that answers the concern that motivated our inquiry in the first place. At the same time, we have seen there is no interpretive method that would lead to a universally acceptable account, one that would be accepted by all sides. And there is no technique, no interpretation-free algorithm or procedure with which we can evaluate an interpretation. As Rosen (1987, p. 143) puts it: "There are no canons by which one can usefully restrict legitimate from illegitimate readings."

However, the four evaluative approaches we have considered have each been judged from a traditional perspective that claims that such canons must exist, and each has been judged flawed. Coherence seems inevitable. The agent's intentions or current view of events seem unreliable. Consensus seems either too easy to achieve or too difficult. Prediction seems impossible. Nor can we dodge this with an appeal to notions of 'partial' validation; with evaluation only within the bounds of probable error. The term "error" itself points to an ideal of "correctness," the ideal of a measuring instrument with perfect reliability, one that will give identical measurements on repeated trials, one that is impervious to unwanted influences, the way an ideal measuring-rod is unaffected by shifts in temperature. In interpretive inquiry we must drop this ideal of universal certitude.

An analogy may help. An interpretive account resembles in some respects a hammer in a workshop. The traditional approach to validation involves a misunderstanding that is like thinking the question, "How good is the hammer?" is similar to "How heavy is the hammer?" Two things are overlooked: the task in which the hammer will be employed, and its place among the other tools (cf. Heidegger 1927/1962, 413). The hammer's weight can be established with no attention to either of these. But the hammer is good only if it advances the current task and only if it works well with its companion tools. This choice is not a fixed one, it will change as new phases of the task arise. Heavy hammers are better for framing walls, and light ones are good for carefully placing molding pins. In the same way, a good interpretive account is one that advances the practical concerns with which we undertake an interpretive inquiry, and one that works well with the other activities we are engaged in.

The four approaches to evaluation stem from forms of persuasive reasoning that have developed over the centuries; reasoning we engage in when questions of veracity arise in our everyday interactions. If we are unsure how to understand someone's action we can see if our interpretation holds together and makes sense (applying the logic of our choice), we can ask her what she meant (with a skeptical ear), we can talk with others (aware we may be seeking their agreement), and we can look to see what happens when we tell her our interpretation. If these checks pan out we are calmed, but if we are wise we don't feel an unwarranted confidence that we've got to the bottom of the matter. Ultimately we will never be quite sure; we may have to change our mind the very next moment: a revolution may take place.

Only in this century has there been a general recognition that the search for epistemological security can never succeed. This suggests that we would be better employed working to open up *new* perspectives, rather than trying to justify whatever perspective we currently hold. The logical positivists' reaction to Einstein's revolution in physics was to hope such a thing wouldn't happen again. Having seen what that attitude led to, shouldn't we learn from their mistake and struggle to stay open to such reorientations? We should, perhaps, be attempting to *in*validate our own interpretations; to look for the cracks in their apparently polished surfaces. We've learned that it is the troubling anomalies, such as the precession of Mercury's perihelion, that catalyze a change in scientific paradigm. In a science such as psychology that will never be paradigmatic in the way that physics and chemistry are, we ought to ferret out anomalies rather than try to prove ourselves correct. Hermeneutics has no magical recipe for evading dogmatism; if we tend to scold empiricist and rationalist inquiry for tending to lionize one view of things as the "true" one (or "scientific," "objective", "accurate," "real") or as the only practicable one ("operationalized," "pragmatic", "functional"), interpretation has its own tendency to slide into tendentious opinions and pronouncements. Claims to demonstrate validity only exacerbate this problem. Instead we interpretive researchers might all be required to spend time debunking our own perspectives: pointing out their flaws and shortcomings; documenting the anomalies and oddities that remain puzzling and unexplained, the fish that have escaped our nets. These things waken us in the small hours to a recognition that, even as psychologists, there is much about people we still can't give a name to.

Notes and References

Overview

References

Aanstoos, C.M. 1985. Psychology as a human science. *American Psychologist*, 40, 1417-1418.

Addison, R.B. In press. Covering-Over and Over-Reflecting: Using personal and professional development groups to integrate dysfunctional modes of being in residency training. In M.J. Little & J.E. Midtling (Eds.), *Becoming a Family Physician*. New York: Springer-Verlag.

Brown, L.M. 1986. Moral orientations and epistemology: A conceptual analysis. Unpublished paper, Harvard University Graduate School of Education.

Champion, R. 1985. The importance of Popper's theories to psychology. *American Psychologist*, 40, 1415-1416.

Dar, R. 1987. Another look at Meehl, Lakatos, and the scientific practices of psychologists. *American Psychologist*, 42, 145-151.

Farrell, E. 1986. Metaphor and psychology: A reply to Gholson and Barker. *American Psychologist*, 41, 719-720.

Faulconer, J.E., & Williams, R.N. 1985. Temporality in human action: An alternative to positivism and historicism. *American Psychologist*, 40, 1179-1188.

Gergen, K.J. 1982. *Toward transformation in social knowledge*. New York: Springer-Verlag.

Gergen, K.J. 1985. The social constructionist movement in modern psychology. *American Psychologist*, 40, 266-275.

Gholson, B., & Barker, P. 1986. On metaphor in psychology and physics: Reply to Farrell. *American Psychologist*, 41, 720-721.

Gilligan, C. 1982. *In a different voice: Psychological theory and women's development*. Cambridge, MA: Harvard University Press.

Heidegger, M. 1927/1962. *Being and time*. (J. Macquarrie and E. Robinson, Trans.). New York: Harper & Row.

293

Jennings, J.L. 1986. Husserl revisited: The forgotten distinction between psychology and phenomenology. *American Psychologist*, 41, 1231-1240.

Kimble, G.A. 1984. Psychology's two cultures. *American Psychologist*, 39, 833-839.

Krasner, L., & Houts, A.C. 1984. A study of the "value" systems of behavioral scientists. *American Psychologist*, 39, 840-850.

Manicas, P.T., & Secord, P.F. 1983. Implications for psychology of the new philosophy of science. *American Psychologist*, 38, 339-413.

Messer, S.B. 1985. Choice of method is value laden too. *American Psychologist*, 40, 1414-1415.

Packer, M.J. 1985a. *The structure of moral action: A hermeneutic study of moral conflict*. Basel: Karger.

Packer, M.J. 1985b. Hermeneutic inquiry in the study of human conduct. *American Psychologist*, 40, 1081-1093.

Ricoeur, P. 1979. The model of the text: Meaningful action considered as a text. In P. Rabinow and W.M. Sullivan (Eds.), *Interpretive social science: a reader*. Berkeley: University of California Press.

Sarbin, T.R. 1986. *Narrative psychology: The storied nature of human conduct*. New York: Praeger.

Selman, R. 1980. *The growth of interpersonal understanding*. New York: Academic Press.

Serlin, R.C., & Lapsley, D.K. 1985. Rationality in psychological research: the good-enough principle. *American Psychologist*, 40, 73-83.

Shweder, R.A. & D'Andrade, R.G. 1980. The systematic distortion hypothesis. *New Directions for Methodology of Social and Behavioral Science*, 4, 37-58.

Silverstein, A. 1988. An Aristotelian resolution of the idiographic versus nomothetic tension. *American Psychologist*, 43, 425-430.

Spence, D.P. 1982. *Narrative truth and historical truth: Meaning and interpretation in psychoanalysis*. New York: Norton.

Steele, R.S. 1982. *Freud and Jung: Conflicts of interpretation*. London: Routledge & Kegan Paul.

Unger, R.K. 1985. Epistemological consistency and its scientific implications. *American Psychologist*, 40, 1413-1414.

Introduction

Notes

1. And Musil ought to know. Although best known as a novelist, Robert Musil wrote his dissertation on Ernst Mach's work (Musil 1908/1982).

References

Bernstein, R. 1983. *Beyond objectivism and relativism.* Philadelphia: University of Pennsylvania Press.

Bleicher, J. 1980. *Contemporary hermeneutics: Hermeneutics as method, philosophy and critique.* London: Routledge & Kegan Paul.

Caputo, J.D. 1987. *Radical hermeneutics: Repetition, deconstruction, and the hermeneutic project.* Bloomington: Indiana University Press.

Cherry, E.C. 1953. Some experiments on the recognition of speech, with one and with two ears. *Journal of the Acoustical Society of America,* 25, 975-979.

Chomsky, N. 1957. *Syntactic structures.* Mouton: The Hague.

Chomsky, N. 1965. *Aspects of the theory of syntax.* Cambridge, MA: MIT Press.

Descartes, R. 1641/1968. (Trans.) F.E. Sutcliffe. *Meditations on the first philosophy.* Penguin Press.

Dreyfus, H. 1979. *What computers can't do: The limits of artificial intelligence.* Revised edition. London: Harper & Row.

Dreyfus, H. 1980. Holism and hermeneutics. *Review of Metaphysics,* 34, 3-23.

Dreyfus, H.L., & Dreyfus, S.E. 1986. *Mind over machine: The power of human intuition and expertize in the era of the computer.* The Free Press.

Gadamer, H-G. 1960/1976. *Philosophical hermeneutics.* Berkeley: University of California Press.

Gadamer, H-G. 1960/1986. *Truth and method.* New York: Crossroad Publishing Company.

Garfinkel, H. 1967. *Studies in ethnomethodology.* Englewood Cliffs, NJ: Prentice-Hall.

Geertz, C. 1983. *Local knowledge: Further essays in interpretive anthropology.* New York: Basic Books.

Habermas, J. 1979. *Communication and the evolution of society.* (T. McCarthy, Trans.). Boston: Beacon Press.

Hacking, I. 1983. *Representing and intervening: Introductory topics in the philosophy of natural science.* New York: Cambridge University Press.

Hahn, H. 1930/1980. The significance of the scientific world view, especially for mathematics and physics. Reprinted in B. McGuiness (Ed.), *Empiricism, logic, and mathematics. (Vienna Circle Collection, v. 13).* Dordrecht, Holland: D. Reidel.

Hahn, H. 1933/1980. The crisis in intuition. Reprinted in B. McGuiness (Ed.), *Empiricism, logic, and mathematics. (Vienna Circle Collection, v. 13).* Dordrecht, Holland: D. Reidel.

Hanson, N.R. 1958. *Patterns of discovery.* Cambridge: Cambridge University Press.

Harris, R. 1987. *Reading Saussure: A critical commentary on the "Cours de linguistique générale".* La Salle, IL: Open Court.

Heidegger, M. 1927/1962. *Being and time.* (J. Macquarrie and E. Robinson, Trans.). New York: Harper & Row.

Hirsch, E.D. 1967. *Validity in interpretation.* New Haven: Yale University Press.

Kohlberg, L. 1971. From Is to Ought: How to commit the naturalistic fallacy and get away with it in the study of moral development. In T. Mischel, (Ed.), *Cognitive development and epistemology.* New York: Academic Press.

Kuhn, T.S. 1970a. *The structure of scientific revolutions.* 2nd ed. Chicago: University of Chicago Press.

Kuhn, T.S. 1970b. Logic of discovery or psychology of research? In I. Lakatos & A. Musgrave (Eds.), *Criticism and the growth of knowledge.* New York: Cambridge University Press.

Kuhn, T.S. 1977. *The essential tension.* Chicago: University of Chicago Press.

Locke, J. 1690/1975. *An essay concerning human understanding.* Oxford: Clarendon Press.

Mach, E. 1896/1986. *Principles of the theory of heat.* (*Vienna Circle Collection, v. 17*). Dordrecht, Holland: D. Reidel.

MacIntyre, A. 1984. *After virtue: A study in moral theory.* South Bend, IN: University of Notre Dame Press.

MacIntyre, A. 1988. *Whose justice? Which rationality?* South Bend, IN: University of Notre Dame Press.

McCarthy, T. 1978. *The critical theory of Jurgen Habermas.* Cambridge, MA: MIT Press.

Musil, R. 1908/1982. *On Mach's Theories.* Washington DC: Catholic University of America Press.

Musil, R. 1930/1979. *The man without qualities.* London: Pan Books.

Nagel, T. 1986. *The view from nowhere.* New York: Oxford University Press.

Nagel, E., & Newman, J.R. 1958. *Godel's proof.* New York University Press.

Packer, M.J. 1985. Hermeneutic inquiry in the study of human conduct. *American Psychologist,* 40, 1081-1093.

Packer, M.J. (this volume). Tracing the hermeneutic circle: Articulating an ontical study of moral conflicts. In M.J. Packer & R.B. Addison Eds., *Entering the circle: hermeneutic inquiry in psychology.* Albany: State University of New York Press.

Palmer, R.E. 1969. *Hermeneutics: Interpretation theory in Schleiermacher, Dilthey, Heidegger and Gadamer.* Evanston, IL: Northwestern University Press.

Piaget, J. 1970. *Structuralism.* (C. Maschler, Trans.). New York: Harper & Row.

Piaget, J. 1977. *The development of thought: Equilibration of cognitive structures.* New York: Viking.

Popper, K.R. 1959. *The logic of scientific discovery.* New York: Basic Books.

Popper, K.R. 1979. *Objective knowledge: An evolutionary approach.* Revised edition. New York: Oxford University Press.

Rosen, S. 1987. *Hermeneutics as politics.* New York: Oxford University Press.

de Saussure, F. 1915/1959. *Course in general linguistics* (W. Baskin, Trans.). New York: Philosophical library.

Taylor, C. 1985. *Human agency and language: Philosophical papers, Vol. 1.* New York: Cambridge University Press.

Taylor, C. 1979. Interpretation and the science of man. In P. Rabinow and W. Sullivan (Eds.), *Interpretive social science: A reader.* Berkeley: University of California Press.

von Mises, R. 1956. *Positivism: A study in human understanding.* New York: George Braziller.

Warnke, G. 1987. *Gadamer: Hermeneutics, tradition and reason.* Stanford, CA: Stanford University Press.

Weinsheimer, J.C. 1985. *Gadamer's hermeneutics: A reading of "Truth and method".* New Haven: Yale University Press.

Williams, B. 1978. *Descartes: The project of pure enquiry.* Penguin Press.

Williams, B. 1985. *Ethics and the limits of philosophy.* Cambridge, MA: Harvard University Press.

Chapter 1

Notes

1. The author wishes to express his thanks to Lu Sucholaski for her help in transcribing endless field notes and to Margo Addison for her excellent comments and suggestions on earlier drafts of this chapter.

2. Primary-care physicians are those physicians who specialize in family medicine, pediatrics, and general internal medicine. Physicians who specialize in obstetrics-gynecology are sometimes also considered to be primary-care physicians.

3. For a description of grounded theory, see Glaser and Strauss, (1967), and Glaser, (1978).

4. For the most part, I was not impressed with the quality or conception of the research I encountered. At an annual workshop of the Society for Research and Education in Primary Care Internal Medicine, researchers admitted that the desired outcomes of medical training were unclear; no one knew what the relevant "variables" were. While this statement indicated the emptiness of positivist research endeavors, I saw the possibility inherent in the statement: perhaps medical researchers would begin to reflect on their own practices.

5. The term "surviving" was usually used metaphorically. It achieved its potency from residents who had attempted suicide, had emotional breakdowns, and/or quit the residency in the past. As Lasch stated:

The concern with the self, which seems so characteristic of our time, takes the form of a concern with its psychic survival. Everyday life has begun to pattern itself on the survival strategies forced on those exposed to extreme adversity. Selective apathy, emotional disengagement from others, renunciation of the past and the future, a determination to live one day at a time—these techniques of emotional self-management, necessarily carried to extremes under extreme conditions, in more moderate form have come to shape the lives of ordinary people under the ordinary conditions of a bureaucratic society widely perceived as a far-flung system of total control (1984. p. 39).

6. Because of space limitations, I have only provided a brief narrative summary of my account. For a more thorough explication, see Addison (1984).

7. The issue of the economic benefit to the hospital gained by seeing greater numbers of patients was never explicitly addressed. See the following section for a further discussion of this issue.

8. See the above discussion on the fore-structure of interpretation for reference to how the account opened up new ways of seeing for the researcher.

References

Addison, R.B. 1984. *Surviving the residency: A grounded, interpretive investigation of physician socialization.* Unpublished doctoral dissertation, University of California, Berkeley. (University Microfilms No. 84-268-89).

Addison, R.B. In press. Covering-over and Over-Reflecting: Using personal and professional development groups to integrate dysfunctional modes of being in residency training. In M.J. Little & J.E. Midtling (Eds.), *Becoming a family physician.* New York: Springer-Verlag.

Bernstein, R.J. 1976. *The restructuring of social and political theory.* Philadelphia: University of Pennsylvania Press.

Bernstein, R.J. 1983. *Beyond objectivism and relativism: Science, hermeneutics, and praxis.* Philadelphia: University of Pennsylvania Press.

Bleicher, J. 1982. *The hermeneutic imagination: Outline of a positive critique of scientism and sociology.* London: Routledge & Kegan Paul.

Bloom, S.W. 1963. The process of becoming a physician. *Annals of the American Academy of Political and Social Science,* 346, 77-87.

Dreyfus, H.L. 1980. Holism and hermeneutics. *Review of Metaphysics,* 34, 3-23.

Dreyfus, H.L. In press. *Being-in-the-world: A commentary on Division I of Being and time.* Cambridge, MA: MIT Press.

Gadamer, H.G. 1976. *Philosophical hermeneutics.* Berkeley: University of California Press.

Geer, B., Hass, J., Vivona, C., Miller, S.J., Woods, C., & Becker, H.S. 1968. Learning the ropes: Situational learning in four occupational training programs. In I. Deutscher & E.J. Thompson (Eds.), *Among the people: Encounters with the poor* (pp. 209-233). New York: Basic Books.

Glaser, B.C., & Strauss, A.L. 1967. *The discovery of grounded theory: Strategies for qualitative research.* New York: Aldine.

Glaser, B.C. 1978. *Theoretical sensitivity.* Mill Valley, CA: The Sociology Press.

Guba, E. 1981. Criteria for assessing the trustworthiness of naturalistic inquiry. *Educational Communication and Technology Journal,* 29, 79-92.

Guba, E., & Lincoln, Y. 1982. Epistemological and methodological bases of naturalistic inquiry. *Educational Communication and Technology Journal,* 30, 233-252.

Habermas, J. 1971. *Knowledge and human interests.* Boston: Beacon Press.

Heidegger, M. 1927/1962. *Being and time.* New York: Harper and Row.

Lasch, C. 1984. February 2. The great American variety show. *The New York Review of Books,* pp. 36-40.

Light, D. 1980. *Becoming psychiatrists: The professional transformation of self.* New York: Norton.

Miller, S. 1970. *Prescription for leadership.* Chicago: Aldine.

Mizrahi, T. 1986. *Getting rid of patients: Contradictions in the socialization of physicians.* New Brunswick, NJ: Rutgers University Press.

Mumford, E. 1970. *Interns: From students to physicians.* Cambridge, MA: Harvard University Press.

Smith, J.K., & Heshusius, L. 1986. Closing down the conversation: The end of the quantitative-qualitative debate among educational inquirers. *Educational Researcher,* 15, 1, 4-12.

Starr, P. 1982. *The social transformation of American medicine.* New York: Basic Books.

Taylor, C. 1979. Interpretation and the sciences of man. In P. Rabinow & W.M. Sullivan (Eds.), *Interpretive social science: A reader* (pp. 25-71). Berkeley: University of California Press.

Chapter 2

Notes

1. This paper was written with the support of the W.T. Grant Foundation and the Spencer Foundation. It reflects a collaborative effort of the four authors, with no implication of primary authorship in the order of the names. The authors all participated in this effort as members of the Group for the Study of Interpersonal Development, directed by Robert L. Selman. The interaction indices analysis was based upon observations

made by B. Caplan and K. Schantz, and further developed by B. Caplan and R. Selman (Caplan 1988). L. Schultz provided an integration of this analysis with two other ways in which the project explores interpersonal development.

2. This introduction is drawn from a paper by R. Selman, Fostering Intimacy and Autonomy, which appears in a volume edited by W. Damon, *New Directions in Child Development: 10th Anniversary Volume*. San Francisco, Jossey-Bass (in press).

References

Blatt, S.J., & Shichman, S. 1983. Two primary configurations of psychopathology. *Psychoanalysis and contemporary thought*, 6, 187-254.

Bronfenbrenner, U. 1979. *The ecology of human development: Experiments by nature and design*. Cambridge, MA: Harvard University Press.

Caplan, B. 1988. A hermeneutic analysis of social interaction. Unpublished qualifying paper, Harvard University.

Cooper, C.R., Grotevant, H.D., & Condon, S.M. 1983. Individuation and connectedness in family as a context for adolescent identity formation and role-taking skills. In H.D. Grotevant and C.R. Cooper (Eds.), *Adolescent development in the family: New directions in child development* (pp. 43-60), No. 22. San Francisco: Jossey-Bass.

Erikson, E. 1963. *Childhood and society*. New York: Norton.

Erikson, E. 1968. *Identity, youth and crisis*. New York: Norton.

Freud, A. 1966. *The ego and the mechanisms of defense*. New York: International Universities Press.

Gergen, K.J., & Gergen, M.M. 1982. Explaining human conduct: Form and function. In P.F. Secord (Ed.), *Explaining human behavior: Consciousness, human action and social structure* (pp. 127-154). Beverly Hills, CA: Sage.

Gilligan, C. 1982. *In a different voice: Psychological theory and women's development*. Cambridge, MA: Harvard University Press.

Hinde, R. 1979. *Toward understanding relationships*. London: Academic Press.

Mishler, E.G. 1979. Meaning in context: Is there any other kind? *Harvard Educational Review*, 49(1), 1-19.

Packer, M. 1985. Hermeneutic inquiry in the study of human conduct. *American Psychologist*, 40, 1081-1093.

Selman, R.L. 1980. *The growth of interpersonal understanding: Developmental and clinical analyses*. New York: Academic Press.

Selman, R.L., & Schultz, L.H. (in press). Children's strategies for interpersonal negotiation with peers: An interpretive/empirical approach to the study of social development. In T.J. Berndt & G.W. Ladd (Eds.), *Peer relationships in child development*. New York: Wiley.

Selman, R.L., & Schultz, L.H. 1988. *The child's quest for collaboration: Theory and practice in a developmental framework.* Manuscript submitted for publication.

Selman, R.L., & Yeates, K.O. 1987. Childhood social regulation of intimacy and autonomy: A developmental-constructionist perspective. In W.M. Kurtines & J. L. Gewirtz (Eds.), *Moral development through social interaction* (pp. 43-101). New York: Wiley.

Stern D. 1985. *The interpersonal world of the infant.* New York: Basic Books.

Sroufe, L.A., & Fleeson, J. 1986. Attachment and the construction of relationships. In W.W. Hartup and Z. Rubin (Eds.), *Relationships and development* (pp. 51-72). Hillsdale, NJ: Erlbaum.

Sullivan, H.S. 1953. *The interpersonal theory of psychiatry.* New York: Norton.

Werner, H. 1948. *The comparative psychology of mental development.* New York: International Universities Press.

Chapter 3

Notes

1. Dr. Norma Haan generously made available to me these video recordings, which she made during a study concerning her interactional theory of morality (cf. Haan, Aerts & Cooper 1985).

2. I am aware of the possibility that quoting Heidegger may puzzle as much as it clarifies a point. I do so with the intention of providing a modicum of assistance to the reader who wishes to refer to *Being and Time.*

3. I have described elsewhere the three modes of engagement that Heidegger distinguishes: the ready-to-hand, unready-to-hand, and present-at-hand modes (Packer 1985c). These are modes respectively of engaged activity, deliberation on a practical difficulty, and disengaged reflection.

4. Here the initial capital letter indicates the session, and the number is the transcript line number. The speaker is indicated with a three-character code: L indicates a member of the losing team, W a member of the winning team; F indicates female, M male; 1 and 2 indicate which of the two team-members of each gender was speaking. So LF1 is the first female member of the losing team. Brackets provide contextual information; parentheses indicate unclear and inaudible speech.

5. For more detail on the fore-structures of interpretation the reader is referred to Addison (this volume), to Dreyfus (in press) and Caputo (1987 p. 70).

6. In the project "Social entry and rejection among preschool children," funded by the National Institute of Mental Health, Prevention Research Branch.

References

Addison, R.B. (This volume). Grounded interpretive research: An investigation of physician socialization.

Anglo, S. 1969. *Spectacle, pageantry, and early Tudor policy.* Oxford Univ. Press.

Aristotle. 1954. *Rhetoric.* (W. Rhys Roberts, Trans.) New York: Random House.

Arnold, M. 1968. *The nature of emotion.* Baltimore: Penguin Books.

Bailey, F.G. 1983. *The tactical uses of passion: An essay on power, reason, and reality.* Cornell University Press.

Barratt, B.B., & Sloan, T.S. 1988. Critical notes on Packer's "hermeneutic inquiry." *American Psychologist,* 43, 131-133.

Blasi, A. 1980. Bridging moral cognition and moral action: A critical review of the literature. *Psychological Bulletin,* 88, 1-45.

Booth, W.C. 1974. *Modern dogma and the rhetoric of assent.* The University of Chicago Press.

Caputo, J.D. 1987. *Radical hermeneutics: Repetition, deconstruction, and the hermeneutic project.* Bloomington: Indiana University Press.

Danner, H. 1986. Review of *The structure of moral action: A hermeneutic study of moral conflict. Phenomenology + Pedagogy,* 4, 95-100.

de Rivera, J. 1977. A structural theory of the emotions. *Psychological Issues,* 10, whole number #40.

de Rivera, J. 1986. Abstract conceptualization may reveal reality. Paper presented at the annual meeting of the American Psychological Association, Washington, DC.

Dreyfus, H.L. (in press). *Being-in-the-world: A commentary on Division 1 of Being and Time.* Cambridge, MA: MIT Press.

Garfinkel, H. 1967. *Studies in ethnomethodology.* Englewood Cliffs, NJ: Prentice-Hall.

Geertz, C. 1983. *Local knowledge: Further essays in interpretive anthropology.* New York: Basic Books.

Guignon, C. 1984. Moods in Heidegger's *Being and Time.* In (Eds.), C. Calhoun & R. Solomon, *What is an emotion?* New York: Oxford University Press.

Haan, N., Aerts, E., & Cooper, B. 1985. *Practical morality: Self and situation in everyday morality.* New York University Press.

Habermas, J. 1979. *Communication and the evolution of society.* (T. McCarthy, Trans.). Boston: Beacon Press.

Habermas, J. 1983. Interpretive social science vs. hermeneuticism. In N. Haan, R.M. Bellah, P. Rabinow, & W.M. Sullivan (Eds.), *Social science as moral inquiry.* Columbia University Press.

Hall, R.L., & Cobey, V.E. 1976. Emotion as transformation of the world. *Journal of Phenomenological Psychology,* 6, 180-198.

Hampshire, S. 1959. *Thought and action.* New York: Viking Press.

Heidegger, M. 1927/1962. *Being and time.* (J. Macquarrie & E. Robinson, Trans.). New York: Harper & Row.

Hoffman, M. 1979. Development of moral thought, feeling, and behavior. *American Psychologist,* 34, 958-966.

Hoffman, M. 1982. Affect and moral development. In (Eds). D. Cicchetti & P. Hesse, *New Directions for Child Development: #16. Emotional Development.* San Francisco: Jossey-Bass.

Hume, D. 1888/1978. *A treatise of human nature.* Second edition. New York: Oxford University Press.

James, W. 1890/1950. *The principles of psychology. Vol. 2.* New York: Dover.

Kenny, A. 1963. *Action, emotion and will.* London: Routledge and Kegan Paul.

Kinneavy, J.L. 1971. *A theory of discourse: The aims of discourse.* New York: Norton.

Kohlberg, L., Levine, C., & Hewer, A. 1983. Moral stages: A current formulation and a response to critics. *Contributions to Human Development.* 10, whole number.

Kuhn, T. 1977. *The essential tension.* Chicago: University of Chicago Press.

Lange, C.G., & James, W. 1922. *The emotions.* Baltimore: Williams and Wilkins.

Langer, S.K. 1967. *Mind: An essay on human feeling. Vol. 1.* Baltimore: Johns Hopkins University Press.

Lather, P. 1986. Research as praxis. *Harvard Educational Review,* 56, 257-277.

Liberman, K. 1980. Ambiguity and gratuitous concurrence in inter-cultural communication. *Human Studies,* 3, 65-86.

Locke, D. 1983. Doing what comes morally: The relation between behavior and stages of moral reasoning. *Human Development,* 26, 11-25.

MacCarthy, V.A. 1978. *The phenomenology of moods in Kierkegaard.* Boston: Martinus Nijhoff.

Mackenzie, B.D. 1977. *Behaviorism and the limits of scientific method.* New Jersey: Humanities Press.

MacMurray, J. 1962/1972. *Reason and emotion.* London: Faber and Faber.

Mandler, G. 1975. *Mind and emotion.* Mew York: Wiley.

Merleau-Ponty, M. 1942/1963. *The structure of behavior.* London: Methuen.

Merleau-Ponty, M. 1945/1962. *Phenomenology of perception.* London: Routledge & Kegan Paul.

Mischel, T. 1974. Understanding neurotic behavior: From "mechanism" to "intentionality." In T. Mischel, (Ed.). *Understanding other persons.* Oxford: Blackwell.

Nagel, T. 1986. *The view from nowhere.* New York: Oxford University Press.

Nussbaum, M.C. 1986. *The fragility of goodness: Luck and ethics in Greek tragedy and philosophy*. New York: Cambridge University Press.

Packer, M.J. 1985a. Concealment and uncovering in moral philosophy and moral practice. *Human Development*, 28, 108-112.

Packer, M.J. 1985b. *The structure of moral action: A hermeneutic study of moral conflict*. Basel: Karger.

Packer, M.J. 1985c. Hermeneutic inquiry in the study of human conduct. *American Psychologist*, 40, 1081-1093.

Packer, M.J. 1988. Hermeneutic inquiry: A response to criticisms. *American Psychologist*, 43, 133-136.

Ricoeur, P. 1979. The model of the text: Meaningful action considered as a text. In P. Rabinow and W.M. Sullivan (Eds.), *Interpretive social science: A reader*. Berkeley: University of California Press.

Ricoeur, P. 1981. *Hermeneutics and the human sciences: Essays on language, action and interpretation*. (Ed.), J.B. Thompson. New York: Cambridge University Press.

Rorty, A. (Ed.). 1980. *Explaining emotions*. Berkeley: University of California Press.

Sartre, J.-P. 1948. *The emotions: Outline of a theory*. (B. Frechtman, Trans.). New York: The Philosophical Library.

Searle, J. 1969. *Speech acts: An essay in the philosophy of language*. New York: Cambridge University Press.

Seung, T.K. 1982. *Structuralism and hermeneutics*. New York: Columbia University Press.

Shweder, R.A., & Much, N.C. 1987. Determinations of meaning: Discourse and moral socialization. In W.M. Kurtines & J.L. Gewirtz (Eds.), *Moral development through social interaction* (pp. 197-244). New York: Wiley.

Solomon, R.C. 1980. Emotions and choice. In A. Rorty (Ed.), *Explaining emotions*. Berkeley: University of California Press.

Solomon, R.C. 1983. *The passions: The myth and nature of human emotion*. South Bend, IN: University of Notre Dame Press.

Staub, E. 1978. *Positive social behavior and morality. Vol. 1. Social and personal influences*.

Thalberg, I. 1971. Acting against one's better judgment. In G.W. Mortimore, (Ed.). *Weakness of will*. London: Macmillan.

Weiner, B. 1980. A cognitive (attribution)-emotion-acting model of motivated behavior: An analysis of judgments of help-giving. *Journal of Personality and Social Psychology*, 39, 186-200.

Zajonc, R. 1980. Feeling and thinking: Preferences need no inferences. *American Psychologist*, 35.

Chapter 4

Notes

1. All names in this essay are pseudonyms.

References

Blasi, A. 1980. Moral cognition and moral action: A theoretical perspective. *Developmental Review*, 3, 178-210.

Blasi, A. 1984. Moral identity: Its role in moral functioning. In W.M. Kurtines & J.L. Gewirtz (Eds.), *Morality, moral behavior, and moral development.* New York: Wiley.

Camus, A. 1956. *The rebel.* New York: Random House.

Coles, R. 1967. *Children of crisis: A study of courage and fear.* Boston: Little, Brown & Company.

Dewey, J. 1922. *Human nature and conduct: An introduction to social psychology.* New York: Henry Holt.

Erikson, E.H. 1968. *Identity, youth and crisis.* New York: Norton.

Gaylin, W. 1970. *In service of their country: War resisters in prison.* New York: Viking.

Geertz, C. 1973. Thick description: Toward an interpretive theory of culture. In *The interpretation of cultures.* New York: Basic Books.

Haan, N., Block, J., and Smith, M.B. 1968. Moral reasoning of young adults: Political-social behavior, family background, and personality correlates. *Journal of Personality and Social Psychology*, 10, 183-201.

Higgins, A., Power, C., and Kohlberg, L. 1984. The relationship of moral atmosphere to judgments of responsibility. In W.M. Kurtines & Jacob L. Gewirtz (Eds.), *Morality, moral behavior, and moral development.* New York: Wiley.

Kohlberg, L. 1970. Education for justice: A modern statement of the Platonic view. In N.F. Sizer & T.R. Sizer (Eds.), *Moral education: Five lectures.* Cambridge, MA: Harvard University Press.

Kohlberg, L. 1971. From Is to Ought: How to commit the naturalistic fallacy and get away with it. In T. Mischel (Ed.), *Cognitive development and epistemology.* New York: Academic Press.

Kohlberg, L. and Candee, D. 1984. The relationship of moral judgment to moral action. In W.M. Kurtines & J.L. Gewirtz (Eds.), *Morality, moral behavior, and moral development.* New York: Wiley.

MacIntyre, A. 1981. *After virtue: A study in moral theory.* Notre Dame, IN: University of Notre Dame Press.

Mantell, D.M. 1974. *True Americanism: Green berets and war resisters.* New York: Teachers College Press.

Mergendoller, J.R. 1981. *War resistance and moral experience.* Unpublished Doctoral Dissertation, University of Michigan.

Merklin, Jr., L. 1974. *They chose honor: The problem of conscience in custody.* New York: Harper and Row.

McDougall, W. 1908. *An introduction to social psychology.* London: Methuen.

McNamee, S.M. 1972. *Moral behavior, moral development, and needs in students and political activists.* Unpublished Doctoral Dissertation, Case Western Reserve University.

Rest, J.R. 1983. Morality. In P.H. Mussen (Ed.), *Handbook of child psychology.* New York: Wiley.

Rothman, G.R. 1971. *An experimental analysis of the relationship between moral judgment and behavioral choice.* Unpublished Doctoral Dissertation, Columbia University.

Rothman, G.R. and Turiel, E. 1972. The influence of reasoning of behavioral choices at different stages of moral development. *Child Development,* 43, 741-756.

Chapter 5

Notes

1. The first two authors shared primary responsibility for the preparation of this chapter. They are listed in alphabetical order.

The work reported here was supported in part by grants from the Cleveland Foundation, the Bardige Foundation, and the Joseph S. Klingenstein Foundation.

Thanks to Martin Packer and Annie Rogers for their helpful comments on earlier versions of this manuscript.

2. In a similar sense we have emphasized, following Mishler (1986), the importance of considering the context from which the interview has come. Specifically, we would argue that while an individual interview can only be understood in terms of the whole context of which it is part, at the same time a full understanding of that context can only be grasped by understanding the meaning it holds for individual interviewees.

3. Specifically the problem of "validity in interpretation," which we will consider briefly later in this chapter.

4. After this chapter was written we discovered two recent and very insightful treatments of Ricoeur's work with respect to the psychological and developmental interpretation of interview texts—pieces that, in many respects, are quite similar to our own reading of his work (see Freeman 1985; Honey 1987).

5. Because the first reading (reading for the story or the plot) requires a full text, and because space limitation prevents us from presenting and analyzing Tanya's complete narrative, we move directly to the second reading—reading for self.

6. See Gilligan, Brown and Rogers (in press) for a more complete analysis and interpretation of this case.

7. A note on the use of the term "code" here: In developing data analysis techniques based on these "Narrative Types" we have used numerical "codes" to summarize and represent the interpretation of the reader. The term "code" thus refers only to this kind of categorical summary and representation—not to the process of interpreting and analyzing the narrative as a whole.

8. We have evidence from other studies in progress that provide additional support for our hunch that the Alignment dimension may be especially sensitive to context. In particular, when adolescent girls attending an all-girls school are compared with the adolescent girls attending the coed school, there is a significant difference in the Alignment distribution. That is, the girls from the all-girls school show significantly more alignment with care than the girls from the coed school (54% vs. 23%, X^2 [3 $\underline{N}$ = 89] = 20.8 $\underline{p}$ < .001). Given our knowledge of, and experience with these two schools, we interpret this difference as indicating that the context of the all-girls school may be more "care focused" than the context of the coed school.

9. We are indebted to Martin Packer for this recommendation.

References

Anastasi, A. 1976. *Psychological testing* (4th ed.). New York: MacMillan.

Argyris, D. 1987. *Exploring moral practice.* Unpublished manuscript, Harvard University.

Bleicher, J. 1980. *Contemporary hermeneutics.* London: Routledge & Kegan Paul.

Brown, L., Argyris, D., Attanucci, J., Bardige, B., Gilligan, C., Johnston, K., Miller, B., Osborne, R., Ward, J., Wiggins, G., & Wilcox, D. 1987. *A guide to reading narratives of moral conflict and choice for self and moral voice.* Cambridge: The Center for the Study of Gender, Education, and Human Development, Harvard University (Monograph #1).

Chronbach, L. 1949. *Essentials of psychological testing* (3rd ed.). New York: Harper & Row.

Chronbach, L. & Meehl, P. 1973. Construct validity in psychological tests. In P. Meehl, *Psychodiagnosis: Selected papers.* New York: W.W. Norton. (Original work published 1955)

Cohen, J. 1960. A coefficient of agreement for nominal scales. *Educational and Psychological Measurement, 20,* 37-46.

Colby, A. & Kohlberg, L. 1987. *The measurement of moral judgment.* New York: Cambridge University Press.

Dilthey, W. 1900/1976. The development of hermeneutics. In W. Dilthey, *Selected writings* (H. Rickman, Ed. & Trans.). Cambridge: Cambridge University Press.

Freeman, M. 1985. Paul Ricoeur on interpretation: The model of the text and the idea of development. *Human Development, 28,* 295-312.

Gadamer, H. 1975. *Truth and method.* New York: Crossroad.

Gadamer, H. 1976. *Philosophical hermeneutics* (D. Linge, Ed. & Trans.). Berkeley: University of California Press.

Gibbs, J. & Widaman, K. 1982. *Social intelligence: Measuring the development of sociomoral reflection.* Englewood-Cliffs: Prentice-Hall.

Gilligan, C. 1977. In a different voice: Women's conceptions of self and of morality. *Harvard Educational Review,* 47, 481-517.

Gilligan, C. 1982. *In a different voice: Psychological theory and women's development.* Cambridge: Harvard University Press.

Gilligan, C. 1983. Do the social sciences have an adequate theory of moral development? In N. Haan, R. Bellah, P. Rabinow, & W. Sullivan (Eds.), *Social science as moral inquiry.* New York: Columbia University Press.

Gilligan, C. 1986. Remapping the moral domain: New images of self in relationship. In T. Heller, M. Sosna, & D. Wellber (Eds.), *Reconstructing individualism: Autonomy, individualism, and the self in Western thought.* Stanford: Stanford University Press.

Gilligan, C. 1987. Moral orientation and moral development. In E. Kittay & D. Meyers (Eds.), *Women and moral theory.* New York: Rowman & Littlefield.

Gilligan, C., & Wiggins, G. 1987. The origins of morality in early childhood relationships. In J. Kagan & S. Lamb (Eds.), *The emergence of morality in young children.* Chicago: The University of Chicago Press.

Gilligan, C., Brown, L., & Rogers, A. (in press). Psyche embedded: A place for body, relationships, and culture in personality theory. In A. Rabin (Ed.), *Studying persons and lives.* New York: Springer-Verlag.

Gilligan, C., Johnston, D.K., & Miller, B. 1988. *Moral voice, adolescent development, and secondary education: A study at the Green River School.* Cambridge: The Center for the Study of Gender, Education, and Human Development, Harvard University (Monograph #3).

Hirsch, E. 1967. *Validity in interpretation.* New Haven: Yale University Press.

Hirsch, E. 1978. *The aims of interpretation.* Chicago: The University of Chicago Press.

Honey, M. 1987. The interview as text: Hermeneutics considered as a model for analyzing the clinically informed research interview. *Human Development,* 30, 69-82.

Johnston, K. 1985. *Two moral orientations—Two problem-solving strategies: Adolescents' solutions to dilemmas in fables.* Unpublished doctoral dissertation, Harvard University.

Juhl, P. 1980. *Interpretation: An essay in the philosophy of literary criticism.* Princeton: Princeton University Press.

Kohlberg, L. 1984. *Essays in moral development, Volume II: The psychology of moral development.* San Francisco: Harper & Row.

Landis, J.R., & Koch, G. 1977. The measurement of observer agreement for categorical data. *Biometrics*, 33, 159-174.

Loevinger, J. & Wessler, R. 1970. *Measuring ego development: Construction and use of a sentence completion test.* San Francisco: Jossey-Bass.

Macmurray, J. 1957. *The self as agent.* Atlantic Highlands, NJ: Humanities Press.

Mishler, E. 1979. Meaning in context: Is there any other kind? *Harvard Educational Review*, 53, 125-145.

Mishler, E. 1986. *Research interviewing: Context and narrative.* Cambridge, MA: Harvard University Press.

Nussbaum, M. 1986. *The fragility of goodness.* Cambridge: Cambridge University Press.

Packer, M. 1985. Hermeneutic inquiry in the study of human conduct. *American Psychologist*, 40, 1081-1093.

Palmer, R. 1969. *Hermeneutics: Interpretation theory in Schleiermacher, Dilthey, Heidegger, and Gadamer.* Evanston: Northwestern University Press.

Popper, K. 1959. *The logic of scientific discovery.* New York: Basic Books.

Rest, J. 1979. *Development in judging moral issues.* Minneapolis: The University of Minnesota Press.

Ricoeur, P. 1979. The model of a text: Meaningful action considered as a text. In P. Rabinow & W. Sullivan (Eds.), *Interpretive social science: A reader.* Berkeley: University of California Press.

Rogers, A. 1987. *Gender differences in moral thinking: A validity study of two moral orientations.* Unpublished doctoral dissertation, Washington University.

Spence, D. 1982.*Narrative truth and historical truth: Meaning and interpretation in psychoanalysis.* New York: Norton.

Tappan, M. 1987. *Hermeneutics and moral development: A developmental analysis of short-term change in moral functioning during late adolescence.* Unpublished doctoral dissertation, Harvard University.

Taylor, C. 1979. Interpretation and the sciences of man. In P. Rabinow & W. Sullivan (Eds.), *Interpretive social science: A reader.* Berkeley: University of California Press.

Chapter 6

Notes

1. Laura Underwood, David Cislo, Linda Webb, and Nancy Sack contributed to the development of the Comprehensive Process Analysis method and helped carry out the study of awareness events. Grants from the University of Toledo Graduate School and NIMH (1-RO3 MH35468-01) provided partial support for this research. Address

correspondence to Robert Elliott, Department of Psychology, University of Toledo, Toledo, OH 43606.

2. Rice and Greenberg (1984) have studied 15-40 minute events defined in terms of a particular therapeutic task (e.g., resolving an internal conflict), events which may encompass many distinct subtasks or topics. A middle ground between very brief and very long events is obtained using a recently developed tape-assisted recall procedure (Elliott & Shapiro, in press) in which definition of events is left up to clients. These events are typically 4-7 minute conversational episodes.

References

Bordin, E.S. 1974. *Research strategies in psychotherapy*. New York: Wiley.

Elliott, R. 1983a. Fitting process research to the practicing psychotherapist. *Psychotherapy: Theory, Research & Practice*, 20, 47-55.

Elliott, R. 1983b. "That in your hands...": A comprehensive process analysis of a significant event in psychotherapy. *Psychiatry*, 46, 113-129.

Elliott, R. 1984. A discovery-oriented approach to significant events in psychotherapy: Interpersonal Process Recall and Comprehensive Process Analysis. In L. Rice & L. Greenberg (Eds.), *Patterns of change* (pp. 249-286). New York: Guilford.

Elliott, R. 1986. Interpersonal Process Recall (IPR) as a process research method. In L. Greenberg & W. Pinsof (Eds.), *The psychotherapeutic process* (pp. 503-527). New York: Guilford.

Elliott, R., Barker, C.B., Caskey, N., & Pistrang, N. 1982. Differential helpfulness of counselor verbal response modes. *Journal of Counseling Psychology*, 29, 354-361.

Elliott, R., Cline, J., & Shulman, R. 1983, July. *Effective processes in psychotherapy: A single case study using four evaluative paradigms*. Paper presented at meetings of the Society for Psychotherapy Research, Sheffield, England.

Elliott, R., James, E., Reimschuessel, C., Cislo, D., & Sack, N. 1985. Significant events and the analysis of immediate therapeutic impacts. *Psychotherapy*, 22, 620-630.

Elliott, R., Shapiro, D. (in press). Brief Structured Recall: A more efficient method for identifying and describing significant therapy events. *British Journal of Medical Psychology*.

Elliott, R., Underwood, L., Cislo, D., & Webb, L. June 1985. *Awareness in psychotherapy: A comprehensive process analysis of awareness events*. Paper presented at meetings of Society for Psychotherapy Research, Evanston, IL.

Frank, J.D. 1974. *Persuasion and healing* (2nd ed.). New York: Schocken.

Gendlin, E.T. 1978. *Focusing*. New York: Everest House.

Giorgi, A. 1983. Concerning the possibility of phenomenological psychological research. *Journal of Phenomenological Psychology*, 14, 129-169.

Goldfried, M.R. (Ed.) 1982. *Converging themes in psychotherapy*. New York: Springer.

Glaser, B. & Strauss, A. 1967. *The discovery of grounded theory: Strategies for qualitative research.* Chicago: Aldine.

Huberman, A.M., & Miles, M.B. 1983. Drawing valid meaning from qualitative data: Some techniques of data reduction and display. *Quality and Quantity,* 17, 281-339.

Kagan, N. 1975. *Interpersonal process recall: A method of influencing human interaction.* (Available from N. Kagan, 491 Farish Hall, University of Houston, University Park, Houston, TX 77004.)

Kelman, H. 1969. Kairos: The auspicious moment. *American Journal of Psychoanalysis,* 29, 59-83.

Keisler, D.J. 1973. *The process of psychotherapy.* Chicago: Aldine.

Klein, M.H., Mathieu-Coughlan, P., & Kiesler, D.J. 1986. The Experiencing Scales. In L. Greenberg & W. Pinsof (Eds.), *The Psychotherapeutic Process* (pp. 21-71). New York: Guilford Press.

Labov, W. & Fanshel, D. 1977. *Therapeutic discourse.* New York: Academic Press.

Llewelyn, S.P. (in press). Psychological therapy as viewed by clients and therapists. *British Journal of Clinical Psychology.*

Luborsky, L. 1976. Helping alliances in psychotherapy. In J.L. Claghorn (Ed.), *Successful psychotherapy* (pp. 92-116). New York: Brunner/Mazel.

Luborsky, L., Crits-Christoph, P., & Mellon, J. 1986. Advent of objective measures of the transference concept, *Journal of Consulting and Clinical Psychology,* 54, 39-47.

Mahrer, A.R., & Nadler, W.P. 1986. Good moments in psychotherapy: A preliminary review, a list, and some promising research avenues. *Journal of Consulting and Clinical Psychology,* 54, 10-15.

Orlinsky, D.E., & Howard, K.I. 1978. The relation of process to outcome in psychotherapy. In S.L. Garfield & A.E. Bergin (Eds.), *Handbook of psychotherapy and behavior change* (2nd ed. pp. 283-330). New York: Wiley.

Orlinsky, D.E., & Howard, K.I. 1987. A generic model of psychotherapy. *Journal of Integrative and Eclectic Psychotherapy,* 6, 6-27.

Packer, M.J. 1985. Hermeneutic inquiry in the study of human conduct. *American Psychologist,* 40, 1081-1093.

Rice, L.N. & Greenberg, L. (Eds.) 1984. *Patterns of change.* New York: Guilford Press.

Rogers, C.R. 1957. The necessary and sufficient conditions of therapeutic personality change. *Journal of Consulting Psychology,* 21, 95-103.

Russell, R.L., & Stiles, W.B. 1979. Categories for classifying language in psychotherapy. *Psychological Bulletin,* 86, 404-419.

Sacks, H., Schegloff, E.A., & Jefferson, G. 1974. A simplest systematics for the organization of turn-taking in conversation. *Language,* 50, 696-735.

Sampson, H., & Weiss, J. 1986. Testing hypotheses: The approach of the Mount Zion psychotherapy research groups. In L. Greenberg & W. Pinsof (Eds.), *The psychotherapeutic process* (pp. 51-613). New York: Guilford Press.

Taylor, S.J., & Bogdan, R. 1984. *Introduction to qualitative research methods* (2nd ed). New York: Wiley.

Wertz, F.J. 1983. From everyday to psychological description: Analyzing the moments of a qualitative data analysis. *Journal of Phenomenological Psychology*, 14, 197-241.

Chapter 7

Notes

1. This chapter is an extended version of an invited address delivered at the 67th Annual Convention of the Western Psychological Association, Long Beach, California, April 24, 1987. It is based, in part, on my chapter in *The Social Construction of Emotions*, edited by R. Harré (Sarbin 1985). Some of the ideas were developed for a symposium on the Role of Emotions in Ideal Human Development, Heinz Werner Institute of Developmental Psychology, Clark University, June 21-22, 1985. I acknowlege with gratitude penetrating critiques of the earlier paper by Dr. Richard Hallam and by Professor Herbert Fingarette. Their reviews helped me immeasurably. Professors Carson Eoyang, John I. Kitsuse, Marvin Rosenberg, and D. Ralph Carney, faithful readers all, offered many helpful comments.

2. Anger appears to be the most common prototype for emotion. The word 'anger' antedated 'emotion' by several hundred years. In the present paper, I have used anger to illustrate my arguments. This should not be interpreted to mean that anger plots are the only models for interpreting the multifarious forms of conduct subsumed under emotions.

3. Limitations of space make it impossible to gloss the brilliant exposition of the agency theme in Robert Solomon's book, *The Passions* (1976).

4. Averill (1982) would include a third descriptor for the passions: the actor's claim that they are happenings. The actor regards self as a passive recipient and does not attribute causality to self. The root of the word 'passion' is to be found in 'passive,' 'patient,' and 'pathetic.' I agree with Averill that common usage does convey the message: "the emotion happened, I didn't do it." Capital crimes are sometimes excused when the defendant convincingly pleads that the criminal act was controlled by passion. In such cases, the jury adopts the premise that passions are happenings, not under the control of the defendant.

5. Because of space limitations, I cannot do justice to a defense of the assertion that rhetorical acts are the most powerful of the adaptive strategies available to human beings in solving their life crises. Suffice it to say that rhetorical acts are instrumental, they are directed to the perceived antecedents of strain. In one of the alternate forms

of adaptive conduct, attention deployment, for example, the actions are not instrumental—they are directed away from the perceived antecedents.

References

Averill, J.R. 1982. *Anger and aggression: An essay on emotion,* New York: Springer-
Verlag.

Averill, J.R. 1974. An analysis of psychophysiological symbolism and its influence on
theories of emotion. *Journal for the Theory of Social Behavior,* 4, 147-90.

Bruner, J. 1986. *Actual minds, possible worlds,* Cambridge, MA: Harvard University Press.

Chun, K.T. and Sarbin, T.R. 1970. An empirical study of "metaphor to myth" transformation. *Philosophical Psychology,* 4, 16-20.

Geertz, C. 1980. Blurred genres: The refiguration of social thought. *American Scholar,*
80, 165-189.

Goffman, E. 1961. *Encounters: Two studies in the sociology of interaction.* Indian-
apolis: Bobbs-Merrill.

Goffman, E. 1959. *The presentation of self in everyday life.* Garden City, NY: Doubleday.

Heider, F. and Simmel, E. 1944. A study of apparent behavior. *American Journal of
Psychology,* 57, 243-259.

Lakoff, G. and Kövecses, Z. 1983. The cognitive model of anger inherent in American
English. *Berkeley Cognitive Science Report No. 10.*

Lazarus, R.S. 1984. On the primacy of cognition. *American Psychologist,* 39, 124-129.

Michotte, A.E. 1963. *The perception of causality,* London: Methuen. Trans. Miles,
T.R. and Miles, E. from *La Perception de la Causalite.* Louvain, France. (Original work published 1946)

Pepper, S. 1942. *World hypotheses,* Berkeley: University of California Press.

Sarbin, T.R. (Ed.) 1986. *Narrative psychology: The storied nature of human conduct.*
New York: Praeger.

Sarbin, T.R. 1985. Emotions and act: Roles and rhetoric, in Harre, R. *The Social
Construction of Emotions,* Oxford: Blackwell.

Sarbin, T.R. 1968. Ontology recapitulates philology: The mythic nature of anxiety. *American Psychologist,* 23, 411-418.

Sarbin, T.R. 1954. Role theory, in Lindzey, G. (Ed.) *Handbook of Social Psychology,*
Cambridge: Addison Wesley Press.

Sarbin, T.R. & Allen, V.L., 1968. Role Theory, in Lindzey, G. and Aronson, E. (Eds.)
Handbook of Social Psychology, 2nd Edition. Boston: Addison Wesley Press.

Sarbin, T.R. and Scheibe, K.E. (Eds.) 1983. *Studies of social identity,* New York: Praeger.

Scheibe, K.E. 1979. *Mirrors, masks, lies and secrets,* New York: Praeger.

Solomon, R.C. 1976. *The passions*, Garden City, NY: Anchor Press/Doubleday.

Turbayne, C. 1962. *The myth of metaphor*, New Haven: Yale University Press.

Zajonc, R.B. 1984. On the primacy of affect, *American Psychologist*, 39, 117-123.

Chapter 8

References

Brenner, C. 1982. *The mind in conflict*, New York: International Universities Press.

Campbell, D.T. 1986. Science's social system of validity-enhancing collective belief change and the problems of social sciences. In D.W. Fiske and R.A. Shweder (Eds.), *Metatheory in Social Science*. Chicago: Univ. of Chicago Press.

Freud, S. 1912. Recommendations to physicians practicing psychoanalysis. *Standard Edition* 12, 111-120. New York: Norton, 1958.

Freud, S. 1925. An autobiographical study. *Standard Edition* 20, 7-74. New York: Norton, 1959.

Freud, S. 1933. The question of a Weltanschauung. (New introductory lectures on psychoanalysis). *Standard Edition* 22, 158-182. New York: Norton, 1964.

Grünbaum, A. 1984. *The foundations of psychoanalysis*, Berkeley: Univ. of California Press.

Holt, R.R. 1984. The current status of psychoanalytic theory. Invited address, American Psychological Association, Toronto.

Jacobsen, P.B. and Steele, R.S. 1979. From present to past: Freudian archeology. *International Review of Psychoanalysis*, 6, 349-62.

Smith, M.L. 1987. Publishing qualitative research. *American Educational Research Journal*. 24, 173-183.

Spence, D.P. 1982. *Narrative truth and historical truth*, New York: Norton.

Spence, D.P. 1987. *The Freudian metaphor*, New York: Norton.

Vickers, B. (Ed.) 1984. *Occult and scientific mentalities in the Renaissance*, New York: Cambridge University Press.

Walker, D.P. 1958. *Spiritual and demonic magic from Ficino to Campanella*. London.

Williams, M. 1987. Reconstruction of an early seduction and its aftereffects. *Journal of the American Psychoanalytic Association*, 35, 145-163.

Wright, E. 1987. Transmission in psychoanalysis and literature: Whose text is it anyway? In S. Rimmon-Kenan (Ed.), *Discourse in Psychoanalysis and Literature*, New York: Methuen.

Chapter 9

References

Bronowski, J. 1981. *The common sense of science.* Cambridge, MA: Harvard University Press.

Chesler, P. 1972. *Women & madness.* New York: Doubleday.

Chodorow, N. 1978. *The reproduction of mothering: Psychoanalysis and the sociology of gender.* Berkeley: University of California Press.

deBeauvoir, S. 1961. *The second sex.* New York: Bantam.

Derrida, J. 1976. Freud and the scene of writing. In J. Mehlman (Ed.), *French Freud: Structural studies in psychoanalysis.* Millwook, NY: Kraus Reprint Co.

Dinnerstein, D. 1977. *The mermaid and the minotaur: Sexual arrangements and human malaise.* New York: Harper & Row.

Fairbairn, W.R.D. 1952. *An object-relations theory of personality.* New York: Basic Books.

Gouldner, A. 1979. *The future of intellectuals and the rise of the new class.* New York: Seabury.

Griffin, S. 1978. *Women and nature: The roaring inside her.* New York: Harper & Row.

Herschberger, R. 1970 *Adam's rib.* New York: Harper & Row.

Irigaray, L. 1980. When our lips speak together. Translated by Carolyn Burke. *Signs: Journal of Women in Culture and Society,* 6, 69-79.

Jung, C.G. 1955-6. Mysterium coniuntionis: An inquiry into the separation and synthesis of psychic opposites in alchemy. *Collected works of C.G. Jung,* 14, Princeton, NJ: Princeton University Press, 1970.

Jung, C.G. 1931. Analytical psychology and Weltanschauung. *Collected works of C.G. Jung,* 8, Princeton, NJ: Princeton University Press, 1969.

McClelland, D. 1961. *The achieving society.* New York: The Free Press.

Merchant, C. 1980. *The death of nature: Women, ecology, and the scientific revolution.* New York: Harper & Row.

Merleau-Ponty, M. 1964. *Sense and nonsense.* Chicago: Northwestern University Press.

Mischel, W. 1969. Continuity and change in personality. *American Psychologist,* 24, 1012-1018.

Murray, H. 1941. In nomine diaboli. *New England Quarterly,* 24, 435-452.

Ricouer, P. 1979. The model of the text: Meaningful action considered as a text. In P. Rabinow and W. Sullivan (Eds.), *Interpretive social science.* Berkeley: University of California Press, 73-101.

Stanley, L. & Wise, S. 1983. *Breaking out: Feminist consciousness and feminist research.* London; Routledge & Kegan Paul.

Steele, R.S. 1982. *Freud and Jung: Conflicts of interpretation*. London: Routledge & Kegen Paul.

Steele, R.S. (in press). Differences: Small and irreconcilable. *New Ideas in Psychology*.

Winter, D. 1973. *The power motive*. New York: Free Press.

Chapter 10

References

Anderson, N.H. 1968. Likableness ratings of 555 personality trait words. *Journal of Personality and Social Psychology*, 9, 272-279.

Austin, J.L. 1962. *How to do things with words*. Cambridge, MA: Harvard University Press.

Betti, E. 1980. Hermeneutics as the general methodology of *Geisteswissenschafen*. In J. Bleicher, (Ed.), *Contemporary methods*.

Bernstein, R. 1978. *The restructuring of social and political theory*. Philadelphia: University of Pennsylvania Press.

Bleicher, J. 1980. *Contemporary hermeneutics*. London: Routledge & Kegan Paul.

Clifford, J. & Marcus, G. 1986. *Writing culture*. Berkeley, CA: University of California Press.

Collingwood, R.G. 1946. *The idea of history*. Oxford: Clarendon Press.

Dilthey, W. 1894. *Selected writings*. H.P. Rickman (Ed.), Cambridge, MA: Cambridge University Press. (vol. first published in 1914).

Doherty, W.J. & Ryder, R.G. 1979. Locus of control, inter-personal trust, and assertive behavior among newlyweds. *Journal of Personality and Social Psychology*, 37, 2212-2220.

Findley, M.J. & Cooper, H.M. 1983. Locus of control and academic achievement: A literature review. *Journal of Personality and Social Psychology*, 44, 419-427.

Fish, S. 1980. *Is there a text in this class? The authority of interpretive communities*. Cambridge, MA: Harvard University Press.

Gadamer, H.G. 1975. *Wahrheit und methode*. Tubingen: Mohr, 1960 *Truth and method*. Trans. Garrett Barden & John Cumming. New York: Seabury Press.

Garfinkel, H. 1967. *Studies in ethnomethodology*. Englewood Cliffs, NJ: Prentice-Hall.

Gauld, A. & Shotter, J. 1977. *Human action and its psychological investigation*. London: Routledge & Kegan Paul.

Geertz, C. 1973. *Interpretation of cultures*. New York: Basic Books.

Gergen, K.J. 1982. *Toward transformation in social knowledge*. New York: Springer-Verlag.

Gergen, K.J. & Davis, K.E. 1985. *The social construction of the person.* New York: Springer-Verlag.

Gore, P. & Rotter, J. 1963. A personality correlate of social action. *Journal of Personality,* 31, 58-64.

Hirsch, E.D., Jr. 1976. *The aims of interpretation.* Chicago: University of Chicago Press.

Hollinger, R. (Ed.) 1985. *Hermeneutics and praxis.* South Bend: University of Notre Dame Press.

Holmes, D. & Jackson, T. 1975. Influence of locus of control in inter-personal attraction and affective reactions in situations involving reward and punishment. *Journal of Personality and Social Psychology,* 31, 132-136.

Kirkpatrick, J. 1985. How personal differences can make a difference. In K.J. Gergen & K.E. Davis (Eds.) *The social construction of the person.* New York: Springer-Verlag.

Knorr-Cetina, K. & Cicourel, A.V. 1981. *Advances in social theory and methodology.* London: Routledge & Kegan Paul.

Lanyon, R.I. & Goodstein, L. 1971. *Personality assessment.* New York: Wiley.

Lefcourt, H.M. 1976. *Locus of control: Current trends in theory and research.* Hillsdale, NJ: Erlbaum.

Lefcourt, H.M. 1981. Overview. In H.M. Lefcourt (Ed.) *Research with the locus of control construct.* (p. 3-27). New York: Academic Press.

Lutz, C. 1982. The domain of emotion words in Ifaluk. *American Ethnologist,* 9, 113-128.

Mischel, W. 1968. *Personality and assessment.* New York: Wiley.

Norris, C. 1985. *The contest of faculties.* New York: Methuen.

Peters, R.S. 1958. *The concept of motivation.* London: Routledge & Kegan Paul.

Phares, E.J. 1965. Internal-external control as a determinant of amount of social influence exerted. *Journal of Personality and Social Psychology,* 2, 642-647.

Phares, E.J. 1976. *Locus of control in personality.* Morristown, NJ: General Learning Press.

Rabinow, P. & Sullivan, W. (Eds.) 1979. *Interpretive social science: A reader.* Berkeley, CA: University of California Press.

Ricoeur, P. 1971. What is a text? Explanation interpretation. In D.M. Rasmussen (Ed.) *Mythic-symbolic language and philosophical anthropology: A constructive interpretation of the thought of Paul Ricoeur.* The Hague: Martinus Nijhoff.

Rosaldo, M. 1980. *Knowledge and passion, Ilongot notions of self and social life.* Cambridge, MA: Cambridge University Press.

Rotter, J.B. 1975. Some problems and misconceptions related to the construct of internal versus external control of reinforcement. *Journal of Consulting and Clinical Psychology,* 43, 56-67.

Sarbin, T.R. 1986. *Narrative psychology*. New York: Praeger.

Schleirmacher, F.D.E. 1959. *Hermeneutik*. Carl Winter Universitatsverlag, Heidelberg.

Shweder, R.A. & Miller, J.G. 1985. The social construction of the person: How is it possible? In K.J. Gergen & K.E. Davis (Eds.) *The social construction of the person*. New York: Springer-Verlag.

Strickland, L.H., Aboud, F.E. & Gergen, K.J. (Eds.), 1976. *Social psychology in transition*. New York: Plenum.

Suleiman, S.R. & Crosman, I. 1980. *The reader in the text*. Princeton: Princeton University Press.

Sundberg, N.D. 1977. *Assessment of persons*. Englewood Cliffs, NJ: Prentice-Hall.

Taylor, C. 1964. *The explanation of behavior*. London: Routledge & Kegan Paul.

Winch, P. 1958. *The idea of social science*. London: Routledge & Kegan Paul (Originally published 1946).

Chapter 11

References

Buber, M. 1970. *I and Thou*. New York: Charles Scribner's Sons.

Gadamer, H.G. 1975. *Truth and Method*. New York: Seabury Press.

Gadamer, H.G. 1977. *Philosophical Hermeneutics*. Berkeley: University of California Press.

Habermas, J. 1971. *Knowledge and Human Interests*. Boston: Beacon Press.

Habermas, J. 1983. Interpretive social science vs. hermeneuticism. In N. Haan, R.N. Bellah, P. Rabinow, W.M. Sullivan, (Eds.) *Social Science as Moral Inquiry*. New York: Columbia University Press.

Habermas, J. 1984. *The Theory of Communicative Action*, vol 1. Boston: Beacon Press.

Heidegger, M. 1962. *Being and Time*. New York: Harper and Row.

Heidegger, M. 1977. *The Question Concerning Technology*. New York: Harper and Row.

Jardine, D.W. 1984. The Piagetian picture of the world. *Phenomenology + Pedagogy*, 2, 224-239.

Jardine, D.W. 1987. Reflection and self-understanding in Piagetian theory: A phenomenological critique. *Journal of Educational Thought*, 21, 10-19.

Jardine, D.W. (in press a). There are children all around us. *Journal of Educational Thought*.

Jardine, D.W. (in press b). Play and hermeneutics: An exploration of the bi-polarities of mutual understanding. *Journal of Curriculum Theorizing*.

Jardine, D.W. 1988. Piaget's clay and Descartes' wax. *Educational Theory*, 38.

Jardine, D.W. & Morgan, G.A.V. 1987. Analogy as a model for the development of representational abilities in children. *Educational Theory*, 37, 209-217.

Merleau-Ponty, M. 1964. Everywhere and nowhere. In *Signs* (126-158). Evanston: Northwestern University Press.

Misgeld, D. 1974. Critical theory and hermeneutics: The debate between Habermas and Gadamer. In O'Neill, (Ed.) *On Critical Theory* (164-184). New York: Seabury Press.

Misgeld, D. 1983. Common sense and common convictions. Sociology as a science, phenomenological sociology and the hermeneutical point of view. *Human Studies*, 6, 109-139. Forthcoming in Van Holthorn, V. & Olson, D., (Eds.), *Common Sense: The Ground of Science*. New York: Universities of America Press.

Misgeld, D. 1975. Research as an occasion for self-reflection: A reply to Heap and Silvers. *Interchange*, 6, 58-62.

Misgeld, D. 1985. Self-reflection and adult maturity: Adult and child in hermeneutical-critical reflection. *Phenomenology + Pedagogy*, 3, 191-201.

Misgeld, D. 1985a. Practical reasoning and social science: From the phenomenology of the social world to radical hermeneutics. In Glynn, S., (Ed.) *European Philosophy and the Human and Social Sciences*. Hampshire: Gower Publishing Co.

Misgeld, D. 1985b. Education and cultural invasion: Critical social theory, education as instruction and the pedagogy of the oppressed. In Forester, J. (Ed.) *Critical Theory and Public Life*. Cambridge, MA: MIT Press, p. 77-121.

Misgeld, D., Jardine, D.W. & Grahame, P. 1985. Communicative competence, practical reasoning, and the understanding of culture. *Phenomenology + Pedagogy*, 3.

Murphy, J.W. 1985. Consideration of computer mediated education: A critique. *Phenomenology + Pedagogy*, 3, 167-176.

Piaget, J. 1970. *The Place of the Sciences of Man in the System of Sciences*. New York: Harper and Row.

Piaget, J. 1971. *Biology and Knowledge*. Chicago: University of Chicago Press.

Program of Studies for Elementary Schools, Alberta Education Document, 1982.

Ricoeur, P. 1984. *Hermeneutics and the Human Sciences*. New York: Cambridge University Press.

Smith, David G. (forthcoming). Children and the gods of war. *Journal of Educational Thought*.

Chapter 12

References

Caputo, J.D. 1987. *Radical hermeneutics: repetition, deconstruction, and the hermeneutic project*. Bloomington: Indiana University Press.

Fischer, C.T. 1987. The quality of qualitative research. *Theoretical and Philosophical Psychology*, 7, 2-11.

Guba, E.G., & Lincoln, Y.S. 1982. Epistemological and methodological bases of naturalistic inquiry. *Educational Communication and Technology Journal*, 30, 233-252.

Habermas, J. 1971. *Knowledge and human interests.* (J. Shapiro, Trans.). Boston: Beacon Press.

Heidegger, M. 1927/1962. *Being and time.* (J. Macquarrie and E. Robinson, Trans.). New York: Harper & Row.

Hirsch, E.D. 1967. *Validity in interpretation.* New Haven: Yale University Press.

Kirk, J., & Miller, M.L. 1985. *Reliability and validity in qualitative research.* Sage University Paper Series on Qualitative Research Methods, Volume 1. Beverly Hills, CA: Sage.

Kuhn, T. 1977. Objectivity, value judgment, and theory choice. Reprinted in *The essential tension.* Chicago: University of Chicago Press.

Lather, P. 1986. Research as praxis. *Harvard Educational Review*, 56, 257-277.

MacIntyre, A. 1984. *After virtue: A study in moral theory.* South Bend, IN: University of Notre Dame Press.

Miles, M.B., Huberman, A.M. 1984a. *Qualitative data analysis: A sourcebook of new methods.* Beverly Hills, CA: Sage Publications.

Miles, M.B., Huberman, A.M. 1984b. Drawing valid meaning from qualitative data: Toward a shared craft. *Educational Researcher*, May, 20-30.

Okrent, M. 1988. *Heidegger's pragmatism: Understanding, being, and the critique of metaphysics.* Ithaca: Cornell University Press.

Polkinghorne, D. 1983. *Methodology for the human sciences.* Albany: State University of New York Press.

Popper, K.R. 1972. *Conjectures and refutations: The growth of scientific knowledge.* 4th ed. rev. London: Routledge and Kegan Paul.

Popper, K.R. 1979. *Objective knowledge: An evolutionary approach.* Revised edition. New York: Oxford University Press.

Ricoeur, P. 1976. *Interpretation theory: Discourse and the surplus of meaning.* Fort Worth: Texas Christian University Press.

Rosen, S. 1987. *Hermeneutics as politics.* New York: Oxford University Press.

Smith, J.K., & Heshusius, L. 1986. Closing down the conversation: The end of the quantitative-qualitative debate among educational inquirers. *Educational Researcher*, 15, 4-12.

Taylor, C. 1979. Interpretation and the science of man. In P. Rabinow and W. Sullivan (Eds.), *Interpretive social science: A reader.* Berkeley: University of California Press.

Taylor, C. 1985a. *Human agency and language: Philosophical papers, Vol. 1.* New York: Cambridge University Press.

Taylor, C. 1985b. *Philosophy and the human sciences: Philosophical papers, Vol. 2.* New York: Cambridge University Press.

Contributors

Richard B. Addison is a clinical psychologist in private practice, Assistant Clinical Professor in the Department of Family and Community Medicine at the University of California, San Francisco's School of Medicine, and a member of the Behavioral Science faculty in the Family Practice Residency Program at Community Hospital of Sonoma County in Santa Rosa, California.

Dianne E. Argyris is a Research Associate in the Laboratory of Human Development at Harvard Graduate School of Education.

Lyn M. Brown is a Research Associate in the Laboratory of Human Development at Harvard Graduate School of Education.

Brina Caplan is a doctoral candidate in Counseling and Consulting Psychology at Harvard Graduate School of Education. She is also a member of the Group for the Study of Interpersonal Development.

Robert Elliott is an Associate Professor of Psychology and Director of the Psychology Clinic and Training Center at the University of Toledo in Toledo, Ohio.

Kenneth J. Gergen is a Professor of Psychology at Swarthmore College in Swarthmore, Pennsylvania.

Carol Gilligan is a Professor of Education at the Laboratory of Human Development at Harvard Graduate School of Education.

David W. Jardine is an Associate Professor of Early Childhood Education at the University of Calgary in Calgary, Alberta.

John R. Mergendoller is Senior Program Director at Far West Laboratory for Educational Research and Development.

Barbara A. Miller is a Research Associate in the Laboratory of Human Development at Harvard Graduate School of Education.

Dieter Misgeld is an Associate Professor of Education at the Ontario Institute for Studies in Education in Toronto, Ontario.

Martin J. Packer is a Visiting Assistant Professor in the School of Education at the University of California at Berkeley and a Research Scientist at Far West Laboratory for Educational Research and Development in San Francisco.

Theodore R. Sarbin is Professor Emeritus of Psychology and Criminology at Adlai E. Stevenson College, University of California at Santa Cruz.

Katherine Schantz is a doctoral candidate in Counseling and Consulting Psychology at Harvard Graduate School of Education. She is also a member of the Group for the Study of Interpersonal Development.

Lynn Hickey Schultz is a Research Fellow at Harvard Graduate School of Education. She is also a member of the Group for the Study of Interpersonal Development.

Robert L. Selman is a Senior Associate in Psychology at Harvard Medical School's Department of Psychiatry, Senior Associate in Psychology at Harvard Graduate School of Education, and Director of the Group for the Study of Interpersonal Development.

Donald P. Spence is a Professor of Psychiatry at Rutgers Medical School, University of Medicine and Dentistry of New Jersey in Piscataway, New Jersey.

Robert S. Steele is Associate Professor of Psychology and Women's Studies at Wesleyan University in Middleton, Connecticut.

Mark B. Tappan is a Research Associate in the Laboratory of Human Development at Harvard Graduate School of Education.

Index